Memoirs of a
Minor Public Figure

Also by Des Wilson

1969 – I know it was the place's fault (on Shelter and the homeless)

1973 – Des Wilson's Minority Report (*Observer* columns)

1979 – So you want to be Prime Minister (an introduction to British politics)

1983 – The Lead Scandal (the case for lead-free petrol)

1984 – The Secrets File – editor (the case for freedom of information)

1984 – Pressure – the A to Z of campaigning

1985 – The Environmental Crisis – editor

1985 – Battle for Power (on the 1987 Alliance election campaign)

1989 – The Citizen Action Handbook (with Leighton Andrews)

1990 – Costa del Sol (novel)

1992 – Campaign (novel)

1993 – Campaigning – the A to Z of public advocacy

2002 – Private Business, Public Battleground –with Sir John Egan (the case for corporate social responsibility)

2006 – Swimming with the Devilfish (under the surface of professional poker)

2007 – Ghosts at the Table (history of poker, the world's most popular game)

Memoirs of
a Minor
Public Figure

DES WILSON

Forewords by
SIR HAROLD EVANS
and
PROFESSOR PETER HENNESSY

To Harry, I AM SO proud to have your name on this book.

DesW.

QUARTET

First published in 2011 by
Quartet Books Limited
A member of the Namara Group
27 Goodge Street, London w1t 2ld

A catalogue record for this book
is available from the British Library

ISBN   978 0 7043 7205 4

Typeset by Antony Gray
Printed and bound in Great Britain by
T J International Ltd, Padstow, Cornwall

To Jane
and
Jacqui and Tim
and in memory of
Albert and Nell Wilson

Contents

'You do not become a 'dissident' just because you decide one day to take up this most unusual career. You are thrown into it by your own personal sense of responsibility, combined with a complex set of external circumstances. You are cast out of the existing structures and placed in a position of conflict with them. It begins with you attempting to do your work well, and ends with being branded an enemy of society.' VACLAV HAVEL

Foreword (1)

HAROLD EVANS

Millions of people in Britain are indebted to Des Wilson, and not many of them know it. We and our children no longer breathe air poisoned by lead from petrol fumes and fewer succumb to lethal cigarette smoke. Wilson led the way. Progressively fewer over many years endured life in a rat-plagued slum or slept rough on the streets, in part because of the agitation Wilson fomented through Shelter's arousal of public awareness. The irony is that one of Wilson's later great achievements was to transform the flow of information in a society affected by chronic arteriosclerosis. He's too sensible and modest to claim that the Freedom of Information Act was all his own work, but he galvanized the campaigners and marvellously discomfited the suppressors.

Every country needs a Des Wilson. No, every country needs a hundred Des Wilson's. The DNA that informs a Wilson comes out clearly in this readable autobiography: A passion to right wrongs – but a passion dis-ciplined by intelligence in identifying achievable objectives. The self-con-fidence to take on dragons – but the prudence to take on one at a time and to recruit allies. The determination to persist through setbacks – but the imagination to avoid becoming a cranky bore.

The inside story of Wilson's campaigns is revealing. Just how did he achieve so much? It is all very well to denounce the devil and all his works, but venting, which is so common in the age of social media and 24/7 cable news, is no more than self-indulgence. One of the striking things about the stories of the Wilson campaigns is how thoroughly he and his supporters studied the case against the cause he proposed adopting. This shrewdly prepared them to have their counter arguments ready – they really had to know their stuff – but it was also armour for the soul against the venom, vilification and lies they'd have to endure. Wilson's campaign against giving comfort to the appalling Mugabe in sanctioning a tour by the English cricket team of Zimbabwe produced a sickening cascade of betrayals in the sport and in government. The refrain he frequently endured, 'He's doing it for personal publicity' was mean and stupid. He'd never have been able to endure so much personal abuse, sacrifice so much time, hazard his livelihood, unless he'd been impelled by a moral imperative. (In this connection, it is pleasing that Wilson freely acknowledges all the assistance he had; his benefactor and partner, Godfrey Bradman, emerges as a very fine citizen.)

The most comparable figure to Des Wilson is the American icon, Ralph Nader. They differ in specific objectives and personal styles but, in addition to individual reform, they have both made a major contribution to the creation of a new active citizenry, a 'countervailing force' against the law's delays, the insolence of office, and now the greedy arrogance of the transnational corporations who casually wreck the financial system, pollute the oceans and degrade the culture.

HAROLD EVANS

(Sir Harold Evans was Editor of *The Sunday Times*
from 1967–81 and of *The Times* from 1981–2)

Foreword (2)

PETER HENNESSY

Des Wilson is a force of nature. I knew this within minutes of first seeing and hearing him, even though we didn't talk face-to-face for another ten years. It was an autumn night in Cambridge in 1967. The hall was packed with students gathered to listen to Des on the homeless and what the still new campaigning group, Shelter, was going to do for them.

Des was sharp featured and terribly young, just a few years older than we undergraduates. For all Shelter's relative novelty, he must have worked crowds like us many, many times before, but the big hall came alight. Des, to adapt the motto of the John Lewis Partnership, has never knowingly been understated. What he said and how he said it bit so deep it is there on the template of my memory more than forty years later.

To warm us up he showed us *Cathy Come Home*. Then he really laid into we gilded youths about the iniquity of a wealthy country that, through sheer neglect, could do such things to people. That night in Cambridge Des was relentless. The flames of outrage flared and roared. It was highly contagious stuff.

When I got to know him later he was leading the Campaign for Freedom of Information. I was bowled over again by his wit, his joy in the absurd, his sheer *joie de vivre*, and his self irony. But Des played to win – and he usually did, eventually.

Quite apart from the Wilson brio in these pages, there lies within a fascinating history of the development of campaigning in the UK. By the time I reached the age of twenty (1967) there had been two quantum leaps in my lifetime. The first was in 1958 with the Campaign for Nuclear Disarmament whose use of words, images, logo and demonstrations produced the kind of impact not seen since the Suffragettes half-a-century before. Des Wilson took the craft on even further, using a multiplicity of instruments – new campaigning and fund raising techniques, vivid posters and advertisements plus his own biting media appearances. All this was fashioned by a recently arrived New Zealander in his mid twenties. It was an extraordinary phenomenon and the Shelter experience, so vividly recaptured in this memoir, provided the basis for a string of Wilson-led campaigns that followed. Des was as much a part of the Sixties as the Profumo Affair and the Rolling Stones. It was a brilliant example of the Empire striking back.

PETER HENNESSY

(Peter Hennessy is Attlee Professor of Contemporary British History, Queen Mary, University of London. In 2010 he became a member of the House of Lords as Baron Nympsfield)

New Zealand in 1950. *A small hall in a small town is packed with farmers and shopkeepers and tradesmen. And their families. A local builder, one of the only men in town who earns serious money, is showing his slides of a driving tour across America. So rare is it in those days for anyone from New Zealand to travel overseas, that hundreds have come to look at his pictures, listen to his stories, and experience the adventure second-hand.*

In the centre of the front row is a small boy. He is nine years old, his knees are scratched, his socks hang around his ankles, his shoes are muddy; he has been playing rugby on the local park.

He can hardly believe what he is hearing and seeing.

The builder is no photographer, nor is he much of a public speaker. So the pictures are poor and the delivery even worse. But that does not matter. What matters is that he has been there.

*Overseas! This man has actually been **overseas** – to America – other places too.*

The boy has always dreamed of travelling, and has devoted hours to poring over pictures in his encyclopaedia of places all over the world. He's told himself that one day he will travel to see them, but it's an improbable dream; hardly anyone from the town has even been to the North Island of New Zealand, let alone another country.

Now, as he hangs on every word and gazes in wonder at every picture, he is consumed by one thought:

It is possible! It really IS possible!

And as he walks home he promises himself: 'One day I will do that . . . one day I will see the world.'

I Never had a Plan

Towards the end of the last century I knew a man with an enormous chip on his shoulder. He clearly believed – with some justification – that his life had been a failure. It was more than he could bear that I achieved even minimal success and one day he launched into a debunking analysis of my career with the words, 'Des, I recall the days when you were a *minor public figure* . . .'

I suppose I could have taken offence, or at least been mildly put out. Instead I found it amusing and filed it away as a title for my memoirs, if ever I were to write them.

And, of course, there's some truth in it.

It was not for lack of opportunity. There were moments when the summit was within reach – moments when, if I had been more ambitious, more compromising, more ruthless, more conventionally upstanding (or, conversely, more of a creep), or maybe just more hungry or more needy, I could have reached The Top, whatever and wherever that was.

My critics, some of whom could even be called enemies – an occupational hazard in my campaigning days – would say that I *was* ambitious, even self-seeking; but they never understood me. The ambitious have a plan; I did not.

No, I never had a plan.

Instead, I took opportunities, not I hasten to add, in the conventional sense, of someone whose eye was always on the main chance. It will become obvious to anyone who reads this book that for many years I worked for what a campaign or a charity could afford, and sometimes for no money at all. As for power, while the more ambitious of my fellow campaigners took the Conservative or Labour route to political power, and two or three of them (including a former PA of mine), even became Ministers, when I turned to politics, I chose a party that at the time offered no chance at all.

Michael Palin, writing of his diaries, says, 'an overall impression is given of a kaleidoscope of characters and events, clarity and confusion, of great strides forward and long and rambling cul-de-sacs, from which a pattern emerges, but only briefly, like the moon between clouds on a stormy night . . .' I suspect the same impression emerges from an account of my life. What I was doing always seemed to make sense, to me if no one else, and there was, more often than not, some pattern; but I do understand that, as it was not 'onwards and upwards' in a conventional sense, it often mystified friends and families, commentators and cynics alike. It probably did not help that I always pursued a policy of 'never apologise, never explain', preferring a self-accountability that probably led to more misunderstanding and allowed more misrepresentation of my actions or motives than need ever have been the case.

It seemed to me that I, and everyone I knew, were all on the same road, but the conventionally ambitious stuck to it without deviation, their foot on the accelerator, eyes fixed on the white line, their only aim to reach the end of it as fast as possible.

I took all the detours . . . what the travel companies call the 'optional excursions'.

I could see what many could not, namely, that we would not be coming back and that if we wanted to experience all that this journey had to offer, we had to do it now.

In any case, I suspected there never was an end; life was the journey itself. So, if we wanted to make a difference, we had to do it as we travelled; not postpone it until we somehow, sometime, finally reached some place somewhere called Power.

I have, I believe, been blessed with more than my share of enthusiasm, optimism, and self-confidence. These qualities have the virtue of being infectious, and they under-pin conviction, and that – the indestructible belief that a particular cause is just and can be won – in turn fuels will-power, and the will to win is the key to campaigning success. So, if this book has a message, it is that you can help make the world a better place without becoming a major public figure. You can do it by practicing the art of the possible.

In other words, if you can't change it all, change what you can. In my campaigning years I was inspired by a poem by Louis MacNeice:

What is it we really want?
For what end and how?
If it is something feasible, obtainable,
Let us dream it now,
And pray for a possible land . . .

To make the aim achievable, the cause winnable, and to campaign for a 'possible land' has not been to me to minimise the challenge, but to maximise the chance of a result. And I did want a result. I did want to make a difference. I did want to leave the world, even fractionally, a better place.

Shelter may not have solved the national housing problem but I'm proud that over forty-five years the charity I helped launch solved many thousands of individual ones.

When I hear and see, almost daily, revelations as a result of the Freedom of Information Act, I'm proud that, at least partially thanks to my initiative, the sun is now shining on the darker corners of our public life, where we have been too easily betrayed or robbed or just plain let down.

When I see environmental concerns now properly understood and acted upon, I think back to the years when environmentalists were seen as eccentric and I'm proud that I was there when it was unfashionable. When I see children trying to buy cigarettes and being turned away by tobacconists afraid of prosecution, or motorists filling their cars with unleaded petrol and thus protecting children from damaging pollution, I'm proud that, while all this probably would have come about eventually, it definitely happened sooner because of campaigns I was part of.

These were all positive outcomes of optimistic endeavour based on realistic hopes; in short, a result.

As for the minor private figure, I don't really think I've ever really changed in character from that New Zealand boy who dared to dream; life was an adventure then and it still is, confronted with the same enthusiasm, albeit at seventy with a little less energy.

For, in addition to the minor public figure, there's been a minor private figure too. Despite the rather humourless and occasionally sanctimonious impression that may have been given by my campaigning (I often received letters addressed to the Rev. Des Wilson), if my life has been a success it is because I have allowed public and private passions to share it, without,

I hope, being too holier than thou in the first, or too frivolous in the second.

Above all, I have enjoyed the whole challenge of getting by, of surviving. As I sit in Cornwall on my seventieth birthday, I realise that 'getting there' is the big thing. After all, we don't choose to come into this incredibly challenging, competitive and complex world. We just find ourselves in it. It's not a democratic decision.

So in my view just confronting life's dangers and demands and conjuring up the courage and strength and skills to survive, to become acceptably, comfortably and respectably old is a real achievement in itself.

And now, three points about this book:

First, I may have chosen to write a memoir, but my family have not. So I have not written one for them. They have always been wonderfully there for me, even when I have been absent or distracted more than a son, husband and father ever should be, and the least I could do to repay them was to respect their privacy.

Second, the story does not flow seamlessly from A to Z, any more than my life has. This is mainly due to my choice of a thematic approach. Readers may, therefore, find the Chronology particularly useful.

Finally, if this memoir has a purpose, it is to find a place one day on the shelves of my old school and local libraries – a record of an improbable journey from the small New Zealand town where it all began. Perhaps, there, it will serve to inspire some kid like me, one who dares to dream he can leave that little town, travel the world and do special things. That would be immortality of a sort. Maybe just the minor immortality of a minor public figure, but good enough for me.

DES WILSON, MARCH 5, 2011

PART ONE

I Will See the World . . .
The first twenty-five years

1

War Memoirs

The Second World War lasted 2,174 days and cost 50 million lives. It caused death and distress and devastation across two thirds of the planet. It ended when I was four years old. For me this came as a surprise, because until the very last day no one had told me there was a war.

Oamaru, a small town half way down the South Island of New Zealand, was about as far from the battlefields of Europe as it was possible to be. We did have one big gun, positioned on a hill above the beach and aimed out to sea, just in case the Japanese came. But they didn't. At no point did the Emperor point to Oamaru on the map and say, 'We must take that town'.

So, having been born on March 5, 1941 – the year when Japan bombed Pearl Harbour – I was alive for most of the war, but missed it completely. We had no television. I didn't, as an infant, listen to the radio news and I couldn't yet read the newspapers. My parents didn't tell me. How could I know?

I do, however, remember the German surrender, because an older boy who lived nearby came running up our path to announce it. He was wearing a gas mask (don't ask me why) and I was so frightened I too began to run and fell over and cut my knee. I have a scar to this day. I call it my war injury.

I also remember a year later my mum reading to the family a letter she had received from a woman in Britain. These were the days when we sent food parcels to the 'home country' and this letter thanking us for one was so touching that even as a small boy I was moved by it. This was the first time I ever knew that some people did not automatically have all they wanted to eat.

So that's my war. I suppose you could say I had a good one.

2

Oamaru

When you are young you get blamed for crimes you never committed, and when you are old you begin to get credit for virtues you never possessed. It evens itself out. I. F. STONE

Oamaru was spotted by the famous explorer and seafarer Captain James Cook as he sailed by in his ship *The Endeavour* in 1770. He didn't see any inhabitants, but some Maoris probably lived in the area. They definitely did by 1814 when a boat-load of sealers landed there and were eaten.

Fortunately this was a practice which had died out by the time I was born; the town was by then home to about 10,000 people and was the base for a farming community. Oamaru was well known for four things.

First, it was the only town in New Zealand with prohibition – under a law passed in 1905 and not overturned until the 1960s. You could not sell alcohol within a thirteen mile radius of the town centre. The effect of this was that at five o'clock every afternoon a lot of the men in town jumped in their cars and raced out to the pubs that circled the town like a Wild West wagon train; by six, when the pubs closed by law, they were unfit to drive back. But of course they did.

Second, it was from Oamaru Harbour that the first New Zealand frozen meat was sent overseas – from the Waitaki Freezing Works nearby. When I first came to London my folks used to send me a whole frozen lamb for Christmas; it would be stored in the local butcher's freezer and I would wander in and ask for 'six of my lamb chops, please.' (By the time you have had lamb chops and lamb cutlets, leg and shoulder of lamb, lamb shank, and lamb stew day after day for several weeks, you *can* go off lamb.)

Third, they mined nearby a unique white limestone that became known as Oamaru stone, and all the main buildings in town – the bank, the post office, the library, the high schools – were built with it. This made it one of the most beautiful and striking towns in the country.

Finally, it achieved some international fame as the home of the acclaimed writer, Janet Frame, who re-named it in one of her books 'Waimaru'.

My father's family came from Lincolnshire. His grandfather is buried there in a churchyard in Stamford. My father was born in Waimate, about thirty miles north of Oamaru. He spent nearly all of his life in Oamaru. He became a painter's apprentice when he was about thirteen but was the bravest and best of the men in the firm and when its owner died, it was Dad who took the lead and re-established the business under his own name. (His name was Albert, but he was universally known as Ab.) He married a Karitane nurse (the elite of NZ nurses) called Ellen Hoskin, and I was the third of their six kids. The Hoskin family came from Cornwall in the UK, where I now live. In fact, if you come to Nancegollan, the place in Cornwall where my home is, and if you start to drill a hole, and if you keep drilling in a more-or-less straight line until you break the surface on the other side of the world, you will find yourself at Oamaru.

My parents were a decent, hard-working couple who stayed together over fifty years till my father died at seventy-six and my mother at ninety-four. For fun they played cards with friends, and my father went fishing for rainbow trout in the fast-flowing local rivers. Otherwise, they worked. Typical of her generation of working class women, my Mum worked from daybreak until well into the evening, cooking, cleaning, washing, sewing, and, above all, knitting. You have never seen knitting needles move at such speed; if knitting was an Olympic sport, she would have won a gold medal. My father provided for a family of eight by leading his team of painters and paper-hangers from the front; it was hard for them to complain about the hours they worked when he always worked longer.

I suppose we were relatively poor when I was small but it didn't seem like it; we always had coal for the fire, warm clothes (admittedly passed down from brother to brother), and plenty of food.

We were a busy and boisterous lot but, on the whole, did well at school and none of us ended up in the cells of the local police station. We lived in a small, overcrowded house, the only heating coming from a coal fire in the sitting room. It had an outside lavatory and this ramshackle place we shared with an army of mice and a succession of cats, whose task it was to keep them under control. In this respect, the place was a war zone.

The house was in two parts, linked by a passage-way with a glass roof.

The passage-way was filled with old shoes. Two adults and six children need a lot of shoes over the years and my mother would never throw them away. So allow for two pairs per person at any one time (day shoes and best shoes) plus three pairs of rugby boots, six pairs of gym shoes, eight pairs of slippers and my sister Helen's ballet shoes, then multiply this by about nine times to allow for increased sizes over the years, and there were at least 150 pairs of shoes there. Imelda Marcos was not in my mother's class.

Crossing this passage-way from the kitchen and my father's workshop, on one side of the house, to the sitting room on the other, was a hazardous business. The wind would often blow pieces of glass off the roof and they would crash down on the shoes and anyone who happened to be passing below. I remember a friend of mine came home to play after school, and his mother had obviously told him to be polite and compliment my mother on our house. As she opened the door and his eyes fell upon the piles of shoes, a piece of glass went whizzing past him and hit the wall, breaking into hundreds of pieces. 'What a nice house you have, Mrs Wilson,' he said, sticking to the script despite the evidence before his eyes and his narrow escape from death by decapitation.

Gradually my father's business developed. He opened a paint shop, added a furniture department and we moved to a specially built house in the same street. One day, the Farmer's Coop – the biggest shop in town – was wiped out by a fire. My father was standing in the crowd watching the blaze when the chairman of the Coop came over and said, 'Well, Ab . . . You can name your own price, because we have to have your shop.' He was able to retire on the money.

Oamaru North School was just 300 yards up the road and it was there where I went until I was ten. Apart from a coaching session with the famous cricketer, Bert Sutcliffe, and a term when one of our teachers was a Commonwealth Games athlete called Harold Nelson (who the whole school chased around the playground at lunchtime in scenes reminiscent from the Pied Piper), I have only one memory. I was nine years old and it was the class Christmas concert. I decided to perform the two magic tricks I had read about in a book.

The first involved breaking a pack of cards into two, even cards on one side and odd on the other. I asked a member of my transfixed audience to take a card from the odds and slip it into the evens. I identified the card which had been transferred and my audience was amazed. My second trick involved placing a glass of water on a desk and covering it with a handkerchief. I told my audience I would drink the water without touching the handkerchief. After a bit of wand-waving, I asked the teacher to remove the handkerchief. This he did and I drank the water without touching the handkerchief. You may not be impressed, but the other kids loved it and their applause was enthusiastic. I was a star. I was euphoric.

After milking the curtain calls to the maximum, I was told by the teacher to stay up front where he produced and gave me a book, *Mona the Welsh Pony*, and informed me I had won an essay prize. I suppose I should have been more pleased than I was, but I was unimpressed – even annoyed – because he was drawing attention away from my real triumph, the launch of my career as a magician.

All the way home, clutching this unwanted book, I re-lived my success, imagining already the career that lay ahead; the black hat and cloak, the woman in tights I would saw in half. I could not wait to tell my mother all about it, and did – at considerable length.

After a while she asked me what the book I was holding was and I grumbled that I had won some essay prize. She opened it and read the certificate and to my surprise became very excited.

'But this is for the whole country,' she said. 'You have won a prize for the *whole of New Zealand.*' My father came home and she told him. I was furious, because I wanted to tell him about my triumph as a magician and she was delaying the moment. Did no one understand? It was the magic that mattered. My performance was the first public success of my life. I had experienced the heady taste of applause.

Later, I realised I had, perhaps, missed the significance of the prize, but on that memorable day there had been revealed unto me two possible careers – one as a magician, one as a writer. At the time, the first offered all the attractions: a spellbound audience, applause, possible fame and fortune. The second seemed like hard work.

Nevertheless, for some reason, I did eventually choose the second. I never performed a magic trick in public again. And I never did read *Mona the Welsh Pony*. But I did make a living as a writer – of sorts.

* * *

Looking back on it, I realise my desire – perhaps my compulsion – to communicate was well-established when I was a kid. I wanted to be the one who broke the news. I just loved those words, 'Have you heard . . . ?' and the attention they got. Inevitably, one of my ambitions when I was only ten years old was to be a newspaper reporter. I also wanted to be a school teacher – a communicator of information, out there in front of the class, breaking the news. The final choice was determined by another one of my characteristics – impatience. I could leave school at fifteen and become a cadet reporter on the local newspaper; I had to wait until I was seventeen to train to be a teacher. So, I left school at fifteen and a reporter I became. (But more of that later . . .)

While I was bright enough, my school record was fairly poor because I didn't study. Like many New Zealand kids, my life was dominated by sport. As a child I listened to the big heavyweight boxing fights on the radio – these were the days of Joe Louis, Jersey Joe Walcott, and Sugar Ray Robinson. After Roger Bannister broke the four minute mile, I listened to the radio when he and John Landy from Australia, the only other four minute miler, clashed at the Commonwealth Games in Canada and heard the commentary on Jim Peters' tragic entry into the stadium at the end of the marathon. And I would hide under the blankets with a tiny radio (they were called crystal sets) and listen in the early hours of the morning to broadcasts of the Ashes tests from faraway cathedrals of the game called Lords and the Oval. But rugby was our big thing. My father had been a respected local rugby player and rugby and the All Blacks were the number one topic in a household containing four sports-mad boys. On the wall of the bedroom we all shared was a picture of the 1949 All Blacks. Each Christmas we would be given a rugby ball as a joint present and would rub fat into it to make the leather more water-resistant and play with it until it needed replacement the following year.

We were a competitive family. Table tennis battles in our garage were brutal affairs. The back lawn was a rugby pitch. The garden was a long-jumping pit. The clothes line was used to hang a cricket ball in an old sock for batting practice and the wall of the garage was used to practice tennis strokes. Hardly a day went by without one sporting encounter or another ending in broken windows and bloodshed.

Most days I was to be found at Takaro Park. This was the town's only soccer pitch, but at one end there was a small piece of grass bounded by a football goal, a fence separating it from the main road out of Oamaru, a concrete cricket practice pitch and a tower built by the Fire Brigade for their practices. On this patch of land, transformed in my imagination into a stadium packed with cheering spectators, I played hundreds of rugby games, pitting my totally imaginary Red Robins team against every province in the country and in tests with the All Blacks. Brilliantly led by its fly-half and captain, D Wilson, it was never beaten. (Wilson was, in fact, an astonishing athlete; he was never beaten at golf, distance running, long-jumping and a number of other sports. Only his modesty has kept this from being better known.) Then, one evening, when I was about ten, as summer approached, some men arrived and put up a net around the cricket pitch. I watched them, enthralled. I had never really been conscious of cricket before, but I fell in love with it and, come Saturday, I went out to my school where the club games were played. From then on rugby took second place. Cricket was my game.

Oamaru did not have Saturday shopping; instead the shops would stay open till nine on a Friday evening. On Friday, the farmers could come to town to stock up for the coming week. The Oamaru Highland Pipe Band would march up and down the main street. And all the boys would hang around on street corners sizing up the local girls. One Friday when I was twelve, after spending the day crawling in dirt on my hands and knees to earn 8/6d pea-picking for a local farmer, I purchased my first cricket book. It described the 1953 Australian cricket tour of England. I read it and re-read it until I could virtually recite the book from memory. To this day I can list both teams in the fifth test, won by England to regain the Ashes. This led me to follow the game internationally. I built up a collection of cricket books, helped by the local library. It sold off old books for a shilling and many of them were cricket books. I still have some of them.

Apart from the radio, such knowledge of the world as I developed came from two sources. One was the Oamaru library, one of remarkable quality for a town that size. I was an avid reader from when I was about seven and probably read more books from that library than any other kid in town. It also had regular copies of *The Illustrated London News*, the world's oldest pictorial magazine (and one that I was to become deputy editor of many years later).

I have a copy of the *ILN* with me as I write: it is the issue of April 11, 1953. The front cover consists of advertising (king-size cigars at one shilling and nine pence each, Imperial Leather toilet soap, and a boot polish). It is dominated by pictures of the funeral of HM Queen Mary. There is a picture feature of a Mau Mau massacre in Kenya, pictures of the Grand National and the Boat Race, and even a picture of the last meeting of the Sudan Executive Council. But the feature that leaps out at me is 'Our Notebook', the weekly column of the right-wing historian Arthur Bryant. When I eventually became Deputy Editor of the *ILN* in 1979, he was still writing the notebook. By now it had become distinctly repetitive and I told the editor I believed he was dead and that his secretary was recycling his columns for the money. One day the editor came into my office waving a newspaper in triumph: 'I told you he was still alive,' he said, 'he's just become engaged to be married.' Bryant was 80 at the time (and died before the wedding could take place).

Anyway, as a boy, the *ILN* was my window on the world. I especially loved its pages of black and white pictures of cricket tests. When the library sold unwanted copies at a penny an issue, I bought them, cut out the cricket pictures and pasted them in my scrapbook.

The other source of news was *The Oamaru Mail*, an evening newspaper that served the town well. Its front page was full of classified advertising and, apart from local news, covered world affairs extensively by simply printing in full all the reports that came over the wire from the NZPA and Reuters. One of the three on the editorial team must have loved cricket because it gave cricket a level of coverage out of all proportion to the rest of the news. This worked well for me, albeit being a bit puzzling to others, who would find news of the outbreak of a major war buried under reports of the latest Ashes test. But, to be fair, it told us all we needed to know. It was in the *Mail* that my parents read what was happening during the Second World War, that the Japanese had bombed Pearl Harbour, and that the Americans had dropped an atomic bomb on Japan. It was in the *Mail* that later I was to read that there was a war in Korea or that there was a Suez crisis. It was in the *Mail* that we read of the death of King George VI and the accession to the throne of his daughter, Elizabeth.

It was also the error-prone *Mail* that published a classified advert seeking a 'dairy maid and randy man'. It also published an astonishing picture of a

Highland band piper resting on a bench in the sun, pipes by his side and his kilt up over his thighs. Alas, the picture answered a frequently-asked question and in this case, the answer was . . . well, embarrassing, albeit also, in terms of what it revealed, hugely impressive!

In those days, there was no television, computers, cell phones, CDs, DVDs, iPods or music centres. The only technology we had was the old fashioned wireless. As kids we were allowed to stay up until eight o'clock on Tuesdays to listen to Cowboy Corner. The radio station only had about six country and western records – Hank Snow's *Stolen Moments* being one of them – so this programme was predictable, but we loved it just the same. Then there were the comedy programmes from London: *Take it from Here, Ray's a Laugh, Hancock's Half Hour, Life with the Lyons, Educating Archie* and *The Goon Show*. And, of course, we crowded round the radio to listen to the famous commentator, Winston McCarthy, describe the rugby tests.

On Saturday mornings we went to the children's matinee at the local Opera House where we cheered the cavalry as it came to the rescue in the cowboy films that we loved – films with singing cowboys like Roy Rogers and Gene Autry.

The moment of truth in New Zealand education was the School Certificate. You sat it when you were about fifteen and had to take it in five subjects which were assessed on the best four scores. You had to average 50 per cent in these to pass. What with my cricket and rugby, I had little time for studies. I chose science as my fifth subject, wrote my name and number on the form, and walked out. To my surprise, I received six marks for that. My other four subjects were English, History, Geography, and Book-keeping. Thanks to the Oamaru library, English was no problem. Nor was History; I was captivated by Gladstone and Disraeli and had devoured every book in the library about them, and that did the trick.

Geography could have been a problem but for a stroke of luck. The local cinema screened a number of short films before the main feature and the owners had purchased an old black and white documentary on nomads in the Sahara. I saw it scores of times and, would you believe, one of the geography questions was to describe the lives of nomads in the Sahara. As I had more or less memorised the soundtrack of the film I must have picked up top marks for that one. How I passed book-keeping I will never know, but anyway I averaged fifty-eight per cent for the four papers and thus had the School Certificate and was now officially educated. I left school and became a journalist.

My career began in the Oamaru office of *The Otago Daily Times* (the ODT), a morning newspaper published in Dunedin, a city seventy-two miles south. My boss was Maurie Tonkin, who worked on the ODT all his life, always in that small office, rode a bike to work for about fifty years and was probably the most humourless, unimaginative and uncommunicative man I ever met. He hammered out brief, factually accurate but colourless reports on a battered old typewriter and was terrified of an elderly and even more humourless woman who took the advertising at the front desk.

It would not have been a cheerful place were it not for the other reporter, Brian Hunter, with whom I have stayed friends ever since. Brian made up for Maurie's lack of humour and imagination and had an extraordinary capacity for remembering phone numbers. You only had to mention a name and Brian would say 883467 or whatever, a skill which saved having to have a phone book in the office. One story sums up the difference between the two. The National Theatre Company was in town and I was sent to interview its leading actor-comedian. I ran the story as a question-and-answer piece, full of his one-liners. The following day Maurie, for once, did communicate. He stormed into the office and told me he had never been so ashamed to be on the newspaper. The piece was, he said, embarrassingly unfunny. Just as he finished his tirade Brian walked in, a big smile on his face.

'For the first time I can remember,' he said, 'people stopped me on the way to work to talk about the paper; said they'd not laughed so much for years. That piece was really funny – brilliant.' Maurie was reduced to his usual state – struck dumb.

Reading them now, some of my stories were a bit naïve. One interview began: 'The opinion that too many who fell prisoner to the Japanese during the war did not make the effort to adapt themselves to the way of life of their captors and refused to look on the bright side of life, was expressed by Father Jose Gonsano in an interview with the ODT today . . . ' What that Alec Guinness character, buried up to his neck in the hot sand, would have thought of that, heaven knows.

While in Dunedin I even managed to insert myself into a story. A local dance hall promoter called Joe Brown organised a talkathon – an attempt on the world record of ninety-eight hours of non-stop talking. A blind man called Archie came all the way from Auckland to win the first prize. He lasted seventy-six hours and won £130. However, my account of the event also stated: 'The third entrant was an Oamaru man, Des Wilson. He made the £5 third prize and left contented after fifteen minutes.' And indeed I was contented. That was more than I earned in a week.

Between reporting for the *ODT* and cricket on Saturdays, I was engaged in two of my passions. Now, I was to discover a third. We had two cinemas in town; one was the Oamaru Opera House which doubled as a cinema and concert hall and the other was The Majestic Theatre. I never missed a film and at fifteen went to see Shakespeare's *Julius Caesar*. It says a lot about a New Zealand education and upbringing in those days that I had never heard of Shakespeare and I was exceedingly fortunate that this film was my introduction, because it was made as a thriller, in black and white and I was overwhelmed by it. While it is best remembered for Marlon Brando's Mark Antony, I was enthralled by the inner torment of James Mason's Brutus, who I felt was the play's real hero, thoroughly deserving of Antony's final verdict: 'This was the noblest Roman of them all . . .'

Then came Olivier's *Richard III*. I could not take my eyes off the screen. I first saw it at a 5 o'clock session, went straight back 8 o'clock and then each of the following two evenings. I spent what little spare money I had on an LP record of it, which I later had to sell to a second-hand record shop in Dunedin. (The following Saturday I did a spot of baby-sitting for my news editor and in his record collection I found my treasured *Richard III* album.)

Both films were a revelation. I wanted to know more about Shakespeare and the theatre and, as usual, having been infected by an enthusiasm, I became unstoppable, reading every book I could find and joining the Oamaru Repertory Society and the Oamaru Operatic Society. Unfortunately, I was unable to act convincingly nor sing in tune, so I took on the publicity for the plays and shows and, as secretary, virtually ran the Operatic Society by the time I was seventeen.

With the plays I often acted as a prompter. The key to being good at this, I discovered, was to avoid as much as possible helping actors when they were rehearsing, because once you had prompted them on a line they seemed to always need to be prompted on the same line; there developed a dependency. There was a local farmer called Chas Brown who developed such a dependency on me for one or two prompts that he never once, in the entire run of a play, remembered his two lines. Chas was at the heart of the most disturbing thing I've ever seen in a theatre. On the night of the dress rehearsal, only twenty-four hours before the play's opening, he suddenly went blank and announced he had never heard one of the other actor's lines before. In the end I took the script onto the stage and showed him, whereupon he announced he had not heard or seen the whole scene before. As far as he was concerned, all the weeks of rehearsal hadn't happened. They were a complete black-out. It was an awful moment. We had to abandon the dress rehearsal and just pray that it would be alright on the night. Fortunately the following night he turned up word perfect – except for his usual two lines.

I loved the whole drama of drama – the rehearsals, the building of the sets, the lighting and dress rehearsals. The Operatic Society hired a professional director from Dunedin called Stan Lawson and his shows were of remarkable quality, especially Noel Coward's *Bitter Sweet*.

I discovered you could achieve considerable influence in almost any community if you volunteered to work and, having boundless energy and precocious confidence, I did volunteer, ending up in my teens as secretary or committee member of a number of organisations. So, given my enthusiasms for cricket and the theatre, I was at the heart of these activities and as I was at nearly every local event or meeting as a reporter, I was more or less everywhere else too. Unfortunately, no one told me that at eighteen there was a lot you didn't know and that you should just shut up and learn. Looking back on it now with some horror, I realise I must have been a real pain in the backside; a bossy young know-all, an un-guided missile, indispensable because of my work ethic but intolerable because of my presumption. In the end the town was not big enough for me; on the other hand, I cannot recall anyone trying to persuade me to stay when I decided to move on.

I fixed an interview with the *ODT* headquarters in Dunedin. Maurie blocked the move so I joined the *Evening Star* in Dunedin instead. The *Star* was an outstanding newspaper, full of fascinating characters and brilliant journalists, amiably led by a good-natured news editor called Buzz Harte who went on to become a big shot in television when it eventually came to the country. (He died in 2009.) The year I spent on the *Star* was one of the happiest times of my life; the older journalists responded to my enthusiasm and, provided I undertook whatever was allocated to me in the daily diary, I was given free rein to do what I liked. I'm still proud of some of the stories I turned in on that paper.

Just as I had loved every aspect of the creation of a theatrical production, so I loved all that was involved in the creation of a daily newspaper. For me, you could not call it work; I would have paid to work on the *Evening Star*. Well after the other reporters had left for home or the snooker hall or a poker game, I would be still there, in the composing room, watching the pages being put together. On Saturdays we published a special paper, *Star Sports*, and we all worked on it. Most of it was put together during the week and the last few pages were produced on the Saturday afternoon, covering the day's rugby, cricket and racing. I wrote extensively for this, building up my experience and winning the goodwill of the editors and sub editors who needed free material.

My life revolved around journalism, cricket and the theatre, but now I discovered girls. Unfortunately, they did not discover me. But, in pursuit of them, I spent most evenings in the local dance halls. One day I was called in by Buzz and told that I was being sent back to Oamaru, to open up a news service for the town and hopefully build up the circulation there; little short of a disaster for me, but I was given no choice. I found myself back at the same meetings, covering the same events and without even a dance to attend at night, except on Saturdays when everyone in the area between fifteen and forty would turn up at the Scottish Hall to dance to a band called *The Rhythm Boys*. The band members were nearly all aged over fifty and, while it cannot be entirely so, as I recall they knew only one tune – *Yes, Sir, She's My Baby*, played at various speeds to serve as a fox trot, quick step or whatever else they wanted it to be.

It's impossible to over-state the innocence and simplicity of these Scottish Hall dances. The dances began at 8 pm and at 10 pm we had the supper dance. It was the practice to ask the girl you danced with to join you for supper (a cup of tea and a bun – the town was dry remember) which was the signal it was probably your intention to ask her for the last dance, which, in turn, indicated you would be asking to walk her home. Except, it was never as simple at that.

For a start, the girls would sit down each of the longer walls of the hall and the boys would mix at the back. When the band leader called out 'Take your partners for a fox trot – *Yes Sir, She's My Baby*', you would have to walk over and ask your chosen partner to dance. She had the right to refuse and often did. The result, of course, was utter humiliation. A near-suicidal embarrassment, especially if she was sat way down the end of the hall, causing a solitary walk back that seemed endless. Condemned men walked to the gallows with a lighter step. You imagined the mocking, unfeeling eyes of everyone in the town upon you. Sometimes, when it happened to me, I walked straight to the back, out the door, and into the night and kept away from the Scottish Hall for weeks, convinced I was the laughing stock of the entire district. Of course, it never crossed our minds to consider the horror that it was for the girls, especially those who were not approached all night and were left sitting there alone, while everyone else danced by.

Nor did the problems end there. In the unlikely circumstances that a girl would actually consider allowing you to take her home, another question then arose: How were you going to do it? Oamaru was built between the sea and some hills and was much longer than it was wide. It was not impossible that the girl lived five miles away. And with no late-night bus and most of us unable to afford taxis or owning cars, you could hardly ask her, in her best party dress, to climb on the back of your bike. So we would have to walk. You try explaining to a girl who is not too enthusiastic to begin with, that if she handles herself right, she could spend two hours in your company in her dancing shoes, walking. As for what you did when you left the hall and found it was raining . . . ! As someone with little appeal to the girls at that time, my strategy, therefore, had to be to aim low – look for a relatively plain girl who was likely to be grateful to be asked to dance and who lived within a mile of the Scottish Hall. Even that strategy achieved little success.

The Scottish Hall dance was hours of embarrassment and humiliation combined with the occasional moments of excitement and exhilaration. Never the less, in a small town without pubs or clubs, where the social centre was the milk bar and dining out could mean a pie and chips from the local stall, the Saturday night dances at the Scottish Hall were the highlight of the week. That's where the town's youth met and from where many became engaged and eventually married. My parents met there and their eldest daughter, my sister Helen, met her husband there.

Having become accustomed to a dance every night in Dunedin, when I returned to Oamaru, I found the Saturday night-only aspect of the Scottish Hall intolerable. So, at eighteen, I booked the hall mid-week, hired a newly-formed band called *The Modernnaires* and ran my own dances. I became an entrepreneur. I began to make serious money. I had never had enough to open a bank account, so kept my new found wealth in an old suitcase under the bed. There was enough to pay for me to leave the country. So I did.

A friend from the *Star* had moved to *The Melbourne Sun* and wrote to tell me there was a vacancy there. Within days I was on my way – and nearly twenty-five years passed before I was to return.

*   *   *

I often look back and wonder how it was, of all the kids of my generation in Oamaru, I was the one who went on to 'greater things'? How did I turn my love of cricket into becoming an advisor to the MCC and a member of the English Cricket Board? How did I turn my love of theatre into becoming Head of Public Affairs for the Royal Shakespeare Company? How did I turn my love of journalism into becoming a columnist on the *Guardian* and the *Observer* and deputy editor of the dear old *Illustrated London News* (Arthur Bryant and all)?

I am now beginning to understand how I became what I am. As a young reporter who was everywhere and knew everyone, and an enthusiast in a town where, without television and pubs, a lot of energy was invested in organised activity, such as sport and theatre, I absorbed the workings of civic life and gained experience as an organiser at a very early point. All this gave me a capacity and confidence beyond my years. I was always the enthusiast who said 'I'll do that'. So by the time I was nineteen I was accustomed to taking responsibility and, given that the sane majority just want to get on with their lives and leave others to do the work, I often ended up running the show, whether it be the cricket club, the theatre company, or the Junior Chamber of Commerce (I joined this to be in the debating team).

Without realising it, I must also have established the foundations for my energy and stamina there. I was, for instance, a winning distance and cross country runner in my teens, never beaten in the local Harriers' junior events. Where did the energy and stamina come from? It's only looking back on it now, more than fifty years later, that I realise it was not because of any special talent, but because I had to bike to school – two miles there in the morning, home for lunch, back after lunch and back after school, every weekday for five years. And all at break-neck speed. I had a rule: no other cyclist would pass me on the journey. This exacting test was to relieve the boredom of the journey. But what I was also doing was building up strength in my legs, and stamina, the qualities essential to distance running. I won as a distance runner because I was fitter than the others. And I had built up a competitive stamina – the mental stamina that comes from concentrating on biking at top speed in relatively heavy traffic while not letting anyone else from school pass me by. That mental and physical stamina has served me ever since. In my mid sixties I played with intense concentration for sixteen hours to survive the first day of the World Series of Poker in Las Vegas, while brilliant kids in their twenties were being knocked out by mistakes caused by complete exhaustion. I put that down to the stamina I built up on those bike rides. Fifty years on, all that cycling is still paying off.

Being one of six children helped too; you had to learn to handle yourself in unrelenting competition for attention and for opportunities. Then there was the good weather, the availability of parks and the proximity of the countryside; all this bred health and optimism and enabled kids to be out of doors in the fresh air playing sport all the year round. I guess not having television helped; it meant that we had to use our imagination to make our own fun. These were all factors which, when I set out to conquer the world, made up for my lack of education or a social base. I was fit, healthy, optimistic, imaginative – whatever lay ahead, I was up for it.

But for me, the key to later achievements was the afore-mentioned Oamaru Public Library. It became my second home. When I was not on the sports field, I went there after school and took out the permitted four books, read them all that night and then was back the following day. I devoured books. I loved that library. I can still conjure up the experience of being there, the warmth, the calm, the sense of anticipation created by the shelves and shelves of inviting-looking books. By the time I was seven I had read every book by Enid Blyton, to whom I will stay loyal until the day I die for she got me reading. I went on to the *William* books, then to Zane Grey, Conan Doyle, P. G. Wodehouse and, of course, Bulldog Drummond and Hornblower. I read the lot – and then more. As I became enthralled by cricket and the theatre and then fascinated by history, I moved on to non-fiction. The only time I was completely stymied was when I took home *Waiting for Godot*. (But then I still don't understand it today.) The library was a treasure house and in it I found a piece of gold – Hugh Cudlipp's *Publish and be Damned*. I read it once, twice, then a third time, and from then my fate was decided: I was going to be a newspaper reporter. I owe my career in journalism to that moment, to that library and to that book.

There seemed to be no limits to the library's range, because there was another big book on the art of journalism. I can't recall who wrote it but I memorised almost every word of its advice and still remember it today. I learned from it the importance of laying out the facts in the right order: what happened, where, when, why, and who was involved. I learned to encompass the whole story in the first paragraph and then develop it paragraph by paragraph. (This was particularly crucial in those days because all our work was set in 'hot metal' and then fitted into the page on an iron table known as 'the stone'. As printing time got closer, there was no time to 'sub' a story on the stone. If it was too long, they would just take an axe to it and cut off the bit that would not fit, thus endorsing the importance of getting facts well-established early on.)

One piece of advice stuck in my mind: it was to the effect that there is no one on earth – not one single individual – about whom a story cannot be written. Somewhere in everyone's life there is a nugget. You just have to dig till you find it. I proved this to myself when I later worked in Dunedin on the *Evening Star*. I was sent out to the suburb of Port Chalmers to write a piece about a police constable who was retiring after forty years in the force. I dug and dug but could not find my 'nugget' . . . the man was unbelievably boring, as I suppose you could expect of someone who had patrolled the same streets for forty years without promotion. The only crime he seemed to have encountered was double-parking in the main street. I began to fantasise a headline: 'World's most boring man found in Port Chalmers'. Finally I gave up. The book was wrong. There was no story which could be written about this man. As I was leaving, his wife said to me, 'Of course, it's the children who will miss him.' 'Oh,' I said dis-interestedly, 'why's that?' 'Well,' she said, 'Bob never takes to the street without a packet of boiled sweets in his pocket. And he gives one to every kid that he meets. Over the years he has made hundreds of friends who have grown up and still remember him for that.' And there it was. My nugget! The story began 'The children of Port Chalmers have lost a friend today. Constable Bob has retired.' It made the front page.

All my reading had to have an effect, and of course it did. It made me good with words. It made me more articulate than my schoolmates. It's the reason I won that New Zealand writing contest when I was nine. It meant that leaving school at fifteen didn't matter – even without a formal education I could in later years still write well enough to hold down a column in some of the world's top newspapers and to argue well enough to debate at the Oxford and Cambridge universities – places which my own education would ever normally get me near.

So while I have, from time to time, been less than generous to Oamaru I can, in retrospect, see that the seeds of what was to come were well and truly planted there.

3

An Innocent Abroad

*A good traveller is one who does not know where he is going
to, and a perfect traveller does not know where he came from.*
YUTANG LIN

Before air travel became affordable for nearly everyone, most New
Zealanders travelled by sea. From the ship rails we would wave back at
those on the quay, and both they and we would sing an old Maori song:

> Now is the hour
> When we must say goodbye
> Soon we'll be sailing
> Far across the sea
> While I'm away
> Please remember me
> When you return
> You'll find me waiting here . . .

It was nearly always sung in tears, to soldiers or rugby teams being sent
off to battle, to family members or friends sailing off to 'the home country'.
There was always a real fear they would never return. There was no one to
sing it to me though when, in October 1960, I left for Melbourne for I'd
already said good-bye to the family in Oamaru. I was not to see them for
nearly twenty years.

I'd been hired as a reporter on the *Melbourne Sun* and took a bedsit near
the sea at St Kilda to work on the *Sun* for about nine months. After a brief
spell as a reporter, I became a sports sub-editor which meant I worked from
about 5.00 p.m. till about 2.00 a.m., before retiring to a café near my bed-
sitter for a Coke and a read of the first edition. I would make it to bed about
three or four in the morning.

It was a strange year. Because of the hours I worked and the fact that all the other sub-editors were much older and had families, I never made any friends. The whole time I was in Melbourne I never really met anybody. For someone so keen to travel, I was incredibly unimaginative. I spent most of my time in front of the television set at the café. Despite being full of confidence at home, I was, once overseas, quite shy. I always had the same food: Porterhouse steak and chips, a slice of bread and butter, and a Coke (all that I would drink then). On Sundays, if I was not working, I would get up about noon, have steak and chips, bread, butter and Coke, and watch the *Westinghouse World of Sport* on the first television set I had ever seen. I would then watch every other programme until about 6.00 p.m. when I would order steak and chips, bread, butter and a Coke. Then, I'd watch every programme until about 10.00 p.m. when I'd order steak and chips, bread, butter and a Coke.

Eventually, when I went into the café, not a word was said and the staff just brought it over, even Christmas Day – steak and chips, a slice of bread and butter and, because it was Christmas after all, two cokes. One other family was there that Christmas Day and the father kindly came over to ask if I would like to join them. I said, 'No thanks – I have to watch the *Westinghouse World of Sport*'. Bit sad really.

I followed my Oamaru-nurtured enthusiasms: helping create the daily newspaper, of course, but also the theatre and cricket. I went to see local club games. If there was any time left, I spent it on St Kilda beach.

As for girls, my incompetence continued. Actually, I did fall in love, inevitably in the cafe. There were a small number of regulars in the early hours of the morning when my work ended, and one of them was a young woman, clearly older than me, but with a striking, sad, world-weary face. She was always alone, as I was. From a few tables away, I would fantasise about her. I never had the nerve to approach her, but night after night for nearly a year, I wanted to. One night she left just before me. I decided the time had come to act. I would follow her out and find a way to start talking. I stood in the café doorway, building up my courage, and watched her stop on the street corner. Just as I was about make my move, a car pulled up. There was a brief exchange with the driver and then she climbed in. It was then I realised the terrible truth. All that time I had adored her from afar, she could have been mine, for five pound's a time.

My other attempt at romance was a complete catastrophe. I had been observing from afar a young female reporter on the *Melbourne Herald* (they shared our newsroom) but I was to shy too ask her out, even assuming I could find an evening when either she or I were not working. In 1960, the worldwide premiere of the movie of Neville Shute's *On the Beach* was to be in Melbourne. The event of the year and tickets were impossible to buy. However, the newspaper was given some and somehow I got my hands on two. I eventually worked up the courage to ask the girl if she would like to accompany me and the tickets did the trick. Come the night I turned up at the cinema to find her waiting for me with a smile that made me tremble at the knees. I reached into my pocket for the tickets and then, to my horror, realised I had left them in my room at St Kilda. I took a taxi at huge expense and raced back for them; by the time I returned she was standing alone in the foyer, her face like thunder, and the film half over. She never spoke to me again. Shortly afterwards I left the country.

*   *   *

When I came to London in the summer of 1960, I came by ship. We all did in those days. It took six weeks and stopped at Aden, Suez (with some Aussies I hired a car to Cairo and then on to Port Said, picking up a tummy problem you really don't want to know about), Naples (it was an Italian ship) and even Cannes, before docking at Southampton.

If anyone could be described as 'an innocent abroad', it was me, at nineteen. I was as green as it gets, with no sense of the country I was coming to. I had no education of any substance to draw upon, and even less experience of life. I had no money (I had £5 when I arrived in London) and I knew no one. I had nowhere to live and no work in prospect. I should, I suppose, have told myself that I had crossed the world without purpose or resources and was now on skid row, but it never crossed my mind that any of this was a problem, even when a few days later I was down to sixpence or, at my lowest point, when a Melbourne guy and I had to carefully cut a hard-boiled egg in half and share it for dinner. I was not even discouraged when poverty forced me to sell my one asset, a portable typewriter. I was living by the hour and the day, and every day was an adventure; every experience exciting.

I had picked the right time to come to London and, as the song goes: 'Summer time and the living was easy'. The shop windows in Earls Court were full of postcards seeking bar-tenders or builders' labourers, cleaners or café workers. I picked up a few pence here and there. And with the money I went to the cricket: Alec Bedser was still opening the bowling for Surrey, Fred Trueman for Yorkshire, and I saw them both on my first visit to The Oval. South Africa were touring and I saw them play at Lords. Pop music still had tunes, and the first show I saw in London was a nineteen-year-old Cliff Richard singing *Living Doll* at the Palladium. When I had no money, I spent hours at the Overseas Visitors Club watching what, to me, was still a new phenomenon – television. Bruce Forsythe was presenting *Sunday Night at the London Palladium*, Patrick McGoohan was the *Danger Man*, and Granada were screening the first-ever episode of a soap called *Coronation Street*. At the other end of the spectrum I saw Alec Guinness at the Haymarket in the title role of *Ross*.

The Queen was in her seventh year on the throne and the Conservatives, their ninth in power, the country having been told by prime minister Harold MacMillan just a year earlier that it had 'never had it so good'. There were signs of a new self-confidence in British fashion and music, and in the theatre. At the Edinburgh Festival a revue called *Beyond the Fringe* was drawing crowds. In a club in Hamburg an unknown group called The Beatles were honing their act; in Chelsea a girl called Mary Quant was designing what she hoped the country's teenagers would wear. At the Old Bailey a jury refused to convict *Lady Chatterley's Lover* under the Obscene Publications Act. Even a newcomer like me could sense it in the air – things were changing.

Like all Australians and New Zealanders at that time, I planted myself in Earls Court. My first landlady was the gloriously friendly Mrs Higgins in the West Cromwell Road, who when I took the room, told me I could do what I like. 'I don't mind if you have girls up there,' she beamed, and then pointing to her daughter, who was sitting, smoking, in an armchair, 'You can even have Patsy if you like.' Patsy didn't so much as flicker an eyelid. I, on the other hand, fled to my room, only to cautiously emerge to buy my egg and tomato roll and a half pint of milk – my daily diet for some time. (As a treat I would sometimes heat up a packet of green pea soup on the one gas ring in my room.) Later I discovered that Mrs Higgins was not always so friendly: tenants were frequently hurled into the street for no obvious reason. However, she seemed to like me, because over time she even offered me a larger room. I finally had space for myself and my suitcase.

Like all journalists from 'down under' who came to London I went to see Monty Parrott, the genial head of the Australian Associated Press bureau in Fleet Street. I can still recall him sighing as he looked at me and groaning,'God, you guys are getting younger all the time'. Fortunately he needed someone to join his Wimbledon team, so there I was, a day or two later, in the press box on the centre court, with an entry ticket for two weeks and all the Chelsea buns I could eat. There in that summer of 1960 I saw Neale Fraser beat his fellow Australian Rod Laver to win the men's singles title and Maria Bueno beat Christine Truman in the women's final.

For a couple of years Earls Court became my home town. This was partly due to the fact that there was a fundamental difference between me and the other young Australians, New Zealanders and South Africans who had colonised Earls Court; they had a plan, and I didn't. Their scenario was to spend a summer either driving in a shared van or hitch-hiking around Europe, then a winter on the ski slopes, and then head back home – their one big trip over. Living, as I had been, from day to day, I not only had no such plan but I had no return ticket.

I spent a lot of time at the Overseas Visitors Club and ended up running the bar there. I also worked at the Café des Artistes in Fulham, a trendy place at the time. Richard Williams, who did the animation for the first Pink Panther films, played in a jazz band there. I was so naïve I didn't have a clue what was actually happening there – the drugs and whatever. One night, about two in the morning, a couple of detectives from Chelsea police station came in for a coffee. 'If you want to see some action, be at the Wimpy Bar in Earls Court Road when you close,' they said. 'We are having a drugs raid.' As soon as I locked the door, I went down there. It was packed. I sat down and said to the couple sitting next to me: 'Hang around – there's going to be a drugs raid in a few minutes.' Seconds later the place was empty. People fell over each other getting out the door. When the police arrived, I was the only one there. Well, how was I to know?

I did another summer with Monty Parrott's AAP but it still never crossed my mind that I should hammer on the doors of Fleet Street, so for a couple of years I worked on a trade paper, and then one or two local newspapers, including one near the film studios at Elstree. Our canteen and drinking hole was the Red Lion; a regular on a stool at the bar at that time was Tony Hancock who was making his film *The Punch and Judy Man* there. I had always been a huge fan and am still sorry I never spoke to him when I had the chance. Even then, a solitary drinker, he looked lonely and rather desperate.

From there I had a brief and rather comical period with a rather bizarre Fleet Street advertising agency, R. F. White and Sons, said to be the oldest in the world. There was even an eighty-year-old woman account executive and the chief executive and his father, the chairman, still came to work wearing bowler hats and carrying umbrellas over their arms.

Looking back on it, I cannot begin to explain how, doing these bits and pieces, I let five years slip away, but I did. Time passed by at the terrifying speed that it does; before I knew it, it was 1965 and I was now married to my first wife, Rita, who I met at the Café des Artistes, and we were living with our first child, Jacqui, in a flat in Twickenham (before later buying a house in Weston Park in Surrey where my son Tim was to be born.) Personally, those five years had been enjoyable (the thing about living day to day is that every day is a fresh adventure). Professionally, they had, I suppose, been a write-off. But, in the context of what was to come, what really mattered was that politically, they had been formative. And, for me, that had actually begun way back in 1960.

* * *

It's fair to say that when I arrived in London in June of that year I had done no harm to anyone, but nor had I made anyone better off. I had already proved way back in Oamaru that, when inspired, I was an organiser. Once my attention was captured, I had both the inclination and the self confidence to become fully involved and take responsibility, even to lead, and when enthusiastic, I did so with an energy that left detractors or sceptics trailing in my wake. But, even so, it's fair to say that my life was about the pursuit of personal enthusiasms rather than the common good, and it was lived by the hour or – at a stretch – by the day. My small but busy world and the real world were different places.

If I had little depth, this is hardly surprising when you consider my upbringing in a small town in a small country hanging onto the edge of the world. No one in my extended family went to university, nor were we raised to aspire to it. There was no discussion of current affairs at home, with friends or at school. I *was* an avid reader, but the books I read had given me a facility with words, but not a great insight into the world beyond my enthusiasms – cricket, the theatre and then work on a local paper concerned with local affairs. So I arrived in London with no learning, experience, or roots upon which to draw; I had not come up via the British class system, so I had no sense of belonging to a social group. I had suffered no injustice and if I was poor (as in a way I was), it didn't feel like it. So I had no personal reason to become politicised.

I was, however, impressionable. On the ship from Australia there had been a pile of old *Time* magazines and, for lack of alternative reading, I devoured them all. It was in *Time* that I learned all about the 1960 US Presidential election and John F. Kennedy. On January 20, 1961, in a small bed-sitter in Earls Court, I listened, spellbound, to his famous speech – 'Ask not what your country can do for you, ask what you can do for your country'. Today it's fashionable to devalue the Kennedy years, but I know from my own experience what Kennedy's real achievement was: if he did little else, he inspired many who had never done so before to think about politics. Up to then politics had been the part of the newspaper I didn't read; as for a concept like 'public service' . . . you had to be kidding! For me, Kennedy was the catalyst that changed all that: he made politics appear exciting and he made public service respectable.

I began reading the *Guardian* and the *Observer* and the *New Statesman* and political books. These were exciting times politically: like everyone else, I was absorbed by the Profumo Affair and then by the resignation of Macmillan and the dramatic battle for the Tory leadership, won by Lord Home. I followed the battle within the Labour Party over nuclear dis-armament, culminating in Hugh Gaitskell's promise to 'fight, fight and fight again'. I was moved by Gaitskell's premature death and (believe it or not) excited by the emergence of Harold Wilson as leader. At this point I joined the Labour Party.

I started attending local party meetings in Twickenham where I then lived. As usual I was hardly in the door before I was volunteering for the work no one else wanted to do, so I quickly became ward secretary, constituency press officer and council candidate. The local Labour Party had its stars, including Jim Mortimer, who was to become the National party's General Secretary; Russell and Anne Kerr and George Cunningham who, were all to become respected MPs for neighbouring constituencies, and party meetings were lively.

Unfortunately we were talking only to each other for we had only one councillor and no other political influence whatsoever. I was writing and delivering leaflets, producing newspapers, drawing up agendas and writing up minutes, recruiting members, collecting subscriptions, moving resolutions, organising fundraising fetes, all with my customary enthusiasm and energy, but all in a complete vacuum (nearly fifty years later Twickenham has still not elected a Labour MP).

Nevertheless, it was a vital transition from a life previously devoted entirely to self-interest and self-survival, to one of public service. Fired by my reading and my increasing involvement in local politics, a door in my brain, previously locked, suddenly opened and out burst a whole philosophy.

No matter what the issue, I found myself coming to it with a clear, instinctive position, and those positions were all consistent. I found I stood for something. My main cause was the freedom of the individual in relation to authority. I never had liked anyone telling me what to do, and I became increasingly astonished how much the State was able to tell people how to live their lives, and at the way we let it do so.

I believed women should have power over their own lives, so I supported the right to abortion. I believed people should be free to end loveless marriages so I supported divorce reform. I didn't think we should be told what to read, or see in the cinema or on the stage, so I supported the end of censorship. I opposed hanging, but supported, and still do, the right of people to end their own lives.

It became my conviction that the State should only have the right to tell us what to do or not to when it was likely to cause harm to others. Of course, these – and more – were all liberal positions, so, by the time of the 1964 General Election when my home was a ward headquarters and I had a picture of Harold Wilson on the wall, I discovered I was a liberal, not a socialist. At first, this didn't matter, with Roy Jenkins as Home Secretary, supporting a series of brave Private Members Bills, ensuring that abortion became legal, the divorce laws were relaxed, and capital punishment and censorship were ended.

In his biography of Harold Wilson, historian Ben Pimlott wrote of this period:

> The post-war revolution in British moral attitudes came to legislative fruition, in a series of historic enactments which gained parliamentary approval either at Jenkins's instigation, or with his encouragement . . . the effect of this exceptional period of reform was to end a variety of judicial persecutions of private behaviour; quietly to consolidate a mood change in British society; and to provide a legal framework for more civilised social values. For hundreds of thousands, if not millions, of people directly affected – and millions who benefited later, without knowing when, or how, their liberation came about – these were the important changes of the Wilson administration.

This is one reason why I have always maintained some loyalty to the memory of Harold Wilson – at that time he appeared to me like a benevolent family doctor presiding over a vast improvement in the nation's health as far as personal freedom was concerned. (Also he kept Britain out of the Vietnam War; if only Tony Blair in later years had had the same judgement and restraint.) But I was no socialist and did not fit comfortably within the Labour Party and increasingly felt I was exhausting my energies in a cause I only half believed in, and, in Twickenham at any rate, I was exhausting them to no effect.

I was rapidly becoming disenchanted with the sheer futility of local constituency meetings passing useless resolutions and though, on the whole, my comrades were a bunch of decent people, what was the point? I yearned for a metaphorical gun to pick up, a barricade to build, a war to fight. I did not want to be in a talking shop; I wanted to be out there putting all my newly discovered and rapidly growing political feelings into action.

And that, as I come to the end of my first twenty-five years, is where we come to Shelter.

PART TWO

Campaigner

4

Helping the Homeless – Shelter

Where, after all, do universal human rights begin? In small places close to home – so close and so small that they cannot be seen on any map of the world. They are the world of the individual . . . the home and the neighbourhood he lives in . . . the school or college he attends . . . the factory, farm or office where he works. Such are the places where every man, woman and child seeks equal justice, equal opportunity, equal dignity without discrimination. Unless these rights have meaning there, they have little meaning anywhere.

ELEANOR ROOSEVELT

By the time I came to London the country had become a 'welfare state'. Both major political parties offered a universal safety net, with the sick served by the National Health Service, the young by enhanced opportunities for education, the elderly by state pensions and the unemployed by the dole. However, in one respect, the State had failed: despite the provision of prefabs in the Forties, and then later in the Fifties, the building of tower blocks, Britain's post-war housing problem had not been solved. It had become worse. By the Sixties, millions of people were either completely homeless or living in misery and squalor. The full extent of the failure became clear when, after thirteen years of Conservative rule, Labour came back to power in 1964 and published a housing White Paper which stated: 'In Great Britain some three million families still live either in slums, near slums, or grossly overcrowded conditions.' Three million families would be ten million people! A later survey found no less than 1.8 million houses in England and Wales were 'unfit for human habitation'. A further 4.5 million houses were 'below standard'.

In 1966, for reasons I will shortly outline, I went to see the problem for myself. I still have my notes on just one house in Church Road, Birmingham. I went from room to room and noted:

There is a family in every room. No repairs have been done for years and no gas or electricity bills have been paid by the owner so these services are about to be cut off. Some of the rooms are terribly damp, the walls are crumbling, the floors are unsafe, there is only one toilet for the whole house (at least 27 people) and, likewise, only one cold water tap. Mr. & Mrs. Wheeler with their three boys are in one room. The electrical fittings are dangerous. When I touched a piece of wallpaper the wall crumbled under my hand and pieces of concrete, brick and plaster fell to the floor. Mice have been eating away at the fringes of the room. The case of Mrs. Anne Wilson and her husband and four children is particularly bad. They have had two rooms for three years. The smell is dreadful and the larger room is so damp and rotten, because rain pours through the roof, that it is impossible to live in it. Their furniture and the walls are crumbling around them. So the whole family has to sleep in a tiny kitchen 6' x 8'. The mother sleeps sitting in a chair with two children in her lap. Their conditions are almost beyond belief. She says that when they were in the big room they would sometimes find their daughter 'like a drowned rat' in the mornings.

Despite the horror of their conditions, at least these families had not broken up, nor were they – as thousands were – living in hostels for the homeless where the fathers were evicted at night and the whole family was sent onto the streets in the morning and not allowed back until ten at night, no matter what the weather.

What they were often experiencing, however, was the brutality of slum landlords. With no security of tenure, until Labour came to power and introduced it, they had been forced to pay exorbitant rents for their hovels; if they didn't pay they were evicted, in some cases by thuggish bailiffs who would turn up with big, vicious dogs.

Every day for many weeks I explored the slums and found myself looking into the desperate and exhausted faces of young mothers trying to hold their families together, and at kids crowded into a corner of the one-room so-called home, expressionless eyes glued to flickering old black and white television sets. Many lived in danger of their lives. In the Sixties, newspapers often reported the cases of children killed in fires. A contrasting problem was damp. It stripped the wallpaper from the walls, entrenched itself in clothing and bedding. The slum-dwellers never stopped talking about, worrying about, and trying to cope with the damp, and, of course, it was the main contributor to their health problems.

Nor did the housing problem only affect the homeless and badly housed. It contributed to crime and delinquency, ill-health, poor educational performance ... and we all paid the price. When a researcher in Newcastle carried out a survey to compare the least overcrowded third of the city with the most overcrowded third, he concluded that 'the relationship is inescapable: overcrowding may be positively correlated with virtually all aspects of social malaise in Newcastle, often in a most marked fashion.'

School teachers complained of the effect of bad housing and overcrowding on their pupils: children being nervous and insecure, even going to school on tranquillisers. A teacher at a comprehensive in North Kensington, told me: 'For ten years I have taught the adolescents of this twilight zone and in that time I have witnessed a heartbreaking stream of lost opportunities, of lives ruined before they even truly started.'

The more I saw of the housing problem, the more I realised that it was a deeper environmental problem. The conditions they endured undermined people's chances in life. In a competitive society, they were not competing – at school and at work – on an even playing field. I took to quoting some words, a kind of slum-dwellers lament, by Philip Hobsbawn:

> I'll not return;
> There's nothing there I haven't had to learn,
> And I've learned nothing that I'd care to teach –
> Except that I know it was the place's fault.

Of course, some had helped cause their own problems, but even so, it was not the children's fault, and anyway the fundamental problem was a deficit between supply and demand. There were more families than houses. Families were competing, not for luxuries but for a basic necessity of life. You did not have to be foolish or feckless to lose in this race. You just had to be unlucky, or maybe doing work that was essential for society but was badly paid.

Why had this not become a national scandal? Perhaps because up to then the authorities had been too overwhelmed by the problem to want it publicised. Perhaps because in the Swinging Sixties the majority were having too much fun and the media did not want to spoil it. Perhaps because the worst slums were hidden away in twilight zones between lively city centres and leafy suburbs; we just didn't know they were there. Whatever the explanation, somehow, just like a cancer can grow inside an unsuspecting person until it is suddenly, horribly there and probably incurable, so the deterioration of property and the increase in the numbers packed into it, had created a hidden cancer at the heart of our society that now appeared beyond the capacity of either the private or public sectors to solve. Someone had to do something.

The beginnings of Shelter

It was this challenge, and a possible response to it, that I stumbled upon at Christmas-time 1965, just as I was I was looking for a way of applying my political energies to some sort of effect, and just as I was beginning to be aware that there was a voluntary movement out there that was not driven by doctrinaire belief, rather, in the words of my friend Sam Smith, (about whom more later): 'by an understanding that the proper end of politics was not a policy, not a budget, not an ideology, not even abstractions like peace and justice, but rather good places, and good days and happy and healthy people – the collective little republics of our individual hopes and dreams.'

It was during that Christmas holiday that I saw a television documentary about the work of the Notting Hill Housing Trust (the NHHT). This was one of a number of housing charities that were raising money and buying old houses in the inner cities, renovating them, converting them into flats, and letting them at affordable rents to homeless families. According to the documentary, it took about £325 to supplement 100 per cent loans and home improvement grants from the local authority and create a home for a family of four. I was impressed. These were real results. How could passing a resolution in Twickenham, to be sent to Labour headquarters to be filed away probably unread, compare with this practical expression of social conscience?

So early in 1966 I met the founder of the NHHT, a Church of Scotland minister called Bruce Kenrick. He was then forty-six, a charismatic personality, who worked alone from a study in a house in Blenheim Crescent in Notting Hill. Bruce had convinced the four main national voluntary housing organisations to come together to launch an 'Oxfam on the home front'. The plan was that they would unite behind one fundraising appeal, the money to be channelled to the homeless via local housing trusts such as the NHHT. Bruce was now busy raising money to cover initial expenses, having the organisation registered as a charity, and over-seeing the research and planning for the launch.

So I did what I had always done. I volunteered. In the summer of 1966 I found small offices in James Street, just off Oxford Street. I was the one who opened the door each day, swept the office, made the coffee for the only employee (me), answered the only phone, and did all the work. My first task was to research the problem thoroughly and come up with a strategy for the launch. For over half a year I immersed myself in the problem and the more I saw of the condition that families were enduring, the more shocked I became and ever more angry. After years of embracing any activity that appealed at the time, I had now found a cause that really mattered. The campaigner was born.

For the next five years, all my past enthusiasms were abandoned; I never once made it to the cinema or the theatre or to a first class cricket match. Shelter took over my life.

I set out my plan for the launch of Shelter in a book with a green card cover (it became known as The Green Book). I still have a battered copy.

First, we had to shock the country into awareness; I was convinced that if this had happened as the result of an earthquake or some other disaster, it would have been treated as a national catastrophe and resources would have been poured into a rescue operation. I began to see how Shelter should be positioned – as a rescue operation in a national emergency. Human stories would matter, but so would statistics, because we had to communicate that the issue was scarcity. That this was not about the 'deserving' and the 'undeserving poor', it was not the families' own fault, there simply were not enough homes to meet the need.

The authorities would down-play the numbers of homeless by counting only those who were literally on the streets or in hostels; Shelter, on the other hand, would talk about the 'hidden homeless', would assert that the home was the basis of family life, and that any family was actually homeless if it was split up, or if it was living in conditions unfit for a civilised family life. And would stress we were actually doing something.

We believed people would like the idea that for a specific sum we could actually re-house a family, and so we would emphasise that for 'just £325 and we can put a family of four into a decent home'. But, if it was to have credibility, Shelter would have to produce quick results and Bruce Kenrick and I also proposed that we concentrate on four black spots and on established housing trusts that had the capacity to quickly upscale their output.

Finally, believing that a passion for involvement, especially by younger people, had swept across the Atlantic in the post-Kennedy years, we would place particular emphasis on involvement in all our publicity. 'Shelter involves you' became a campaign theme, and the slogan on T-shirts and badges.

Incidentally, the name Shelter did not emerge overnight. We spent hours considering lists of possible names; Shelter appeared on a number of them. Some who were consulted reacted unfavourably, saying that it would be confused with air-raid shelters, or places for tramps (one person was later to collect £26 in the north of England in the belief that he was raising money for a new bus shelter), but once it was chosen it seemed inconceivable we could have called the campaign by any other name.

So that was the plan. We decided to launch Shelter in the crypt of St Martin in the Fields. The date we chose was December 1, 1966. And then, with just a few days left before the launch, we had an extraordinary stoke of luck.

Cathy Come Home

It has been widely assumed that Shelter was launched as a response to *Cathy Come Home*. In fact, we had no idea that Jeremy Sandford's TV play, a groundbreaking drama-documentary destined to become the most talked-about play ever shown on British television, was being made. It was sheer coincidence that it was screened just a week before our launch. I was working at the James Street office till late that evening and did not even see it, but I learned all about it the following day because everyone was talking about it.

The words 'stirred the conscience of the nation' are used too lightly, but this story of the destruction of a homeless family really did shake viewers to the core. They were moved by the harrowing scenes of a family being broken up. They were stunned by its revelations of the sheer size of the housing problem and of the inhumane treatment of the homeless. As the *Independent* said in an obituary of Sandford when he died in 1990: 'television has rarely created such shock waves and spurred on real change in society as when *Cathy Come Home* hit viewers like a punch in the stomach.' By the weekend the problems of the homeless had become a major political issue. Our dream of creating a sense of national emergency had been realised before the campaign was even launched.

Sandford, who was then 36, was an idiosyncratic old Etonian and Oxford graduate. After *Cathy*, he wrote another powerful play called *Edna the Inebriate Woman* but other works about gypsies and prostitutes had less impact. In his later years he became heavily involved with gypsies and his ramshackle country home became a rather bizarre gathering place for all sorts of New Age folk. He became increasingly eccentric: there were bizarre stories that after seeing Ionesco's *The Chairs*, Sandford came to 'distrust furniture' and insisted on sleeping on the floor.

But back in the Sixties, Sandford had become angry about the way a family that lived near him and his wife, Nell Dunn, in Battersea was evicted and taken to a hostel. He launched a small campaign of his own in newspapers, made a radio documentary and then went on to write *Cathy*. Initially called *The Abyss*, the BBC rejected it twice until Nell, whose *Up the Junction* had also been a TV play, persuaded her producer, Tony Garnett, to read it.

The play traced the lives of a young couple and their children. It showed them desperately trying to find a home, ending up in a hostel for the homeless that (as they did in those days) locked their doors at 10.00 p.m. and sent the man of the family out into the night. It ended with Cathy on a railway station platform, crying out 'Don't take my baby,' as it's torn from her arms by so-called welfare workers. As one writer said, 'it was angry, it was humane, and it was authentic'.

Would Shelter have succeeded without *Cathy*? I believe so, but it would have been much harder work and it would have taken much longer. *Cathy* helped Shelter immeasurably. It set the scene. It showed what we were talking about. It propelled helpers and supporters to the campaign in a way we could not have dreamed possible. Above all, it was a scream of pain from the homeless so authentic that it was not only heard but believed. No politicians' platitudes could erase the memory or discredit its basic theme.

Such was its impact, the BBC screened it a second time just a few weeks later, on January 10, 1967. This was the occasion of my first appearance on television, on ITV's *The Frost Programme*. Later I was to make scores of television appearances but this always remained one of the most crucial, because viewers were not only angered by the problem but crying out for an answer. I was able to describe Shelter's 'rescue operation' and create a positive impression of someone with a constructive plan.

Perhaps *Cathy*'s main value to Shelter was that we were allowed to use it at public meetings up and down the country. We showed it more than 400 times in our first year. Literally hundreds would come out to a local church, town or school hall to see it. I confronted audiences in churches, schools and town halls after special screenings. I would walk on just after the dramatic ending with Cathy's anguished cry and I still have vivid memories of the stunned silence and shaken faces of those who had just seen it. They say you make your own luck; all the work we put into the launch of Shelter earned some. And *Cathy* was it.

The launch of Shelter

Helped by the uproar and by weeks of advance work with the media, the launch took place at a packed press conference and the next day there was massive coverage. We had decided to invest in a full page advert in *The Times* headed 'Home Sweet Home' showing a child in a slum room. Its text began: 'This family is one of three million in Britain condemned to spend Christmas in the slums'. It stated 'this is an emergency' and described Shelter as 'a rescue operation'. It said £325 would give a desperate family a home. In other words, all the key words and messages from The Green Book were there. It had cost £1,800 but raised, on its own, over £12,000 – a hell of a lot of money in those days.

We advertised in other newspapers and in church magazines and they paid for themselves many times over. By Christmas we had raised £50,000 (I guess that would be over £1 million today). Many of the donations were small but inspiring. Kenneth More, the film actor, telephoned on Day One and offered a contribution. At the other end of the social scale, a woman sent £10 and said 'I was just about to do my Christmas shopping; this is what I would have spent.' A man offered to sell his car for Shelter. Scores sent money saying 'in thanks for having a decent home'.

After the repeat of *Cathy* in January 1967 and *The Frost Programme* that night, a follow-up advertising campaign took Shelter beyond the £100,000 mark. Offers of help were flooding in and I decided to mobilise it behind two campaigns, one to start Shelter Groups and one to involve schools.

To be Groups Organiser I chose an effervescent twenty-two year-old idealist called Elizabeth Wills who wrote hundreds of letters to those who had offered help and travelled round the country with such energy that she became known as Whiz Liz. She went on to develop a movement of over 300 local groups, creating a team of Regional Organisers to co-ordinate their work. The groups not only raised money on their home turf but added to the publicity we achieved all over the country. When Liz later became Communications Director, I appointed as her successor Joan Ruddock, who at twenty-four came straight from university to Shelter as Groups Organiser for the Home Counties. Less feisty than Liz but quietly determined, she later went on to become a superb chair-person for CND, a Labour MP, and ultimately served as a minister under Gordon Brown.

Within a few weeks we had enough Shelter Groups to hold a rally for them in London. We were to repeat this every January. The aim was to inspire them to undertake another year's fundraising, but they inspired me just as much with their enthusiasm, their loyalty, their unquestioning trust. Whereas our youth support came via schools, universities and organisations such as the Young Liberals, the groups mainly comprised their parents.

Eileen Ware, a Young Liberal at that time, was desperately keen to work at Shelter and at twenty-two came in to be Youth Director. A tall young woman, she became famous for her miniskirts that were short even by the standard of miniskirts. This made her hugely popular in boys' schools – school assemblies were riveted – and is probably why we even raised substantial sums of money from public schools like Eton, Radley and Malvern College; schools then not known for a social conscience, they each raised over £6,000 with sponsored walks. Eileen was eventually to lead a team that raised nearly a third of all Shelter's income.

The third young woman I recruited at the start was Cindy Barlow, also in her early twenties. As well as being secretary of Shelter, she became responsible for spending the money Shelter raised, as our coordinator of housing projects and housing aid and advice activities. Cindy's mixture of social conscience and commonsense did much to establish and protect the voluntary housing movement's confidence in Shelter. Liz, Eileen and Cindy stayed with me the whole time I was with Shelter and their contribution to its success cannot be over-stated. While others also became valued team members, these three and I, the pioneers if you like, always remained particularly close. We were there when it was a dream; we remained an inner team of confidants until the day I left.

Shelter was not planned as a youth movement, but to some extent it became one. I suppose it was inevitable, given that I was twenty-five when I was appointed director, that I appointed a young team and it attracted young supporters. As Susan Barnes wrote in the *Sun* 'when you go to Shelter's offices in the Strand you get an instant impression of miniskirts, blue jeans, efficiency, good humour, dedication.' Anthony Howard came to have a look. In the *New Statesman* he wrote: 'What sort of job would you think is most sought after nowadays by students coming down from a university? I suppose at one time it was the BBC – and years before that it may even have been the Foreign Office. But today, I'm told, the fiercest competition is to get into Shelter, the national campaign for the homeless run by Des Wilson. Having been taken last week round its national head-quarters in the Strand, I can't say I'm surprised: outside a Kennedy presidential bid I've never seen dedication and professionalism to equal it.'

Of course we had one or two grey hairs as well. One of them was Ken Willson, who helped run the 1966 World Cup and who I recruited to co-ordinate all our fundraising. Another was John Willis, who came as housing director and added experience and wisdom to our spending of the money. John eventually succeeded me as director of Shelter.

This was a time of student protest, primarily over the Vietnam War, but also on issues such as race and third world poverty. Shelter was the right cause at the right time; its combination of outspoken criticism of the ruling generation and constructive action attracted those who, while in rebellion from their parents' generation, wanted to do more than attend demonstrations and sit-ins. I spoke at many universities and youth events and was encouraged by the way the majority of the students wanted to be positive, even if there was always at least one revolutionary who believed we were sticking a band aid over the problem when what we should be doing was overthrowing the whole system. It did no harm that I was not dressed like a conventional charity director and was ready to speak for them when they were in conflict with their elders. For instance *The Times* twice asked me to write articles for its leader page at the time of student protest. I sided with idealistic youth, who, I wrote: ' . . . add a cutting edge to the voluntary movement – they add impatience and intolerance of intolerance. They seek to be articulate for the inarticulate; energetic for the exhausted; enthusiastic and idealistic for those whose spirit has been crushed . . . Youth is no threat to the elder generation. It challenges only rigidity, prejudice, selfishness and bigotry.'

The more popular we became with the young, the more the parents liked us too. If their children were going to get involved, they preferred it to be with what they perceived as a 'worthy' organisation. We had help from kids who were only six or seven years old. (It was helpful when Blue Peter chose Shelter for its Christmas Appeal and asked its young viewers to collect stamps; seven year-old Prince Andrew was one of those who responded, with the help of a tiny Prince Edward.) Also the young involved their parents by getting them to contribute to their fundraising activities, especially sponsored walks. This was the decade of the sponsored walk and Shelter was the most popular cause. At weekends you could hardly move for youngsters walking for Shelter. In one week alone, thousands of walkers went on 500 walks.

Kids loved collecting things; not only was the stamp-collecting a success, but when it was announced in 1968 that 960 million halfpennies in circulation were to be eliminated from the currency, we launched an appeal to kids to collect them. We found ourselves with six and a half million halfpennies, enough to re-house 45 families. Then there was 'Tycoons for Shelter', kids being asked to persuaded their parents to give them two shillings and sixpence and then to make the money grow. Some kids in Surrey helped re-house two families with this scheme. (Only one boy came back without the money – he had put it all on a horse and it lost.)

For a while I became a popular choice as the speaker at school speech days. I made a real effort to make each prize-winner feel special, but I also cheered up the rest by telling them that I never won a prize either. Often the school had raised money for Shelter and I would often leave with a cheque.

By March 1967, Shelter was well established. We had reached half of our first year's target after only 16 weeks. We had become both a professional and popular movement. We had put together a young and dynamic team and moved to larger premises at 86 The Strand. We had recruited some marvellous people, not all of them in the front-line. I will just mention two who may have been older than the rest but whose spirit was representative of the whole team: First, there was a retired accountant called Lionel Beale, a bespectacled, mild-mannered man in his Sixties who joined the Shelter team to do the books when we were in our infancy and who stayed the whole time I was there, rarely leaving his desk in the accounts office, but utterly devoted to Shelter and loyal to me. Thanks to him our financial management was flawless. I can still remember him coming into my office from time to time, his eyes glistening as he showed me a particularly generous cheque. Then there was Charlie Austin. He came to head up our dispatch section and over-saw the volunteers who mailed posters, leaflets etc to Shelter Groups, schools, and individuals all over the country. When he reached sixty-five Charlie retired and we had a party on his last Friday evening. Gifts were given; tears were spilled. It was a memorable event. The following Monday I passed the dispatch office and glanced in the door and there was Charlie. He had given up paid work but was back on the first possible day, working full-time as a volunteer.

About this time we began to reveal our penchant for shock tactics by taking a stand at the Ideal Home Exhibition and installing a slum room into the midst of this show of luxury housing.

We also began to accelerate our activities in the slums. Housing trusts had already been asked to apply to Shelter setting out a programme to show how they could re-house the maximum number of families in the shortest possible time; we now showed our confidence by asking them to plan housing programmes in advance so that the rescue operation could keep pace with the flow of income.

This confidence reflected a sense that, while we were still raising much less than the famous and well-established charities, we were rapidly becoming the country's most popular one. However, for the Trustees and me, there remained one small problem.

'A little local difficulty' – The personal tragedy of Bruce Kenrick

While it never surfaced publicly, there was what could be described as a 'little local difficulty' in Shelter's first year, leading to its 'founder' Bruce Kenrick walking away, never to return. When he died at 86 in January, 2007, his obituaries touched on 'acrimonious exchanges' and a 'battle for power'. In fact, those were exaggerations: it was for Shelter a relatively minor crisis, albeit a personal tragedy for Bruce himself.

To his credit, Bruce had assembled a formidable Board of Trustees. Few, if any, histories of the twentieth century will mention Lewis Waddilove, but they should. Conservative in appearance and manner, he was in fact a highly influential radical. In a self-effacing way he was associated with as much innovation in British social policy over forty or more years as anyone in the country. A leading Quaker – he was chairman of their world conference in 1967 – his base was a trust established by the Rowntree family. From this he injected millions of pounds into research and social planning and practical experiment. He was a rock of commonsense and stability at Shelter and my respect for him was unconfined. He died at eighty-five in the year 2000.

Edwin Barker was just as conservative in style but without as much of Lewis's accompanying radicalism. He was director of the Church of England's Board of Responsibility – in fact he had a dome-like, balding head that made him look a bit like a human cathedral. A gentle man who I cannot imagine ever raising his voice, he was definitely embarrassed, even horrified, by some of our more abrasive activities, notably some of our advertising, but he too made his point in private. He was kindly, understanding, and generously supportive and he did much to help Shelter raise money within the Church of England.

But the star trustee was Father Eamonn Casey, the effervescent Catholic priest who was so shocked by the housing problems of his parishioners that he founded the Catholic Housing Aid Society, pioneering the concept of housing aid centres in Britain. Casey was to become chairman of Shelter for most of my time there; our views on Catholicism and such issues as birth control, could not have been further apart, but we became the closest of friends and confidants. Indeed, he was much loved by the whole Shelter team.

Unlike those three, David Reid did not last the distance with me, but not for lack of loyalty. A young member of the aristocratic Douglas Home family, he befriended Bruce Kenrick in the mid-sixties and was his closest advisor during the planning of Shelter. He loaned money for its launch. The word 'integrity' was written with David in mind and this is why, when problems arose between Bruce Kenrick and myself after I became director, I never feared David. I relied on his sense of fair play and his intelligence to lead him to the right decisions. And they did. But, having chosen to desert his friend when it came to a choice between Bruce and me, his integrity was such that he felt it only right to leave Shelter after the deed was done.

I write about these Trustees not only because their contribution to Shelter should be properly recorded, but because it was they, not I, who had to make a crucial decision in 1967. When Shelter was launched, Bruce was executive chairman and I was campaign director. For a brief time in early 1967 David Reid spent a lot of time in the office. He could see that Bruce was not in tune with the young, irreverent, full-time team, and recommended that Bruce should have a more hands off role, as chairman of the Board, and that Shelter should appoint a full-time director. With Bruce a lone dissenter on the Board, I was appointed director with Bruce still there as chairman. Surprisingly, considering the strength of his feelings, Bruce and I never had what you could call a row. Maybe it would have helped if we had; maybe then we would have found an accommodation. But we never clashed directly, and consequently, when, even after I became director, he went back to the Trustees to say that he wanted me out, it actually became a dispute between him and the Trustees, not he and I.

So what was it all about? There were two problems. The main one was motivational. Bruce, admirably in my view, was not happy to just talk Christianity; he believed it should be expressed practically by engagement in people's day to day lives, especially those living in poverty or suffering from social injustice. As a later *Times* obituary said of him: 'he nurtured his belief that faith was expressed in struggle and that the church's role was to aid the suffering, indeed to suffer with them.' Inspired by a year's experience with a church community project in East Harlem in New York, he wrote a widely-respected book called *Come Out the Wilderness*. Published in 1962, it advocated a more participatory form of Christianity.

While I was not a Christian, I greatly respected this philosophy of

combining faith or principles with practical action. You could exchange
Christianity for Politics and I could have written similarly. So I understood exactly where Bruce was coming from and it never crossed my mind
that it would be the cause of a rift between us. In my view our differing
motivations were irrelevant; he was driven by a Christian sense of
responsibility for others; I was driven more by straight-forward instinctive
anger at the injustice and lack of necessity of poverty and bad housing in
what was, generally speaking, a rich country. I could not see why our
differently motivated energies could not be equally applied to equal affect.
But as we approached the launch it became clear that he intended the
Christian motivation to not only be the primary driving force within the
organisation but to be intricately linked to the projection of Shelter outside it. He felt that by omitting a Christian message in the campaign I had
devised, we were missing the point – for him it was not enough that this
was Christianity in action; it had to be seen to be so. I, on the other hand,
believed that if Shelter was to succeed it had to reach out to everyone,
Christians and non-Christian alike. We could not afford to lose the
majority of the population who, even if they professed to be Christians,
never went to church and never allowed it to influence their lives. Also, I
was already developing a vision of Shelter as a charity with unique appeal
to the young for whom the Christian message could not match a direct
appeal to their burgeoning social-cum-political conscience.

So in mid 1967 Bruce found himself isolated, the victim, as he saw it, of
betrayal and injustice, convinced Shelter was being taken away from him.
His dream of it being the practical expression of his belief was, as he saw it,
being shattered, and the director who he blamed for all this was rapidly
becoming a familiar public face of the campaign and, unless he acted
quickly, would soon be too well-known to remove without publicity
and damage to everyone involved. He pressed the Trustees to revise their
decision, and eventually he came to a Board meeting and made his pitch.

I was not there, but I can imagine the thrust: they had made a mistake. I
was the wrong man. The campaign was losing its Christian motivation and
becoming too associated with me, and I was of unproven character. I did
not have the experience. I was bound to make some cock-up and would
not be able to maintain public confidence. I was making the organisation
vulnerable because the team was too loyal to me personally and because

my version of Shelter was too angry and strident and risked alienating people. He then moved a resolution that I should be asked to leave, but it was followed by a stony silence. He could not find anyone to second it, not even one of the two close personal friends he had placed on the Board to ensure he had personal support. One of them was David Reid, the man who had persuaded the Trustees to appoint me director and who now despaired of his friend's campaign. Bruce was to sever his links with him too.

It is worth considering further the differences between me and the men who were deciding my (and Shelter's) fate that day. I was twenty-five, completely unknown before Shelter and with no executive experience, whereas the Trustees averaged over fifty and several were chief executives of their organisations, and national figures. I was a non-Christian, whereas the Trustees included one of the world's leading Quakers, a Catholic priest, an Anglican clergyman, and the Director of the Church of England Board of Social Responsibility. I had no previous relationship with any of the Trustees, whereas a number of them, and two in particular, were close personal friends of Bruce's. Finally, these were respectable gentlemen in suits, whereas I was just a lively and irreverent enthusiast in jeans and jumper. In other words, I was as far removed from them in experience, motivation and style as it was possible to be. Taking the above into account you would have expected them to be sympathetic to his points and impressed by his call for a 'safer pair of hands' – someone more like themselves. Yet those Trustees unanimously supported me. Bruce resigned as chairman on the spot, Eamonn was elected in his place, and as a first item of business I was confirmed as director. In doing this they were com-mitting themselves not only to me but the way Shelter was developing. There could be no going back; Shelter and I were now bound together, for better or worse, and Shelter was now confirmed on the course that would change the face of British charity.

The unvarnished truth is that Bruce self-destructed. It was a personal tragedy. A number of us could credibly claim to be 'one of the founders' but we would all gladly concede Bruce pride of place. Shelter was his idea. Unfortunately he remained bitter and it ruined the remainder of his life. Years later *The Times*, while describing him in his obituary as 'passionate, committed, inspiring and difficult' went on to say, 'having stoked the fires, Kenrick's combative personality caused him to become increasingly isolated from his peers . . . eventually he chose geographical isolation too, by moving to Iona in the Inner Hebrides.'

Shelter, now united, never looked back. For the four and a half years I worked with those Trustees, they were always wonderfully supportive, as was the Shelter team. And even within an eventual nationwide movement of over 350 Shelter Groups, we never had discord of any kind. From start to finish we did what we should have done. We concentrated entirely on the homeless.

Eamonn Casey

Somewhere in this memoir I must write of Eamonn. He was a great innovator in the housing field and a great chairman of Shelter. He devised the idea of housing aid centres that is still the basis of Shelter's work today. Everyone in Shelter loved him. The debt I personally owe him for his loyalty and support can never be repaid. He left Shelter after being appointed Bishop of Kerry and then Bishop of Galway. While Bishop there, he went on behalf of the Irish church to the funeral of the murdered Archbishop of San Salvador and was in the cathedral to see the massacre of many who were there. As a result, he became a public critic of US policies in Central America and refused to meet President Reagan when he came to Galway.

Sadly his career was destroyed when he later became involved with his housekeeper and fathered her child. Eamonn was deeply devout, but he was a fun-loving man; when in London he enjoyed socialising with the Shelter team and others in the housing movement. He was the life and soul of any party. I could see how and why it all happened, and, perhaps because I was not a Catholic, just a loyal friend, and was therefore not someone who ever related to him as a Bishop, I couldn't see why it really mattered. But when it hit the headlines he would not answer the one-sided accounts of the affair. No one could save him, nor would he allow anyone to try. At least I was able to have a letter published in *The Times* recording all he had done for the homeless and for Shelter. From a position of some eminence in Ireland he went to become a missionary in a rural parish in South America. He learned Spanish and would travel miles in difficult conditions to say Mass for tiny handfuls of people. With his usual energy, he raised money for a medical centre and school for his parish.

Eamonn is now eighty-five, living quietly in a village in Ireland. He has never in my presence complained about the hand that fate dealt him, yet his story is a tragedy, not just because of what humiliation he must have suffered, but because of what we all lost, because he could have achieved so much more. If I was to be the driving force at Shelter, it was from Eamonn's loyalty and wholehearted support that I drew the confidence. And if I've got it wrong, and there is a God and a heaven, they had better be waiting for Eamonn. Otherwise, I'll have to launch another campaign . . .

The changing face of charity

There were over 100,000 charities in Britain when Shelter was launched but in no time at all it was one of the best-known and popular, and definitely the most controversial. Obviously *Cathy* helped. So did the exuberance and visibility of its young supporters. But its rise can really be attributed to the three characteristics which made it a pioneer that changed the face of charity forever.

First, there was the deliberate fusion of campaign and charity – the creation of a campaigning political (with a small 'p') charity that broke all the rules. We knew that for every family we could help, thousands would remain homeless; we would be letting the homeless down if we let the politicians off the hook. Second, there was a new approach to charity advertising, aggressive, shocking – as much a demand for attention as an appeal for a response. Third, there was the deliberate promotion of a personality – the creation of a 'charity celebrity' to realise the opportunities provided by a new celebrity-conscious media.

I was greatly influenced while I was working on my pre-launch report by an experience I had in Notting Hill. I had climbed three unlit floors of a typically decaying old building and knocked on the door. When it opened I saw one family in one room – mother, father and four children. There was one double bed for the four children to sleep on and one single bed for the two adults. There was one light bulb hanging from the ceiling, wallpaper peeling off the wall, no heating in the room at all and for cooking, just one gas ring. It was in chaos. I had, of course, seen such families before, but I was particularly struck by the mother. She was quite young, and under the surface of exhaustion and shame, I could also see she was very beautiful, though like so many other mothers in those circumstances, she was ageing before her time. I asked her if I could come back with a photographer and she said that was fine. When I came back with the photographer the following Sunday, they had cleaned, washed and polished until that room shone. The children were lined up in their Sunday best like a football team, with the four children in the front, the parents in the back. It was a stunning transformation from squalor and despair to a show of pride. But, of course, for my purposes it was useless.

As I walked away I was struck by the realisation that I had actually got the whole thing wrong – because I had been motivated to that point by pity, the last thing such a family needed. They had more courage, personal dignity and pride than you could believe possible of people living in such circumstances. They didn't need pity, what they needed was a home. They didn't need charity, but justice. They didn't want a hand-out. They wanted a chance. I knew then that it wasn't sympathy we had to generate, but anger. To achieve a real result we had to do more than get a few quid into our collection box. We had to create pressure on the authorities and that could only be powered by public opinion fuelled by outrage. When I got home I wrote a crucial sentence in The Green Book – 'This has to be more than a charity – it has to be a campaign'. And we changed the proposed name from the 'national charity for the homeless' to the national campaign.

To do what I now wanted to do, we had to trample all over the charity laws. These made clear that a charity was not supposed to engage in what was termed 'political activity'. I deliberately chose to interpret this as meaning that we were not to engage in *party* politics and argued that we were earning the right to speak out because we spoke from a platform of achievement in relieving human need, and because we had real answers to the problem through experience in tackling it.

Some MPs challenged Shelter's right to be, as they described it, 'political'. I recall the then MP for Dorset South, Evelyn King (described by Alan Clark in his diaries as 'a nasty old buffer') launching a vicious attack on Shelter. It was, he claimed, a violently left-wing organisation. In numerous forums I replied that some political matters were too important to be left just to party politicians with their conflicting agendas. The *Observer*'s influential Ivan Yates wrote an article on the developing controversy over the challenge to traditional charity: 'Charities used to be anxious to keep out of politics for fear that their fundraising may slacken or dry up . . . Shelter, which raises nearly a million pounds a year, is especially vulnerable to attack because the housing shortage is bound to be the stuff of domestic politics. But Des Wilson, its young Director, is adamant that he will not separate the two sides of Shelter's work.' The *Guardian*, in a leading article, picked up this point: 'Shelter's (creditable) performance has been not only in fundraising, but in its clear, decisive recognition that a charity of this sort must also get into the political arena, shake up ministries and parties, and help focus public opinion on Government policies.'

The Charity Commissioners did not like this at all. In an annual report, they issued a carefully-worded warning that straying into political activity would be 'a breach of its trust' and those responsible could be sued to repay to the charity any funds that had been spent outside its purposes. They complained about volunteers becoming too 'involved'. I replied: 'What on earth do they expect? Do they expect that people can come face to face with serious social problems, help to tackle them every day, and yet not be 'involved'? What this says to me is that they believe volunteers should be some form of manual labour to tackle symptoms of problems, but not actually think about the real causes and fight for their eradication.'

As far as I was concerned this was now war. I talked to the team about it. My view was that if we stood our ground we could not lose. Just imagine the uproar if the Charity Commissioners tried to take away our charitable status to punish us for the crime of speaking out for the homeless and for admitting that our charity could not solve the problem alone. Anyway, I argued, we were so popular and so many people were involved that there would be a national outcry if they tried to stop us.

The Commissioners must have been taken aback by the presence of Prime Minister Wilson by my side at the opening of some Shelter-funded homes in Birmingham, especially as he more or less endorsed Shelter's approach:

> Shelter represents a healthy voice of protest, a voice which speaks always in the accents of urgency. Some would find it occasionally speaking in uncomfortably strident terms. But this housing problem is not going to be solved without the idealism, the protest – but also the constructive approach – which Shelter provides. There is one thing I want of Shelter. That it is never satisfied.

We were now involving ourselves in public confrontations with ministers and housing chairmen of the big local authorities. We were holding packed meetings at party conferences. And our comment on housing performance was uncompromising. We had become a completely new kind of charity – one that did not appeal for compassion but campaigned to engender and organise expressions of anger. And the public loved it. The more we extended beyond the traditional charitable approach, the more they supported us. We broke our fundraising targets three years in a row and I am convinced that as many people gave to Shelter to support our campaigning as to support our rescue operation.

As other charities began to follow our lead, the Charity Commissioners lost control of the debate and ultimately had to cave in. For years they silently watched the charity world change, but eventually, years after they had warned charities about 'becoming involved', the Chief Charity Commissioner, in a remarkable public letter, came out firmly on the side of the Shelter-style campaigning charity: 'Many charities very successfully use political campaigning as part of their work. Many charities speak for those they help, sometimes among the most vulnerable in society. It is right that charities are able to speak out on behalf of such people, whether to government or to the wider public.' What an amazing contrast that was with their attitude when Shelter began its campaign.

Looking back on my Shelter years, I believe that our success in changing the face of charity, of adding anger to compassion, reform to rescue, and creating the now familiar campaigning charity, was a huge contribution in itself. Shelter was not only having a huge impact on the housing problem but also on all voluntary activity. It was the pioneer. And was there a practical return from this political pressure? Did it help the homeless? You bet it did. One fact says it all: In only two years in Britain's history has the country built more than 400,000 houses a year. They were 1968 and 1969 – the two years when Shelter's pressure group activities were at their peak. That can't be a coincidence.

'Christmas – you can stuff it.'

Another way Shelter helped change the face of British charity was in the aggression of its advertising. From the start I had insisted that all Shelter materials should be in black and white, and that the emphasis should be on striking pictures and hard-hitting copy. I did not want them to look too neat; I wanted them to look as if they had been done overnight, and thus enhance the impression of a rescue operation in a national emergency. Early on we had the good fortune to strike upon a brilliant team of copy-writer and designer called Peter Hodgson and John Booth. Together they came up with a dramatically fresh approach. It was all-out aggression. They recommended that instead of the usual sentimental Christmas advertising appeal, we should reflect the bitter feelings of families spending Christmas in the slums. I doubt whether any other charity director at the time would have accepted it. But for me there was no question: this was what I had been reaching out for ever since I saw that family in Notting Hill. This was the new face of charity.

The headline of the main advert said: 'Christmas – you can stuff it for all we care' over a picture of a family huddled in a slum doorway. The advert caused a sensation. Many people were horrified by the approach. Even one or two Shelter trustees expressed reservations to me privately; public figures complained in the media. As a result, the advertising achieved a considerable amount of editorial publicity, notably an article in the *Observer*, reporting 'brutally direct advertising campaign that is a world and a half away from conventional tinselly images of the fund-raisers' best season'. The adverts were so controversial I was asked to comment on it to a Working Party on Charities set up by the National Council of Social Services. I wrote to them: ' . . . there was a risk that we might alienate some of our supporters. But we were truly representing the feelings of the people that we were formed as an organisation to represent. The response was that more money came in from that ad than from any other. And I believe it proved that people respond to truth. They respond to urgent need when it is presented to them in an urgent way.' We went on from there to even more stunning, black and white advertising and posters.

Another Gorbals' photograph was accompanied by the headline: 'Christmas in the Gorbals is just like any other day. ROTTEN.' Another showed a family packed into one room. The headline said: 'Even if Father Christmas came, we couldn't ask him in.' The copy went on: 'As the landlord says, this room's a bargain for a fiver. After all, it does hold seven people.'

Once more, we found that the public liked them. They raised more

"Christmas? You can stuff it for all we care."

Christmas – the bright lights, the big spend-up, the family get-togethers, the sentimentality – it's an insult to a family like this.

You are looking at the hopeless, helpless anger of Britain's 3 million slum dwellers. People who have been rejected so often that they reject everything.

Yet, surely, the Christmas message was meant to bring hope to people like these?

Get them out of their dreadful, overcrowded rooms. Give them a decent home. Let them start living again.

This is what SHELTER wants to do. The voluntary housing groups that SHELTER helps, are doing just this. But we need money.

This Christmas you are going to spend money. So spend some of it to help people live like human beings.

SHELTER
Help SHELTER to house a family

money than earlier ads which had also been fairly uncompromising. They excited our Shelter Groups and our younger supporters. And they had the effect of maintaining the sense of national emergency. I've little doubt that this advertising campaign changed the face of British charity advertising. And it strengthened the overall image of a campaign that was uncompromisingly urgent – a legitimate voice of the spirit of the Sixties.

Shelter's own celebrity

In one other way Shelter was different, by promoting one individual as a 'personality'. If you like, a charity celebrity. It was not in the plan; there was no reference to it in The Green Book. It just happened. The more Shelter captured the public imagination, the more the public wanted to know, and someone had to do the talking. We soon realised that by projecting me as a personality we were creating opportunities no other charity appeared to have, so we unashamedly set out to exploit them. We found ourselves where no charity had been before; on programmes like *Any Questions* and on all the chat shows who never asked organisations to appear. They wanted names. So we gave them one.

The charity-campaign approach, the need to trade blows with politicians in public, and the need to create a visible leadership for what was rapidly developing into a national movement, meant that I was becoming a politician of a kind myself – a new-style politician with no traditional party base or seat in the House but called upon to practice all the political skills – dealing with the media, public speaking, appearing on radio and television, and 'inspiring the troops'. And I was becoming famous, asked to speak at major conferences and other events, and asked to comment on the 'have opinions, will travel' slots in the media. As I've said, at first much of this just happened; later, we set out to achieve it. If eyebrows were raised, and they were, because this shameless seeking of media opportunities was unheard of in charity circles, I replied that all I ever did on these programmes was talk about Shelter and the homeless.

Benedict Nightingale, theatre critic for *The Times* for many years now, wrote a book on charities, published by Allen Lane. He devoted a chapter to Shelter and defended its use of me as a spokesman:

Wilson's campaign had achieved more than those who appointed him can have dared hope . . . making over 100 television appearances within Shelter's first three years and seizing every opportunity to dramatise the cause . . . All this made him enemies and one was apt to be told that he 'stinks of publicity'. The proper answer to that may be that it was his bounden duty to stink of publicity. Without it, he would have been failing in his ambition to 'speak the language of the homeless and express their despair'. . . Those who resist his line of reasoning should ask themselves if Shelter would have half the effect it undoubtedly did without Des Wilson.

The respected journalist John Lloyd later wrote an extensive article about Shelter for Time Out. He endorsed the Nightingale view: 'While Wilson ran Shelter very much with himself up front, he was capable of merging his eminently marketable persona with the organisation to the enhancement of both.'

Was I constantly seeking publicity? Of course I was. I had no choice. Publicity was the currency of my business. In fact, publicity was my business. At Shelter, and in other campaigns to come, my fundamental purpose was to create awareness, mobilise opinion, and create change by public pressure. And the only place where we could do that was in the media.

Ironically, many of my critics on this issue were not adverse to publicity themselves, often to further their political or other careers. I suspect their real complaint was not that I pursued publicity, but that I succeeded in getting it, where they often did not. I was stealing the column inches they believed were rightfully theirs. It was no coincidence that over the years these critics were nearly all backbench MPs (alas, often Liberals). Their own political ambitions frustrated, they found it inexplicable that someone who had not taken the conventional route to political power could achieve colossal coverage while they languished in the House of Commons providing a vote but an effective voice for no one. Yet it was happening partially because of their failure. I recall a London MP, a nasty piece of work called Reginald Freeson, who became a junior housing minister. He hated Shelter and hated me because he felt that the housing problem was his business, not ours. At a meeting I was having with his boss, Anthony Greenwood, he completely lost his cool and told the minister and his civil servants, 'We don't need this. I don't understand how they get all this publicity.' I replied: 'If you were doing your job, Mr Freeson, we would not be getting it.'

No one at Shelter complained about my emergence as a personality; they saw its value every day in every cheque that came in, in every new group formed, and, above all, in every family housed. Liz Wills knew where my priorities lay; when the television programme *This Is Your Life* came to seek her help for a show they wanted to make on me, she warned them off: 'He'll never do it,' she told them. And she was right.

Anyway, however it happened, a personality I became, and this opened up all sorts of other opportunities. This is where my journalistic training was a real asset. I was no Shakespeare, but at least I could churn out words that made some sort of sense. Soon I was given a weekly campaigning column in the *Guardian*; I was asked to write a series of feature page articles for *The Times*; and I wrote articles on the homeless and housing for the *New Statesman*.

I was out most nights head-lining meetings organised by Shelter Groups. We would 'hit town' in the late afternoon, I would record interviews for local television and radio shows, talk to local newspapers, do the public meeting and often stay to speak to a local school or a women's organisation in the morning. This is where the 'star' factor really came in to its own. The halls were invariably packed. I think it is fair to say that no charity director has ever found such an audience, before or since. Once I spoke at seventeen venues in Norfolk in two and a half days and still did local media interviews. Needless to say this was exhausting, but it meant we were promoting Shelter all across the country.

Another benefit we obtained from having our own 'home-grown' personality was that we did not need to seek out the more conventional kind of celebrity to help publicise the cause. Given our confrontational relationship with authority, it made little sense to seek the kind of active Royal support that was available to more conventional charities. We did not need that many show business stars either, though Edward Woodward was one who was generous with his time . . . then at the peak of his fame and popularity as star of the series *Callan*, he said he knew from his own experience what it was like to be homeless.

The then television talk show star Simon Dee was another who helped.

One of our London team was married to Joe Steeples, a comedy writer who was working on Simon's Sunday night show on London Weekend. Joe persuaded Simon I should appear on this and, wearing a blue jumper and jeans, I did, in a show whose star guest that week was the actress Jean Simmons. It was probably my most effective television appearance, perhaps because someone talking with passion about the homeless was such a surprising guest for a peak-time Sunday evening chat show and so, as a result, both the studio audience and the 10 million viewers at home actually listened.

In particular I talked about a woman who had turned up at our office and how, when I asked her if she would like a cup of tea, she burst into tears. I asked what the matter was and she said that she had spent the whole day walking across London from one so-called welfare office to another and no one had even asked her to sit, let alone offered her a cup of tea. It is simple stories like that which make an impact on television and the following day the phones at Shelter went wild; the programme had struck a chord.

Of the politicians, Anthony Greenwood, himself the son of a former Labour Minister, was Minister of Housing in my Shelter days. Unlike some of his junior Ministers, he had the sense to realise that a war with Shelter could only be harmful and he went out of his way to be friendly, visiting our offices and attending various Shelter events. He took the brunt of our campaigning with good humour. Harold Wilson, the Prime Minister, behaved similarly. He was always friendly and even asked me to the House of Commons for a chat about the problem. If he saw me at party conferences he would come over for a friendly word. He even came to my farewell party when I retired. I liked him and I believe he was genuine when he spoke publicly in support of our work.

A senior Minister with whom I became friends was the formidable former don, Richard Crossman, Secretary of State for Social Services. I met him in what became a famous debate at the Cambridge Union. It was described in the *Guardian* the following day:

For the first time the Union let loose Mr Des Wilson, the vehement and successful young director of 'Shelter', the National Campaign for the Homeless, on the man who at one time or another has masterminded policy in all the Government departments with which Mr Des Wilson is angry – Mr Richard Crossman, MP, sometime Minister of Housing, now Secretary for Health and Social Security.

The motion 'that poverty in Britain is self-perpetuating and meant to be so' was a savage rejection of gradualist reform. In proposing it, Mr Wilson, a New Zealander who had never been to university or debated, pitted himself against an ex-Oxford don, who is one of the virtuoso debaters of his generation. Mr Wilson was slightly scared, but he went hewing at the motion with a sword of outrage, while Mr Crossman waited in ambush with the trident of logic and the net of Ministerial statistics.

Mr Wilson saw poverty 'in the lines that ravaged the faces of women struggling to keep families together in the face of permanent insecurity and unhealthy housing conditions'. It was partly the result of a cold-blooded decision to maintain a pool of unemployed – 'a decision defended with astonishing lack of shame'.

After Mr Wilson's two-minute standing ovation . . . Mr Crossman prudently disguised himself as the most open-minded, amiable of college tutors when he began his attack. Of course, he agreed, minority poverty was dreadfully undermining . . . then he began to get in some discreet, but increasingly lacerating trident jabs. 'There is nothing this university likes more than a piece of profound pessimism, couched in morbid language,' he said of the motion.

In later years I spoke many times in both the Oxford and Cambridge Unions, three times on the same side as Michael Foot, and opposed to people like Michael Heseltine and John Biffen, but the Crossman encounter was my most memorable moment in these cockpits of debate. After Labour lost the 1970 General Election, Dick Crossman became editor of the *New Statesman* and asked me if I would like to join his small group of advisors who met on a Thursday morning. This included Barbara Castle, Tony Benn, Harold Lever, and Thomas Balogh as well as the NS journalists. Alan Watkins and Anthony Howard. These meetings often exploded into arguments about what happened when Labour was in power and were fascinating to me. I wrote occasionally for the magazine and Dick and I would sometimes have dinner together and he came to parties at my house. Compared with me he was an intellectual giant, but he loved the

CAMBRIDGE UNION SOCIETY

EASTER TERM, 1969

FIRST DEBATE

THURSDAY, 24th APRIL, 1969
8.0 p.m.

"Poverty in Britain is self-perpetuating and meant to be so"

Proposed by Mr. HUGH ANDERSON, Trinity College, Vice-President.

Opposed by Mr. JON VAUGHAN JONES, Magdalene College.

Mr. DES WILSON, Director SHELTER,
　　　　　National Campaign for the Homeless, will speak third.

Rt. Hon. RICHARD CROSSMAN, O.B.E., M.P.,
　　　　　Secretary of State for Health and Social Security, will speak fourth.

FOR THE AYES	*Tellers:*	FOR THE NOES
	Floor :	
Mr. D. J. SAUNDERS, Christ's College.		Mr. J. C. CORR, Peterhouse.
	Gallery :	
Mr. R. W. J. DINGWALL, St. John's College.		Mr. C. R. S. SHEPPARD, Trinity College.

Newnham College,　　　　　　　　　　　　　　HELENE MIDDLEWEEK,
　16th April, 1969　　　　　　　　　　　　　　　　　*President*

gossip and intrigue of political life and I always found ministers in the Blair and Brown years pygmies compared with him.

I first met Michael Foot at a dinner at the home of the Hampstead MP at that time, Ben Whitaker. It was a glittering evening, and Foot was in a group with the theatre critic Kenneth Tynan and the journalist Nick Tomalin. He asked me how he could help Shelter and I said we would love to have a spot at the annual Tribune Rally at the Labour Party Conference. A couple of days later he wrote, asking me to speak, and I did for two years in a row. He was a remarkable man and it was a real thrill when he and I later formed a team to speak two or three times at other Cambridge Union debates where he was always given a hero's welcome

Did it all go to my head? I don't think so. For a start, I was having to learn as I went along; every experience was a new one, and for all my self-confidence, these experiences were often nerve-wracking. Also, I was just too busy working, and, for much of the time, just too tired, to be fully aware, let alone enjoy, what was happening to me. The secret of success in campaigning (or, for that matter, in all forms of human endeavour) is focus. Applying one's emotional, intellectual, and physical energy on an activity in an intense concentration of willpower that allows for little else. If I won more battles than I lost over the coming years, I believe it was because I was driven by an almost overwhelming will to win. That did not allow a lot of time for enjoying 'being someone'. There was another pressure: I felt an enormous responsibility to repay trust. The Trustees, the team, the local Groups trusted me. Everyone who gave money to Shelter trusted me. There was no way I was going to let them down. If I ever performed poorly as their representative on television, and I always knew when I did, I was overcome with shame. And, finally, if by any chance I allowed myself to be tempted to put self before Shelter, perhaps appear on a television programme that was more about self promotion than the campaign, I had a human conscience in the form of Eamonn Casey. When I told him what I planned, he would always ask: 'How will that help the homeless, Des?' If I couldn't look him in the eye, I wouldn't do it.

The Queen and I

While we did not seek Royal sponsorship when I was at Shelter, I did have an encounter with them. In those days, and possibly still today, the Queen had a monthly lunch for a cross-section of people in public life. Presumably this had the double-objective of keeping her in touch with what was happening in her realm and giving a Royal pat on the back to those who her advisors believed worthy of it.

I was in a downstairs office at Shelter one day when the telephone operator called to say a Lord Plunkett was on the line. I took the call and he explained, albeit not in these words, that he was a senior flunkey in Buckingham Palace and HMQ wondered if I was free for lunch on a date some three weeks hence. I said I would have to pop upstairs and check my diary. There was an intake of breath at the other end and I realised that this was not exactly the enthusiastic response he was accustomed to. Anyway, I was free and told him so, and it was left there.

About three weeks later I was woken at six in the morning. It was my family, all talking on the phone at the same time. Over the babble I could hear my father saying 'It's a proud day for the Wilson family' Now, I had not heard their voices for nine years and I was amazed. What had happened? It turned out that Buckingham Palace had released the list of those attending that day's lunch and it had been picked up by the New Zealand media and by the *Oamaru Mail* in particular. Because they were twelve hours ahead of British time, my family had read about it over their tea and nearly choked on their buttered scones (or whatever they were having).

Now up to now this point, the lunch had been just another date in the diary. Frankly, I was not particularly keen on royalty. To me, it was an institution that helped prop up the class system and that was part of the British problem, not part of the solution. So I had not been impressed by the invitation or given it much thought. But this call made me nervous. Perhaps this was a bit more of an event than I had allowed for.

So I put on my one suit, hurried to London (I was by then living in a place called Weston Park in Surrey), booked a hair cut, and went down into the shops below our offices in the Strand and purchased a new shirt and tie. By 12.30 I was looking as smart as I had in my whole life and standing under Admiralty Arch, having left myself half an hour to stroll down to the

Palace. At that point the heavens opened and we were hit by a torrential rain storm. Within a couple of minutes I was soaked to the skin. My beautifully ironed suit became shapeless; my new shirt and tie looked like wet rags; my beautifully cut and combed hair was ruined. I headed for the nearest doorway, which turned out to be some kind of gentleman's club. When I burst into its hallway a porter (who, I still remember, was clad in a green uniform) came over, clearly determined to evict me. I all but fell on my knees: 'Help me,' I cried, 'I am due to have lunch with the Queen and its pouring with rain and I'm soaked. Can you call a taxi?' He looked at me for a moment and then sprang into action. I arrived at the Palace twenty minutes later, still soaked, but at least on time.

I was met at the door by the Queen's then Press Secretary, an Australian called William Heseltine, who took one look, summed the situation up, and took me off to be dried out and made to look semi-respectable. I was then taken to meet the other guests. They included Richard Lester, who had just directed *A Hard Day's Night* and Angus Wilson. Somehow I succeeded in upsetting every member of the Royal Family present. Prince Charles was attending one of these events for the first time and sat between Richard Lester and me. I seem to remember telling him he should get out into the real world and find out how people really lived. He politely declined my offer to act as his guide. Then, over coffee afterwards, a Labour MP and I found ourselves in dispute with Prince Philip over some issue of the day. He made little attempt to hide his disdain. Finally, I found myself talking to the Queen who began brightly by telling me she was about to visit the Ideal Home Exhibition. I explained this was a fantasy land that bore no relation to the real lives of her subjects. 'Oh come now, Mr Wilson,' she said rather more sharply than I would have expected, 'I would have imagined you would have welcomed it. After all, they are building houses.' Lord Plunkett hastily ushered me away and, convinced I had alienated all three, I slunk into a corner to await the first opportunity to depart before I was forcibly taken to the Tower.

Some weeks later I was on a plane to Scotland and who should sit next to me but Lord Plunkett.

'I'm afraid I did not perform terribly well,' I said. 'Oh, I would not worry, Mr Wilson,' he said. 'Her Majesty is used to meeting all sorts.'

Oh dear.

The Propaganda Wars (I): The Housing Surplus

One effect of our disrespect for the rules of 'charity behaviour' was to make it impossible for the authorities to cover up the problem. As soon as some hapless minister spoke publicly to claim the problem was solved, we came down on him like a ton of bricks.

There were two major confrontations in 1969. The first was over the so-called housing surplus.

Britain had achieved a surplus of homes over families in Britain. This did not mean, however, that the housing problem was solved, because it was not about an equal number of homes to families over the country as a whole, but having homes in the right place (where people had to live in order to work), at the right price (at rents and prices people could afford), of the right size, and of the right condition.

The question of the housing surplus arose in 1967 when the then Minister of Housing, Anthony Greenwood, referred to it in a speech, but to his credit he put it in some perspective, saying:

> 'I have seen it said recently that the demand for housing will fall sharply in the 1970s. I am absolutely convinced that this is wrong. We know that over 100,000 houses a year will be needed simply to keep pace with the growth in households. More, we know now that we have between two and three million slums and potentially unfit houses. This indicates our major housing problem in the 1970s.'

Unfortunately, abbreviated press reports of this speech concentrated on the potential surplus and Shelter decided to destroy the myth as soon as possible. On the whole Greenwood fell into line, but in February 1969, under attack from Conservatives in the House of Commons, his junior minister, Kenneth Robinson, predicted a surplus of one million houses by 1973. Although he qualified this to some small extent, he used the housing surplus as the main plank in his defence of the Labour administration's record, and the tone of his speech was reflected in a *Guardian* headline: 'Cathy may come home to housing surplus in 1973'.

We loaded up the guns, determined to reverse the trend of the publicity.

Hours after the Robinson speech, the *London Evening News* reported: 'Mr Kenneth Robinson's claim in the Commons yesterday that there would be surplus of a million houses by 1973 was described by the Director of Shelter today as 'either a cruel joke, an unscrupulous deception, or an indication of Mr Robinson's abysmal ignorance of the realities of the housing problem.'

The *Guardian* ran a leader describing Robinson's 'kind of calculation as an exercise in inexcusable complacency'. The television programme, *Twenty-Four Hours* (now *Newsnight*) invited me to debate the issue with Robinson. That evening just before I left home, I was telephoned to say that Robinson would only appear if he was alone. I could, therefore, not represent our side of the story. I saw no reason why he should be allowed to escape that easily, and immediately issued to the Press Association the facts about the programme. The result was that the story made the front pages of every newspaper the next day. Robinson had, by refusing to debate, made certain that the maximum attention would be drawn to my answer to his claims in the House of Commons. And we heard little more about the housing surplus after that.

The Propaganda Wars (2): Face the Facts

For our Autumn campaigns we took to producing a black and white 'shock report' – full of dramatic pictures and case histories, but always with a theme consistent with our campaigning objectives at the time. The first was 'Back to school from a holiday in the slums', showing that hundreds of thousands of children went to school each day from housing conditions so oppressive that their capacity for education was restricted. In 1968 we followed it with a shock report on bad landlords. The report 'Notice to Quit' and accompanying campaign helped to end the complacency that existed after the introduction of the 1968 Rent Act. Then came the 1969 report, however, called 'Face the Facts'. It was to be our greatest campaign.

In March 1969, Dick Crossman announced an inquiry into the homeless. Later, on April 29, his Junior Minister, David Ennals, announced the details of the survey, saying: 'I am speaking of truly homeless people'. What did he mean by 'truly'? He later made that clear: he was talking about those who were in hostels for the homeless or literally on the streets. The hidden homeless were not included.

We were determined that ministers should not be allowed to pull the wool over people's eyes about the real nature of the housing emergency, and so we decided to devote our autumn campaign to hammer home our wider view of the problem, The title of the report 'Face the Facts' summed up its message. Excluded from the homeless, by most official definitions were :

1 Families 'on the streets' – sleeping in an abandoned car, or in the open. (This again shows the absurdity of the official definition; having lost the four walls and a roof, the family have to regain them – 'in temporary accommodation' – before they are homeless!)
2 Families living in squalor
3 Families hopelessly overcrowded
4 Families split up (including those with children 'in care')
5 Families taken in under stress by in-laws or friends
6 Families in physical danger because of the unfitness of their property
7 Families lacking many or all of the essential facilities, toilets, hot water etc

The report was packed with stories about such families, underlined by the question: are these not homeless too? The publicity achieved was massive; the media all supported the thrust of he campaign. The *Sunday Telegraph* understood exactly what we were on about:

> Divided families, like those who share overcrowded accommodation with others or lack the elementary means of preserving privacy and health, can fairly be regarded as homeless. SHELTER does well to remind us of this. If there are only 18,689 homeless people in Britain, as official statistics claim, the problem is marginal, and its victims can too easily be linked with meths drinkers and layabouts as the inevitable sediment of a complex society. Raise the figure to a million, and a big social question presents itself causing all of us to think again.

This was a triumph. The media were hammering home our key messages. But much more was to come because we were to be helped by the incompetence of the Labour machine in sending two junior ministers into battle, the hapless Kenneth Robinson and David Ennals (actually a decent man, but in this case seriously off-key). These two made speeches on the same night that so clumsily defended their position, I almost felt sorry for them. Even their politician opponents could see it. The

Conservative shadow housing minister Peter Walker announced his party would 're-define the homeless to take in all families living in conditions unacceptable in a civilised society'. The Liberal leader Jeremy Thorpe said the Liberal Party too would re-define the homeless.

And all this set the scene for our most effective party conference season. Our Liberal Party conference meeting was packed. And in his major televised leader's speech to the conference, Jeremy Thorpe was most loudly applauded when he said: 'The worst social evil in this country is bad housing. The Shelter report Face the Facts should be compulsory reading for every MP and councillor in the country.' Our Labour Party conference meeting was also packed. Ennals sat in the front row and tried to defend himself but his remarks were heard in silence. The next day the Prime Minister himself, in his televised leader's speech, said: 'First among the priorities of the seventies is to get rid of the scandal of bad housing and no-housing. That is why all of us here are on the same side as SHELTER.' We achieved a hat trick when Tory leader Edward Heath followed: 'The next Conservative Government will give high priority to the problems of the homeless. We have already agreed to redefine the homeless and to make a genuine endeavour to redefine the problem properly.'

Can any pressure group in history have forced all three leaders of political parties to respond to their campaign on the occasion of their big speech of the year? Of course, we knew that there were bigger issues to confront than how a few Ministers defined the homeless. But we had seized on their incompetence and complacency to hammer home our point – that there was a national emergency and the real problem was the hidden homeless. We had shown we could force the politicians on the defensive. We had forced housing to the top of the political agenda. It was a ruthless campaign, but every day the numbers appealing to our housing groups for help were growing and sounding ever more desperate. We were in no mood to compromise.

These days the political parties make much of their early response units. These pick up stories and feed in the party's point of view even before you and I have heard them on radio and television. Shelter had showed them how.

Housing Programmes

By March 1970, just over three years after its launch, Shelter had helped housing trusts to re-house 3,103 families and homes for another 2,840 were in the pipeline. We had helped to re-house three families every day since the launch. These statistics probably do little to convey the joy we created in the lives of many thousands of people living for the first time in decent homes with caring landlords. Alas, I was now too busy to meet more than a handful.

If I do not devote much space in this book to the rescue operation itself, it was because I was not heavily involved. One of my strongly-held beliefs is that power corrupts, and the real power in Shelter lay in the distribution of money. I was controversial enough without getting into any issues that may arise about who should get what. (In fact no serious issues did arise.) So I had what I still think was the good sense to keep out of the decision-making about where the money went. Fortunately in John Willis and Cindy Barlow I had two team members I would have trusted with my life, and they put together a high quality committee to allocate the money.

I was, however, always boosted when I received letters from families re-housed. I kept those letters and whenever, because of exhaustion or a bad day, I wondered whether it was all worthwhile, they were a source of reassurance. In the end it was the housing of such families that it was all about. And to do that we needed the housing associations. It would be unforgivable to write about the work of Shelter without recording the work that these local groups did, dealing with the homeless face to face, day in and day out, finding the houses, buying them, getting them repaired, and then helping families into them. I think of people like David Mumford, who ran the Birmingham Housing Trust and was still there, working away in the local voluntary housing movement, over 30 years later.

Fortunately I met with these heroes fairly frequently, at housing conferences and whatever, but, looking back, one of my regrets is that I did not see more of those we re-housed. It would have been hugely motivating and no doubt even today would fill me with great memories of what we were doing then. But there was so much to do. In 1970 I was able to report to the Shelter Rally three experiments – in housing aid and advice, in neighbourhood rehabilitation, and community relations.

SNAP – The Shelter Neighbourhood Action Project –was created as a shop window for the rehabilitation of a whole neighbourhood with the full participation of the people. Architects, planners, politicians and the press were flocking to Liverpool 8 to see what SNAP was achieving, a community life that was not being demolished and destroyed, but instead revived by our pioneering concept of neighbourhood action projects and rehabilitation.

SHAC – The Shelter (family) Housing Aid Centre – built on the work of Eamonn Casey and the Catholic Housing Aid Society – was to be the basis of a campaign by SHELTER to further the concept of housing aid and advice throughout England, and now also in Scotland we were pioneering a concept that I was convinced would grow and grow. (As indeed it did – there are now many hundreds of such centres throughout the country, many of them still funded by Shelter.)

SHARE – The Shelter Housing and Renewal Experiment in Bradford – was also under way, and forcing authorities and volunteers alike to take a fresh look at community relations, linked with better housing, both in that City and in the rest of the country.

Homes for the Irish, or 'Why we Wanted to Borrow an Aircraft Carrier from the Ministry of Defence'

The Sixties saw the return of 'the troubles' to Northern Ireland. They had created a breed of homeless family I had never come across before – near the end of 1969 I first met families literally afraid to return to their homes in case they were murdered. Joe Connelly, slight, softly-spoken, bespectacled, mild and essentially a family man told me that the strain of living 'near the front' – the Falls Road – had been beginning to tell and so on the night of August 15 he took two sleeping pills. He slept through a riot, and woke to find houses burning in the street, and, in his own words 'all hell let loose'. The next day, Joe, who is father of six children, got the message: 'Get out – or else.' As he put it: 'With six kids, who was going to stay around to find out what they meant?'

Although the Northern Ireland authorities had in some respects moved remarkably quickly, many families were faced with a grim Christmas.

This was the situation on Monday, November 24, 1969, when Desmond Plummer, leader of the Greater London Council, and Horace Cutler, Chairman of the Housing Committee, came for a working lunch with John Coward, John Willis, Cindy Barlow and myself at Shelter. After chatting about mutual problems for some time, Plummer said he had something to offer: 500 mobile homes over two years. It turned out that the homes were high-standard, temporary houses, purpose-built by the GLC to help with the decanting of slum clearance areas. The GLC was running out of land, and finding the cost of moving them prohibitive. They offered 100 homes immediately – 'You can have them today' – and the rest over the next couple of years.

After Plummer and Cutler left, I had an idea: what about Belfast? Should we offer them to the Northern Ireland authorities as emergency housing. A fast-moving operation could get at least some of them over for Christmas. The telephones buzzed for a couple of days as I firstly confirmed that the 100 homes could be made available quickly and that we could use them anywhere in the UK, and then contacted Des McConaghy, director of Liverpool SNAP, who had contacts at national and local Government level in Northern Ireland. A Belfast official soon arrived, and was shown the homes. He confirmed that the houses were of sufficient quality, but two major problems remained: firstly, transporting them to Northern Ireland quickly; secondly, persuading the Northern Ireland authorities to pay the costs.

I rang David Owen, the Under-Secretary for the Royal Navy, to ask him for an aircraft carrier. To my surprise he both returned my call and took the whole matter seriously ('who have you declared war on, Des ?' he asked), and after investigations said that the Navy could perhaps help out in an emergency. Fortunately, by then, John Willis had found out that it was easier and quicker to take them up the M1 on lorries and across the Irish Sea by ferry, and so we didn't need to bother David Owen any further.

Des McConaghy and I got into Belfast by the Sunday morning, and drove past soldiers with machine guns and walkie-talkies, past the so-called 'peace line' of rolls of barbed wire, to begin a day of frantic meetings, with the homeless on the site, representatives of the Catholic community, and local officials, who turned up in a voluntary capacity to have talks about what could be done. The locals were somewhat sceptical about our ability to persuade the Ministry to act quickly, and we were told that the only hope was to get Brian Faulkner, the Minister of Development, behind the scheme. A meeting was fixed between myself and Faulkner for half past ten on the Monday morning, and in order to build up the pressure on him, stories were leaked to the Irish newspapers and to the *Guardian* about the offer.

On December 1, 1969, three years exactly since the launch of Shelter, the *Guardian* reported:

Mr Des Wilson flew unannounced to Belfast at the weekend and apparently gave the Northern Ireland authorities a brisk ultimatum: to cut red tape and accept £200,000 of housing within 48 hours, or face the political uproar which would result if they lost the chance of re-housing 100 families immediately.

This crucial day was only one week after the GLC made their offer of the homes. I made some Diary notes for that day and they read:

Woken up at 6.30 a.m. by the BBC who wanted an interview for *Today* programme via the telephone . . . a few minutes later heard it broadcast back. The newspapers were full of the story, with the main local news-paper making it their front page lead, and the *Guardian* giving it pro-minence. This publicity was in my view essential to the success of the negotiations . . . By the time we arrived at Stormont we judged the atmosphere was on our side . . . by the time I was hauled in he was surrounded by his own officials, representatives of the Northern Ireland Housing Trust, and the Belfast Corporation. I laid down four conditions: the homes were to be used as quickly as possible to help families in emergency circumstances and all efforts were to be made to get the families in by Christmas; they were to be treated as temporary and should not prejudice in any way the provision of good standard per-manent housing; the Northern Ireland authorities must meet the costs involved – about £1200 per house for transport and installation; proper arrangements must be made for maintenance of the housing and services. There was a slight brush with Faulkner over the radio broadcast in the morning and the *Guardian* story. Faulkner seemed fairly deter-mined to keep me in my place, and I was tempted to tell him what he could do with himself, but I decided that no matter what he said, he was being forced into taking the houses, so I shut up. It was finally decided that they should take 50 houses immediately and attempt to install them by Christmas and that we would hold another 50 in reserve for them.

In the meantime, John Willis had been performing miracles in lining up the transport of the mobile homes. The first of the shipment left London on December 9, having been picked up by cranes from a site in Battersea, put on giant transporters and sent to Preston, from where they were shipped to Northern Ireland. Two homes left London each day and 25 families were actually in their homes by Christmas. We soon received an order for the remaining homes.

From Shelter's point of view this had all made for a most exciting Christmas. It was heart-warming to see the families preparing to spend Christmas in much more comfortable conditions than they had dreamt would be possible. It was also exciting to think that we had been capable of pulling off a remarkable operation in only 22 days. In all this teamwork had been the key and the two heroes of the exercise were John Willis, who was responsible for getting the homes over there, and Des McConaghy, who did most of the negotiating with the Northern Ireland officials to make the success possible. Inevitably it helped our Christmas Appeal. We were to end the year on a high.

Time to Leave

That 1969 Autumn-Winter with the Face of the Facts campaign and the Belfast operation was probably the peak of my contribution at Shelter. The following year was relatively uneventful. We now had to raise a million pounds every year to finance our operations but we fell short in 1970, partly because sponsored walks were losing their novelty appeal, but mainly because the General Election was called at the same time as our Shelter Week and seriously under-mined our main money-making event of the year. Otherwise it was a year of consolidation.

For my part I was beginning to tire. From the summer of 1966 I had enjoyed little in the way of holiday while working 15 to 18 hour days and many weekends. But the real problem was that I was becoming stale. I had observed how many charities were run by the same powerful individual for many years and I was determined not to stay too long, and risk undoing much that I had done, either because I was exhausted or because I was getting in the way of fresh energy and ideas. By then I was up and running by 7.00 a.m. every day and after taking part in meetings, giving interviews, writing articles and speeches, dealing with correspondence, etc., in the evening I would drive to some far-flung place to do a public meeting. Often I would be expected to attend a reception afterwards. It would sometimes be the early hours of the morning before I got home. No matter how much you care, if you make speech after speech about the homeless, you start to lose your edge.

One day, having been in the office all day, I drove up to Nottingham in the evening to speak at a meeting. Afterwards I drove back to London in the pouring rain, crossed the city, and had reached some traffic lights at Teddington on my way to Weston Park when they turned red. It was now four in the morning and I had been going for 20 hours. The rain was torrential. I rested my head on the steering wheel and suddenly felt over-whelmingly tired, utterly exhausted. My system had endured enough and was literally closing down on me. I could feel the energy and life in me draining out of me just as blood would have drained away if I had been shot. Tears began to run down my cheeks. I knew then that I was finished. I knew that if I could only get home to bed, I would stay there and never get up. I had no more to give. As I peered through the rain pounding on my windscreen, I noticed something white on the back window of the car in front. I leaned forward to look and could just make out the words. They were: Shelter involves me.

It was one of our car stickers. I could not believe it. There I was, all alone at four in the morning in the pouring rain, and at just the moment when I needed some inspiration, when I needed to believe this exhaustion was worthwhile, when I needed someone to do something – anything – to make me feel it was all making a difference, someone had come from nowhere and without knowing that they were doing it, they were signalling their support. The weight in my heart and on my shoulders lifted. My optimism and self-purpose returned. I had been saved by a car sticker.

Even so, I knew that night that the time was coming when I had to go. Shelter was now an established national institution. It had raised over £3 million, it had 350 local groups, and helped to re-house 6,000 families. It had made housing the major domestic political issue of the late Sixties. And it had provided a vehicle for the idealism of a considerable number of younger people. It had also shown that a charity could be highly effective as a spokesman for the cause, and an advocate on policies and expenditure priorities. It had demonstrated the importance of professionalism. It had pioneered a number of new techniques – the more hard-hitting advertising, the periodical reports with reinforcing advertising and direct mail, the barnstorming of local areas, the use of dynamic campaign newspapers and professional, integrated design, and the realisation of the full potential of public meetings. Helped by a Labour Government that, to be fair, was well motivated and genuinely responsive to our campaign, and that did give housing far greater priority, much had been achieved: house building records had been broken; a lot of older housing had been saved so that new building was genuinely improving the housing stock; tenants had been given greater security; the 'Cathy-style' hostels for the homeless had either been closed or made more humane. Between the Government and Shelter we had not solved the housing problem but we had set the country on the right road.

The Shelter of my directorship has been criticised for not giving Labour sufficient credit at the time. It is a fair criticism. But our task was to campaign for the homeless, not for Labour, and it was never possible to be satisfied when we knew how long the waiting lists remained and how bad many of the slums still were. We were also criticised for being unsophisticated in our political objectives. There is some truth in that too; I believe we would have benefited from having a more sophisticated set of policy objectives to bring to direct talks with ministers and council leaders. But housing policies by the end of the 1960s were not that unsound – there was a mix of new building and rehabilitation, security of tenure for unfurnished tenants, proposals for extending rent subsidies to the private sector, discussion of the concept of neighbourhood rehabilitation and we were much more humane in our approach to the homeless. There is no question in my mind, therefore, that Shelter's priority should have been exactly what it was – to convey the nature of the housing problem to the majority of the population, to campaign for greater priority for housing for social as well as compassionate reasons, and to put so much steam into the issue that no party could afford to do other than commit itself to keeping housing at the top of its agenda and – and this was the point of all that – build more houses. I mentioned earlier that in two separate years while I was at Shelter, Britain broke all housing records and twice passed the 400,000 a year mark. That had not been done before and has not been done since. Our main political objective – more houses – was achieved.

Shelter now needed to consolidate, review its role, re-launch itself afresh, and it needed fresh energy and enthusiasm. So late in 1970, I called a small meeting of the key Trustees and told them that the time for change had come, and by January 31, 1971, I was gone. I was just coming up thirty and had been working for Shelter virtually every minute of every day for four and a half years. John Willis was appointed to succeed me. This had my support. John was in many ways the opposite of me but I believed this was what Shelter needed. I had provided the energy to get the rocket off the ground. Now it needed a safe pair of hands to steer it to the stars.

5

The Consumer Champion
who never was

At the time I never saw myself as a 'campaigner'. Shelter had been special, but a one-off. I was a journalist and it was time to return to journalism. I now had a formidable list of contacts and had written for newspapers from *The Times* and the *Guardian* to the *Daily Mirror*. For the first time I had the confidence to aim for Fleet Street. Then, out of nowhere, I had a call from Dame Elizabeth (Betty) Ackroyd, who was about to retire as director of the Consumer Council. They had considered over 200 applicants to replace her, but she and her chairman Lord (Jack) Donaldson had been unimpressed. She asked me to come for a chat. I did, and the upshot was that at the last minute I was added to the short list.

Betty Ackroyd was a remarkable woman. A former senior civil servant with a distinctly upper class accent and manner, she was also a formidable fighter for her cause, with both an instinct for what was fair and at the same time a sense of fun. She had established the independence and in-fluence of the Consumer Council and it was respected both in Whitehall and in industry. But, it lacked public visibility; she hoped I would achieve a higher profile for it, and sharpen its political teeth. I was immediately taken with the idea, and I saw no inconsistency with what I had been doing. As with most issues it was the already-disadvantaged who suffered most from lack of choice or safety, and from inadequate information or legal protection.

The interview with the Council was lively. One or two members, fearing a more populist approach, made up their minds before we met; they did not want me at any price. One, a university professor, made his hostility clear. 'You may know about the homeless,' he all but snarled, 'but what do you know about, say, ladies' tights?' I smiled sweetly: 'I've had some acquaintance with them,' I said. This had them laughing, but at a price – the professor's hostility turned to hatred before my eyes. Another Council member, a battleaxe of a woman from Scotland, would not even come to the meeting, saying she felt it inevitable I would be chosen and wanted no part of it. Anyway, I won the day.

The decision was widely publicised. The *Sunday Telegraph* said: 'One prospect that strikes terror into various hearts is Wilson Unchained.' And Richard Crossman, now editor of the *New Statesman*, wrote in his weekly diary: 'It is exciting news . . . I am willing to predict that in terms of scandals exposed and injustices put right he will get more done than most minsters of the cabinet.'

The Conservatives were not amused. Betty Ackroyd had been convinced for some time that newly-elected Prime Minister Heath, was looking for an excuse to shut the Council down, and she was proved right. The PM and his chancellor Anthony Barber were having none of me. The Consumer Council was closed down, its demise a one-line public expenditure cut in a special emergency Autumn 1970 budget. More than 90 highly professional staff and all their experience and expertise were thrown on the scrapheap to save no more than £250,000 a year. The decision aroused considerable anger. Richard Crossman, in his *NS* diary, described it as the 'pettiest and meanest of all the Chancellor's economy cuts'.

The one positive to come out of it all was that I became a friend of Betty Ackroyd and remained so for the remainder of her life. Betty never married and lived what I suspect was a lonely life in a spacious flat in St James Street. But she was good fun and a marvellous public servant, later founding and giving 25 years of leadership to the Patients Association. When we launched the Clear campaign for lead-free petrol she kindly came on board as chairman of its charitable trust and was wonderfully supportive (she insisted on chair*man* – she had no time for 'chair'). Betty didn't suffer fools gladly. When the Consumer Council closed its doors, she had the telephone calls re-directed to the desk of the civil servant she held partly responsible, so that for weeks he received calls reminding him how much in demand the Council's advice had been.

Many years later, when she was involved with Clear, she took the trouble to study all the arguments. Then one day she found herself at a conference in Europe and, to her surprise, at the lunch table some know-all suddenly raised the subject of leaded petrol and explained to everyone that the concerns about it were a nonsense. The last thing he must have expected was that this elderly, upper class woman from the UK would begin to demolish his case by correcting one point after another. By the end of the lunch he was so embarrassed he tried to save face by saying in a loud voice: 'Madam, it has been a pleasure debating with someone who one can say is an equal.' Betty replied in an even louder voice: 'I only wish I could say the same.'

One of my dreams since childhood was to see the Great Wall of China, so when Betty told me she was going on a guided tour of China I was green with envy. When she came back we had dinner and I asked her how it went. 'Well,' she said, 'it started badly. I arrived at the airport without my passport and by the time I went back and found it and returned to the airport I had missed the flight. So I arrived out there a day late.' 'Oh Lord,' I said. 'That was bad luck.' 'Well, not really,' she said. 'At least I missed having to go and see that tiresome Great Wall . . . ' For once I was speechless.

Betty's adjective for anyone she did not like or who she was exasperated by was 'tiresome'. If Betty called you that, believe me, you *were* tiresome and in her view you stayed tiresome. But she was brave, loyal, a genuinely dedicated public servant. Towards the end of her life I organised a dinner in her honour. It was held at the Reform Club and was a memorable evening. And I'm so glad I did because soon after that she became ill, and succumbed quickly to cancer. Yet, even as she was visibly shrinking away, she still fought her way to the Patients Association offices (once being mugged on the way). I went to see her in hospital. She looked terribly weak and a few days later she died at 87.

I was the speaker at the small funeral at Golders Green crematorium (she would not have a church service, nor would she allow a memorial service) and I concluded by quoting the words of Adlai Stevenson in his eulogy to Eleanor Roosevelt: 'She would rather light candles than curse the darkness, and her glow has warmed the world.'

6

Back to Journalism: Campaigning with the *Observer* (1)

'To succeed as a journalist you need a little literary ability, a plausible manner, and rat-like cunning.'

NICHOLAS TOMALIN

For a number of years I was torn between my love of working for newspapers and my tendency to become the story. Of course, there was a relationship between the two. As a campaigner, I owed much to my instincts and training as a journalist. But, I also loved newspaper offices, especially those of my younger years before computers took away the atmosphere. Apart from the smell of the hot metal and the roar of the printing machines, the cynical good nature of the subs' desk and the organised chaos of the reporters' room with its old wooden desks and battered typewriters, I loved the unique access that journalists had to people and places. A press pass is a pass to the world. If you have the nerve to wave it about with a show of authority, it can take you to places and to meet people that few others can access. Of course, you do need to have the nerve –in fact, to be honest, sometimes sheer cheek.

A press pass has enabled me to come face to face with presidents and prime ministers, and travel to countries all over the world. For the *Illustrated London News*, for whom I wrote freelance features for over ten years, I wrote a series on other people's work and spent weeks with a police detective and a London fireman. I spent time with a Concorde pilot, a jockey, a farmer, a coal miner and a country vicar, and on the HMS *Ark Royal* in the Mediterranean and with paramedics in New York. Who but a journalist could race about London on a fire engine, enter backstreet criminal clubs 'under cover' with real detectives, fly across the Atlantic in the cockpit of a plane, explore the depths of a coal mine, or pick up a phone wherever he or she is and get such ready access to places of interest and people of power?

On many of these *ILN* stories I worked with a photographer called Richard Cooke, perhaps the only photographer in the world who was as enthusiastic as me. Richard would tie himself to the wings of planes to get the best possible pictures of the Red Arrows. Typical of the fun we had was a feature on the Scots Guards in the year they were leading the Trooping of the Colour. For this we first went to Germany where they were stationed. We got there in time for St Andrew's Day and the battalion's party to celebrate it. Everyone got hopelessly drunk. About three in the morning I bumped into one officer leaning on a wall for support; 'Can I get you a drink?' I asked. 'No, laddie,' he replied, 'I've had enough.' 'Well, a soft drink then?' 'Good idea,' he said. 'I'll have a double Scotch.'

Richard and I were appalled at the class elitism that meant twenty-one-year-old young 'gentlemen' who had never been shot at in their lives were fast-tracked into becoming officers and allowed to order about experienced veterans of real wars. We were particularly struck by a conversation over dinner in the officer's mess: 'I say,' said one. 'Did you know that a couple of years back we had a tank driven into the barracks wall over there – nearly brought the whole place tumbling down.' 'My God,' said another. 'Were they young officers or men?' 'Officers.' 'Oh, so it was high spirits then, not vandalism.'

We observed also that in the planning of the party there was much talk of the 'officers and their ladies, the men and their women'.

Richard got his own back on one particularly arrogant young officer. He flattered him by asking whether he would pose for a picture leading his men out of a troop-carrier and throwing himself face-down in the mud, rifle at the ready. The officer burst from the vehicle and dived forwards into mud a foot deep and virtually vanished under it, emerging covered from head to toe in it. 'Oh dear,' said Richard. 'Sorry – I forgot to put film in the camera.' We followed them out to the Gambia where the officers, still determined to have their own mess, hung a sign 'Officers' Mess' on a tree and then created a little circle of leather armchairs brought from England to maintain standards and traditions. But we also went to Northern Ireland and saw them risking their lives every time they left the barracks. Arrogant, maybe; cowards, no.

I owe an enormous debt to those journalists I worked with as a teenager. My local newspaper experience was in the days when local papers were seen as providing a public service. There were no celebrities on the paper; we did not have by-lines. We were not in the business of exposes; people's private lives remained private. We told people what was happening in their courts and councils, farmers' unions and women's clubs, on their playing fields and at their places of work.

Brian Hunter in the Oamaru office of the *Otago Daily Times* taught me the importance of accuracy; if you work on a national newspaper and you make an error – misspelling someone's name, for instance – this is obviously bad, but at least you may never have to face them and admit the mistake, but if you work on a local paper you are likely to meet them in the street the next day. Locals did not care about the standard of the writing or the importance of the story; they just wanted to know what was happening in town and they wanted their name spelt right.

Buzz Harte and my colleagues on the *Evening Star* in Dunedin, especially the brilliant team of sub editors led by the genial but authoritative Bill Cave, taught me the importance of writing a story that would 'sell' to the subs: because every reporter was competing for space and prominence in the paper, you had to capture the attention and imagination of the 'subs' if your story was to appear later that day. And you really did want it to appear.

There was no greater private humiliation than picking up a paper, still warm off the press, and flicking from page to page to find your story had been discarded, It was a slap in the face. It was the equivalent of someone with a megaphone storming into the reporters' room and saying: 'Wilson, that story did not matter. It was boring. It was a non-story.' Or, even worse, 'that story was badly written.' Of course you could go to the Chief Reporter and say, 'I don't really think this is a story,' but your thanks for that would be: 'Since when were you a chief reporter, laddie ?' Or worse, even worse, he would take it back, stick a piece of paper in his typewriter, hammer away, and later that day you would see the story on the front page . . . because he had seen what you had missed.

Looking back over the years, there's no doubt that my time on the *Evening Star* was as happy as any time I have had. We were a particularly united and uncompetitive team; we worked and played together. Because our final deadline was about 2.00 p.m., we worked from early morning non-stop till the print machines began to roll, afterwards playing poker together or in the local snooker hall until it was time to go our separate ways to cover meetings or other city activities. At weekends we had a cricket team, its activities hampered somewhat by constant reference to a keg of beer kept in the shade of a tree. When it came to the 'home brew' season we would all go to each other's official sampling. Most would get drunk fairly quickly, because of the potency of the brew. Fortunately I did not drink in those days; one Monday I was the only journalist who made it to work; all the rest had been poisoned by the chief sub's home brew.

I was always a pound short of what I needed to survive. One week I borrowed a pound off our religious reporter. Or should I say reporter on religion? No, actually, he was our religious reporter on religion. He believed the stuff he wrote. Anyway, he put a note above his desk: 'Des owes me £1.' Each week I would ask him if I could have another week to repay it. Each week he would solemnly take down the note, screw it up, throw it away, and then replace it with a brand-new one: 'Des owes me £1.' He said it was good for my soul.

To succeed as a journalist you need, above all, an eye for the story. The pressures of a big daily paper in a relatively small locality with a limited team of journalists meant you learned to work quickly. Sometimes I would be given a 300 page report with half an hour till deadline and be told to write 500 words on it; somehow in that brief time I had to find the point of the report – the story – and then tell it. Once you develop this skill you find it works in every aspect of life; it's about seeing quickly what matters and what does not. And I could see the story; I thought in stories. This talent was to be a huge asset to me in the years ahead. It became the key to my success as a campaigner; I was always, first and foremost, an identifier of issues and a teller of stories. That's why, even today, whenever I am asked for my occupation, I always reply: journalist.

A Column on the *Observer*

When it became clear that I was not to be director of the Consumer Council, I reminded myself that I was a professional journalist, albeit one who had been diverted. And I began to wonder: could I combine the two – be a campaigner and a journalist. Or more precisely, could I become a campaigning journalist? Fortunately someone else had been wondering the same thing. Inspired by the Consumer Council controversy, the *Daily Express* asked me to become their consumer champion. It was an exciting offer: my own page, a team to help me, and oodles of money. I would have been a star. However, there was a problem: politically, the *Daily Express* was just not my paper. Mine would have been the only words in the paper with which I agreed. Fortunately for me, the executive who made the offer had a daughter who worked on the *Observer* and he must have talked about it over dinner because, family loyalty not being her strength, I was now phoned by the paper's deputy editor Donald Trelford to ask whether 'the rumours' were true. 'Well, Donald,' I said, 'they may be – unless, of course, the *Observer* wants to make me an offer.' An hour later we were having lunch together. And a day later I had a weekly column on the leader page.

I could hardly believe it. I had, of course, been proud of my weekly column on the *Guardian*, especially as it was usually edited for me by the great Peter Preston, then the paper's features editor, but, because it was written while I was at Shelter, it was just one thing I was doing of many – the *Observer* column was for real. Of course, I knew I had not earned this break; there were scores of journalists in and around Fleet Street who better deserved this prominence and who could write better than me. I had no illusions; I was being hired for my name and image. It was vital, therefore, that I carved out a special niche and occupied territory that was more or less exclusively mine. We decided to call the column Des Wilson's Minority Report and, week after week, I set out to publicise injustice and human need and to chip away at the nation's conscience on one issue after another. Mostly, I followed the approach that had succeeded at Shelter, focusing on individual cases histories and controversies to highlight wider issues.

The deal was that I would write 45 columns a year (930 words to be delivered by four o'clock on Friday afternoons), plus some features for the *Observer* magazine. The editor of my column at first was a wonderfully eccentric Fleet Street legend called John Silverlight and later Donald Trelford took over himself. Donald, who went on to become editor of the paper, became a good friend. We played occasional rounds of erratic golf together on Wimbledon Common, over the road from where he lived. Perhaps because he followed the great David Astor, Donald's strengths have perhaps not been fully recognised; he was fair and, above all, he was a fighter and he helped the paper survive some difficult times after the Astor family relinquished its ownership.

He was my second golfing editor. When I first joined the paper I would often hack my way round Highgate golf course on a Monday (the paper's day off) and one day nearly hit a man coming down the opposite fairway who turned out to be the then editor David Astor, who incidentally was born on the same day as me, March 5, a man for whom I was particularly proud to write and who showed his courage as far back as the Suez affair when the *Observer* charted a relatively lonely course opposing the actions of Anthony Eden. David, with whom I now played golf regularly on Mondays, was wonderfully supportive of my column and it was always a real thrill when occasionally he took the trouble to phone on a Friday night to say he had been reading the proofs and liked it.

He was, of course, a rich man and was not always in touch with the lives of ordinary people, but he was instinctively on their side and he put the *Observer* on their side too. In his funeral address, Donald Trelford said that 'David always insisted that nobody was too important, or too un-important, to write for a newspaper. . . for him a journalist should be someone who had something to say or wanted something done in the world.' When I heard those words I understood why he had hired me and why he allowed me to stay on the leader page for over four years, always feeling I had his full support.

While I was on a freelance contract and worked from home, I also had one quarter of an office and a secretary, shared with three reporters, Peter Wilby (later to the editor of the *New Statesman*), Robert Chesshyre (later to be the paper's man in Washington, and still a friend today), and Peter Deeley (who went on to become one of the country's leading cricket writers). Aware I was earning for one column as much as they were for a week's work, they always enjoyed trying to put me in my place whenever I came in. In response, I took to entering the room by saying 'Please don't stand . . .' and gradually either I or the column won them over because they made me feel increasingly welcome. I took to coming in earlier on a Friday in the hope of joining some of the *Observer* clan at the Black Friars pub next door. There I would sit in the shadow of such greats as the moody but brilliant reporter Laurence Marks, the famous sports editor Cliff Makins and his star writer Hugh MacIlvanney, the renowned books editor Terry

Kilmarten, and occasionally the television critic Clive James. I was so excited by being in the company of these journalists and having my own column in this famous paper that every Saturday night I would drive down to Blackfriars to pick up one of the first copies off the press. Only when I physically saw my column there would I believe it would actually be there to be read the following day.

I had no difficulty getting material. Over the Shelter years I had became friendly with two other high profile campaigners, Tony Lynes of the Child Poverty Action Group and Tony Smythe of the National Council for Civil Liberties. We worked well as a team, often sharing platforms at conferences and other events. I was elected to both their national committees and, after Tony Lynes moved on (to further the cause from inside the civil service) I was at the meeting that appointed Frank Field (later to become a controversial Labour MP) in his place. I was also on the NCCL selection committee when Tony Smythe left to work for the American civil liberties movement in New York. One of the candidates we reluctantly turned away was Jon Snow, who was then running a shelter for London's young home-less. We did him a good turn; he went on to a distinguished career as the presenter of Channel 4 News. The CPAG committee in those days involved two of Britain's most effective anti-poverty campaigners, Brian Abel-Smith and Peter Townsend. The NCCL committee included Jack Dromey, who became a leading trade unionist, Labour Party Treasurer and now an MP, and the husband of Labour deputy leader Harriet Harman (who after my time worked for the NCCL herself).

My main sources of causes and stories were organisations like these. Their offices were packed with research material, and they had moving case histories to back it up; this all formed a rich seam of stories that no one else in Fleet Street was mining.

Bail Refused

If you ever have a spare day and it's raining, go to court. There you will find out what is really happening in your town or city. I spent a lot of time in courts. Sometimes I was directed there by the NCCL who knew of a par-ticularly controversial case. Sometimes I went there because I had learned that every case is a story, and – from my experience – these may have been the 'law' courts, but they were not palaces of justice. There is no greater infringement of individual freedom than to lock someone away, and a constant theme of my *Observer* columns was the refusal of bail by the courts.

I had always believed that an accused person was presumed innocent until proved guilty, but I discovered that at that time 30,000 people each year went to prison without being convicted; of those nearly 2,000 were later acquitted and 18,000 did not return to prison after sentence. There appeared to be three main problems: the reluctance of magistrates to overrule police objections or to insist on compelling evidence to support their objections; the setting of sureties so onerous that the accused were unable to meet them; and magistrates were often failing to inform the accused of their right to appeal to a judge in chambers against the refusal of bail, or the conditions imposed.

I wrote about Albert Cooper, a gipsy in his early thirties, who had just spent a Christmas in Brixton Prison. Cooper was illiterate, very inarticulate, and depressive – indeed, his doctor said he was a potential suicide risk. One December day – it was the 10th I believe – he left home to buy a Christmas present for his father and never returned. On the 14th a solicitor who was one of the voluntary workers helping the Coopers telephoned both the police in St Mary Cray, Kent, near where Cooper was living, and Brixton Prison, but was told by both that they had not heard of Cooper. On the 16th he inquired again. This time he was told that Cooper had, in fact, been charged at St Mary Cray on the 11th – with stealing a pair of pliers worth 62 1/2p – and had been remanded to Brixton by Bromley magistrates until 20 December. It was too late to obtain legal assistance, so a Community Service Volunteer went to the court on the 20th to speak for Cooper, saw on the list that he was to appear in Court One, and sat waiting there all morning. In the meantime Cooper was switched to Court Three, was further remanded in custody over Christmas, and was taken away. On the 29th Cooper appeared at Bromley Court again and this time was granted bail on his own recognisance of £10. So this 'potential suicide risk' was kept in prison by one magistrate for eighteen days, including the Christmas period, for an offence so minor that immediately after Christmas another magistrate granted bail for £10 and didn't think it worth bothering about sureties. Further, neither the police nor the prison bothered to notify the Cooper family, who for a week couldn't even find out where he was.

One of my readers wrote a lengthy letter of much-needed encouragement to a man awaiting trial in Brixton. With the prisoner's reply came a card from the prison authorities. It said: 'You may answer letters received [from prisoners]. Matters of special importance to a prisoner may be communicated to the Governor who will inform him. Two pages of ordinary notepaper written on both sides is considered sufficient for the reply. Letters in excess or of inordinate length will be returned.' If I were being held awaiting trial, especially if I were innocent, this was the kind of pin-pricking treatment that would drive me to a frenzy of anger and bitterness. Who did prison authorities think they were to say what is a 'sufficient' number of pages for people to communicate their feelings to prisoners (who may also be husbands and fathers) at a difficult time? Who decided what was an expression of affection of 'inordinate length'? I returned frequently to this issue and, while I can't claim a clear victory, over time there was some reduction in bail refusals.

I thought I had been angry at Shelter, but I got even angrier at the arrogance I saw in the courts: barristers who appeared before judges to defend clients they had not even bothered to meet; judges who appeared to automatically add time onto sentences of people who were black or even white working class; and, above all, an unforgivable contempt for people's rights to freedom – at least until proven guilty. By the end of my first year on the *Observer*, I was showing that a column devoted to minority causes and injustices would every week have more stories to tell than space could ever allow; clearly David Astor wanted these causes taken up in his paper, because my contract was renewed, as it was for the next three years.

My columns over four years were ultimately published in a book called Des Wilson's *Minority Report*, so I will illustrate them with just one of the many causes I took up: Gypsies. There was no way I could win every cause I adopted, but every now and then I had a success, usually by resolving a specific case. Of all the stories I told, this was the one that had the most impact:

When it rains they huddle together for warmth under wind-whipped canvas held up by sticks cut from the tree, and sadly watch their open fire dampen and die. The nine-month-old baby cries pathetically, half-buried in the pile of grubby clothes and blankets that form the bed-cum-floor in the tent. The four other children are 'little Cinderella' (nine), Marianne (five), Israel (four), and Edward (two).

Cinderella (her real name), the mother, is twenty-five but looks forty. Most of her day is spent collecting bits of wood for the fire and cooking in a big black pot. She sits cross-legged in front of the fire, smoking her own peculiar brand of home-made cigarettes. She is proud of the watch, worn round her neck, but she can't tell the time. Nor can she read or write. She is lonely and frightened, but she tries hard to hide it.

Her family look like refugees from a terrible war, and in a way they are, for all their lives they've been fighting ignorance and prejudice, and nearly always they've lost. The defeat that drove them to this lonely camp was suffered at the hands of a law that in practice does not protect them but harasses them and their fellow-gipsies until their lives become perpetual misery.

Cinderella was born in a tent – near Oxford, in 1946. Since she was sixteen she lived with Snowy (his real name is Israel Butler; he's called Snowy because he is fair-haired, which is rare for a gipsy). Their love for each other has survived nine years of poverty and persecution and is exceptional even in the gipsy culture, renowned for the closeness of its family life.

Like other gipsies they've suffered from the intolerance of a wider society that seems to find it so hard to make room for, let alone welcome, people whose way of life harms absolutely nobody but doesn't conform. Their own life has been a hard one, all the harder because Snowy, too, is illiterate, and neither of them has adjusted to the changing pace of life, even gipsy life, as have their family and friends. It is almost as if the world has moved on and left Snowy and Cinderella behind.

For years Snowy has tried to feed his growing family by collecting old rags in a pram, and then selling them, but it became hopeless and he got hold of an old lorry. That's when his troubles really intensified, because he couldn't get a licence (he couldn't read the Highway Code, let alone remember it), and he couldn't afford to tax the vehicle. So he became a frequent visitor to the courts for a variety of motor offences.

No one tried to sort out the problem; Snowy was a sitting duck for arrest, and arrested he was, time after time. It was all totally destructive.

Then, last year, they charged him with theft. He denied it but he was not represented and made a sorry spectacle in a courtroom he didn't understand. He was sent to prison.

When the Gipsy Council heard that he was due out, they found him a job as a builder's labourer and set out to raise the money for a horse-drawn caravan, thus solving the housing problem and the motor offences problem at the same time. It looked as if Snowy and his family were going to be okay. But everyone had reckoned without the majesty of the law.

Sixteen days after he was released, the police pounced once more – with twelve warrants for £152 of unpaid fines for motor offences. His guilt, the law had decided, must be purged whatever the cost, and he was sent back to prison for six months.

What is the cost? To the taxpayer, it is about £750 in prison upkeep and welfare payments for the family – five times the fines he owed. To Snowy, it is the loss of the chance to lead the kind of stable life the law has persecuted him for not leading. To Cinderella, it is the loss of the chance of a caravan home; it's back to a tent, and loneliness, and fear in the night, and worry about the children.

No one in officialdom asked, when Snowy was imprisoned, what would happen to his family. But then, when it's a matter of gipsies, they hardly ever do.

Readers reacted with anger. Money poured in. Gipsy Snowy was released and quickly reunited with his wife, Cinderella, and with some of the surplus money was able to buy the family a caravan. The rest was put in a welfare fund, administered by the Gypsy Council, to help other such families. A small victory, but, for me, these were the victories that mattered. They meant the column was making a difference.

7

Campaigning with the *Observer* (2)

The dark side of the United States

After a couple of years the paper began to allow me to travel. For over 20 years, ever since I saw that local builder's slides in Oamaru, I had dreamed of going to the United States and in particular New York, and in 1972, at 31, I finally made it (I was later to return at least 70 times). On this first journey I went first to Washington, then to the Appalachians, and then to New York itself. In those days I had endless energy and, enthused by just being there, I walked for miles across those two famous cities. In Washington I climbed the hill to the Kennedy grave at Arlington Cemetery and then walked down to the bridge across the Potamic to the marble Lincoln Memorial, then all the way up the graceful mall past the Jefferson and Washington memorials and the White House to the Air and Space Musuem where I saw Lindberg's airplane the Spirit of St Louis and the capsule in which Armstrong and the others landed on their return from the Moon. From there I went on to my favourite museum, the Museum of American History, ending the journey at the Congress Building and then the Supreme Court and the Library of Congress.

In New York, too, I walked and walked – from the wharf where you catch the Staten Island Ferry or the boat to the Statue of Liberty, up past the Empire State Building all the way to Central Park . . . I went to Little Italy and Chinatown, to the Garment District and Greenwich Village, and to the banks of the Hudson where I gazed across at Hoboken where Frank Sinatra was born. I could not have enough of these places and after a day walking from one piece of history to another, would head for one those superb old New York bars and listen to and watch the locals into the early hours. I loved the lines of fire escapes on the old brownstone buildings, the steam rising from vents in the pavements, the rattle of the subway trains as they passed under-foot, the crazy conversation of the taxi drivers who seemed to come from every country in the world except the US, the smell of pea-nuts roasting or hot dogs being cooked on street corners, the mayhem on the streets at rush hour – the constant tooting of horns and squealing of brakes, breakfasts of beautifully scrambled egg and crispy bacon and unbeatable coffee obtainable from cafes on every corner, the skyscrapers. I could not get enough of it; I felt as Christopher Hitchens, who believed that 'time spent asleep in New York was somehow time wasted.'

I was in Washington on election day and briefly called in on the McGovern headquarters, full of gloom as Richard Nixon took state after state, and then I heard his concession speech on television in the basement of a church in one of the city's black (and poor) districts – the election headquarters of the Statehood Party. The Statehood Party was trying to get some democracy into the capital of the world's most powerful democracy. It had, after all, 750,000 people – more than 10 other States of the Union and more than 20 nations in the world. Even so, it had been refused statehood and had no vote for a Senator and Congressman (only a non-voting delegate).

I quoted one Statehood campaigner, Sam Smith, who ran a little news-paper on the issue, as 'thinking of getting some African countries to insist that the US is called upon, as others are, to submit an annual report to the United Nations on its progress towards granting self-determination to its colonies – in this case, its own capital!' It was Sam Smith who had taken me to this unlikely venue on election night. At the time of writing, nearly forty years later, Washington DC still has no Senator or Congressman, but I will always remember that night because Sam Smith asked me home to have dinner with he and his wife Kathy; it was the beginning of a friendship that has lasted nearly forty years.

Sam Smith

Sam could have been a world famous journalist or writer if he wanted to be; his talent is predigious. Instead he has devoted his life to alternative journalism, beginning with a paper called the *DC Gazette* that became the *Progressive Review* and is now an alternative web site with literally millions of hits every year. Sam may not have been poor himself (he came from a wealthy family and had when I met him a small farm in Virginia and beautiful homes in the Cleveland Park area of Washington and on Casco Bay near Freeport, Maine), but his heart was with them; his writings have never ceased to flay those in power for the inequalities and injustices of the land of the free.

Sam wrote in the *Review* that I came to dinner in 1972 and never left; and it's true.

I have stayed in their homes in DC and Maine so many times it is embarrassing. I have played baseball with their kids and seen them grow from tiny children to adults in their forties with their own flourishing careers and marriages. I have seen Kathy develop into DC's leading historian; only recently she edited what is probably the best book ever published on the history of the nation's capitol. (*Washington at Home* by Kathryn Schneider Smith, John Hopkins University Press). I have sailed in their boat on Casco Bay, made raids on the famous LL Bean store up the road for my jackets and jeans, eaten Maine lobsters that have been out of the water for only an hour, walked in their woods and on their farm and devoured many tons of their unique Wolfs Neck steaks. I went all the way to Washington for his fiftieth birthday and was the official photographer at his mother's seventieth. I have become friends with their friends. There was a time when I could sit on the front steps of their house in Cleveland Park and say hullo by name to everyone who walked by. (One of their neighbours was the Pulitzer-prize winning journalist Seymour Hersh, who many years later I persuaded to come to London to present our Freedom of Information awards.)

What Sam says is true – I came to dinner and never left. And if you knew Sam and Kathy Smith you would know why. How fortunate can one be in one's friends.

America's Darker Side

Excited and enchanted as I was by my first experiences in America, I was still the author of a 'minority report', and so set out to see its darker side. I took a driving trip to the beautiful but sad Appalachian mountains. There I found Harlan County, and from there I wrote this:

Can this, too, be America? This poverty, this illiteracy, this ill-health, this despair? This place where over 40 per cent live below the national poverty line, where many can only sign their name with a cross, where men cough up coal dust and many children have all their teeth out in their teens because it's cheaper that way? This place where men sit for hours on the steps of ramshackle huts and stare in despair at the ravaged hills?

You come to it alone. I was the only person in Harlan's main motel. The nearby hotel was deserted. America has raped this land and shamelessly robbed its people, and now prefers to pass it by.

This is, perhaps, the most depressed area of the United States. Over three million people in Appalachia are poor; one-fifth of its 397 counties, including Harlan, are officially described as 'extremely poor'. Yet it need never have been so, for when frontiersmen like Daniel Boone first contested it with the Indians it was a land of rare beauty and rich in minerals, especially coal. Even now many of its mountains are covered with beautiful trees and a wide variety of plants and flowers.

Coal, the main economic asset of much of Appalachia, has also been its curse. It attracted to the area speculators and absentee owners of massive stretches of land. They have taken hungrily from the land, while paying practically no taxes and leaving behind only a pittance in wages.

Instead of becoming rich from the coal industry, the ordinary people of counties like Harlan have been forced down into poverty – many of their homes are miners' shacks, black with coal dust, cold and in poor repair.

It was about towns like this that the famous song 'Sixteen Tons' was written – the words 'Sixteen tons and what do you get? Another day older and deeper in debt' ring true for a lot of men around here. Many really can say, 'I lost my soul to the company store,' the only place where in the past they could purchase their necessities, and where they were often deliberately enticed into debt.

Then, about twenty years ago, the mine owners decided to cut back. They started 'strip-mining' – cutting away the coal from the surface, rather than digging down. Employment in the mines has been reduced 75 per cent in the last twenty years as machines have taken over. The environmental effect has been horrific – strip-mining leaves gaping wounds in the hills, destroying the area's natural beauty. Trees are felled, bushes and flowers and fields are buried, and creeks and streams polluted.

In Kentucky alone 12,000 acres a year are being strip-mined. Near Harlan, the world's biggest earth-moving machine – they call it Big Muskie – lifts 325 tons of soil at a gulp. It is as tall as a 32-storey building and consumes enough electricity for a small town. Its power of destroying the landscape is unlimited. So Harlan County has become a place Americans prefer not to know about – it shows only too clearly where the mindless pursuit of profit can lead. The people of Harlan have become the invisible poor, part of the silent majority (one in five) of poor Americans.

New York – the day Leon died

I had never actually seen a dead man until I found myself one day sharing the back seat of a police car with one. His name was Leon and he had a bullet hole in his chest. It was New York, February 1974, and I was spending a day with the police in Harlem. For a few hours even that famous ghetto had looked calm and clean, but by noon the snow had turned to ice and slush and the 17 blocks of tenement slums that made up New York's 28th police precinct looked miserable.

The patrolmen I was with had only half-an-hour of their shift left. For over seven hours they had driven round the 15 miles of streets of a precinct that was distinctive because it was the smallest in the city and had for the past three years experienced the most murders – nearly three a week (more than in the whole of Britain).

An elderly black woman came over to the car. Would the patrolmen escort her into her house because the hallway was so dark and she was afraid? It turned out to be a condemned slum. Pinned on the front door was the council report – 'The house has no heat, no water supply, no electricity, no operable sanitary facilities. It has already been extensively burnt by fire. The staircases are defective. There are no fire escapes and the use of kerosene lamps furthers the possibility of disaster by fire.' It reminded me of my Shelter days.

We helped the woman down the dark corridor to her unlit, unheated bare room. There were three other families in the house. Some 50,000 people lived in the precinct in conditions like this. Many were on drugs. Circles of addicts huddled round the open fires they made in rubbish bins in the streets. Sometimes a whole line of bins was aflame so that the street was lit up and the thin, nervy bodies of the addicts, shuffling round and round the fire, became shadows that seemed to dance on the walls like massive puppets.

In was near such a bin that we found Leon. He lay face down in a puddle. Around him some twenty addicts shuffled, some, apparently indifferent to his fate, some plainly scared by the still body but none sufficiently concerned to move from the warmth of the fire.

He looked dead. The cops picked him up and put him on the back seat of the car where I was. We all piled in the front and raced four blocks to the hospital, where he was confirmed 'dead on arrival'. Within 15 minutes a detective from the local Homicide Squad was in the emergency ward to examine the body. He looked at the bullet hole and commented that Leon had been struck in the heart and probably killed instantly. I asked what chance there was that the killer would be found. 'One in a thousand', I was told. 'This is a typical Harlem homicide – it took place on the streets after dark, no obvious motive, and the witnesses not keen to talk.'

In fact, it was the one in a thousand. The precinct's anti-crime squad later picked up a white youth who had been involved in a car accident in Harlem. They took him to the police station, where, by a stroke of fortune, there waited the only witness to the murder who was prepared to talk. The witness picked out the youth and the next day he confessed his involvement in the murder. Apparently he and a friend had come to Harlem the previous day to buy drugs and had been robbed of $200. So they came back with a gun and vengefully pumped four or five bullets into the circle of addicts huddled round the fire. The only one to be hit was Leon.

About thirty-three, black, a 'freelance' car washer, he was not even an addict – just sitting in the circle to keep warm because he had no home. His pockets were empty – he didn't have a cent to his name. He died without family or a friend to mourn him. As one of the cops said, 'He just got in the way of a passing bullet.' He was wheeled off to the morgue. The cops filed their reports and went home, their shift completed. In a few months' time they would appear in court to testify to the discovery of the body. A detective would be there to present the confessions. The two white youths would then disappear to prison.

Not one of the New York newspapers reported the murder. There were stories about white people who had been mugged, but were still alive and a story about a white woman who had been raped. But Leon was black, poor and lived in Harlem. And everyone knew that people got themselves killed in Harlem. So he didn't rate a mention. I was within 24 hours probably the only person in the world who was thinking about Leon. I still sometimes do today. He is still the only dead man I have ever seen.

And thanks to my unlikely presence in that car, and an *Observer* column that followed, and thanks to whoever is reading this book, he's still remembered. Let this chapter be a flower on his grave . . . wherever it is.

8

Campaigning with the *Observer* (3)

The Third World

In 1971 and in 1973 I spent a few weeks in Third World countries – in West Africa and in South and Central America. These were my first encounters with poverty at this extreme level. Like so many people, I had only really been conscious of Third World poverty when a major disaster made it to our television screens; now I saw it for myself and came to realise for the first time that the crises that hit our headlines did so mainly because they met our criteria for concern – i.e., they were sudden, their ill-effects were immediate, they were dramatic, and they obviously could not have been prevented. Above all they were 'news'.

But I now learned that most people in the poorest countries lived with day-by-day, permanent disaster; for them, gruelling, life-sapping hardship and loss of life were not occasional stories, they were the reality of lives that consisted of a series of little unpublicised individual disasters with the occasional major, mass disaster thrown in; the former never hit the headlines, for whoever heard of a British headline: 'West African farmer loses year's crop in rainstorm'?

I was stunned by the suffering and dying that occurred every day of every week of every year. Yes, I had seen the statistics – that, for instance, fifty million children would die of malnutrition in that decade alone. But you had to see the kids dying to appreciate what it meant . . . you had to learn at first hand that for *every one* of the fifty million children there was a mother who carried the child for nine months in hot desert or humid forest, suffered the fears and pain of childbirth without medical help, drained her resources to feed it, and then saw all the effort and love wasted with its death. And before each death there were the weeks, months or even years of suffering by the child: some just went on having diarrhoea or vomiting until they literally shrivelled away.

Also, one could not help but observe with mounting alarm the flight to the cities of the many who could no longer tolerate the isolation and antiquity of life in rural areas, and the resultant social problems this had caused – unemployment and shanty-town slums. In one under-developed country after another I heard stories of the break-up of centuries of tradition as the new generation, beaten by years of crop failure and hardship and the depressingly frequent death of their children, moved to the cities to seek a new life. When they got there, they found no work, or only badly paid work, and no homes. So they lived in slums – slums many times worse than those we knew in Britain.

In Dakar I saw people living in conditions of indescribable filth. Unwanted in the city itself, they had built with their own hands a series of appalling shanty towns, known as bidonvilles (after the metal drums that they tore apart for the roofs and walls). Over 100,000 people lived in these massive warrens of cardboard and metal and bits of wood, packed ten or more to a room, without electricity, water supplies and sanitary services. Sometimes they slept with their animals. Many suffered from malnutrition, for they were usually unemployed and without money. The overcrowding, linked to the piles of rubbish lying out in the open, created major health problems. The shanties stretched, row after row, for hundreds of yards, linked by complicated, intertwining passages only two feet wide. The smell was sickening. They were at best an enormous rubbish dump for unwanted people and contrasted sharply with some of Dakar's modern buildings and motorway.

The shanty towns had their own shops, usually dirty little shacks where almost nothing was really fit to eat. One of the most hideous sights I saw in West Africa was one of these, an open-air butcher's shop with awful yellowish meat displayed, and just above it a sickening number of swarming flies. I also saw a little boy, about three years old, sent into a huge pile of rubbish, at least six feet high, with a little bag to search for food. I hoped he wouldn't find any, for it would probably have killed him. I was later to see such shanty towns, albeit with different names, in South Africa, and in South and Central America too.

In November 1971, I went to Upper Volta, the poorest country in the world. (It is now known as Burkina Faso). This friendly, proud, little-known country in West Africa was poised on the brink of famine that was to come soon after with disease and death that struck down many of its children – and this in a country where already one in five babies died and life expectancy was one of the lowest in the world, thirty-five (half that in Britain).

The famine was caused by too little rain. It should have fallen steadily from June to mid-October, the traditional rainy season, but the last fall was in mid-September, and when it did come it was in torrential downpours that burst the clay wells and washed them and the crops away.

The rain also washed away most of the year's toil and the hopes of the farmers, their wives and their children, for they all worked together in the fields and lived on what they produced. In a good year a farmer with a working family of five could hope to earn about £30. That year many earned no money at all, for the harvest was pathetic and many of their animals died of thirst, a disastrous rainfall for them was disaster for the whole country. As an American Peace Corps Volunteer said to me: 'In a subsistence society you can only sit and wait – wait for God to do His thing, and if He doesn't . . . that's it.'

Their lives were dominated by the need and quest for water. Most people in Britain, accustomed to being able to turn a tap on and off scores of times a day, could never appreciate the value of a drop of clean water in that dry, burnt-out place.

After being in Upper Volta and Senegal, I wrote in the *Observer*:

If the Third World had a trademark, it would undoubtedly be the corpse of a child. The phrase 'they die like flies' is a terrible one, but too often it is the truth.

In Senegal 42 per cent of children – two out of every five – die before they are five years old . . . an infant mortality rate ten times worse than Britain's.

The children are struck down by malaria, severe forms of dysentery and diarrhoea, pneumonia, TB, and a variety of other diseases that thrive in tropical or sub-tropical conditions and occasionally sweep with special venom from country to country, town to town, and even hut to hut, to cause the most dreadful human devastation. Many die, too, of malnutrition, and many more are so weakened by it as to be especially vulnerable to a fatal disease. Even measles and chickenpox frequently kill the weakened children. Once a child is picked out by a potentially fatal disease, it has little chance.

The difference between Britain and the underdeveloped countries can be seen in this simple fact: in Britain there is a doctor to every 870 persons; in Upper Volta there is a doctor to every 80,000 persons.

The Nicaraguan Earthquake

I was travelling in South America when the 1973 earthquake happened. After consulting with the *Observer*, I diverted to Managua. I had not considered the possibility that the airport would be affected, but all the electricity was still out and we landed in the dark. I was the only one disembarking.

I walked out of the little airport building into the humid night air and found only one old taxi standing there. I had the name of a town just outside Managua where I knew there were some Oxfam volunteers and I asked the taxi driver to take me there. We drove through the capital where over 27 square kilometres had become rubble. It was disconcertingly quiet and still. Occasionally a ghostly figure could be seen searching for a few possessions, or maybe even a lost member of the family. The whole journey was taken up with the radio listing names of people who were trying to find relatives. I eventually found the Oxfam volunteers in an old school building. Their leader was a man called Reggie Norton, a well-known Oxfam personality. I reported:

> The first emergency is over, the 10,000 'known dead' have been buried and outbreaks of diseases like cholera and typhoid have been averted. (No one knows exactly how many died. Many bodies remain under the rubble and every day the radio broadcasts pathetic appeals for lost ones.) The 20,000 injured have been treated. The 250,000 homeless have been temporarily sheltered in 'tent cities' in impromptu shacks, or mainly with friends and relatives scattered all over the country.

> This problem has to be tackled despite the loss of 40 per cent of the gross national product in a few minutes, the loss of the whole governmental apparatus, many of the country's small businesses, and nearly a million square metres of commercial buildings, factories and offices from which much of the nation's income has previously come.

More than 50,000 homes have been demolished and 24,000 have been extensively damaged, and also lost are 956 schools and the four main hospitals comprising 40 per cent of hospital bed capacity of the country. Ironically, their wooden shacks on the outskirts took the blow like punch-drunk boxers and refused to fall down.

The following day Reggie took me to meet the British ambassador and he, in turn, fixed for me to meet the man who ran the whole country like a cross between a family business and a political dictatorship – General Anastrasio Somoza. He saw me for 30 minutes in the room of his hacienda in the hills where all the decisions, from the purchase of an electric generator to the priorities for rebuilding the nation, were taken. It was the first time I had felt myself to be in the company of pure evil.

His hacienda was built in two parts with a covered sitting area linking them. There sat a group of men in suits, all with attaché cases, all looking to profit from the earthquake – salesman for construction firms, and the like. And who did they have to win the business from and to whom would they write their cheques? Samoza. The people may have been made homeless and hungry by the earthquake, but Somoza exuded the assurance of someone who saw no problem. Despite plenty of evidence, he blandly denied that his soldiers were shooting at or had killed pillagers (often people desperate for food). Even as he did so, I could hear gunfire in the distance. For a moment we both listened to it in silence. Then he smiled. What else could he do for me?

I asked him how he could consider rebuilding Managua on or near the site hit three times by major earthquakes. The land, he pointed out, equally blandly, was worth up to $400 million.

How much would he make out of it all? Well, let's put it this way: the new Managua would require a massive amount of cement. Guess who owned the cement company.

Padre Lira

While I was deeply shaken by what I saw in the Third World, I also found inspiration in the work of some amazing people, from the Peace Corps volunteers in Upper Volta to the Oxfam team who were helping in the aftermath of an earthquake in Nicaragua. One I will remember all my life was a priest in the north of Brazil. It was Oxfam who sent me to meet Padre Lira. The sheer size of Brazil came as a shock. Now, in the northern interior, I became acutely aware of it: the roads were so bad that it took hours to make relatively short journeys – you really just crawled from crater to crater. The scrub, grey for lack of water, stretched for hundreds of miles and dotted about in it were the farmers, living alone miles from anyone, only just surviving on what they could grow. Their only transport was by donkey. The graves of their children popped up at the roadside as often as you saw live people – little crosses circled by a picket fence, each testifying to another defeat in the battle with extreme deprivation. The hardship of the farmers was increased by difficulty in storing water when there was rainfall, by poor seeds, by the non-existence of fertilisers or modern equipment, by lack of any shared labour or services.

Father Lira Parente was one of the most remarkable men I'd ever met or heard of. He had come alone to that parched, dusty, lonely, fly-ridden territory and over ten years he had built a new community as an experiment in how farmers can be educated into cooperative activity to better their lives. Out of this wilderness he had somehow carved 175 miles of roads, created an airstrip, and built schools for 550 children, nine reservoirs, a brick factory, and a shoe-manufacturing factory, and launched a programme for improving the quality of the livestock. He had begged and borrowed money from all over the world, and he then acted as the voluntary provider of community services for an area of nearly 4,000 square miles.

The aim of this small, bearded man, his faced blackened by years toiling under the sun, was to show how it could be possible for people to survive and to thrive out there. It must be, he said, by cooperative effort, built around certain basic requirements – a reservoir, a central provider of fertiliser, some shared equipment, and seeds, and a way of obtaining credit. With this, he said – and he had proved it with the Fundacao Ruralista he had created – men could have dignity on the land instead of the indignity of being dish-washers in the cities.

It was an incredible experience to drive for miles across that inhuman land and then to see ahead that remarkable little village created by a man with amazing willpower and sense of mission. This desert was the last place in the world where I would have expected to find such a ray of hope.

Julian Latham

Julian Latham was an even more difficult man to find. To start with, I had to go to Lima, Peru. From there I caught a plane to Ayacucho, 500 miles from Lima, a market town thousands of feet up in the Andes. Ayacucho was the last stop in the twentieth century; from then on I travelled backwards in time. To visit Julian Latham I had to travel another 120 miles across mountains, valleys and streams, on a road so bad that the journey took twelve hours on a good day and sixteen or more if the weather was bad. That day it was bad.

It was the rainy season, and transport was provided by one of several open-topped trucks that made their way from Ayacucho to the banks of the Apurimac River. It was packed with peasants, and their babies, chickens, dogs, fruit, vegetables and other belongings. Everyone stood – all the way. Occasionally the road disappeared under water or mud from a landslide; often the truck hung over ledges with a steep drop of 5,000 feet or more. Throughout the journey I was soaked. In more comfortable circumstances I would have been entranced by the contrasts between the bareness of the mountains and the richness of the valleys; by the donkeys and llamas; by the Indian descendants of the Incas, beautiful people in colourful costumes that hadn't altered in hundreds of years. But I was too tired and often too scared; I just stood and hung on for dear life and wished I had never come.

Few people did. And when I reached San Francisco I found out why. I saw it first from the brow of the hill – at first it looked like one gigantic dilapidated tin marquee, because the shanties were so closely packed that their tin and wood roofs were linked. The rain dripped through thousands of cracks and turned the dirt floors into mud. Barefooted children carried rain water out in buckets and poured it into the yellow-brown stream that, when dry, was the 'main street' (there were only three streets).

About 1,000 sierranos (mountain Indians) lived in less than a hundred shacks, an abandoned hotel (no one wanted to stay there), a couple of 'cafes', a few makeshift stores, and a few score chickens and pigs. There were no banks or insurance houses. It was a town without money. There was no sanitation of any kind and no water supply.

In the house I stayed in, easily the best in the town, there were fourteen Indians and a dog, and a rooster was tied to the end of my bed. But there was more than one room, and that made their home exceptional: most families lived in one room, crowded together on dirt floors or on old wire beds, usually without mattresses, sharing their dreadful conditions with what animals they had. There was no roof over my room and it was raining. Julian Latham's last words to me before he went to his own room were 'Look out for the bats; they have rabies'!

Julian was the only European in town. Tall, broad-shouldered and dark-haired, he was thirty-seven. He was born in Rhodesia, and for thirty-odd years lived the good life there; then, in 1968, a friend persuaded him to fly out to Peru to work as a volunteer adviser to the Indians living in San Francisco and the valley, five miles wide and a hundred miles long, through which the Apurimac River (one of the head waters of the Amazon) flows, always swiftly and at times turning into dangerous rapids.

He found little communities of peasants living up and down the river, on the edge of thick, steeply sloping jungle, scratching out a meagre existence by growing vegetables or fruit, and then selling them to middle-men who came up the river from San Francisco, paid a pittance for the products, and then transported them by truck to Ayacucho – sometimes to Lima – for sale at a considerable profit.

All the water the people consumed came from the river; it contained nine types of parasite. All the children had worms, and all suffered from malnutrition. There were snakes, flies that bit viciously, mosquitoes, and even vampire bats, most of them with rabies.

As a result the people were ravaged by malaria, hepatitis, pneumonia (from the combination of humidity, wetness and cold winds) and almost every other tropical disease.

The only hospital around was unmanned and had no medicine. A badly burned man dragged himself out of the jungle to an abandoned hospital in the village. He found it locked, but assumed someone would soon be back. He sat there for three days and then died. No one knew what to do or how to help him.

With the money that would have paid his return fare to Britain, Julian built a little wood-and-tin shop with the help of two local boys, Armando and Mario, then, seventeen. They stocked it with food, rice, sugar and suchlike, and used the back of the store as a home for themselves and any orphan who wished to come for warmth and food.

The turnover of the shop in such a poverty-stricken place couldn't keep all the children who wanted to come, so Latham and the others went some forty miles into the jungle and found a giant torneillo tree, which they cut down and hollowed out to make a canoe. They lived on root crops and jungle fruit, and worked until their hands were black and bruised. It took two months to hollow the tree out. They carried it eight miles to the river, floating it back to San Francisco, sold it for £100, then went back and built another one. They then sold the shop and with the proceeds, plus the £100 from the first canoe, they made a down payment on an outboard motor.

Now, with the orphans organised into a team, and supporting each other, Julian set about the second stage of his operation: he formed a transport cooperative to carry fertilisers, tools, and foodstuffs up the river to the farmers, and to buy their produce at fair prices. The farmers leapt at the first chance they had ever had to get a decent return for their efforts, and the cooperative grew in size. Julian now made contact with British charities and with some money from them the cooperative built three more boats and bought motors for them.

It all sounds simple, but in that part of the world you were constantly being drenched by sudden tropical downpours and attacked by flies and mosquitoes. As if that was not bad enough, the merchants, who had previously exploited the farmers mercilessly, were naturally furious at the introduction of justice into the trading set-up. Julian was warned on three occasions to get out or he would be killed. Once he was dragged from his tent at midnight by friends who had heard merchants planning to dynamite it.

Julian's constant appeals for medical help, both in Peru and Britain, had had their reward: the St Joseph Hospice Association in Liverpool had decided to man the empty hospital in San Francisco with a doctor and three nurses, and to supply an ambulance, a river ambulance and local radio communication. At least the people of San Francisco and the surrounding valleys would have some chance of survival when they were ill or injured.

I did not spend one comfortable second in that place but by the time I left, my spirits were soaring, because I had seen courage and perseverance and self-sacrifice that was beyond imagination. When I left Julian, he was full of other plans . . . for a crude oil extracting plant to be built at San Francisco, which would cut transport costs by 80 per cent, and mean more employment and income for the area, for technical help for the valley's coffee farmers, for a small hydroelectric plant: and for a timber mill, in the first instance simply to produce wood for local use, to improve the housing.

Julian was not motivated by a religious drive, nor by political beliefs. He was a man who found himself in an area of need, identified with it, and decided to become part of it. Julian was a complete answer to those who, overwhelmed by the extent of the Third World's problems, would say: 'There is nothing that one person can do.' Whenever after that people spoke favourably of what I had done for one cause or another, I would often think of Julian and remind myself that he was worth a hundred of me.

All I could do was help persuade British charities to give him money, and I supported his fundraising with publicity, devoting an *Observer* magazine article to him. When he became ill and needed to come to London for treatment, he stayed in my home. What was remarkable about Julian was that he did not think he was remarkable. It was almost as if he had no choice to do what he did. But he did have a choice. He just made the hard one.

Women

I have written of two men who were, by any standards, heroes. But there were heroines too, and almost every woman in the Third World was one. Some 40 years later, my main memory is of women walking – women walking to fetch water, women walking to the fields, women walking to the markets, women walking to clinics, women walking from the country to the cities – walking many miles a day, often with a baby on their backs and goods or water on their heads.

I recall being driven across a West African desert by a Peace Corps volunteer who pointed to a woman walking slowly across the baking, cracked soil. On her back she carried a small child. On her head a big pot. He explained to me that every day she walked 9 miles to a well to collect water and 9 miles back to the small piece of land her family farmed. That water would be drunk by the humans and the remainder used for washing or given to the animals or used for their meagre crop. He told me how one day she had walked that 9 miles there and 6 miles back when a wild goat leapt from behind some shrubs in the desert and startled her so that the pot fell off her head and the water trickled down the cracks in the sand. She had no choice but to turn round and walk a further 12 miles – 6 back to the well and 6 back to that point before she could continue her journey – all this was with no food and the baby on her back in the heat of the African sun. She had to do it because they had to have the water. And as we drove on, I counted in my mind the number of times that we turn on a tap. A turn of the wrist and there is plentiful water, piped into our homes, hot or cold, often available in 3 or 4 rooms, and apparently limitless. In Britain the absence of a cold water tap would make a home officially 'unfit for human habitation'.

I recall, too, sitting at a street bar in Dakar in Senegal. As I've said, into cities like Dakar every day come hundreds of thousands of people, fleeing the poverty of the countryside. One such woman, probably in her late twenties, with two small children in rags, came walking wearily and slowly down the street and sank into the doorway opposite. As I sat and looked at her, I saw a large tear begin to run down her cheek. For some reason that affected me more deeply than all that I had seen before and it took me several days to realise why. It was because nobody had ever told me that they cried. They were not supposed to cry.

Like so many others, I had protected myself from the reality of the third world by unconsciously believing that they were different, that their lives may well be hell but that they had a particular immunity. They did not suffer in the way we suffer, they did not feel in the way we feel and did not cry. Well, they do.

9

Away from it all and an editor at last (by way of the RSC)

'Nobody made a greater mistake than he who did nothing because he could do only a little.'

EDMUND BURKE

It takes a saint to spend their whole life in the service of humanity, and I was never a saint. I have written of my anger and impatience when confronted with much that I have seen, but the Lira's and Latham's of this world do not appear to be driven by anger and impatience, or even a burning desire for justice. They share a remarkable acceptance of humanity for what it is, and they have the courage, humility, patience and astonishing selflessness to endure themselves the worst of conditions and horrors. I am proud to have made the effort to travel to where Padre Lira and Julian Latham worked, but I was also always pleased to leave. I did not like being there. I could not stay there for any length of time.

I learned something about myself from such people and such places: I learned that I could be deeply touched by what I saw, that I did care, but not enough to bleed or starve, be bitten by mosquitos or snakes, live with discomfort and disease. These were heroes. I was no hero. I can still remember the shame I felt when I left Julian Latham alone with his Indians. I can still remember the sense of guilt as I waved goodbye to Padre Lira from the truck taking me back from his heartless desert to decent food and wine, a warm bed and clean clothes.

Eventually I came to terms with myself and my limitations. I simply could not do what they did. It was not in me. But, there were things I could do without being a hero. Things I could do to support them. Things I did best. I could see, hear, remember and describe. In other words, I could tell their story. I could use my access to the media, I could give them a voice, help them raise money, and at home, I could help apply pressure on uncaring authorities and try to change unjust laws. Good enough? Probably not, but that was what I did.

For four years I campaigned away in the *Observer*, served on the executive of the NCCL and joined in the work of a variety of other campaigning groups. And I did all I could for Oxfam, writing and speaking for it. But, you could only write so many columns on the same themes before they lost their impact, and by 1974 I had written over 150 of them. The *Observer* still seemed to be content, but I knew I had become too predictable. I was in danger of becoming a bore. It was time to move on,

What I did next made little sense to those who had assumed I was a better man than I was. It also made little sense to those who had assumed I was making my way carefully up the steps of some preconceived career path. What I did, was walk away. Not with a sense of permanence. Never that! But I was in my mid-thirties and I had been on a campaigning roller-coaster ride for nearly a decade, I had heard and seen too much. I had lost some of my capacity for anger and my sense of shock. I desperately needed a change. OK, more truthfully, a holiday, even a holiday from reality.

Never a long-term planner, I never the less made a small plan. I would take some time out. Then I would return to the 'front', wherever or what-ever that would be. But what to do to now?

There was television, of course. I enjoyed the challenge of making tele-vision. And I had shown I could do it. While at Shelter and the *Observer*, I had guest-presented an edition of BBC2's *Late Night Line-up* and been co-presenter on one Sunday evening discussion series and sole presenter of another. I had made a 50 minute documentary in the One Pair of Eyes series. I was regularly on radio's *Any Questions* and particularly useful to the two radio programmes *The World at One* and *The World This Weekend*, then edited by Andrew Boyle. He employed and nurtured such up-and-coming reporters as Jonathan Dimbleby and Roger Cook. Because I was involved in a number of issues and was only a few minutes away from Broadcasting House and had become a proven performer, they were always calling me over to comment on one controversy or another. I appeared so often I should have been on a retainer. However, before I could explore these possibilities, there arose an opportunity that I could not resist.

What greater change could there be than to join The Royal Shakespeare Company?

At the RSC

I know, when it was announced that I was joining the RSC, it baffled most people, but it actually made complete sense to both parties. The RSC was looking for someone to head up their public affairs activities as they moved towards their 1975 Centenary Season. They desperately needed to use this event to raise money to pay for repairs to the main Stratford-upon-Avon theatre. To them, I was somebody who combined publicity skills with experience in mobilising supporters and raising money. For me, the attraction was a complete change, the chance to explore and express my earlier enthusiasm for the theatre, but with a clear exit route after a year and a half. Everyone a winner! At least, that is what we hoped.

Punch magazine were kind enough to write my first press release for me:

Though they have been in print some little while, this is the first time I have read the Collected Works of William Shakespeare, and highly disturbing reading they make too. A series of reports on the state of Britain, with some further looks at the Continent, they reveal a state of affairs so shameful that it is hard to know where to begin.

Housing being the area I know best, I can heartily endorse everything that Mr Shakespeare says in his indictment of British housing policy. As elsewhere, he presents unforgettable case histories rather than theories. He tells in some detail the plight of a certain Lear, homeless and friendless, who had made the mistake of settling his estate prematurely on his daughters. When they threw him out, he had no legal redress against them whatsoever, which supports the case I have always made for legislation which would oblige children to provide basic accommodation for their parents. Sadly, Lear died before Mr. Shakespeare finished his report, but there are thousands of similar cases still suffering from this legal oversight.

And if anyone doubted that security of tenure, now promised by the Labour Government, was long overdue, he needs merely study the case of John Falstaff, an elderly man lodging in Windsor, who only escaped eviction and homelessness by sheer cunning and resourcefulness. But should such people have to rely on their own ingenuity? In a modern society, should there not be safeguards against temporary absence of funds? Mr. Shakespeare is very fair-minded about this; he admits that cases like Falstaff are not easy to deal with, being often deceitful, semi-alcoholic, and even criminal, yet concludes that humanity over-rides all these considerations.

Lack of rented accommodation is yet again behind another tragic story, that of an engaged couple he calls Romeo and Juliet. Other factors are involved, it is true – unsympathetic parents, a muddled family planning policy, teenage gang fights – but the root cause of their ill-starred attempt to set up house was simply the difficulty of finding suitable flats or obtaining a reasonable mortgage. Family pressures eventually became too much and the couple committed suicide: another nail in the coffin of complacent Tory property policies. Mr. Shakespeare, incidentally, makes a moving plea in this report for the immediate improvement of nurses' conditions, which I have always fought for.

That all this is nothing new is proved by an interesting series of historical essays in which the author damningly indicts the continued laisser-faire of British governments through the years, whether reflected in the appalling conditions of the army in Henry V's day, the wretched wage levels of peasants or the corruption present in Scottish politics even a thousand years ago. But the big question which I have always asked, and which Mr. Shakespeare asks too, is: Why? How does it happen? What is behind the constant resistance to the redistribution of wealth?

Not for the last time, I discovered that if you come into a fairly senior position in a company, everybody assumes you must know what you're doing. Unfortunately, it is not always so. No one sat me down and said: 'Look, you're entering a world of rampaging egos, great sensitivities, high intellectual and professional standards; you need to get yourself fully briefed and you need to proceed with care.' Of course, I should have worked that out for myself. But, in a way, I was still an innocent abroad, completely unprepared to hold my own with world class theatre directors, all of whom appeared to have been at either Cambridge or Oxford, and with actors, who were often either riddled with insecurity and crying out for reassurance or, alternatively, convinced they were on the brink of becoming the next Olivier. Into this I came like a bull in a china shop.

Fortunately, if you come from my limited beginnings, you become adept at learning from your mistakes and on the whole, I did not do too badly. But the subtlety of theatre company politics and the complexity of the characters who work in it, led me to stand on more than a few toes. Part of the problem is that I was an instinctive enthusiast, whereas theatre people were, on the whole, laid back – even cynical. Actors, in particular, had been lied to and let down too often to respond to my 'we can achieve miracles – let's do it' kind of leadership style.

Having said that I did get by without causing any major disaster. And I did some good, making a number of small changes that proved worthwhile, improving relationships between the theatre and the town, extending the service to members, and merging the booking schedules of all three theatres so that the Aldwych regulars were now receiving details of Stratford publications and vice versa. To do this I had to win over the highly suspicious box office managers of the two main theatres. I came to learn that box office managers everywhere tend to reign over their tiny kingdoms with a rod of iron. They are almost universally conservative and resist change as a matter of principle. However, after a meeting at Stratford, the RSC box office managers all accepted my idea, and I was even invited for morning coffee at the home shared by two of them, an honour, I was told, enjoyed by few in the history of the company.

While the whole idea of the RSC was that it would be an ensemble, the company in fact changed personnel considerably from season to season. There was, of course, a hard core of actors who were not widely known outside the RSC but were familiar and respected faces within it; I think of people like Emrys James, Jeffery Dench and Tony Church. But to me it was clear that the RSC, at least at that time, was not so much a company of actors, as a company of directors. The most powerful were Trevor Nunn, Terry Hands, John Barton and David Jones. It was the directors who chose the programme for the year and, as often as not, the choices were made on the basis of what they personally wanted to do, (i.e. where they were in their own career plan), rather than what was necessarily right for the company. Thus the season emerged from a process of bargaining between them.

I liked the actors, and I understood their vulnerability. This was a profession with 90 per cent unemployment and many were paid a pittance. One day they could be a star, applauded by full houses; the next day they could be signing on for the dole. The RSC offered no guarantees from season to season. And in what other profession can you perform your duties and the next day be savaged in the media if you have made a mistake, or because you do not perform to the satisfaction of a handful of critics? No wonder they were so insecure and, in my view, the director-orientated RSC did not make it any less so. Never the less they were, with the usual exceptions, as generous and hard-working as any people I had known.

I will always be pleased I spent time at the RSC. As a theatre-lover I had been briefly allowed behind the scenes, to be part of a great company in vintage form. I had the chance to see, and even be associated with, the intellectual firepower, the scholarship, the unbelievable attention to detail – the sheer hard work that went into some outstanding productions. At Stratford, Ian Richardson and Richard Pasco were memorably swapping roles nightly as Richard and Bolingbroke in a riveting production of *Richard II*. At the Aldwych, John Wood was brilliant in the world première of Stoppard's *Travesties*, and then equally brilliant as Sherlock Holmes. (I went to New York to help launch the Sherlock Holmes season there. There was a tradition that leading actors would dine at Sardis after the first night and, as in the case of Wood, get a standing ovation when they entered the restaurant. Wood enjoyed it so much he went out and came back for seconds.)

Then Nicol Williamson and Helen Mirren came to Stratford to act in *Macbeth*; this began as the RSC at its worst, with Nunn's Stratford production a self-indulgent, rambling three and a half hours, but by the time it transferred to the Aldwych it was the RSC at its best, the production down to 90 minutes without an interval. Outstanding as Nicol Williamson was, I enjoyed him even more as a hilariously gloomy and precious Malvolio. Williamson was a mild enough man until he had a few drinks; then it was wise to keep your distance. My main memory of Helen Mirren was of her self-effacement off the stage; I often saw her, without makeup and in a shapeless cardigan and skirt, sitting alone in the corner of the Green Room knitting or doing needle work.

While I am pleased to have been there, it was not a happy time. For one thing, years of being away from home while working for Shelter or undertaking other engagements had already made me too much of an absentee husband and father, and now spending the weeks in Stratford while my wife Rita and Tim and Jacqui lived in London finally caused me to lose touch with what should have mattered most, my family. Eventually we parted. It was all very painful and it was entirely my fault, a cruel irony that while spending years campaigning to help families stay together, I had become so wrapped up in it that I had caused my own to fail. It was a bad time but I have no excuse and deserve no sympathy.

It's typical of Rita that, having found a new life with her new husband Jeff, she has not only always been forgiving but has remained friends to this day. She and Jeff took up 'the good life' with a small farm in Sussex. Thanks once more to Rita, the whole family has remained united. She and Jeff and I would all turn up at school parents' evenings and confuse teachers who usually had placed only two chairs in front of them. We have often all joined together for family events. But at the time it was deeply distressing and inevitably I found it difficult to work professionally while I was privately deeply disturbed at my negligence.

Also, it was probably naïve of me to believe that, after campaigning for over a decade, investing my energies in a theatre company would work. Much as I still loved attending the rehearsals, chatting to the costume makers and scenery builders, all master craftsmen, and gossiping with the actors, and, above all, becoming part of the audience on first nights, full of pride in the performances, I could not escape the feeling that, while the RSC was not frivolous – far from it – it was a frivolous use of my particular experience and skills. Fortunately, just when I was concluding that I was the wrong man in the wrong place, I found that it all made sense after all, because I proved the right man to work with Terry Hands on the centenary season.

It was decided that the season would consist of four related plays – *The Merry Wives of Windsor, Henry IV Parts One and Two*, and *Henry V*. There would be only one director for the whole season, Terry Hands. And there would be one company with Alan Howard playing Hal throughout, Brewster Mason playing Falstaff and other actors sticking with the same characters. The company, which for the only time I was at Stratford really became a convincing ensemble, was not only impressively led by Howard but produced a number of extraordinary performances in lesser roles, notably the trio of Tim Wylton as a memorable Bardolph, Richard Moore as an exuberant Pistol, and Philip Dunbar as a hilarious Nym. Clement McCallin, who first played at Stratford in 1937 came back to play the King of France, and nearly the whole of the 1968 cast of *The Merry Wives of Windsor* including Brewster Mason, Ian Richardson and Brenda Bruce were reassembled for the final production of the four. Everyone working on these four productions was managed by a fabulously committed and hilarious gay Australian called Hal Rogers with whom I had become friends. (Hal was once put in charge of a fireworks display to mark some RSC occasion and accidentally set light to the shed that contained them and blew the display to pieces.)

I went to Terry with what was for the RSC a fairly radical proposal: instead of four posters and four programmes, why not have one for the whole season? And instead of four separate photographers, why not appoint just one for all four productions. Thus, just as he was producing four productions as a cohesive whole, we would represent it and market it that way too. Terry loved the idea. Terry's effort in directing all four productions and creating a glittering season of theatre was monumental. Of their *Henry V*, the veteran *Sunday Times* critic Harold Hobson wrote: 'no words of mine can adequately convey its theatrical and above all visual splendour . . . the production is packed with brilliances . . . Alan Howard is a superb, and I had almost said, eclipsing Henry . . . he utters some of the most ringing and thrilling calls to valour ever heard in the theatre.'

To help the centenary appeal I proposed a huge Elizabethan Fair on the park over the river from the theatre. We put together a committee from both theatre people and the town. We planned an Elizabethan food fair, an actors' tent (the RSC actors grasped the idea with great enthusiasm), a procession of hundreds in Elizabethan costume, jousting, falconry – the lot. Over 20,000 people came on the day and it was a huge success. What was particularly pleasing for me was the way the whole community took part – the local council appointed a special sub-committee with the power to suspend any by-laws that got in the way; a local architect so brilliantly designed a fairground layout that we did not have to make a single change; every local club and society had a tent. It became such a spectacle that the *New York Times* devoted a whole page to what it described as, 'a combination of Old World pageantry and New World salesmanship'.

Even with the organisation of the fair, I was still an innocent abroad: about two weeks before the big day two rough-looking and untidily-dressed men turned up in my office. They explained they ran a fun fair and wanted to be part of our show. I explained that this was an Elizabethan Fair and that their presence with roundabouts and a ferris wheel would not be appropriate. So, sorry, No. They all but fell upon their knees. Times were hard, Guv. Their children were starving. This was their only opportunity to benefit from a big crowd and build up their stores for the winter. Have a heart, Guv.

This was all too much for a campaigner for minorities; I said that provided they would site their fun fair well away from the main fairground, they could come. But what would they pay towards the theatre fund? This virtually had them in tears. I had a repeat performance. Times were hard, Guv. I did not know how their families suffered in the winter if they did not make some money now. Be fair, Guv. I caved in and settled for £100 and they left. A few minutes later I glanced out the window and saw them climb into a brand-new Jaguar that had been parked outside and drive away. And we never did get the £100.

The four productions eventually transferred to the Aldwych and the climax was a day when the two *Henry IV's* & *V* were performed together, one at 10.30 in the morning, one at 2.30 in the afternoon, and the last at 7.30. By the end of the night the audience and actors were equally exhausted and exhilarated. Each applauded the other. Hal Rogers, carried away, ran down to the front of the dress circle crying 'Bravo! Bravo!' tears running down his face. Flowers were thrown and standing ovations given to Howard and the others.

It was a great and glorious moment and I will always be grateful I was there. But it was time to move on. I had come from promoting the Oamaru Operatic Society to promoting the Royal Shakespeare Company, one of the top theatre administrative positions in the world and there was satisfaction in that. But I had learned something too. That the theatre world was not one that would ever satisfy me, and nor was I really the right man for it. It had been the change I needed. It had been an experience. Now it was time to get back to where I belonged. I thought that was newspapers.

Back to Journalism

Throughout my time at the RSC I was still writing for most issues of the *Illustrated London News*, and also had a column on the *Birmingham Post*. But what I really wanted was to become an editor and I jumped at the opportunity to show what I could do with the social workers' magazine *Social Work Today*. For a journalist with a national profile, it was a modest publication, but I had the chance to learn my trade as an editor where relatively few would see my mistakes, and it covered the social services, the area I knew best.

My plan for this deeply worthy, but essentially dull fortnightly, was to turn it into a weekly and promote it to the whole social services world. As an exercise in magazine management it was a success. I inherited a loss in that financial year of £30,000 and a declining circulation of around 12,000. By the time I left it was making a profit of over £150,000 (despite an increase in the staff from four to 24) and the circulation was 30,000. I am rather proud of having discovered Steve Bell, who has become a star cartoonist for the *Guardian*. He was unknown at the time and I paid him a few pounds a week to design my covers.

The editorial team was a happy little band; we worked hard and we played hard, mainly squash and snooker. We had a little squash 'ladder' but in fact it became so competitive that I had to ban it after people would come back to the office not talking to each other. When the news editor came back with blood pouring from his head, having been struck by the sub-editor's racquet – he claimed it was accidental – I decided that enough was enough.

All the time I was there I was still writing the column for the *Birmingham Post*, a monthly column for the *Observer* on social services issues, and feature articles for the *Illustrated London News*. I also did a phone-in show for BRMB in Birmingham and a series of interview programmes. And I wrote a book on politics for schools. Then Jim Bishop, *ILN*'s editor, asked me if I would like to become his deputy, with the possibility eventually of becoming editor of the famous old magazine that I had first seen in the Oamaru library.

To be fair, Jim gave me plenty of opportunity. I persuaded him we should strengthen the London aspect of the magazine and introduced an events section at the front, in the style of the *New Yorker*, and a news section on London. I introduced a number of talented friends to the magazine – Sam Smith became our man in America (and became the first man in 150 years to get the word 'fuck' into the magazine, a feat of which he is inordinately proud); another friend, Andrew Moncur, who was to become diary editor on the *Guardian*, was commissioned to write some colour features; and John Morgan, former *Panorama* reporter, became restaurant critic, a role he fulfilled with considerable gusto.

It was a comfortable and rewarding life. We produced some impressive issues and I was able to travel and write on any subject I liked, but it soon became clear that there was going to be no vacancy as editor. Jim was going nowhere. It was not really his fault; we were hit by a recession and the magazine fell from over 170 pages to only 50 or so. Jim's second problem was that he did not really fit into the pocket-calculator world of the non-journalist guys who were now running the company. The manager in charge of the ILN and some other magazines came to Thomson Magazines from Colman's Mustard. He did not know a thing about magazines. I discovered what he and the other managers were like at the beginning. I had gone into the office the Friday before I was due to start, to drop a few things off, and found there was no desk or chair in my office. It was empty. Jim was away, so his secretary and I decided that I should go round to Gray's Inn Road where there were a number of second-hand office furniture shops and buy a desk and chair and put it on expenses. About two weeks later Jim came into my office looking embarrassed. 'I'm sorry about this, Des,' he said, 'but you are supposed to choose furniture from an approved catalogue. You're going to have to write an apology to the Finance Director. He's furious.' I looked at the catalogue and saw that the approved desk and chair would have cost £600 whereas I had spent only £200.

So I wrote my letter:

Dear Finance Director,
I apologise for saving the company £400. This will never happen again.
   Yours,
   Des Wilson

This was as near as I got to becoming an editor, because, in 1981, I woke up and found I was forty years old. The years had slipped by. I had enjoyed my break, but I could not but feel that these few years had not made me a better person, that my life was more hedonistic than heroic, that I was going with the flow instead of making a difference. It was time to re-inject some purpose into my life.

One night I was on my way home and the taxi-driver asked me, 'Weren't you once that Des Wilson?' I said, 'I still am.'

'What are you doing these days?' he asked.

'I think I'm about to become a campaigner again,' I said.

10

The Story of Clear – the Campaign Classic

'Those who profess to favour freedom, and yet depreciate agitation, are men who want rain without thunder and lightening. They want the ocean without the roar of its many waters.'

FREDERICK DOUGLAS

I've often been asked what campaign I'm most proud of. Obviously Shelter has a special place, because it was my first. But if I had to choose one on a technical basis – for the quality and success of the campaign, irrespective of the cause – then it would be the Clear campaign for lead-free petrol. Not only did a small number of people achieve complete victory over powerful political and industrial forces in little over a year, but, as the *Observer* said in a leading article, it achieved 'the first major success of the Green movement in Britain'.

As with Shelter, I cannot claim to be Clear's sole founder, because it would never have happened without the concern and resources of a remarkable man who I met in the Autumn of 1981. His name was Godfrey Bradman and he was to have an immense influence on the next ten years of my life.

Godfrey Bradman – my campaigning partner

Born into a Jewish family in Willesden and evacuated to Suffolk during the Second World War, Godfrey, like me, left school at fifteen, so we were both minimally educated. In so much as we had talents to overcome that start, they could not have differed more. Mine was for words, his was for numbers. Godfrey read numbers as if they were poetry. He could read beyond numbers and related jargon in a way no one else could, and as a result reduced even the Treasury to tears as he became the country's leading authority on tax avoidance. Some took a dim view of this, but Godfrey's reply was that if the authorities wanted to eliminate tax avoidance, all they had to do was close the loopholes that he, Godfrey, was uncovering. In fact, said Godfrey, he was doing them a favour by exposing them. While it would be naïve to believe that he was not at least partially motivated by money, because he became extremely wealthy, it was also obvious to anyone close to him that what he really loved was the intellectual challenge of all this. In a rare profile of him (by Michael Davie in the *Observer*), it was said: 'Far from lying awake at night worrying about the social morality of abetting tax avoidance, he seems to have regarded the Revenue purely as antagonists to be outwitted.' What for you and I would have been deeply boring, albeit rewarding work, for Godfrey was fun; the money he made was a way of keeping the score. He just loved what he did.

Later he turned to developing property. In 1979 he purchased an old tea company called Rosehaugh. It had the smallest market capitalisation of any company on the London Stock Exchange, just £180. When I met him two years later it was valued at £600 million. When it came to making money, Godfrey was a genius.

In my experience, those who are really obsessed with money are usually mean. John Paul Getty had a public telephone box in his house so that guests could pay for their calls. Godfrey was the opposite. While he lived in beautiful homes, provided well for his extended family, and entertained liberally, he also gave huge sums to charity and other causes he adopted. He was very modest about his philanthropy; time after time he refused me permission to draw public attention to one kind deed or another. He only became known as a philanthropist because in some cases, such as Clear, it became impossible to keep the source of their funding secret. No doubt he gave many millions to Jewish causes, but he would also respond instinctively to individual cases. He was once on a plane returning from Israel when he was told there was a family on board who had a boy suffering a life-threatening illness and needed to see a particular specialist in the United States urgently. Godfrey went up and down the aisle identifying a number of rich Jewish friends, and then with their combined resources they put a Concorde on standby in case it was necessary to transport the boy at short notice.

When 1500 sufferers from the side effects of the anti-arthritis drug Opren wanted to undertake a class action and sue the manufacturers Eli Lilly for compensation, Godfrey offered to put up £2 million to fund their case. He and l launched a campaign to shame the company. Not only did we achieve columns of editorial publicity but he paid for full-page ads in the *Wall Street Journal* and other newspapers, identifying the directors of the company and pressing them to meet their moral obligations. When I told him that the local newspaper near their British headquarters, the *Basingstoke Gazette*, would not take the advert because it did not want to embarrass a local firm, Godfrey said: 'In that case I'll buy the Basingstoke Gazette.' I assumed he was joking but the next time I was in his office he showed me a Dun and Bradstreet report on the company. He was actually proposing to do it. I had to work hard to persuade him to let it drop. We eventually forced the Lilly company to settle. It was, said the *Guardian*: 'Their worst hour and Bradman's finest.'

As a property developer he became concerned that there could be health hazards in the buildings he was responsible for, so he tried to persuade the authorities to research the hazards to human health caused in construction and then pay for the publication of proper guidance. When they failed to do so, he quietly financed an inter-disciplinary study by academic specialists at Salford University and paid for the publication of a book that he circulated throughout the building trade. Davie described him well in his article as 'gentle and humorous, with his conversation studded with statistics'.

He quickly became bored if he was not working. He had a team of secretaries working around the clock and when I left him sometimes late at night he would be heading for home with a taxi full of big boxes of papers to prepare for the next day's meetings. Always busy and always late, Godfrey was travelling in a taxi one day when he noticed it was being driven down what appeared to be a street closed to traffic. When the driver explained there were some streets that only taxis could use, Godfrey immediately bought the taxi, hired the driver, kept the meter running and thus kept his journey times as short as possible. (This habit nearly caused me a heart attack. I was being driven to the airport in it and dozed off. When I woke, I glanced at the meter, as one does, and it was showing £750. The driver explained that the meter had to be on all the time if he was to be a lawfully employed taxi driver. £750 represented two day's driving.)

Driving Godfrey around must have been an adventurous business: he once saw a tramp lying in the gutter, asked his driver to stop, picked him up, and booked him into a luxury hotel. He once spotted an attractive woman struggling with a heavy suitcase. He asked his driver to stop and insisted he take her to wherever she was going. (Her name was Susan and he has now been married to her for over 40 years.)

Godfrey was unpredictable and yet conservative, intuitive, intolerant of any delay or incompetence and yet often remarkably thoughtful. He would appear indifferent to the hours he was making others work, or the pressures he was placing upon them, and then suddenly realise they could be hungry and send them to Claridges where a table would be waiting. He did not drink or smoke, was meticulously (even obsessively) clean and tidy, but he never imposed his way of life on others. Once I drove him home after a late night meeting and he insisted I come in for a drink. He searched the empty house until a cupboard opened and a whole stack of champagne bottles fell out – there were scores of them there. He looked at them, clearly bewildered. 'Will this do, Des?' he asked.

Quietly spoken, mild of manner, courteous and with a quick sense of humour, he could, however, drive those around him near-insane by his attention to detail (the quality that made him rich) and his persistence in pursuing a particular and sometimes utterly irrelevant point. Godfrey was an obsessive – about his work, about the health and safety of his family (he was one of the few individuals in the country to have a nuclear bomb shelter in the garden), and about any issue he happened to seize upon.

All the broadsheets tried at one time or another to find some ulterior motive for his support of my campaigns, but, once he was persuaded by me that he should allow an interview, his courtesy, good humour and modesty enabled him to emerge from them all with flying colours. The *Daily Telegraph* explored him in depth and in 1988 concluded:

> Bradman is what many of his fellow businessmen would call a crank. But of all the tycoons of his day, Bradman perhaps best embodies the spirit of his age. He lives by market forces . . . but he sees that man cannot live by market forces alone: that a businessman's responsibilities extend further than his shareholder's pockets . . . in that he may be more representative of the Nineties than the Eighties.

Godfrey and I met in 1981 and were to forge a partnership that lasted for 12 years. We would settle on a cause we both shared, I would devise and run the campaign, and he would finance it. He liked to be involved and to feed in his ideas, some brilliant, some completely over the top, but he never took the view that 'he who pays the piper calls the tune'. He never told me what to do. He trusted me to spend the money well, I trusted him to let me do it. My freedom to take decisions and to act without consultation was essential to our success. Sometimes I had to ask him for substantial sums of money, and once he understood why and how the money would be used, he never refused. I think he would say, however, that he and I had a lot of fun. The atmosphere in his office was formal, even strict, and everyone, including Godfrey, was properly dressed. I would turn up in jeans and jumper and tease him about his eccentricities and he liked that. I think he saw me and our campaigns as a way to express an anarchistic side of him that no one else knew.

We eventually created an organisation called Citizen Action that was a kind of holding company for our campaigns and we had four or five operating simultaneously. I suppose over those twelve years I spent a couple of million pounds of Godfrey's money. It says a lot about him that I never felt embarrassed about that; I always felt that this is what he wanted me to do. I was, of course, extraordinarily lucky to find him. But I like to think he was lucky to find me too. He could not have achieved what he did without me and I could not have achieved what I did without him. We became close friends as well as partners.

Lead in Petrol

When I met Godfrey, his concern was lead pollution. Lead had since the 1930s been added to petrol to boost the octane rating and was ultimately released into the atmosphere from car exhausts. Godfrey's concern, and that of a group he had collected around him, was that lead was a neurotoxin, a brain poison, and one that particularly affected children. To him, blasting this poison into the air in considerable quantities from car exhausts was an act of irresponsible folly.

Determined to protect his own children from any threat, he now became obsessed with the need to remove lead from petrol. As was his practice, he consulted everyone who knew about the subject, and then began a search for a campaigner who could help him have the menace removed. That is how he came upon me.

We had dinner in his 'staff canteen' (the dining room at Claridges, where he often had lunch and dinner, and where he terrorised the waiters with his insistence on clean cutlery and immediate service; he once tele-phoned Pizza Express from his table to order a pizza delivered to him in the restaurant to make the point that the service was too slow.) I liked him immediately. For all the formality, he had an air of mischief about him, a twinkle in his eye. He may have been serious about whatever he was doing, but he still had a sense of humour. He was very amused by my stories of past campaigning; he was almost rubbing his hands with glee.

But, while I liked Godfrey, I was not immediately convinced about his cause. I didn't even know that lead was in petrol and my initial reaction was that this was all a bit loopy, a view reinforced when I met a steering committee that Godfrey had already set up, some of whom struck me as having a screw loose. But I promised to look into it. So (what I learned to be) the inevitable motorbike came and the endless papers and a lengthy list of those I should consult. Godfrey had also recruited the help of three scientists and they were impressive: they were Professor Derek Bryce-Smith from Reading University; Dr Robert (Bob) Stephens, a reader in chemistry at Birmingham University, who had together done con-siderable work on lead pollution, and a London doctor, Robin Russell-Jones, who was concerned about all forms of pollution and their effect on health.

I concluded that there were three key questions: Was there a serious health threat from lead at the relatively low levels of exposure involved? If the answer was 'yes', was lead in petrol the main threat, or should we be more concerned by lead in paint or plumbing? And if the main threat was lead in petrol, what could be done about it? My scepticism only lasted a few days.

I found there was indeed a growing body of evidence that lead could affect children's intelligence and behaviour at lower levels than previously understood and considerably lower than those deemed as safe by the British health authorities. And that the main source of this exposure was from car exhausts. Also, I was impressed by the fact that major car-manufacturing countries such as the United States and Japan had decided to eliminate lead from petrol altogether – a thing that our own British industries were telling us could not be easily done.

The difference between me and the others gathered around Godfrey Bradman was over the objective for a campaign. My view has always been that a campaign needs aims that are not only achievable and realistic but are accepted as such by the public and the decision makers. Credibility is everything. It's the first question anyone asks about any campaign: 'Is what you are asking for actually possible? Can it be done?' To put it bluntly, if you look or sound even a bit nutty, you don't stand a chance. While Bryce-Smith was clearly a brilliant and well-intentioned man, and others were equally well-intentioned, they wanted to have lead removed from petrol immediately. I was neither an engineer or a scientist, but it appeared to me that this was not a credible objective: it appeared impractical because most cars had been manufactured to run on leaded petrol, and even if, as Bryce Smith claimed, they could be adapted to run on unleaded petrol and every car in the country was taken to a garage for that purpose, they would still not be useable on the continent of Europe where unleaded petrol would not be available – at least, not immediately.

The obvious answer, therefore, was to press the authorities to phase lead out of petrol over a generation of cars. It would take longer but it was practical and, in my view, proportionate, and it would enable us to come across as sane and reasonable people. So when I met Godfrey a second time (at Claridges, naturally) I told him I was convinced there was a genuine threat to health, but that I would have to abandon his steering committee and put together my own team and that we would have to adopt the 'phasing out' approach. The team would include Bob Stephens and Robin Russell-Jones (both of whom accepted the case for phasing out) but not Bryce-Smith and the others. Godfrey asked me if it could be done within a year; I said it would be closer to 18 months. He asked me how much money it would need and I said about £100,000 (in 1981 money). We shook hands on the deal and I resigned my position as deputy editor of *The Illustrated London News* and set off on my lead-free course.

My first task was to fully understand the problem. I discovered that until fairly recently it had been officially assumed that if we were exposed to blood lead levels of 35 ug/dl (micrograms per decilitre) or less, we were safe. This was the official safety level. But scientists were now suggesting that children were at least four to five times more vulnerable to the ill effects of lead than adults, and also that children in particular could be adversely affected at much lower levels of exposure than 35 ug/dl.

The most respected study on the effects of low level lead exposure on children was conducted by an American scientist, Dr Herbert Needleman, who studied lead in teeth. He showed an IQ deficit of 4–5 points between the children with the highest and the lowest tooth lead, a deficit which could not be explained away by social class or any of the other 39 variables analysed in his study. This study, and other work, indicated that at every-day levels of lead exposure, especially in towns and cities, children were at risk of:

- reduced IQ
- learning difficulties because they were more easily distracted or frustrated
- behavioural problems
- hyper-activity.

In other words, they were at risk of not achieving their full potential in life.

However, there was another point: lead was non-degradable. Unlike many other environmental pollutants, it did not eventually disappear. It just continued to build up around us, to the tune of over 3.5 million tonnes every year. It was in the air we breathed, in the dust the children picked up on their fingers, in the water we drunk, and in our food. So as well as the short-term case for protecting children, there was also a long-term environmental case for action.

The United States' Environmental Protection Agency had decided as far back as 1970 that it made sense to remove lead from petrol. Apart from the immediate health hazard, they had another reason for doing this, namely, that they wished to introduce catalytic converters to cars to control other emissions, and the lead was shown to be damaging the converters. So for both reasons the US ruled that all new cars coming on the market from 1975 should run on lead-free petrol, and that lead-free petrol should be available at all petrol stations. By 1981, when our campaign was about to be launched, US petrol was already over 60 per cent lead-free (by 1990 it was totally lead-free). Japan was over 95 per cent lead-free in 1981 and Australia had decided to introduce lead-free petrol from the mid-1980s.

Britain in 1981 allowed 0.40 grams per litre of lead in petrol and the car manufacturers and the petroleum industry wanted this to continue. To the credit of Bryce-Smith and Stephens, their campaigning had forced the British health authorities to set up a working party, chaired by Professor Patrick Lawther, to look into the matter. Unfortunately, while it recommended a number of steps to reduce lead exposure, it fell short of recommending lead-free petrol and this led to a compromise measure, namely the reduction to 0.15 by the mid-1980s.

So it looked as if that was that. Given the strength of the Conservative Government at that time, and the influence of the Lawther report, the anti-lead lobby appeared to be defeated. After all, we had a Prime Minister in Margaret Thatcher who prided herself on the 'resolute approach'. This was a woman who was not for turning! How could we hope to change the position so soon after her ministers had proudly announced what they believed to be an adequate measure?

And how could we overcome the wealth and influence of big industry, for the more I looked at it, the more it seemed to be a case of multinationals with enormous economic and political power, ruthlessly persisting with a potentially hazardous practice with complete indifference to its health effects. It was a classic case of the way some industries developed far greater clout in Westminster and Whitehall than the public ever could.

If that seems a bit strong, consider these words from *The Times* newspaper which conducted an investigation into how the decision was made and concluded: 'Our findings show that it was a prolonged barter over tangled priorities, and in the end the ministers went down the line of least expensive resistance. Muddled evidence that the invisible and tasteless lead aerosol emitted by car exhausts may damage children's intelligence was traded against the health and safety of British Leyland and the government's unwillingness to do anything which cost money . . . If the (Clear) campaign wins, it will be a rare example of moral politics defeating real-politik.'

Up to now, this issue had been dealt with in the corridors of Whitehall, rather than out in the public domain. It was clear to me that we had to change that, a strategy which meant that we and our opponents would be occupying contrasting territory. We would be claiming that the health risks called for action irrespective of costs and inconvenience to industry and they would claim the risks did not justify the technical and economic penalty involved.

We then added the 'risk factor'. Our argument went like this: 'if there is scientific debate about whether a practice is damaging to children, and if no one study seems to be decisive, and if there is a possibility that the evidence, one way or another, will never be 'conclusive' – at least, not in the eyes of the industries and their Whitehall accomplices – should we not act out of prudence?'.

Thanks to Godfrey Bradman, we had over £100,000 to finance the launch and build-up of the campaign. We had taken a small top-floor office in a building near King's Cross, staffed by myself, and by two colleagues, Susan Dibb, administrator of the campaign, and Patricia Simms, who acted as research assistant/PA. Our two top volunteer helpers and advisers were Bob Stephens and Robin Russell-Jones.

I was determined that when we launched the campaign we would not look like a bunch of cranks. To a nation that, like me, had not known lead had ever been added to petrol, the issue was in danger of sounding weird enough without adding to it by 'eccentric' appearance or behaviour. We had to convince them this was a serious problem identified by serious people. We produced print material of a much higher quality than would normally have been possible or necessary. We ruled out any kind of demonstration. And we did our best to look professional. Maybe we were being excessively sensitive, but from the start this was about credibility.

I was also determined that we would be proved right. We assembled filing cabinets full of reports, studies, and books on lead pollution; not only did we set out to build an answerable case for action on the balance of the evidence, but we carefully considered all of the arguments and so-called 'evidence' of the other side and established convincing answers. We slowly developed a solid scientific case based on a relatively cautious interpretation of the best studies.

Reflecting my determination that we should avoid looking like a small emotional minority, we set about building up the numbers so that on Launch Day we would come across as formidable and substantial. We constructed a coalition with other organisations, and compiled an impressive list of supporters. We set up a charitable trust, and recruited such public figures as my friend Betty Ackroyd, the noisy but helpful trade unionist Clive Jenkins, conservationists Lord Avebury and David Bellamy (who I accidentally met and recruited on a train), Jonathan Miller, former Whitehall adviser Professor Christopher Foster and the influential journalist, Sheila Black. Invitations for the launch were issued not just by Clear but by a list of eight national organisations. We had sent a circular to MPs and by this time we could also list 130 Members in support. In addition, I went to see David Owen, parliamentary leader of the SDP, and wrote to the Liberal leader, David Steel, and the Labour leader Michael Foot. All replied with supportive letters that we were able to quote at the launch of our campaign. Then we had a stroke of luck. What became famous as the 'Yellowlees Letter' was for Clear as fortunate as *Cathy Come Home* had been for Shelter.

The Yellowlees Letter

A friendly journalist had in mid 1981 been leaked a confidential letter sent to senior Whitehall colleagues earlier that year by the Chief Officer of Health, Dr Henry Yellowlees. Because leaded petrol was not a major issue at that time, no one had appreciated its potential impact and even his own newspaper had barely noted it. Now he wondered whether it would be of use to me. In fact it was dynamite. In it, Yellowlees noted that there was a dispute within Whitehall between the environmental and health authorities and the energy and economic advisors. The first were 'recommending a very considerable reduction of lead in petrol' and the latter were opposed 'on economic grounds'.

> Further evidence has accrued (since the Lawther Report) which, although not in itself wholly conclusive, nevertheless strongly supports the view that:
>
> (a) Even at low blood levels there is a negative correlation between blood lead levels and the IQ of which the simplest explanation is that lead produces these effects.
>
> (b) Lead in petrol is a major contribution to blood lead acting through the food chain as well as by inhalation.

There is a strong likelihood that lead in petrol is permanently reducing the IQ of many of our children. Although the reduction amounts to only a few percentage points, some hundreds of thousands of children are affected. I regard this as a very serious issue. [My italics]

For Clear, this was the equivalent of an army with bows and arrows suddenly being handed a nuclear weapon. If, as a campaigner, you obtain a leak, a number of questions immediately arise: What can we achieve with this? How shall we handle it? Who should we entrust with it? When should we use it? Naturally, the temptation was to employ it at the launch of the campaign. There was no question that by dramatically producing this letter at the launch press conference, we could achieve considerable effect, and get the campaign under way with a bang. In fact, we did not. We entered that press conference with the Yellowlees Letter in our pockets and never referred to it. Why?

Well, firstly, we knew that because of the number of organisations involved in our launch, and because of the strength of our case, we could virtually guarantee ourselves substantial publicity from the press conference. We did not need the letter yet. However, we would need it to answer the main charge that would be levelled *after* we launched – that we did not have a convincing scientific case. We knew that the industries and Whitehall would say that our campaign was over emotive and not based on any medical evidence. Imagine, therefore, what it meant to us to have ammunition up our sleeve that was in our view totally devastating and completely vindicated our campaign.

Secondly, most people were completely unaware of the issue; thus the letter emerging before they had been made aware of it would cause few ripples (as our journalist friend had discovered when he first obtained it). We felt that to obtain maximum benefit from it, we had to get a debate going, and then produce the letter. Thirdly, as a leak on a controversial issue, it was an extremely good story for the media generally, but as an 'exclusive' to one newspaper, it clearly was a real scoop. If we held it back to after the launch, we could choose the most appropriate newspaper – perhaps one that up to now had not adequately covered the story – and negotiate the best possible terms for its publication on an exclusive basis.

We decided, therefore, to hold our weapon back, open the attack with

News Extra

CLEAR

Newspaper of **CLEAR** – The Campaign for Lead-free Air

CLEAR publishes on this page what can only be described as remarkable evidence that last year's Ministerial decision to reject a ban on lead in petrol was taken either in ignorance or after behind-the-scenes rejection of a powerful warning by its Chief Medical Adviser.

We can reveal that in what he himself describes as an "unusual step", Sir Henry Yellowlees wrote to three Permanent Secretaries because "the risk to children is now shown to be too great for me to take any other course.

In the till now confidential letter, he:

Rejected the key findings of the Lawther Committee, the basis of all governmental thinking.

Doubted that there was any point in further research.

Stated that "there is a strong likelihood that lead in petrol is permanently reducing the I.Q. of many of our children . . . some hundreds of thousands of children are affected".

Said that the accumulating evidence "always points in the same direction as existing evidence, so that the health case becomes steadily stronger and stronger".

In discovering this letter, CLEAR confirms a report in The Observer last year that the Chief Medical Officer was deeply concerned about the situation.

Exclusive

Health coverup exposed–Govt. was warned 'Action should now be taken'

His letter is unequivocal and its publication by CLEAR should cause a storm of considerable proportions. It is not known whether the responsible Ministers ever saw the letter or how much they knew of the serious view that the Chief Medical Officer took of the situation.

What is clear, however, is that Ministers can expect to have to answer searching questions, for this high-level advice was never made public, or given to MPs.

The Lawther committee was set up by the DHSS to look into the whole problem of lead pollution. It was criticised when it published a report that completely failed to acknowledge that lead emitted from car exhausts would not only be inhaled directly but also eaten because of its interception in the food chain.

Sir Henry Yellowlees makes his own position perfectly clear: "Lead in petrol is a major contributor to blood lead acting through the food chain as well as by inhalation". This is a direct contradiction of Lawther.

Sir Henry also reveals that new evidence subsequently arrived at the DHSS to contradict Lawther.

His memorandum in support of his letter ends with the remarkable sentence:

"So the pieces in the jigsaw gradually fit together and become complete".

What the Govt. expert wrote

Sir Henry Yellowlees, Chief Medical Officer at the DHSS, wrote the following letter to the Permanent Secretary of the Department of Education and Science on March 6, 1981, prior to a crucial meeting to discuss lead in petrol:

I am taking the unusual step of writing to you about this matter which is to come before E(EA) Committee next week because the educational implications seem to me to be potentially important to DES.

It has been known for many years that lead is a hazard to health and the signs of overt lead poisoning – plumbism – are known to every medical student. More recently disquiet has grown that lead at comparatively low blood levels which are insufficient to give rise to obvious signs of lead poisoning may cause central nervous system damage to the population at large and particularly to children, with resulting minor intellectual deficits and minor behavioural disorders.

Although a good deal of environmental action has already been taken to reduce exposure to lead it was decided to set up a working party under the Chairmanship of Professor Pat Lawther to assess the situation especially with regard to children in whom low levels of exposure to lead had been detected. The Report of the Lawther Working Party was published in March 1980 and it was clear that at that time they were not convinced of the harm done by lead at low blood levels but they considered that at intermediate blood levels the risks could certainly not be discounted. Nevertheless because of the general uncertainty the Working Party recommended that the Government should take a number of measures to reduce population exposure to the metal. Further research into the problem was known to be in the pipeline and was recommended to be continued and increased.

Some of the recommendations are uncontroversial, but on one important matter that of lead in petrol—officials from several departments involved have been unable to reach agreement and a comprehensive report will go on Monday next to E(EA) Committee of the Cabinet leaving this major item for Ministerial resolution. There is no doubt that the simplest and quickest way of reducing general population exposure to lead is by reducing sharply or by entirely eliminating lead in petrol. The Environment Departments Health Departments and Ministry of Transport are recommending a very considerable reduction of lead in petrol, but this is opposed by the Department of Energy and the Treasury on economic grounds.

I must now make my own position clear. A year ago when the Lawther Report was published there was a degree of uncertainty that lead from petrol was in itself wholly conclusive, nevertheless though supports the view that:

(a) Even at low blood levels there is a negative correlation between blood lead levels and IQ of which the simplest explanation is that the lead produces these effects.

(b) Lead in petrol is a major contributor to blood lead acting through the food-chain as well as by inhalation.

Further research is being mounted but we are dealing here with the biological sciences where truly conclusive evidence may be unobtainable and it is therefore doubtful whether there is anything to be gained by deferring a decision until the results of further research become available.

There is a strong likelihood that lead in petrol is permanently reducing the IQ of many of our children. Although the reduction amounts to only a few percentage points, some hundreds of thousands of children are affected and as Chief Medical Officer I have advised my Secretary of State that action should now be taken to reduce markedly the lead content of petrol in use in the United Kingdom.

The risk to children is now shown to be too great for me to take any other course and I am therefore conveying this advice to you as Permanent Secretary at DES and I am copying the letter to the Permanent Secretaries at the Home Office and the Department of the Environment being the other Government Departments to which I owe responsibility.

You will know that several other major industrial nations faced with similar problems have opted for lead-free petrol or for petrol with a very low lead level despite the substantial costs and the energy penalties so incurred.

I regard this as a very serious issue on which I should give you my opinion as Chief Medical Officer.

> *Sir Henry Yellowlees*
> *Chief Medical Officer*

More recent health evidence

Sir Henry added this note:

The Health evidence, persuasive though it is already, cannot yet be regarded as conclusive. The important thing is that new evidence is accumulating all the time – and it always points in the same direction as the existing evidence, so that the health case becomes steadily stronger and stronger.

Paras 5-7 of Annex A to the E(EA) report describe the outcome of three studies since the Lawther Report was published about a year ago. I am particularly concerned about the pilot study on blood-lead and intelligence, attainment and behaviour described in para 6 which was supported by the Medical Research Council. It obviously not possible to sum up the results in a sentence but (subject of course to a the usual reservations applicable to pilot study) the study shows a average IQ loss, related to lead, of seven points across the entire range of intelligence, so that everybody is liable to suffer, from a PhD to a educationally subnormal individual.

Paragraph 8 of Annex A draws attention to points where the Lawther Report is considered to be on uncertain ground. One of these is the contribution of lead in petrol to the food chain by fallout over land. Lawther (para 61 of his report) mentioned some work being carried out at Isper in Italy at an ERC lab, which using a lead isotope, has attempted to estimate this contribution. Evidence just arrived at my Department indicates that petrol lead may contribute on average about 27 per cent of total blood lead in adults, from all sources (including food) and about 40 per cent of total blood lead in children.

So the pieces in the jigsaw gradually fit together and become complete.

Comment

We believe the letter and attached memorandum published on this page raise very serious doubts about how the decision not to ban lead in petrol was taken.

CLEAR makes the following points:

1. What is the point of the nation having a Chief Medical Officer, presumably employed because of his ability to pull together all the strands of medical evidence and opinion and advise the nation on the most appropriate steps to take to protect its people, if his advice is either suppressed or over-ruled in cavalier fashion?

Did Ministers ever see Sir Henry's letter? Did anyone else other than the Permanent Secretaries to whom it was addressed see it? Does any document exist within Whitehall which answers or discredits Sir Henry's evaluation of the position?

2. Sir Henry's rejection of the fundamental findings of the Lawther report are the most powerful expression of high-level medical opinion to support CLEAR that has yet been published. It simply cannot be brushed aside. His letter makes clear his most serious concern and it confirms what CLEAR has said – that all of the evidence accumulating "points in the same direction as the existing evidence, so that the health case becomes steadily stronger and stronger".

3. Sir Henry makes the totally valid point that on this issue "truly conclusive evidence may be unattainable" and he is correct to say that research that first points one way and then the other does not discredit the consistent line of evidence suggesting a threat to children.

4. It is astonishing that a document from the Chief Medical Officer of Health expressing the "strong likelihood" that "some hundreds of thousands of children are affected" should not have been fully published until now.

Finally, it is of course a fact that Sir Henry refers to either lead-free petrol or for "petrol with a very low lead level". He may attempt to defend itself by saying that the reduction to 0.15 grams per litre was a move to that low lead level. If Sir Henry is to be consistent, he would have to admit that the evidence not only continues to confirm earlier work, but that children are affected at even lower levels of exposure than had been realised. In any case it is clear he would have preferred complete ban. And he was right.

the remainder of our artillery, and let the opposition fire back. When their initial ammunition was wasted, we would hit them with the big gun.

The launch was planned for the third Monday in January. I spent the night before in the Odeon, Leicester Square watching the Super Bowl beamed live from America. It was not only terrific fun but, with fans of the two teams downing beer and popcorn and rising from their seats to cheer the action as if they were in the stadium, it took my mind off what was to be such a big day. (Another reason why I will always remember this campaign launch – a happening that was to prove for me much more momentous than seeing the Super Bowl – was that when the press conference ended I found myself confronted by an attractive woman editor of a small environmental magazine who seemed to me to be deeply sceptical about the campaign. Afterwards I said to the team that I felt I should phone her and take her to Joe Allen's for lunch and try to 'neutralise her'. I never succeeded in that but, to be fair, I am still trying – Jane and I have now been together for twenty-nine years and married for twenty-six.)

The press conference took place in a building in Westminster Square and was packed. Not only did we receive widespread news coverage, but also considerable support in leading articles, both in national and provincial newspapers. Immediately after the London launch, Bob, Robin and I set off on a provincial tour, holding receptions and making presentations in media centres, each with television stations covering the surrounding counties. While we were on the tour we watched closely what was happening in the national media, where the petroleum industry and car manufacturers were trying to fight back, either with scare stories about the cost of lead-free petrol, or claims that there was no health hazard. Ten days after the launch we were in Liverpool and it was there that we decided that it was time to play our trump card – the Yellowlees Letter.

We were not particularly happy with the coverage in *The Times* and decided that there were two reasons why we should offer the leak exclusively to that newspaper. First, it was a highly influential newspaper. Second, because the editor at the time, Harold Evans, was known and rightly respected for his campaigning journalism and we felt that he would appreciate the nature of the story and welcome an issue that he could credibly campaign on. I telephoned a friend, Tony Holden, the deputy editor, and told him that I had a leaked document I believed to be 'dynamite'. I said I was prepared to offer it to *The Times* exclusively, but wished to come and see Harold Evans personally. Holden knew that I was trained as a journalist and not likely to make a dramatic gesture without reason. He fixed for me to meet Evans at 3.00 p.m. the following day.

I had followed Harold Evans' campaign for the sufferers from Thalidomide while he was editor of the *Sunday Times* and as a journalist had been hugely impressed with the newspaper under his leadership, but this was my first meeting with the famous editor and I took to him immediately. He was friendly, insightful and he and Tony Holden accepted without reservation that it was a major newspaper story.

I said that I would like it on the front page, and that I would like the opportunity to write a back-up feature article putting it in its perspective within the lead controversy. These were not unreasonable terms and, in fact, Harry Evans clearly took the view without any pressure from me that this was a front page story, even a potential lead.

The publication of the Yellowlees letter hit the lead in petrol issue like a time bomb, spread-eagling the opposition and convincing almost everybody that Clear's case was vindicated and action had to be taken. By the following Tuesday, the matter was on the floor of the House of Commons and the Prime Minister herself was faced with the issue by both David Steel and Michael Foot. The letter was the big break-through in attracting public attention. It was also crucial to establishing our credibility. From then on people trusted us, not the authorities and not the industry.

Clear had become a genuinely popular cause. The letters of support and money were flooding in and we had almost 100 per cent media backing. The number of MPs who had signed up as supporters increased dramatically. It was crucial to maintain the momentum, so we now undertook a public opinion poll. What we wanted to prove was that the public supported a ban on lead in petrol and were prepared to pay more for unleaded fuel. It revealed overwhelming support for Clear. Nine out of ten people wanted lead out of petrol, and 77 per cent said they wanted action even if petrol prices went up by 'a few pence per gallon'.

We had now succeeded in maintaining the momentum for over six weeks and both the industries and the government must have wondered how long we could sustain it. What we now saw was an extraordinary set of lies, distortions, evasions, and prevarications.

When Government policy is under attack by single issue pressure groups, the relevant Secretary of State is often considered too high and mighty to confront them in person. This is left to junior ministers whose success is judged by how well they communicate the briefs they are given by civil servants. This happened with the Clear campaign. Their lead junior minister was a man called Giles Shaw who, on the day Clear was launched, co-signed with Ken Clarke, then a Health Minister, a letter to all MPs to say that the demands were unrealistic. He later accused us of 'extremist pressure' and later said 'The trouble with Clear is that it misleads through a selectivity which I can only assume is deliberate.'

On the whole, the car manufacturers and the petroleum industry tried to avoid the health debate altogether. While they claimed that this was not within their area of expertise, and we replied that no manufacturer had the right to adopt a position of neutrality on the safety of its product, the only fighters for leaded petrol were the manufacturers of the lead additive, Associated Octel. This company, operating from Ellesmere Port on Merseyside, was actually owned by a consortium of petroleum companies. To Octel, our campaign was clearly a frightening prospect, because if we won their business would be seriously under-mined. So they began by attacking our motives. One senior executive wrote: 'Clear is probably supported by anti-capitalists. We can see only three reasons for the anti-lead movement: support by precious metal producers who want the catalytic converters; support by engineering groups who believe they will have new facilities to install; or support by leftist-sponsored, anti big business groups. We think the third is most likely.'

Once it became clear that everyone was treating this analysis with contempt, Octel tried to join in the health debate, producing its own print material claiming there was no problem and quoting all sorts of people out of context, keeping up the same series of charges: that our campaign was 'emotional'; that there was no evidence to link low level lead exposure with health; that the costs and technical difficulties would be too great. We countered these by saying that rather than being emotional, we were presenting scientific material in a scientific context coolly and factually. We countered the 'cost' argument with our own survey of petrol prices in

America. We established that on the American experience petrol prices would increase by between one and two per cent in Britain if we moved to lead-free petrol.

And in April 1982 we received a breakthrough in the scientific argument in the form of two major studies, both of them supportive of our position. The first, a massive study in the US, showed that by the time 55 per cent of the lead had been eliminated from petrol in America, blood lead levels across the country as a whole had fallen by 37 per cent. Statistical analysis of the studies, led to the conclusion that the key factor in the reduction in blood-lead levels was the reduction in lead in petrol. This helped to demolish the case of the industries that petrol-lead was not the main contributor to body lead burdens. Our case in this respect was further boosted by the first results of an Italian study. This, too, showed a clear relationship between petrol-lead and lead in blood. We worked hard to publicise these studies and achieved a major article in the *Sunday Times* and also news stories in other publications. But now we came to our next major initiative, one that was to have as much impact on the final result as the Yellowlees letter. Enter the debate Professor Michael Rutter.

The Unimpeachable Judge

From the start we had been keen to pull all the evidence together in one forum, a major international symposium to be held in London. We raised the money, including a £15,000 donation by a food company, to invite to Britain all the scientists who had produced major studies on lead and health, and we now invited everyone concerned with the issue in Britain to come and hear and cross-examine the studies' authors. We invited representatives of the relevant Ministries, all of the members of the Lawther Committee, environmental health officers, and the scientific media, and advertised it widely, so that representatives of industry, including Associated Octel, would be in the audience as well. We had the whole event professionally staged to meet the standards that would be expected of a high-quality scientific symposium. In a nutshell, we were putting our evidence on the line.

However, we still had to overcome the inevitable charges from Octel and others that the conference was loaded in support of our case. We decided its authority would come down to the choice of chairman. This had to be someone who all sides of the debate respected, an unimpeachable scientific judge whose credentials, integrity and independence would lead to a summing up that would virtually decide the issue. So we took an enormous risk. We chose a man who could not be presumed to be sympathetic to Clear's position, a former member of the Lawther Committee. He was Professor Michael Rutter, at fifty perhaps the leading child psychiatrist in the world. I went to see him at the Maudsley Hospital where he was a consultant psychiatrist, and told him what was planned and who would be involved. I promised him it would be professionally run and he would be fully in control. Even so, I was astonished when he accepted.

I did not know whether to be pleased by, or frightened by his decision. If, after hearing all the evidence, this distinguished scientist was to conclude there was no health hazard, it would be a major set-back. Not only would it mean that all the money we had invested in the symposium had been wasted, but it would give our opponents a field day.

I did not hear most of the presentations, having been hit by a vicious attack of food poisoning on the opening night. I was still very weak when I half-crawled into the hall at the end to hear Professor Rutter's summing up. Had we blown our case? Our faith in Rutter and in our case proved justified. What happened is perhaps best independently described – by Geoffrey Lean in his article in the *Observer* the following Sunday:

> To experts in the audience the meeting took on the atmosphere of a tribunal rather than a symposium, with Professor Rutter keenly questioning each speaker. By the end of the three day conference most were expecting a cautious and qualified endorsement of lead-free fuel. But after a thoughtful 5,000 word review of the evidence, Professor Rutter called trenchantly and unequivocally for immediate action. He described the reduction announced by the Government last year as an unacceptable compromise without clear advantages and with definite disadvantages. He added 'The evidence suggests that the removal of lead from petrol would have a quite substantial effect in reducing lead pollution, and the costs are quite modest by any reasonable standard.' In passing he demolished many of the basic arguments of the Lawther Committee's report . . . His statement demolishes the entire platform on which the Government has stood.

So, Professor Rutter had discredited the official safety threshold. It was a remarkable finding from a man whose credentials were accepted by all sides as impeccable. It must have sent a shudder down the spine of all those on the other side. This simply was not a man whose expertise they could mock or whose motives they could question.

Unfortunately, the Falklands War was now under way and even Clear could not compete with that for editorial space, so the symposium did not get the publicity it may otherwise have done, but nevertheless it had been a major set-back for all of our opponents, none of whom could have been comfortable with the way the scientific ground was falling away beneath them. It was one thing to take on Des Wilson in a scientific argument; another to take on Michael Rutter.

Some months later Professor Rutter and I spoke again. I pointed out that the proceedings of the symposium were about to be published in a book and that it would be helpful to accompany that event with a lecture. This took place in London and he was now even more emphatic: No further research was necessary to resolve the key issue: 'Personally, I have no doubt that they should take that step, in spite of the scientific doubts . . . The point is that we do not need any further research . . . No good can come from keeping lead in petrol and harm may result.' The onus of proof on this issue needed to be placed on those who advocated no action, rather than the other way round. 'It is obvious that, if viewed purely in health terms, the risks lie entirely in the maintenance of the status quo'. The Lawther Committee 'very substantially underestimated the risks from lead in petrol'. The link between reduced IQ and high lead levels could not be blamed on chance – 'in my view the hypothesis that lead does have an effect is substantially more likely than the hypothesis that it does not'.

Professor Rutter (now Sir Michael), had justified our faith in his independence and integrity. And he had rewarded us for having the nerve to gamble everything on that faith. For just imagine the stick we would have taken if he had come down on the other side.

Into the Autumn

When we finally took a break for the summer, we were content that we had won every battle so far, but this was a complicated issue and one that was difficult to keep before the public in a way that would apply the necessary pressure on the politicians. The problem now was how to maintain momentum. We devised two fresh initiatives. First, we sent a van, manned by one of our keen supporters, Brian Price from Bristol, and a student, to schools in cities all over the country, to collect dust samples from playgrounds and pavements. The van was painted white with the words 'Clear lead-testing unit' painted on it and looked impressive. Brian and his helper would arrive at schools while parents were dropping off or collecting their children and they would hand out leaflets, scoop up dust samples and provide pictures for local newspapers and television. The local publicity was colossal and came in two bites, firstly when the samples were collected, and secondly when the results were published. The tests provided fresh evidence of the relationship between lead emitted from car exhausts and lead in the vicinity of school buildings. Many local newspapers made it their front page lead.

Then we raised the money from a trust to finance a study of lead in vegetables grown in allotments and gardens in London. The aim of the experience was to see whether the lead levels in vegetables in areas of higher traffic density was higher than the lead levels in outer suburbs. The study discovered that 40 per cent of land in inner London and 20 per cent in outer London was unsuitable for growing vegetables. We fielded at the same press conference Dr James Bevan, senior medical consultant to the Automobile Association. More publicity; indeed it was the front page lead in the *Evening Standard* that night.

Next we launched a major assault on the party conferences. Fringe meetings were fixed for each, and material dispersed widely. As a member of the Liberal Party, I was able to move a resolution at the Assembly with full television coverage and widespread publicity the following day. We launched our autumn campaign with a press conference attended by a Shadow Cabinet Environmental Spokesman, who irrevocably committed Labour to a ban on lead. At the same press conference we unveiled our survey of local authorities showing that 85 per cent of those that had taken a policy decision on lead in petrol supported the drive to have it eliminated. We also published the results of our survey into monitoring.

Our opponents must have been in despair. Whatever we did appeared to work; whereas they showed an extraordinary capacity to score own goals. They spent a small fortune on full-page ads in all of the major national newspapers presenting their case under the absurd heading 'The Health and Wealth of the Nation'. This proved totally counterproductive.

First, it was so hopelessly inaccurate that it actually led to condemnation by the Advertising Standards Authority, who upheld a considerable number of public complaints. In its judgment, the ASA concluded that Octel was 'expressing what was no more than their own opinion in terms likely to be interpreted as incontrovertible fact.'

This expensive advertising actually contributed to drawing widespread attention to the issue without achieving any credibility for Associated Octel. They had effectively spent over £100,000 giving us new issue visibility and momentum that we possibly could not have achieved without them. With enemies like this, we thought, who needed friends?

Throughout all this I had been working on a 182-page book called *The Lead Scandal*. When this was published, from morning to night I was on radio and television programmes talking about it. Our opponents were now in disarray. It must have seemed to them that we had an endless list of initiatives up our sleeve. They could never relax. And whatever we did, it appeared to work; whatever they did, it seemed to backfire. They had one hope left: the Royal Commission on Environmental Pollution.

The Royal Commission

The Royal Commission on Environmental Pollution, chaired by Professor Richard Southwood, had been following the debate with interest and now announced they were having an inquiry into sources of lead pollution and the implications of their elimination. In our eyes this equalled the Rutter intervention in terms of the pressure it applied to the legitimacy of our case.

However, we were particularly concerned that it had excluded from its inquiry the health hazards created by lead pollution, on the grounds that that this had been explored by the Lawther Committee. In our view the Commission could not adequately approach the task it had set itself without beginning with the fundamental question: Do we *need* to eliminate lead from petrol? That question could only be fully answered by consideration of the evidence related to its effect on human health and behaviour.

We submitted detailed evidence and Robin Russell-Jones and Bob

Stephens and I also appeared before the Commission. On the issue of whether it addressed the health threat of lead in petrol, our arguments appeared to have won the day. We were reassured by hints that the Royal Commission was becoming more flexible on its brief. Just the same, our fears remained: as we put it at the time, 'was this to be Royal Commission on lead or on whitewash?' We were soon to find out, for the Royal Commission wasted no time in coming to a conclusion. Our opponents were about to suffer the knockout blow.

The *Observer*'s Geoffrey Lean had been diligently exploring the activities of the Royal Commission and on April 3, 1983, he wrote that their report, to be published on April 18, would in fact come down on the side of Clear. If this was so, it was fantastic news, but it also was not coming a day too soon, because the campaign was facing its first set-back.

Two years earlier the DHSS had commissioned research on the link between low level lead exposure and health. Unfortunately the research had been given to scientists who were members of the Lawther Committee, or who were part of a group who had publicly consistently denied the strength of the evidence on the issue. Clear had consistently warned for over a year that this research would have no standing in the campaign's eyes. In fact it did identify an IQ deficit in children with higher lead levels, but attempted to show that there were other probable reasons, such as social class, for this. The DoE, for a year so frustrated by its defeats and humiliations at the hands of Clear, leapt upon this dubious finding and took the unusual step of releasing their version of the evidence plus their interpretation of it.

Once more the value of the pressure group was made apparent, because when Clear was telephoned by the newspapers, we were able to quickly react by condemning the way the material was being released to create the impression that the reports wholly supported the DoE view when they did not. As a result, the Government was angered to find headlines 'Government delivers verdict without releasing studies' in the *Guardian* and 'Lead reports cause fury' in the *Birmingham Post* with the stories largely dominated by our protest about the way the research was being manipulated by DoE public relations people. Once more their clumsy handling of the issue had back-fired.

A morning visitor – the concession

And then one morning I had an unusual call from Godfrey Bradman. Could I drop what I was doing and come to see him post-haste. I jumped into a taxi and went to his office at Queen Anne Street where I found him having coffee with a friend of his, David Wolfson, who worked at No. 10 as the Prime Minister's chief political advisor. Wolfson asked us to sum up the state of play on the issue and, having listened quietly, then said that the Prime Minister had concluded that there was a case for action. His request was a simple one: if the Government caved in, how could it be done so that it did not lose too much face. Mrs Thatcher, he pointed out, did not take kindly to public humiliation. Godfrey and I looked at each, amazed. Were we really hearing this? Was the Government not only admitting defeat but asking to negotiate acceptable terms of surrender? Had we won?

Fortunately I was able to help David Wolfson. 'If the *Observer* story is correct,' I said, 'the Royal Commission is about to come down on our side. The Prime Minister will be able to say that the government had rightly and responsibly waited for this advice, and having received it, would act promptly upon it.' But would we jump all over them with glee, he asked – or words to that effect. Godfrey and I looked at each other again, and then almost fell over ourselves to assure Wolfson this was the last thing we would do. We would accept the decision with enthusiasm and praise the Government for its swift response to the Royal Commission.

We now knew it was only a matter of days. What was extraordinary was that even the Government's junior ministers did not know. Even after this meeting they were still appearing to the last minute on radio and television defending their stance.

On Friday April 15 the Westminster lobby was tipped off that there could be a change of position on lead in petrol and that it could come as soon as Monday. This was reported on the intervening Sunday. The fact that Mrs Thatcher was now personally involved was demonstrated by the breadth of the leaks and references such as that in the *Mail on Sunday* that 'the decision by Mrs Thatcher and other ministers effectively steals some of Labour's political clothes', and in the *News of the World*, 'Premier Margaret Thatcher has decided to respond swiftly to a Royal Commission report'.

On Monday, April 18, hardly able to contain my impatience, I was in the office early when I was called upon by Tom Radice, the secretary to the Royal Commission, who gave me in confidence the key recommendations from the report being published later that morning. I could see that the Royal Commission had struck the final blow. It said the current permitted levels for lead in petrol should be seen as just an intermediate stage before its phasing out altogether. The Government should begin immediate discussions with the relevant industries to fix a timetable for the introduction of lead-free petrol.

At 2.30 p.m. Professor Richard Southwood, chairman of the Royal Commission on Environmental Pollution, duly published his report at a press conference. I was in the Strangers Gallery in the House of Commons at 3.30 p.m. that afternoon to hear Tom King accept that recommendation and announce that the Government would press for a Europe-wide ban on lead in petrol. As he waited to speak, King looked up to the public gallery. Our eyes locked. He reddened and looked away.

King then called a press conference and we followed it with our own, calling for the introduction of a definite date and saying that if there were delays in Europe, Britain should act unilaterally. I did my best to keep our promise to Wolfson but could not totally let them off the hook:

'The battle between ourselves, the industries, and the ministers responsible on this issue has been vigorously fought in public. There can, therefore, be no doubt that this is a triumph for the mobilised concern and determination of the parents of this country over the power of multi-national industries and the obstinacy of ministers and bureaucrats. It is to be hoped that they have learned their lesson that the people of this country will not accept environmental pollution, demand the measures to eliminate it, and are prepared to pay for them. If that message is taken on board, then the prize for our victory today will be much greater than just lead-free petrol – it will be a healthier and safer country for our children to grow up in.'

That night an exultant Godfrey Bradman and I met for a celebratory dinner at the Connaught (it had temporarily replaced Claridges as his canteen). Afterwards we drove round to the *Guardian* to pick up an early edition at the back door. The story was, of course, on the front page and a leading article said: 'Rout of stout party: environment ministers seen

heading for the policy hills with the Royal Commission on Environmental Pollution and Clear – the Campaign for Lead-free Air – in full
pursuit.' The *Observer*, in a leading article, was equally gratifying. It praised
the Royal Commission and went on to say: 'Credit is also due to Clear and
its energetic chairman, Des Wilson. Even its opponents admit that the
pressure group, formed only 15 months ago, carried out a brilliant and
effective campaign. It's victory, surely the fastest in the history of
environmental campaigning, is the first major success for the Green
movement in Britain.'

So the battle on the principle was over. Of course, we did not have lead-
free petrol overnight, and Clear remained in being to fight for a definite and
early date, to persuade other European countries to move to lead free petrol
as well, and to make sure that there is no sell out. But the aim of the
exercise had been to get a decision by ministers who did not want to take
that decision, a decision in the face of Whitehall opposition and in defiance
of the vast resources spent by huge industries and a decision that was a
reversal of an earlier Governmental decision two years earlier.

Looking back over that 15 months, one can see that all the initiatives I
have described were crucial, but what really mattered was that we were
right. Our case withstood all examination and there were lessons to be
drawn. The authorities had to learn that the people now gave higher
priority to environmental protection – they rated the health of their
children much more highly than the performance of their cars or the price
of petrol. The industries had to learn that instead of trying to fight growing
environmental concerns, they would be better to respond positively to
them, for, if they did not, they would end up being forced to act, often
more expensively than if they had acted voluntarily. And hopefully, the
public had learned that when the democratic process fails them, when
their institutions fail to respond, there is still hope – hope in the alternative
ways of becoming involved – in voluntary organisations, charities and
pressure groups, with a legitimate role in the democratic process and
offering another way to exercise power.

It took another year to achieve a final result in Europe, but we did. In
May 1984 the European Commission announced a time table towards lead
free petrol. Our campaign had spread its wings and now hundreds of
millions would be protected from increasing exposure to lead.

A lead-free New Zealand

At this point I received a letter from John Horrocks, the leader of Friends of the Earth in New Zealand. Would I do a brief tour there and front a call for lead free petrol in my home country. So I went out in the summer of 1984. I was preceded by a series of articles and interviews in all the major newspapers and my tour of the country received saturation coverage in the press and on radio and television. I spoke to packed audiences in all four major cities and also to a sell-out crowd in my home town. I even went and spoke to my old school's assembly. It was both enjoyable and effective; and the impact of the campaign on what is, after all, a relatively small country was amazing.

New Zealand had, at 0.84 grams per litre, six times as much lead in petrol as Europe's projected 0.15 grams per litre. Once more I found myself confronted with the lobbying of Octel, who had managed to have the issue kept within the preview of the energy and transport ministries. My main opponent in New Zealand was an intellectually-challenged Energy minister called Bob Tizard. For a week I went toe to toe with him. Interviewed soon after my arrival in New Zealand, he said of me on television, 'I just laugh at him – he's a fool.' We then clashed in the newspapers. 'I have seen no link between leaded petrol and health,' he said, an astonishing comment considering the evidence we had produced. I was quoted in reply: 'Mr Tizard has set himself up for a crushing defeat . . . he has made a disastrous personal blunder, completely ignoring overseas advice and experience.'

When I went to see the Minister for the Environment, Russell Marshall, it became clear to me that the government was divided and, thanks to our campaign, the health and environmental interests were beginning to make headway. A newspaper, arguing that the matter should not be decided by energy interests, headlined its attack on Tizard: 'Right argument, wrong minister'. By now the whole country was caught up in the row. One argument of mine was making real headway; it was the simple question: 'In what way are New Zealand children better able to withstand the ill-affects of lead pollution compared with the US, Australia, Japan and the whole of Europe?'

The campaign, which began on a Monday, took only four days. On the fifth day, the Friday, the Ministers responsible for energy, health and environment issued a joint statement: 'The Government will be acting as rapidly as possible to reduce the lead content of petrol, and to remove the hazards to health . . . we confirm that it is Government policy to introduce lead-free 91 octane petrol as soon as possible.' That night I appeared before another sell-out crowd in Wellington, the nation's capital, and was greeted with cheers as the press release was read out. It had been a stunning victory.

Friends of the Earth released a statement welcoming the decision and kindly saying: 'There is no doubt our campaign has been immensely helped by the visit to New Zealand of Des Wilson . . . as an expatriate New Zealander himself, it is particularly appropriate that he should still be in the country at the time this historic move was announced.' On my last night in New Zealand the whole of its main weekly television programme was turned over to an interview with me. I was asked: How did it happen? How could it happen in only four days?

My reply was that the moment the issue was moved from the business influenced ministries of energy and transport to the health based ministries, the affair could only have one outcome. I also pointed out that it was impossible for politicians in a small country to maintain they were right on an issue when much of the rest of the world was, on the basis of carefully considered evidence, taking a different view – and acting upon it. The programme showed Tizard calling me a fool. What did I think of that? I replied that on Monday he said I was a fool, and on Friday he announced he was taking my advice: What did that make him?

11

Friend of the Earth

'Everywhere in the world there is evidence of a deep-seated failure to use the competence, the wealth, the power at human disposal for the maximum good of human beings. The environmental crisis is a major indication of this failure . . . '

BARRY COMMONER, *The Closing Circle*

A decade into the twenty-first century the environmental movement is now mainstream, but this was not so at the beginning of the 1980s. The Green Party had achieved their first electoral success in Germany, but 'Greens' (as environmentalists were now being called) were still seen as eccentric in the UK. I myself had no fully formed view of the environmental movement. The Clear campaign was as much a public health campaign as an environmental one, and, while helped by local Friends of the Earth groups, it existed largely in isolation from the environmental movement. It was a cause unto itself. Clear was, however, seen by Friends of the Earth UK as one of the UK's first environmental success stories and this so heartened its Board, that Steve Billcliffe, then its director, was asked to approach me to enquire whether I would consider becoming its non-executive (i.e. unpaid) chairman.

FoE was part of an international network, founded in the United States, and in the UK was a collection of local groups, many fighting only on local issues, but coordinated for national campaigns by a small full-time team in an overcrowded building near the Angel Islington. It had made some impact, but suffered from spreading its resources too wide and not having sufficient focus. Some of its stunts made it seem more eccentric than serious. In particular, its cause needed to be seen to be more relevant to people's everyday lives; campaigns to 'save the whales' were, of course, worthy, but they defined the movement in a rather airy-fairy way. If you were unemployed or struggling on a low income, this was not an issue that grabbed you.

But it had some talented and idealistic campaigners, notably Chris Rose and Charles Secrett, both clever, dedicated and likable; what it lacked was leadership, a coherent overall strategy, and an effective spokesman. While I did not have notable environmental credentials, this, I presumed, was what they hoped I could provide. My first Board meeting came as a shock. The staff were on strike. And the organisation was more or less bankrupt. It was sad, really. For some reason that I never did fully fathom out, there had been a complete breakdown in understanding between the full-time team and the Board; the team was in a state of insecurity and paranoia and the Board seemed to have no idea how to handle the problem.

This presented me with a dilemma. To become chairman of a success was one thing; to step into an organisation in crisis was another. I talked to Godfrey Bradman about it, explaining that FoE was too necessary and valuable to be allowed to die. As always, he responded generously and said he would pump £30,000 into FoE, but only if I became chairman for at least three years.

Steve Billcliffe was a decent, good-hearted man and an able manager, but he was not really an environmentalist and he was not a leader. It was clear to me, over that period, my main challenge would be to find a leader-director who could do for FoE what I had done with Shelter: both run the full-time operation and lead the national movement. But the first problem was to get the team working.

After I was formally elected. I had lunch with Charles Secrett, the most influential member of the team and spokesman for the 'strikers'. Charles was the wild-life campaigner and I encouraged him to talk about these issues. I was touched by his enthusiasm and his articulate intelligence. After about an hour I said to him, 'Charles, what you are talking about really matters. And it's obvious you care passionately about it. We have to get you back to it, instead of wasting your energies on petty disputes.' I offered him a deal: if he and the team would just return to campaigning and give me six months to sort the organisation out, I would see that Godfrey's £30,000 was injected into FoE, thus solving the financial crisis and giving them some resources to campaign with.

From that day on I never heard another word about the strike. Everyone just forgot about it. And I never did really learn what it was about. All they had ever wanted was to feel valued and to be given the sense of hope and security that came from having leadership that could boost their confidence, give them a sense of direction, and help to increase their resources.

That is what I did my best to provide, stressing the importance of focus on priorities, realistic objectives, careful planning, and quality research.

Despite its problems, FoE had maintained a reasonable contrasting public reputation as a research-based campaign in contrast to Greenpeaces's more spectacular approach, but now it needed to re-establish its importance and underline it distinctive role. It needed a higher profile. It needed an attention-grabber. My response was to propose a series of big 'Green Rallies' across the country with headline speakers like America's Ralph Nader and home-grown 'stars' such as David Bellamy, CND's Joan Ruddock, and Jonathan Porritt. Convinced that the key to their success was Nader, I went to Washington to find him in his offices near Dupont Circle.

Ralph Nader

While I had been aware of Ralph since the Sixties when I read about his campaign for automobile safety in the United States and the impact of his explosive book *Unsafe at any Price*, this was our first meeting. He is one of the few people I have admired from afar and found equally impressive in person. A tall, dark-haired man, with a dark brown complexion reflecting his Lebanese family background, he had an intense, driving personality balanced by a lively sense of humour. Both these qualities were reflected in his only half in jest order to me at a restaurant: 'Eat your greens, Des . . . How can you be a Green when you don't eat your greens!' His office was packed with young zealots, many of them lawyers and they in turn were dwarfed by piles of documents, leaflets and posters. His own room was knee-high in paper and he typed all his own letters, speeches and reports on a battered old typewriter. He was, I gathered, so committed to his campaigns that he lived a monk-like existence alone in a bed-sitter.

He was not an easy man to work with because he never let you off the hook. While, like me, he was not past engaging in, even enjoying, confrontation with 'the enemy', he also tended to fix his accusatorial eye on those around him. Night after night he would confront local communities with their need to help themselves. He stressed how each of us was made up of a number of personalities – husband (or wife), worker, taxpayer, consumer, etc. – whose activities and desires could so conflict with one another that we threw away with one hand what we achieved with the other. He had in mind the man at work who, by failure to control the pollution he caused, could be the enemy of himself at play, because he no longer had fresh air to breathe or clean water to swim or fish in. Or of the woman at work who, by neglecting safety factors in her products, could be the enemy of herself and her children as consumers (who stood to be poisoned) or as motorists (who stood to be injured or killed). And he had in mind, too, the taxpayer, who demanded cuts in taxes and cuts in public expenditure, and then, as a father or mother, complained about slum schools or the weaknesses of the Health Service, or as a commuter complained about the failures of public transport – all of them poverty stricken because of the cuts in taxes and public expenditure.

Nader's was a call for our participation by carrying out what he called our 'civic duties', but it was also a call for involvement in the real issues. He argued that people were blinded to 'the more sophisticated forms of violence'. By that he meant the imposition on us and our children of polluted and poisoned air, noise, unsafe cars and other appliances, of foods that harmed health. He would, for instance, cite the increasing concern at that time about criminal violence; why, he asked, was there not a similar uproar over a spectacular death on the roads, possibly caused by the criminal negligence of a driver, a manufacturer or a repair man? One day when he was in the UK he drew my attention to two stories that appeared on the same day: one said that the number of indictable violent offences for the whole of the previous year had been just over 40,000; the other showed that 10,000 child pedestrians were knocked down by cars in only one quarter of the same year. That could add up to 40,000 a year – and that was 'only' the children! Altogether, 84,000 casualties occurred on the roads in those three months and 1,700 people were killed (compared with fewer than 200 murders in a whole year).

Ralph and I were to become friends. He wrote the foreword to *Pressure*, my book on campaigning, and he asked me to join him in a workshop on citizen action in Maine. I have only admiration for his consistency and sheer hard work in the cause of responsible citizenship over nearly sixty years. I have only ever differed from him on one issue: while I understood his political position – he believed, just as I did in the UK, that the problem was not just the two major political parties but two-party politics – I will always believe it was a mistake to participate in the 2000 Presidential election. While it cannot be conclusively proved that his candidacy let George W. Bush in, many of his most devoted supporters felt that even the risk of it should have been enough for him to withdraw. Ralph strenuously and plausibly rejects this position, claiming that if the Democrats had been behaving as they should, his candidature would not have been necessary. Of course he had a point, but was letting George Bush become America's worst-ever President a worthy end result of the Nader candidature? I don't think so. But back in the latter part of the twentieth century, Ralph was a figure with a justifiable international reputation as a voice for the citizen. His decision to come to the UK to speak at the FoE rallies was a major coup. And he proved an entertaining and inspiring guest.

The Green Rallies

For our 'Green Week' we set up a heavy programme of press conferences, schools events, meetings for industry, and three major rallies in London, Bristol, and Leeds. I was somewhat discouraged in the planning stages when I called a meeting of the London FoE Groups and was told by one bearded cynic that he preferred 'reading to rallies', and I was not exactly heartened when I drove all the way to Leeds in snow to meet a local FoE Group of four who planned to hold the 'rally' above a library in a room that would take about 40. They thought I was mad when I said we would book the town hall and they thought I was even madder when I announced we would be charging people to come – in those days, unheard of.

I knew we had a triumph on our hands when we turned up at London's Central Hall Westminster and found a queue right round the block, over 2,500 people ready to pay £5 a head (it was £3 in the provincial cities). Later we got nearly 1750 in Leeds and packed a smaller hall in Bristol with 450. All three events were a sell-out. In addition we had 2,500 fourth to six formers at a schools rally and also sold out three other smaller events. Altogether over three days more than 8,000 people attended these events. The British environmental movement had never experienced its like and it's fair to say it has never looked back.

The London rally was an inspiring affair. The biggest ever environmental meeting in Britain to that point, it packed the Central Hall to the rafters. It was nearly derailed by a woman speaker from Germany's Green Party who could not be stopped until we had to virtually pull her away from the lectern, but, to be fair, she went down fairly well with the audience. Ralph Nader had the audience on the edges of their seats and Jonathan Porritt, Joan Ruddock and David Bellamy were all enthusiastically applauded.

The result of all this was new members and a much higher profile for FoE as the re-established leader in the environmental field. Its success also helped establish me as one of the leaders of the movement at that time and led to my first appearance – and the first ever appearance by an environmentalist – on *Question Time* on BBC Television. This went well enough for me to be invited back a number of times. This publicity gave a real boost to FoE and proved once more the value of projecting a personality at the head of a campaign.

One of our first big decisions was whether to become an objector at the public inquiry into the Central Electricity Generating Board's plan, warmly supported by Energy ministers, to introduce a pressurised water reactor to Britain – at Sizewell in East Anglia. I have always been more open-minded about the benefits of nuclear power than many environmentalists, given the polluting effects of other forms of energy and the finite nature of some energy resources, but by the time I came on board, the movement was almost committed to being an objector at the Sizewell inquiry.

The Sizewell Inquiry

It took place at the Snape Maltings under the Chairmanship of Sir Frank Layfield. From the start FoE alleged that the inquiry was financially fixed, because the Secretary of State for Energy, Nigel Lawson (later to become Chancellor of the Exchequer) refused public funding for objectors, although the CEGB was said to be spending up to £10 million of electricity consumers' money on the inquiry. Anyone who made the journey to Snape and who saw the huge contingent of expensive lawyers and technical experts on the CEGB side, and, often, only one or two lonely researchers at the objectors' tables, could see how unsatisfactory it was. This is why FoE, faced with an enormous fundraising challenge, considered boycotting it altogether. In the end we concluded that the there were aspects to this project that were unsafe and the Inquiry provided a chance to argue this in public. Also, if there were no effective objectors, both Lawson and his successor, Peter

Walker, were capable of claiming that this proved the lack of public concern and the lack of a real case on the other side. Finally, participation in the Inquiry put FoE in a position to demand information and force facts out of the CEGB that otherwise would have remained secret.

Thus I found myself leading the team into the first day of the inquiry. It was, I hasten to say, a symbolic appearance as chairman. As we took our positions, directly opposite the CEGB and its array of lawyers, I saw the Inspector look across and smile. I knew then that he, at least, was glad we were there, not because he was on our side, but because he wanted a balanced debate.

Of course it was not balanced; how could it be when the CEGB had vast resources and we had basically just a team of two. At the inquiry the CEGB offices were comfortable, well-heated, spacious and filled with telexes, word processors and electric typewriters. The objectors shared rooms, four or five groups to a room, inadequately heated, containing only rudimentary equipment – a few desks, filing cabinets and telephones. The CEGB spent over £10 million on the inquiry; FoE had only £100,000. Despite all this, FoE's two-person team, William Cannell and Rene Chudleigh, backed up by our America consultant, Walt Patterson, were, after three weeks, able to report that FoE was playing a crucial role exposing just how hollow the commitments were to 'put safety under a microscope' at the inquiry.

The team did a brilliant job. They underlined one of the crucial roles of pressure groups like FoE; without them, the ordinary citizen is often simply not represented at inquiries of this sort and the proposers of such things are unchallenged. Whether one was for or against nuclear energy, the proposals had to be tested. Despite the financial and other dice being loaded against them, the FoE team did that. Sometimes it matters just to be there. At Sizewell, being there really mattered.

Beyond Sizewell, my main task was to give FoE a sense of direction. As our membership began to grow, more money flowed in, and we were able to strengthen the full-time team and undertake a range of fresh initiatives. We began to promote environmental and conservation projects as sources of employment and thus recruit the support of the trade unions. We promoted energy conservation and renewable energy, and alternative agricultural policies to protect wildlife habitats, reduce pollution, and conserve soil resources. We launched an anti waste campaign and we promoted alternative countryside and wildlife protection policies.

In all of this, FoE nationally was boosted by the activities of local groups. Typical of their imaginative approach to campaigning were the activities of Joe Weston and other Oxfordshire Friends. In their fight to stop the M40 motorway destroying one of Britain's most famous fields at Otmoor, they had the field divided into thousands of plots and sold these to environmentalists around the world in order to make it extremely difficult for compulsory purchase orders to be served. This idea has since been copied countless times all round the world. (I still own a square foot of that land.)

Jonathan Porritt

One of my main objectives was to replace myself. From the moment I met him, I knew Jonathan Porritt was the man. One of the founders of the Ecology Party (now the Green Party), Jonathan seemed an improbable anti-establishment figure, having been the son of a former physician to the Queen and a former Governor General of New Zealand. He had gone to Eton and Oxford before becoming a teacher in a London grammar school. In fact, I don't suppose he was that anti-establishment (he became a friend of Prince Charles), but he became the most articulate, intellectually compelling spokesman for the environmental movement, and for sustainability, of his generation.

Despite being clever, charismatic, and having impeccable credentials as the driving force behind a then rather ramshackle Ecology Party he did not, when I met him, appear to assume he had any rights to leadership of the wider environmental movement, nor did he appear to have seen a way whereby that could happen. He was genuinely astonished when, over dinner at Joe Allens, I asked him to put his name forward as the next director of FoE.

Once he came on board, we worked well together and have remained friends ever since, but it was clear to me that once he had settled in he should take over 'fronting' the movement, so, as planned, I began to pull back from the front line and give him the space to make his mark. This he quickly did. It was said of Jonathan that he had an 'ego'. Well, of course he had. So did we all – those of us who were ready to step up to the plate and take the responsibility others either could not or would not take upon themselves. A *controlled* ego is, in fact, a vital necessity for leadership, because what most people call ego can be no more than self belief and self confidence and, without it, who would step out in front and say, 'Yes, I will take that responsibility … I will get that done.' I believe the test of whether the leader has a sense of proportion and has his ego under control is whether the leader retains the genuine support of the senior people closest to him (or her) and thus most exposed to his personality. Jonathan always had that support, and that is saying something, because his growing team was not short of abrasive, idealistic and sometimes difficult personalities. Jonathan became an assured and trusted spokesman for the whole cause, so much so that he went on to be made chairman of the nation's Sustainability Commission and now has a world-wide reputation as an advisor and speaker on environmental issues.

For a couple of years I worked harmoniously in partnership with Jonathan, while devoting most of my time to FoE International where I helped out by becoming an unpaid Campaign Director. FoE International was at that time a rather shambolic organisation without funds, a director, or much credibility, and I made my contribution from my offices at Citizen Action, concentrating on helping to make others more effective, rather than building a long term role for myself. As well as producing an international FoE newspaper and campaigning books, I made tours of New Zealand, Australia, and Canada, speaking at public meetings and holding campaigning workshops.

I left the chairmanship of FoE UK after four years. I had inherited a weak, near-bankrupt, deeply divided organisation, but in my last annual report was able to tell the movement that it had just achieved 'a record income, record individual membership, record number of FoE groups, and record media coverage'. And I left it I in the hands of a powerful director who was giving it the intellectual and political weight it needed.

Most people are assessed by their publicly-known achievements; I prefer to privately assess my own performance by the nature of the problem I faced and by what I know I had to do to solve it. Little of what I did for FoE was that obvious outside of the organisation at the time, and even less of it appreciated over a quarter of a century later by a generation I suspect who has never heard of me, but it is a contribution that I have always been as proud of as the better known campaigns I ran. With Godfrey's help, we had turned a troubled organisation into a going (and lasting) concern and at FoE at least, I felt I kept faith with Ralph Nader's motto: 'It is the duty of leaders to create more leaders, not more followers.'

Fiasco of the Decade

As we neared the end of the Eighties, my time as a front-line environmentalist appeared to be about to reach a gratifying climax. ITN were planning a block-buster three-hour special on the full ITV network on New Years Eve 1989 to present awards to the heroes of the past decade. Primarily for the lead-free petrol campaign, I was chosen as Environmentalist of the Decade and was to be so honoured before an audience expected to be close to 15 million viewers.

The event was to be filmed in advance at the London Palladium. I was about to tread the boards that had in their day been the preserve of Bob Hope, Jack Benny, Frank Sinatra and Judy Garland and where I had seen Sammy Davis Jnr. Motivated more by the prospect of live performances by Phil Collins and Blondie than my own cameo appearance, my wife Jane and my son and daughter, Jacqui and Tim, came too. While they made their way to the Dress Circle I was taken to the Green Room where I found a pack of celebrities headed by Michael Caine (Film actor of the decade) and Daley Thompson (Athlete of the decade), all tucking into canapés and drinks. As we had to be there an hour in advance and filming took forever, we were there for four or five hours before the evening ended with a big party and more canapés and drink. (The family somehow ended up in the Groucho Club in the early hours where even more food and drink were consumed; I don't recall how we made it home.)

I filled in the time before my appearance unsuccessfully trying to persuade Michael Caine to make a film of my first novel *Costa del Sol* and successfully persuading the boxer Barry McGuigan to support a celebrity campaign I was about to launch to reduce tobacco sales to children. Eventually it was time for my Palladium debut. I was taken to the side of the stage and watched a short film about environmental issues introduced by the show's presenter Cilla Black and by the presenter of my award, Pamela Stephenson. Then it was my moment. I stepped on the stage to friendly applause and proceeded towards Pamela. What no one had told me was that she was standing on a small platform. When I was about a yard away from her I hit the platform and was catapulted forward, landing in her arms and bringing us both crashing to the floor, with me lying on top of her in what can only be described as a compromising position. Needless to say the audience was in hysterics. Somehow I got to my feet, dusted myself off, made a brief speech and, humiliated, fled back to the Green Room and a desperately-needed drink.

Worse was to follow. There was a rumour that the American Ambassador was coming to receive an award on behalf of Ronald Reagan. Eventually this distinguished looking, white-haired gentleman did arrive, immaculate in full evening dress. He was left to sit alone in front of the television monitor and it seemed to me that he was ill at ease and feeling rather neglected. So I wandered over. How good to see him. What a good decade it had been for America. As for the Russians, they had been humiliated. The country was in ruins. No awards for them. Tee hee! The man in the dinner jacket looked up and growled. 'I am Leonid Zamyatin, Ambassador Extraordinary and Plenipotentiary of the Soviet Union.'

12

Our Right to Know – the Campaign for Freedom of Information

'Liberty cannot be preserved without a general knowledge among the people, who have a right . . . and a desire to know; but besides this, they have a right, an indisputable, unalienable, indefeasible, divine right to that most dreaded and envied kind of knowledge; I mean of the characters and conduct of their rulers.'

JOHN ADAMS

It all began in 1983 in Ralph Nader's crowded office in Washington DC. 'What you need to do is attack secrecy, Des,' he said. 'We have freedom of information laws in the United States. That is our starting point. I don't know how you can campaign effectively without it. Why don't you launch a campaign for the right to know?' So we decided there and then that, while he was in the UK for our Friends of the Earth campaign, he would help us launch a campaign for freedom of information.

Back in London, I set out to explore the issue and, the more I looked into it, the more I understood why Ralph had been so passionate about it. I discovered that of all democratic countries in the world – those that were not dictatorships or subject to one party rule – Britain's institutions were the most secretive. The habit of, and instinct for, secrecy, was totally entrenched in the psyche of the governing elite.

Governmental secrecy was institutionalised by the Official Secrets Act. Section 2 of this Act, in the words of a 1972 report of a Committee of Inquiry under Lord Franks:'catches all official documents and information. It makes no distinction of kind, and no distinction of degree.' And, as well as the Official Secrets Act, there were over one hundred statutes making the disclosure of information by civil servants or others a criminal offence.

Additionally, there were civil service rules and a civil service classification system based on an implicit assumption that virtually all documents fell within one of four classifications: Top Secret, Secret, Confidential, or Restricted.

Reinforced by these laws and regulations, secrecy had become a disease which had spread from Whitehall to envelop local authorities as well as national authorities, other statutory bodies and quangos, nationalised industries and private commerce.

The price we paid for this was huge. Secrecy was the enemy of rational decision making and of accountable, responsible administration. It allowed governments to cover up errors, suppress dissenting views, and conceal the fact that their policies may not be working. The sources of power and influence were obscured. Public servants were not properly accountable and citizen participation was seriously hampered. Justice was either obstructed or not seen to be done. Inefficiency and error and waste were made more likely. Nor was this just about public affairs. Secrecy affected us in very personal ways. With so much of our lives controlled by the State, and given the unprecedented technology that existed to collect and record information, there had never been a more urgent need to carefully balance the rights of the individual and the community.

In one respect, in particular, there was an unacceptable imbalance; it occurred because files were kept on individual members of the public but access to them was reserved for public servants and 'professionals' alone. Not only did the individual not know what is in his or her file, but he or she did not know how many people had seen that file and in what circumstances, or what decisions they had taken on the basis of what information. Parents were held responsible in law for the education of their children, but had no right of access to their children's school files. Social workers maintained extensive files on their so-called 'clients', but the clients had no right of access to those files. Patients had no right of access to their own medical records. Tenants of local authority housing, or those on local authority waiting lists, could not check their files to see that they were accurate. It really was an extraordinary state of affairs when people who, at the end of the day, were the servants of the individual, could deny the individual crucial facts about his or her own life.

The main argument of the professionals was that, somehow, all this was in our 'own interests'. They said that patients could be upset, and their health problems made more serious, if they discovered the truth about their illnesses. Families could be disturbed by the frank comments on their children by school teachers. So-called 'clients' of the social services could be caused distress by having the realities of their lives stated frankly on paper. At its best, this argument was paternalistic. It assumed that adults did not want to, or could not, face the facts about their own lives. It was an unwarranted assumption. The real reason why professionals wished to deny the public the right to their own files was that they wished to preserve the exclusivity and the mystique that were both necessary for their self-esteem and to protect them from their own mistakes or misjudgements.

There was, however, an over-riding reason why the individual should have the right of access if he or she desired it, and that was the extremely high possibility of error. There was simply no guarantee whether the file entries were fact or fiction.

Sometimes the instinct for secrecy led to absurdity. For instance a local newspaper reported that Newcastle City Council 'met in secret to discuss a confidential report congratulating them on how they conduct the city's affairs so openly'. Another reported that a combination of Whitehall and Somerset County Council refused the Chairman of the Exmoor Society to have access to papers relating to the birth of Exmoor National Park in 1954 so that he could prepare a history for the Exmoor Society's 25th birthday and the Park's own thirtieth birthday. But usually the effects of the secrecy were far from funny. The path to adequate environmental protection in Britain was also blocked by an unacceptable level of secrecy demanded by industry and supported by the governmental agencies. Because of this, an uncertain public was unable to obtain the information it needed on what the hazards were, where they were, or whether safety limits required by law were being observed.

A classic case was the Bradford fire. Ten months before 56 people were killed when the football club's grandstand burst into flames in 1985, two public authorities wrote to the club pinpointing the dangers and urging improvements. But the letters appeared to be confidential; they were made public only after the disaster, and club officials even claimed they did not know about them. But if they had been released at the time they were sent, they would have been the subject of considerable local newspaper coverage; you can imagine the headlines. The club would have been forced to act and 56 lives could well have been saved.

To illustrate the extent to which the individual was being denied information affecting his or her life, I invented for my book, *The Secrets File* the case of a not unusual family – mother and father and two children of school age, living in a council house . . . say Mr and Mrs Smith and their children, Ben and Nat (the names of American friends who I often included in my campaigning books and that had the effect that they, at least, were avid readers of them):

- The Smiths are not allowed to see the school files on Ben and Nat.
- The Smiths are not allowed to see any of their family's medical records.
- The Smiths cannot go to the Town Hall and see their file in the housing office, nor can they go to the social services office and see a file on them that exists there.
- They have been recipients of welfare benefits, but they are not allowed to see their social security file.
- Like all members of the public, they cannot attend sub-committee meetings of their local council, nor are their local newspapers allowed to report them.
- They cannot attend meetings of their local water authority, nor can they find reports of them in their local newspaper.
- They live near a big factory handling chemicals, and Mr Smith, as an employee, is entitled under the Health and Safety at Work Act to be told of the potential hazards and safeguards. However, he is not allowed to tell Mrs Smith because this information is restricted to employees only.
- The Smiths have been refused a mortgage by two building societies but have been given no reason why. They cannot see their file to see if the building societies have based their decision on accurate information.
- The Smiths have had some difficulty with their insurance company, and are convinced that the insurance company is acting on the basis of incorrect records, but are not allowed to see their file to check what it says.

- Mr Smith is very concerned about the location of sites in England for the disposal of radioactive waste, believing that one is planned for his own locality. His Member of Parliament raised the question in the House of Commons but was told that 'the sites are not comprehensively listed' (i.e. are not named).
- Mr Smith is a keen cyclist and wrote to the Ministry of Transport to ask for a report he knew existed on options for better cycle safety. He is told this is 'a restricted document' (this actually had happened to a member of Friends of the Earth).

Sitting before their gas fire one night, Mr and Mrs Smith considered all these facts, and came to the conclusion that they lived in a highly secretive society. At that moment the gas fire exploded and considerable damage was caused. Months afterwards, the Smiths still had no idea what caused the explosion. The Gas Board informed them that their report on the incident was confidential!

This, then, was the issue that, thanks to Ralph Nader, I now adopted for my next major campaign. My first step was to persuade Friends of the Earth to be one of the sponsors of the launch of the campaign, and then I set out to build a coalition of individuals and organisations to join it. Then, on an FoE platform, Ralph Nader and I jointly announced it at a press conference.

There had been efforts to achieve FoI in the past. Clement Freud, when a Liberal MP had tried with a Private Members Bill. And there had been a number of individual campaigners on the issue over the years, the most prominent being the then head of the Nuffield Foundation, James Cornford. I went to see him and while he was, on the basis of past experience, sceptical about the chances of success, he accepted my invitation to chair the Council (there was also a campaign committee that I would chair.) Other key recruits were a fine Labour MP, Chris Price, a former Nader associate and health campaigner Charles Medawar, a former head of the National Council for Civil Liberties, Tony Smythe, one of my successors as director of Shelter, Neil McIntosh, a veteran campaigner on many local issues, Ron Bailey, and an NUJ leader, Jake Ecclestone. The full time administrative office was to be led by Laura Thomas, who had joined me in my Northdown Street office. She became a popular and committed administrator of both the CFOI and Citizen Action. (Laura was to die of cancer at a tragically early age but would never be forgotten by those who worked with her.) All of the above were to play valuable roles, but my outstanding recruit was Maurice Frankel, a researcher who had previously worked with me on a pesticides campaign for Friends of the Earth and who I now proposed should be director of the CFOI.

Maurice Frankel

Maurice was highly intelligent, hugely industrious and unhesitatingly supportive. If I was the voice and motivator of the campaign, he was the prime source of its conscience and credibility. We worked together in perfect partnership. At the time of writing he has been with the Campaign for over twenty-five years and has to take the most credit for its success. Maurice emerged on the pressure group scene in the Seventies, influenced by Ralph Nader and by his friend Charles Medawar at Social Audit. He had three special qualities that are worth describing, because there are many campaigners who could learn from them.

First, he never researched an issue just to prove himself or the campaign right; he relentlessly sought the truth, modifying the strength of his argument to fit the strength of the facts supporting it, absorbing within it any value of the opposing point of view, salvaging workable ideas from even the most destructive quarter. Thus his case had an integrity that its opponents rarely equalled. Second, he never acted bigger than the cause or the campaign. For instance, the FoI campaign had to be a coalition, and to hold it together its leading employee needed to sustain the liking and respect of a highly experienced and widely diverse group of campaigners. Maurice was the man. For all his strength of purpose and strongly held views, and his ever-growing stature in the movement, he never changed his personality, always remained the servant of the cause. Nor did he campaign by attacking opponents; he never resorted to aggression (leaving the confrontational stuff to me) but simply argued on, with good humour and seductive sincerity. This really was a man without enemies. In this last respect he was the perfect foil for me; in so much as a campaign cannot avoid controversy and even confrontation, there was a case for a 'good cop, bad cop' team at the top. Maurice was the good cop. His third quality was persistence. On FoI for instance, Maurice was to work day and night. He had few other interests. He would leave the office only to go to a meeting or to his computer at home. He became the world's leading authority on the subject.

Building the Campaign

We put together an impressive coalition. The committee was kept small, but the Council contained over sixty names and we had hundreds of MP supporters and a substantial list of supporting organisations. We even had a list of overseas advisors, headed, of course, by Ralph. It was 'a cast of thousands'. As with Clear, the aim was to create an impression of respectability. And, as with Clear, the big debate was over the objectives, because this was going to be a campaign where what we did *not* seek would be key to whether we achieved what we did seek.

In particular we were aware that there would be total Whitehall hostility unless we protected civil servants from publicity about the advice they provided to ministers. So we decided to concede this point.

To promote our aims we would propose a 'Freedom of Information Act to establish a public right of access to official information subject to those exemptions required to protect confidentiality genuinely necessary to the proper conduct of government, its relations with other governments and organisations and the privacy of individuals.' We would seek repeal of the Official Secrets Acts and their replacement by an Act to give such protection to official information as may be necessary for national security.

We then listed what we would not seek:

'The Campaign accepts that an element of confidentiality remains necessary, and in particular this campaign will not seek the disclosure of information that would:
   (a)   endanger national security;
   (b)   impair relations between the government and other governments or organisations;
   (c)   adversely affect the value of sterling or the reserves;
   (d)   adversely affect law enforcement or criminal investigations;
   (e)   breach genuine commercial confidentiality;
   (f)   invade individual privacy;

(g) breach the confidentiality of advice, opinion or recommendations tendered for the purpose of policy-making. (This does not include expert scientific or technical advice or background factual information.)

With 1984 approaching, the year of Orwell's novel, we decided that for the launch we would call ourselves The 1984 Campaign for Freedom of Information and that we would drop the '1984' when we reached 1985. All was now set for the launch, an event that since the Nader press conference had been keenly anticipated by the media. Not least by *The Times*'s White-hall watcher, Peter Hennessy, who wrote:

Mr Wilson realises his freedom of information campaign has a formidable opponent in Mrs Thatcher, whom he describes as 'a simple black-and-white thinker.' He intends to win skirmishes in the foothills – opening up local government, getting people access to personal files held on them by government – before launching the final assault. Des versus Margaret promises to be an epic worthy of Cecil B De Mille. It opens on Thursday in Westminster.

And, indeed, on that Thursday, and with Godfrey's financial support, we were able once more to launch a campaign in Westminster with a range of impressive booklets and newspapers and once more the media coverage was huge. It made the television news on all channels, every radio news bulletin, and the pages of nearly every newspaper. We sought to explain the difference between this campaign and earlier attempts to achieve freedom of information:

'First, this is an issue that has always been debated within a relatively closed circle of politicians, civil servants, journalists, academics, and pressure groups. Our campaign is the first attempt to make this a sub-stantial popular issue and thus one with real political clout.

Second, the coalition we have formed is almost unique in its size, prestige within the voluntary movement, and the input of resources by the organisations involved. In addition to their contributions to the main campaign, each will undertake their own campaigning activities on the same issue in 1984, emphasising specific objectives related to their work. This 'merger' of resources is almost unique in pressure group activity in Britain.

Third, although at various times in the past, the opposition parties have committed themselves to freedom of information, often betraying the promise after they were elected, there are two distinct differences now: first, key figures in both major opposition parties have on the same day and at the same time clearly committed themselves and their parties; second, there will be a substantial pressure group in existence to maintain surveillance on the issue and to demand that promises be kept. To put it bluntly, we believe we have the opposition parties committed, and thus freedom of information legislation is now inevitable in Britain.

Finally, we believe there is considerable movement in our direction within the civil service.'

A *Guardian* leader welcomed the campaign with a leading article, saying: 'It would be quite wrong to dismiss it with a weary sigh as yet another spin-off of the Des Wilson rolling road show. It is a more than worthy cause; the campaign is being organised with considerable intelligence and impressive support; and perhaps most significant of all, there is already a perceptible nervousness in Whitehall about its chances of success.'

Now, just as *Cathy Come Home* was a stroke of luck for Shelter, and the Yellowlees letter was for Clear, we had one for this campaign as well (I can only assume the campaigning Gods approved of my choice of issues). It came from an unlikely source, Margaret Thatcher.

We had earlier written to the party leaders seeking their support. I had not intended to write to Mrs Thatcher, knowing her likely response, but my committee, who usually trusted my instincts, were strongly opposed to me on this one and, as it turned out, they were right, because she chose the morning of the launch to publish a reply to me slamming the door in my face. The effect of this was to dramatise our launch by adding to the sense of occasion. She was, in effect, telling the assembled media that this was a campaign that concerned her; she was creating a confrontation that, had she kept her head down, she would have avoided. She could not have done more to help us make an impact.

In her letter she said she would 'welcome any move to help ensure that public demands for information are heard and as far as possible satisfied', but she added: 'we already have a clear policy to make more information available and the necessary machinery to do so.' She went on to argue that ministers were accountable to Parliament and:

> a statutory right of public access would remove this enormously important area of decision-making from Ministers and Parliament and transfer ultimate decisions to the courts. No matter how carefully the right were defined and circumscribed, that would be the essential constitutional result. The issues requiring interpretation would tend to be political rather than judicial, and the relationship between the judiciary and the legislature could be greatly damaged. But above all, ministers' accountability to Parliament would be reduced and Parliament itself diminished.

This was clearly absurd and at the press conference I adapted my prepared remarks to reply by asking:

> Why are we denied freedom of information? We are told it is because parliament must remain sovereign. But the other political parties don't believe freedom of information would threaten the sovereignty of the parliamentary system. Australia, Canada, and New Zealand operate a Westminster-style parliamentary system, and they have freedom of information legislation. We are told it will be expensive. But every projection made in other countries about the possible costs of freedom of information has turned out to be vastly exaggerated – in fact, because it can lead to increased efficiency, it can save money. We are told it is because some information has to be kept confidential. We accept that – that's why we have always accepted the need for some exceptions to FoI.
>   There is one simple reason why we are denied freedom of information laws in this country and that is because the Prime Minister does not accept that people have a right to know – in fact, when we recently asked a Conservative MP to sign a letter supporting an aspect of citizens' rights, he actually asked for the word 'rights' to be replaced by another, because it was not an acceptable word in Conservative circles these days. They don't believe they have been given the power to serve – they believe they have been given the power to control.

The *Scotsman* described the Prime Minister's view that availability of information would undermine ministers, and, ultimately, parliament as 'a well-rehearsed piece of banal nonsense', while *The Times* charged that the openness of administrations overseas, particularly those with West-minster-Whitehall style administrations, 'ruins the traditional alibi of British Prime Ministers – which was wheeled out on cue by Mrs Thatcher yesterday – that such arrangements may be alright for foreigners, but they sit ill in the British system with its convention of ministerial accountability to parliament'. But what Mrs Thatcher had done was make the fatal mistake of drawing further attention to a campaign that in reality she wished was never there. Now her administration sunk to an almost childish level thanks to the actions of her civil service minister, Grey Gowrie

When the 1984 Campaign had been launched I had written, as a matter of courtesy, to the Permanent Secretaries as follows:

Dear Permanent Secretary,
I enclose the material published at the launch of the 1984 Campaign for Freedom of Information.
　Additional copies can be purchased for circulation to colleagues.
　We are anxious to have a constructive and friendly dialogue with Whitehall on this matter and would welcome your views.
　Yours sincerely

Des Wilson

The following correspondence then took place:

2 February 1984

Dear Mr Wilson
I understand that you have written to the Permanent Secretaries of a number of Government Departments, suggesting a 'friendly and constructive dialogue' with your Committee about the material which you enclosed with your letter.
　The Government's view has been made clear, and was set out in the Prime Minister's letter to you of 9 December. Other political parties, as you yourself have emphasised, take a different view. I am sure you will understand, therefore, that given these political differences, the

principle of Civil Service impartiality should be preserved. This would make it altogether inappropriate for Permanent Secretaries or other Departmental civil servants to take part in the kind of discussion which you have in mind.

Yours sincerely

Lord Gowrie

7 February 1984

Dear Lord Gowrie

I have to say that I find your letter of 2 February astonishing.

First, my letter to Permanent Secretaries and the enclosed material about our campaign was clearly an act of courtesy on behalf of our campaign, and I have no doubt was understood to be so by the majority of them, and your response is, therefore, at best heavy-handed and borders on paranoia.

That said, we do of course have arrangements in hand to meet Civil Service unions, and I have no doubt they would take the same dim view as our campaign of your attempt to stop reasonable dialogue between civil servants and well-established public organisations on the way our governmental system operates and how it can be improved.

I know this is 1984, but your position that once the Prime Minister and colleagues have made up their minds, a subject no longer exists for discussion, is Orwellian in the extreme.

It will be noted by all objective observers that a government that puts so much stress on the rights of the citizen, individual freedom and democracy, is literally terrified of discussion on how the rights of the citizens can be better protected and our democracy made more healthy.

Yours faithfully

Des Wilson

22 February 1984

Dear Mr Wilson

I have to say that I find your letter of 7 February no less astonishing than you have found mine. I don't think you have understood what I wrote.

The Government does not have any intention of trying to inhibit general public discussion of the objectives of your campaign or to suggest that 'a subject no longer exists for discussion' just because we have a particular view about it, and it is absurd on your part to suggest that it has. My letter was concerned with something quite different – discussion with serving civil servants who are advisers to Ministers. The rule is that civil servants should not take part in public discussion of any matter of current or potential political controversy. That is not a new rule: successive Governments have adopted it, and the principle is of very long standing. Its purpose is to maintain the political impartiality of the Civil Service. If civil servants are to serve impartially ministers of any political party, they cannot expect or be expected to engage in public discussions on matters which, like your campaign, involve party political controversy.

Yours sincerely

Lord Gowrie

24 February 1984

Dear Lord Gowrie

Thank you for your letter of February 22.

You appear to miss the two fundamental issues at stake:

First, we are still a democracy, not a dictatorship. The election of an Administration of any political party makes that Administration the temporary custodians of our affairs, not the permanent controllers. Continual debate should take place involving all sections of the community about all aspects of national life. It has been made clear to me that there has been widespread dismay at every level of public life at the way the Prime Minister and yourself have in such a heavy-handed and obstinate way tried to destroy any debate on the issue of freedom of information before it has even begun. Fortunately, such an objective is beyond even your powers to achieve. In our initial approach to the Prime Minister, we sought only dialogue, and it is deeply regrettable that her response was to display a completely closed mind and to attempt to forcibly close those of her colleagues and senior civil servants.

Secondly, the issue at stake is not just one of broad political policy, but about the administrative workings of Whitehall and other statutory bodies. An open-minded Administration should always be prepared to encourage its servants to participate at least to some extent in dialogue on such matters, if only to put their expertise about how Whitehall works, and their reservations about the advantages or disadvantages of any proposed measures, on the table for the benefit of all concerned parties. In the case of freedom of information, a coalition of twenty-five respected national organisations with a considerable combined record of public service, some of them partly funded by government, sought a friendly and constructive dialogue with civil servants on a matter that directly affects them in their work. Had you written to say that you would like to feel that there were some boundaries to the involvement of civil servants in the debate, this could possibly have made some sense (at least in the context of the way your particular Administration works), but a refusal to allow them to discuss the matter at all is simply unacceptable.

Yours faithfully

Des Wilson

The Civil Servants

In its leader on the day the campaign was launched, the *Guardian* had said:

'Perhaps the most significant indicator of possible success is the amount of support for the campaign from civil servants. Among young and youngish high flyers, the permanent secretaries of the future, there is a growing scepticism about secrecy that would have been rare ten years ago. In addition, civil servants are becoming increasingly frustrated and despairing as a result of this government's cavalier attitude towards decision-making, and as a result want more and more to open up that process to the public. Maybe this perceptible melting of the great iceberg of Whitehall cynicism, on which open government is said to have foundered in the past, will enable Mr Wilson to notch up another success.'

The *Guardian* was right. Given the tradition of secrecy that had been nurtured by the civil service for generations, there were a surprising number of them who were sympathetic to at least the broad aims of the campaign. The first real evidence of this came when nearly all the civil service trade unions affiliated to the campaign, including the Civil and Public Services Association, the Society of Civil and Public Servants, and the Institution of Professional Civil Servants (all of whom passed resolutions at their conferences in support of the Campaign, as did the National Union of Public Employees).

But the most surprising supporter was John Ward, the head of the Association of First Division Civil Servants (FDA). While initially he did not have the support of his union, John indicated there was hope and set up a meeting with his committee. We knew that the main concern of senior civil servants was that when they provided advice to ministers, it should remain confidential, so when we met Ward's Committee I began by saying that it could be of help if I started by listing what we did not want. As I made clear that their advice to ministers would be exempt I could feel the atmosphere in the room change.

Shortly after, the FDA at its annual conference firmly committed itself to freedom of information and took the unprecedented step of affiliating with an outside pressure group. An amazed Peter Hennessy said to me, 'it's like the Salvation Army voting for sin'. Alan Healey, chairman of the First FDA Machinery of Government Sub-Committee, told his members: 'We were favourably impressed with the approach adopted by the Campaign. This is certainly not just another campaign with a self-interested or political axe to grind. They know their stuff, are serious-minded and realistic in their expectations. We found them willing to listen to alternative argument and take on board points about practical and ethical difficulties.'

It became even more difficult for anyone to write the campaign off as a group of trouble-making hot-heads when one of the country's top law lords, Lord Scarman, stepped into the debate in a Guildhall lecture. He called for repeal of the Official Secrets Act 'lock, stock and barrel' and its replacement by a much more narrowly defined protective measure and by a Freedom of Information Act.

The citizen's right to know is not confined to public affairs. It arises also in his private and family life, his employment, the education of his children, the health and social security of his family, and justice to them all. In short, a free democratic society requires that the law should recognise and protect the right of the individual to the information necessary to make his own choices and decisions on public and private matters, to express his own opinions, and to be able himself to act to correct injustice to himself or his family. None of these rights can be fully effective unless he can obtain information.

About this time I appeared on television with a former Permanent Secretary at the DHSS, Sir Patrick Nairne, who I took an immediate liking to and who proved reasonably sympathetic. I set up further talks with him and this led to him announcing he was a convert to the case for FoI legislation. But we were about to catch an even bigger Whitehall fish: Sir Douglas Wass, former Joint Head of the Civil Service, and Permanent Secretary at the Treasury. We had noted that in his Reith lectures he had condemned excessive secrecy, and, after discussions with us, he now went a step further and identified himself with the campaign. Next to 'come out' was Lord Croham, another former head of the civil services. This was highly significant because Lord Croham was the author of the *Croham Directive* which in 1978 called for greater voluntary publication of information and warned civil servants that unless it was effective, legislation could follow. His support could be read, therefore, as an acknowledgement that the voluntary approach had failed. The iceberg had indeed melted.

Soon we were able to announce a new panel of advisors to the campaign: including Wass, Croham and Nairne. Of course the cynics said that all these people had only joined up after they had retired and when they would not be affected by a more open approach. The television programme *Yes Minister* made fun of it all by having the Head of the Civil Service retire and become chairman of the Campaign for FoI. 'How is the campaign going,' asks Sir Humphrey over lunch. 'I'm afraid that's a secret,' comes the reply. Of course, they had a point, but the additional support of the First Division Association showed that our Whitehall supporters were not only past figures and in any case to have supporters of such distinction made it very difficult for the campaign to be misrepresented as irresponsible or unrealistic. Whitehall watchers did not quite know what to make of all this.

The Guerilla Strategy

The Times' Peter Hennessy quickly identified our strategy: 'The Wilson strategy is reminiscent of General Giap's in Vietnam – he is picking off the soft targets of the periphery first with Bills on personal files and access to local government and water authority material, before attacking the Whitehall citadel direct with a full blooded freedom of information Bill.'

He was right. It was clear to me that while Mrs Thatcher was there, a full-scale FOI Act was impossible. But she would not be there forever. In the meantime, we would campaign for what was possible. So we broke the problem down into a number of specifics, like the denial of access to personal files, environmental secrecy, excessive confidentiality within local authorities, the refusal of water authorities and health authorities to meet in public, and we designed campaigns on each of these issues. Our plan was that each would be introduced by a Private Members' Bill. John Hunt, in the *Financial Times*, also noted the approach:

> 'To all appearances the Campaign for Freedom of Information, which was launched with a great deal of publicity in January, has been strangely subdued in recent months.
>
> But the comparatively low profile being maintained by the campaign and its organiser, the normally flamboyant Mr Des Wilson, is highly deceptive.
>
> In fact an elaborate strategy of guerrilla warfare is being stealthily pursued at Westminster. It is probably the most meticulously planned piece of lobbying since the Law Society tried to defeat the Private Member's Bill on house conveyancing.
>
> Careful siege is being laid to Miniture-Orwell's monolithic ministry for the distortion and suppression of information. The walls are being steadily undermined and it is hoped that the breach will finally be made between three and five years from now – either in the run up to the General Election or in the first year of the next Government.

The approach was a success. Within four years we had achieved four pieces of legislation, a feat achieved by no pressure group before. We began with local authorities. Here we had the help of one of our committee members, the extraordinary campaigner Ron Bailey, who had over the years always been on the periphery of my world but now moved to its centre. As well as being on our committee, he had set up a separate organisation called the Community Rights Project and had become concerned about the secrecy of local councils and had persuaded a cheerful and popular Conservative MP, Robin Squire, to introduce a PM Bill. We joined up with Ron.

Ron was once found combing the confidential files of the Greater London Council in the early hours of the morning. He was arrested and charged with trespassing and theft. During his trial he was cross examining the police officer who arrested him and asked that the officer repeat the words Ron uttered on being apprehended. The police officer tried to duck it, but Ron insisted that the police officer consult his notebook. Eventually, the police officer admitted that Ron's response had been to say 'It's a fair cop, Gov'. The court fell about, even the magistrate was forced to hide a grin. (Incidentally, Ron sent a team round to local councils to check whether they were complying with their obligation to allow people to check a number of registers; one council later wrote to protest that the researcher had 'been masquerading as a member of the public'.)

The Local Government (Access to Information) Act introduced under the private Member's procedure by Robin Squire MP, was passed by both the Houses of Commons and Lords, and came into force on April 1 1986. It extended existing public rights to attend council meetings to also include committee and sub-committee meetings, provided for agendas, minutes, and reports to be more widely available, and created a new right to see background papers used in compiling reports considered at meetings. It also improved access to documents by councillors.

Our next success was the Access to Personal Files Act introduced as a private members' bill by Archy Kirkwood MP. It provided a right of access to their own files to tenants in 5.5 million council dwellings; and to more than 1 million social services clients. (While not part of the Act, we also ensured the authorities would introduce regulations giving 8.7 million parents the right of access to their school files.) We had to make some compromises to have it passed before a General Election wiped out all pending legislation, but it moved things in the right direction.

Then, for a second consecutive year, Archy Kirkwood won the right to introduce a private members' bill in the ballot, and this time introduced the Access to Medical Reports Act which took effect from January 1 1989. This was also drafted and promoted by the Campaign. People now had the right to reports supplied by their doctor to insurance companies and employers, the right to correct inaccurate information, and the right to withhold consent for it to be forwarded if they find the report unacceptable. Then, in 1990, Doug Henderson introduced a Bill giving patients the right to see and correct their health records. The Access to Health Records Act came into force in 1991.

Chris Smith, another MP with an outstanding record of support for freedom of information, introduced with our support a bill requiring the setting up of public registers containing details of enforcement notices served by safety and environmental agencies on matters affecting public health and safety and environmental pollution. This ultimately became the Environment and Safety Information Act 1988.

By the time the country began to move towards a full FoI Act, the campaign had been centrally involved or the sole initiator of no less than five pieces of legislation: The 1986 Local Government, (Access to Information) Act; The 1987 Access to Personal Files Act; The 1988 Access to Medical Reports Act; The 1998 Environment and Safety Information Act; The 1990 Access to Health Records Act. But now the Campaign for Freedom of Information found itself in more defensive mood: not so much in fighting for openness as fighting against secrecy and, in particular, the brutal use of the Official Secrets Act.

The Sarah Tisdall Affair

In March 1984 the ability of the State to use Section 2 of the Official Secrets Act to strike fear into the hearts of potential leakers within the civil service was underlined by the Sarah Tisdall affair. She had worked in the private office of Sir Geoffrey Howe and obtained a memorandum written by the Secretary of State for Defence, Michael Heseltine, on how he would handle the public relations aspect of the arrival of cruise missiles in Britain. She photocopied it and delivered it in a brown envelope to the *Guardian* which duly published it.

The government took the newspaper to court to force it to hand over the photocopies in order that the whistle-blower could be detected. The *Guardian* assumed that its position was protected under legislation entitling it to keep confidential the sources of its information, but the court ruled that it must hand over the documents. Shortly afterwards, Sarah Tisdall, a 23-year-old clerk, admitted that she was the leaker. She was subsequently sentenced to six months in Holloway by Mr Justice Cantley who stated: 'It must be made perfectly clear by example that any person entrusted with any material classified as secret, and who presumes to give themselves permission to publish it, shall not escape custodial sentence'.

The sentence caused uproar. It was pointed out at both the *Guardian* hearing and at Tisdall's trial, that the prosecution had emphasised national security had not been endangered. Comparisons were made between Miss Tisdall's relatively trivial offence and that of the late Sir Anthony Blunt, who had been a major spy, but avoided prosecution. Our Campaign made a number of points about the Tisdall case:

First, we pointed out that Miss Tisdall had been imprisoned under discredited legislation. The use of an Act condemned by a Committee which had been specifically set up to look into it (the Franks Committee) and by politicians of all parties, including the present Home Secretary, was unacceptable. Second, we pointed out that Miss Tisdall had no right of defence on the grounds that she had acted in the public interest. We were not saying, of course, that she would have been able to make such a defence in this particular case, but we argued that she should at least have the right, as she would have done in the United States. Third, we stressed our view that it was wrong that any unauthorised disclosure, except that which endangered national security, should involve a criminal prosecution and prison sentence. Internal disciplinary proceedings, and probable dismissal, would have been more than adequate.

The controversy raged for days, with only *The Times* and the *Daily Telegraph* defending the prosecution, and even those newspapers admitting that the sentence had been exceptionally severe. While it would have been of little consolation to Miss Tisdall in her Holloway cell, the case did much to intensify criticism of excessive secrecy and the particularly secretive approach of the government of the day.

The Clive Ponting Case

Clive Ponting, a senior official at the Ministry of Defence, was charged under Section 2 of the Official Secrets Act 1911 after anonymously sending two documents to the Member of Parliament for Linlithgow, Tam Dalyell in July 1984. Both documents related to the political controversy surrounding the sinking of the Argentinean cruiser, *General Belgrano* with the loss of more than 300 lives on May 2 1982 during the Falklands conflict.

At the time he sent the documents, Clive Ponting was head of Defence

Secretariat 5 in the MOD, and had particular responsibility for policy and political aspects of the operational activities of the Royal Navy. He was one of the few people with full access to information about the Belgrano affair, and had prepared the highly classified account of the matter – which came to be known as 'The Crown Jewels' – at the request of Defence Secretary Michael Heseltine. Ponting did not believe there was anything sinister – as some had suggested – about the sinking of the Belgrano. He said in court that he felt the action was fully justified on military grounds. But he did object, and most strongly, to the way in which ministers withheld information about the sinking from Parliament, made misleading statements, and refused to correct earlier mistakes on the grounds – which he knew to be spurious – that any disclosure would harm national security.

During the trial he commented that 'as time went on it was clear ministers were refusing to give information because to do so showed their previous statements to Parliament were incorrect.' However, the turning point for him came when a strategy for responding to an enquiry by the House of Commons Select Committee on Foreign Affairs was devised within the MOD. He told the court: 'The ministers were sending to parliament a document that was misleading and deliberately misleading in an attempt to conceal the information.' 'Somebody somehow' he said, 'had to tell Parliament how it had been misled and how the Government proposed to mislead a committee of the Commons.'

He decided to send two documents to Tam Dalyell. One was a draft reply that he himself had prepared for ministers to use in replying to questions about the Belgrano. The other was an internal minute which outlined the government's strategy for withholding information from the select committee.

On receiving the documents, Dalyell passed them to the chairman of the foreign affairs committee, Sir Anthony Kershaw, who in a much criticised move, immediately handed them over to Defence Secretary Michael Heseltine.

Important evidence for the defence was given by Merlyn Rees MP, former Labour Home Secretary and Secretary of State for Northern Ireland – both posts with vital security responsibility. Mr Rees told the court he would not have agreed to give evidence if he believed Mr Ponting's action had breached national security. He stressed that he put 'truthfulness to

Parliament above all else' and said that while a civil servant must be loyal to ministers and to the government 'loyalty to his nation is far greater.'

This was not the view of the judge. 'I am directing you on the law' said Mr Justice McCowan, 'and you have to accept the law from me.' He went on: 'If the case is proven in accordance with the law as I direct you then you must convict.' But the jury may well have attached greater weight to the final words of Mr Ponting's defence counsel. He told them that if what Mr Ponting had done was a crime then it could be 'a licence for ministers to withhold information from Parliament with the full acquiescence of civil servants, and so infringe your civil liberties.' 'If what Mr Ponting did was a crime, God help us – because no government will' he concluded. In refusing to accept the judge's rulings, the jury clearly showed that they agreed. Ponting was cleared.

The case made a huge impact. A rally we organised in Westminster Central Hall was packed to the rafters. Speakers included opposition leaders who were united in saying the time had come to deal with the obsession with secrecy and its draconian enforcement. The newspapers were equally forceful. Even the *Daily Mail* took a strong line:

> With the Prime Minister, it is a matter of discipline; of authority; of discouraging the others. She wants to see all leakers keel-hauled. This time, a British jury (vetted) – and after a summing up by a judge which can have promised no comfort to Mr Ponting – has given Mrs Thatcher her come-uppance. It should be a salutary lesson. The public may not hold much brief for civil servants who play the holy democrat when they are caught being disloyal to the Government. On the other hand, a dozen good citizens and true are obviously not much impressed either by a Government that seeks to prosecute, and, it may be, jail those who dare to reveal Ministers of the Crown keeping the whole truth from parliament. Hindsight or not, this prosecution was a misjudgement. . . the Government should not have trundled out that obsolete and now utterly discredited blunderbuss, Section 2 of the Official Secrets Act, to defend its virtue (which in terms of naval strategy was impeccable, but in terms of parliamentary veracity scarcely spotless). Vengeance is the Lord's. Politicians should remember that justice here down below can cut both ways.

We welcomed the Ponting acquittal for three reasons. First, it was a deserved humiliation for the Attorney General who cynically used an Act he had himself condemned when he did not have it as a weapon at his own disposal. Second, because we believed, wrongly as it turned out, that the Attorney General or any of his successors would never dare to attempt another prosecution under the Section. And third, because it appeared to establish a precedent for a public interest defence in such cases. At no point did we defend indiscriminate leaking of confidential information. Our case was a simple one: if a civil servant leaked a document, he or she should at least have the opportunity to argue that it was in the public interest that the information was disclosed, and that the public interest was better served by its disclosure than by its confidentiality. Surely now, we thought, we stood a chance of demolishing the Official Secrets Act once and for all. But we had overlooked the Prime Minister's obstinacy. She was, in fact, infuriated by the Ponting case and, instead of learning the lesson that the opposition politicians and the media learned, she decided that rather than the OSA being an anachronism, it was not strong enough.

A Step Backwards: The Official Secrets Act

The Official Secrets Act 1911 was enacted in extraordinary circumstances in the House of Commons. These circumstances were subsequently described by the Under Secretary of State for War at the time, Major General J. A. B. Seeley:

'I got up and proposed that the Bill be read a second time, explaining, in two sentences only, that it was considered desirable in the public interest that the measure should be passed. Hardly a word was said and the Bill was read a second time; the Speaker left the Chair. I then moved the Bill in Committee. This was the first critical moment; two men got up to speak, but both were forcibly pulled down by their neighbours after they had uttered a few sentences and the committee stage was passed. The Speaker walked back to his chair and said: "The question is, that I report this Bill without amendment to the House." Again two or three people stood up; again they were pulled down by their neigh-bours, and the report stage was through. The Speaker turned to me and said: "The third reading, what day?" "Now, sir," I replied. My heart beat fast as the Speaker said: "The question is that this Bill be read a third time." It was open to anyone of all the members of the House of Commons to get up and say that no bill had ever yet been passed through all it stages in one day without a word of explanation from the minister in charge . . . But to the eternal honour of those members, to whom I now offer, on behalf of that and all succeeding governments, my most grateful thanks, not one man seriously opposed, and in a little more time than it has taken to write these words that formidable piece of legislation was passed.'

By 1972, it was clear, as Professor H. W. R. Wade commented to the Franks Committee, that 'Section 2 is a blot on the Statute Book which needs to be removed'. The Franks Committee, set up specifically to look at Section 2, reported in 1972 that 'we found Section 2 a mess. Its scope is enormously wide. Any law which impinges on the freedom of information in a democracy should be much more tightly drawn.' The Franks Report said:

'According to one calculation over two thousand differently worded charges can be brought under it. . .the main offence it creates is the unauthorised communication of official information by a Crown servant. The leading characteristic of this offence is its catch-all quality.'

The debate began with a private members' bill introduced by Richard Shepherd, a Conservative MP who was a passionate supporter if the campaign and who came top of the ballot. He sought to repeal Section 2 of the Official Secrets Act and replace it with new measures to protect a much narrower range of information whose disclosure would clearly be damaging.

The Campaign had its reservations about Shepherd's initiative, both because it was secrecy legislation rather than freedom of information legislation, and because it was vulnerable to interference by the Government which could seize the opportunity to amend it and create even more draconian secrecy laws. But the Government went further than that. It used a three-line whip and all of its power to block it completely. And in doing so, it suffered a considerable humiliation. Not only did nearly one hundred back benchers rebel, but its own newspaper supporters lambasted it for its behaviour. The *Sunday Times* called it an 'ignominious victory'. *The Times* reported that 'the Government and the Prime Minister received a rebuff as they crushed the Conservative backbench attempt to reform the Official Secrets Law, but suffered in the process the biggest revolt since the General Election and one of the most serious since 1979 . . . Mrs Thatcher's tactic of ordering her MPs to attend to see off a private members' measure was savagely condemned on her own side of the House . . . without the three-line whip Mr Shepherd would undoubtedly have won.'

In the House itself, protests were led by former Prime Minister Edward Heath, who was supported by a number of former Cabinet Ministers, including Sir Ian Gilmour, Merlyn Rees, Dr David Owen, and Roy Hattersley.

You would have thought that by now Mrs Thatcher would have learned that this was an issue which she would do well to avoid, but there were no limits to her fury and obstinacy. So she ordered her hapless Home Secretary, Douglas Hurd, to introduce a reformed OSA that would be even more draconian than the existing one.

It was about the control of information – not about access to it. It would lead to a new secrecy law, not greater freedom of information. The campaign was horrified. I myself had to consider the possibility that for once a campaign I was responsible for was going to lead to things becoming worse, rather than better.

We called for support: 'All of our supporters should be in no doubt of the importance of the debates that lie ahead. If a Prime Minister whose obsession with secrecy is greater than any other this century is allowed to prevail, despite considerable disquiet within her own party as well as anger from the opposition, then our cause will suffer a blow that will far outweigh all of our achievements to date.' We had support in the Commons and in the media, The *Observer* describing the lack of a public interest defence as 'intolerable in a peacetime democracy'. But the so-called 'reform' was rammed through with three-line whips and there was little we could do.

At the conclusion of this sorry affair, we said in our campaign newspaper:

As campaigners for freedom of information we see no virtue in the new Act whatsoever. Not one additional piece of information, no matter how trivial, will necessarily become available where it was not available before.

From the start, the Home Secretary attempted to convince politicians and public alike that this was a notable step towards greater openness. It would be 'an earthquake in Whitehall'. It would be 'a substantial and unprecedented thrust in the direction of greater openness'.

He hoped that many people would assume that because the information was no longer protected by the criminal law, that it was no longer protected at all, and unfortunately in this exercise he partly succeeded. Yet it was always a lie. And it was one of the achievements of our Campaign that after a few weeks he was forced to abandon such phrases because of our relentless exposure of their fraudulence.

From all sides he was pressed for a public interest defence. In his refusal to consider this he undoubtedly was acting under orders from Number 10. The effect has been to make it clear beyond dispute that it is the view of the Thatcher administration that the first priority of information policy is to avoid any possibility that it can be embarrassed by the publication of information unhelpful to it no matter how much that information may be needed by the public.

The Official Secrets Act sets out to reverse the decision of the jury in the Ponting case that the interests of the public do not necessarily coincide with the interests of the government of the day. We must now hope that when a similar case comes to trial, a jury will once more refuse to accept this.'

I move on – and FOI is achieved

Despite this set-back I never doubted we would eventually win. Throughout my five years as chairman of the Campaign for Freedom of Information I kept telling myself 'Thatcher will go – the Tories will go' and our primary strategy became to handcuff the Opposition parties to freedom of information. The main way we did this was by offering them platforms; they got the publicity and goodwill that came from speaking out for freedom of information; we got yet another promise in the bank. Opposition leaders or shadow home secretaries were always asked to our rallies. But the main tactic was to have them present the prizes and make a speech at our annual Freedom of Information Awards. Attended not only by campaign supporters, but also by newspaper editors and senior politicians, the awards were presented over the years by both contemporary Labour leaders Neil Kinnock and Tony Blair and by both third party leaders David Owen and David Steel. All used the platform to promise repeal of the OSA and the introduction of an FoI Act. These promises were recorded and heavily publicised in our campaign materials. Gradually we were pinning them down, committing them to a policy.

When Labour came to power there was no way they could duck the issue. The promises had been repeatedly made and, to be fair, the politicians themselves convinced. By now it was clear to me that after the setback of the Thatcher OSA Act, we had created the circumstances where a right to know bill was inevitable. Unfortunately I would not be there to help make it happen. I knew that once I undertook to run the Liberal Democrat's General Election campaign (see chapters 15 and 16) I would be disturbing the party political independence of the campaign and so I made way for James Cornford to extend his role. This I did reluctantly because I was both devoted to the cause and liked everyone I was campaigning with. (To be fair, no one raised it with me. It was entirely my own decision.)

Fortunately I did not have to worry about the health of the campaign. James would be a good chairman and Maurice had by now become a hugely respected and influential figure on the issue. So it was that when Labour finally came to power, James was actually recruited into the civil service to help draft the FoI white paper and Maurice was a constant and valued advisor throughout the process. In the year 2000 the campaign achieved its objective. Britain was given a Freedom of Information Act (it did not come fully into force until 2005). It could easily have been a half-hearted attempt to do just enough to enable Labour to appear to keep its promise. But it was not. It was a thoroughly respectable law. We had won.

Secrecy is an incurable disease. It is built into the genes of those in power, because it protects them from exposure of fault or honesty. The Freedom of Information movement has not cured the disease. No one ever will. But the Act is a way whereby the disease is controlled. It has swung the balance of power from the State to the individual. For that we have reason to be proud of the FoI Campaign and, especially in the crucial latter days, of the roles of James Cornford and Maurice Frankel; the latter is still there today, maintaining surveillance over the Act's implementation. Other campaigners have been making full use of it.

As for myself, well I am proud too. Without my decision to launch the campaign, Freedom of Information would no doubt have come to the UK one day, but even with the campaign's activities, it took over 20 years from its launch until the full Act was achieved; it is, I believe, fair to argue that without the campaign, it would have taken much longer and may not have been as useful as it has been. As for giving the individual more power in relation to those in 'authority', this, above all, was what my life was becoming about. Nothing I had done, or would do, would be more important than this, for every other citizens' group could now be more effective in their campaigns too.

13

Life in 'The Hotel Vacancy' and Citizen Action

'Grievances cannot be redressed until they are known; and they cannot be known but through complaints and petitions . . . where complaining is a crime, hope becomes despair.'
BENJAMIN FRANKLIN

From the mid Eighties, Godfrey Bradman and I were housing our campaigning activities in the basement of a building in Endsleigh Street, near Euston. As for my own housing, whenever anyone asked me where I lived, I replied 'The Hotel Vacancy'. In fact, I had a small cottage in Bewdley in the Wyre Forest, but I was only occasionally there at weekends – most of the time I was in London and living out of the boot of my car. After I had finished work, or after dinner, or after a meeting, I would drive to Carlisle Square near the office, a place full of cheap bed and breakfast places where a room sometimes cost as little as £5 a night. I would look for the word 'Vacancy', park outside, take my suitcase from the boot of the car, and check in. The following morning I would leave to be in the office by seven or eight; by lunchtime I could not tell you where I stayed. So I began to think of them all as one – the 'Hotel Vacancy'.

When I told people what I was doing, they tended to be shocked, thinking that it was a lonely and anonymous existence, but looked at from my point of view, all I needed was a place to sleep and have a shower; I did not have to make the bed or tidy the room or deal with the scores of little problems that accompany being responsible for a rented flat (assuming I could afford one). Admittedly I sometimes had to push past hookers on the stairs, and often found heroin needles in the bathrooms, but the only bill I had was the £5 for the room and I had accommodation in the centre of London that I was only paying for when I was actually using it. Anyway, it worked for me. I liked the 'Hotel Vacancy'.

The campaigns were coordinated within a holding company called Citizen Action. As most of the campaigners worked from home, they were always coming and going, delving into the piles of leaflets, posters, and press releases, occupying any corner where they could clear space to make phone calls or use their lap tops. To others in the campaigning world, it was a place where they could find friends and obtain advice and even inspiration; to our detractors and enemies, this was a nest of vipers, a factory for fermenting revolution.

And of all our detractors, the main one was the Prime Minister herself, Margaret Thatcher.

To her, we were more than just a nuisance; we were an assault on the walls of democracy itself.

In 1985, beaten by Clear and suffering widespread media condemnation for her obsession with secrecy, she finally blew her top and made an astonishing speech at the Carlton Club linking terrorists like the IRA and the 'hard left' with 'campaigning pressure groups' as what she called the 'enemy within'. Of campaigning pressure groups, she said, 'we must never give into the oldest and least democratic trick of all, the coercion of the many by the ruthless, manipulating few. As soon as we surrender the basic rule which says we must persuade our fellow citizen, not coerce them, then we have joined the ranks of the enemies of democracy.' It was a classic case of truism employed out of its context.

This arrogance and contempt for pressure groups reflected not only the Thatcherite dislike of any form of dissent, but showed ignorance of the crucial pioneering role that the voluntary sector had played. Nearly all of the great social changes of the past century had been fought for by individual campaigners or pressure groups against the policies of the government of the day – from the abolition of slavery to votes for women. It's indeed ironic to think that Mrs Thatcher would not even have had a vote, let alone been Prime Minister, if it had not been for the courage and defiance of one of the great campaigners, Emily Pankhurst, and her single issue pressure group. Mrs Thatcher's complaint, in a nutshell, was that we made the country more difficult to govern. Well, maybe we did. That did not worry me a bit. I thought a country should be difficult to govern; countries that were easy to govern were easy to misgovern.

Pressure groups had no power. They were advocates in the court of public opinion. They presented their evidence to the court – the public – either on their own behalf or on behalf of their cause, and hoped to persuade the jury of their peers – the public – that they were right. All I ever asked for pressure groups was the right to a voice, the right to argue their case reasonably and responsibly, but always – always – fully accepting the rights of others to argue their own case.

I was no believer that a pressure group had the right to inconvenience its fellow citizens just because it believed itself to be right. I would not consider violence or violent demonstrations; in fact, I didn't really like demonstrations at all. They occasionally had their place, but only occasionally, and preferably where they inconvenienced those who caused the problem, not the public. I believed pressure groups should be positive, they should be *for* something. They should be for lead-free air, rather than against lead in petrol, and for freedom of information, rather than against secrecy. This is not just a matter of semantics; it was about being positive; it mattered that we promised a better world, not just rage at the one we were in. And I believed they were at their best when they actually dirtied their hands confronting the realities of the problem, as well as speaking out; Shelter's success came from the balance we kept between the two. As I would tell audiences: 'We have a right to speak on this platform; we built it with hammer and nails.'

Over the years I was often called upon to argue the case for pressure groups, and I built that case around five main points.

1 There is more to democracy than the occasional vote

Government 'of the people, by the people and for the people' is not achieved by a vote every four or five years and then blind faith that all will be well. To be healthy, a democracy has to be participatory at every level. Are we really saying that, when we vote for a government, we are giving it unlimited powers to do what it likes, to take any course it sees fit, without any further right to challenge and comment and criticise? If we are not saying that – if we believe the opposite – then pressure groups are one way – an alternative to the media, or the opposition parties – whereby people can exercise their right to know and to comment.

2 Pressure groups give a voice to minorities
Leaders are elected by the majority and, to be re-elected, they have to satisfy that majority. That is a simple fact of political life. The inevitable effect of this is that politicians' priorities and policies are designed to appeal to the majority. Thus minorities have little bargaining power; many pressure groups exist for no other purpose than to give them a voice. Whether it be groups for the disabled, one parent families, gypsies or prisoners, the fundamental role of their pressure groups is to draw attention to their special needs and, in most cases, their neglect.

3 Pressure groups combat other pressure groups
There are many kinds of pressure group, and a fundamental difference between the Citizen Action kind of pressure group, and its opposition, is that the latter, often companies and whole industries, usually do not rely on public opinion. They exercise their enormous power behind the scenes. One of the roles of citizen pressure groups is to balance or reduce the influence of these huge vested interests. As one who has worked for a big company, I, of course, accept the right of big companies as well as citizen groups, to communicate with and seek to influence or petition those in power. The right to petition the source of power was enshrined in the Magna Carta and it was meant for everyone – industries and institutions as well as individuals. But in the past government often only heard one side of the case; they did not hear the conflicting arguments, well-presented and well-researched; today it is often pressure groups that make that possible. Pressure groups do not distort debate; they enable debate to take place. They don't replace the voices of their opponents; they balance them.

4 Pressure groups give causes their stamina
One characteristic of the media is its tendency to pick up issues and then drop them. If it senses its readers, listeners or viewers are getting bored, it moves on: Another day, another story. Another crucial role of the pressure group, therefore, is to keep the story there, to maintain the momentum and put the stamina into an issue. While government or its other opponents hope to ride out unfavourable publicity and public pressure in

the hope that both media and the public will lose interest, the pressure group has to have the persistence, the ingenuity to find fresh ways of promoting its cause and keeping the pressure on. Clear was a classic case of a small group keeping what was, when all is said and done, a small issue, in the forefront of public attention day after day, week after week, until its opponents caved in.

5 Pressure groups offer people the weapons to fight on their own behalf
Many pressure groups are quite simply the providers of weapons with which individuals can unite in their defence and sometimes literally fight for survival. These weapons are organisation, skills, talents, money and the like, but also they offer individuals confidence in numbers, the ability to share their experiences and create a platform for them to express their desires and needs. Pressure groups are, in the final analysis, collections of individuals most of whom could not achieve their objectives on their own but who seek strength and unity.

I make no pretence to propose that pressure groups are an alternative to political parties, even less to government, nor do I believe they should be done any special favours. They are a component of our democracy, a healthy, creative, challenging component of democracy, a shiner of light on dark corners, a counter-balance to complacency and indifference and neglect, invaluable for the reasons I have just attempted to argue, but not infallible and at their most worthy when they fight their corner with truth and tolerance.

14

The Citcom Campaign

'The law of England is the greatest grievance of the nation, very expensive and dilatory'   BISHOP BURNET: *History of His Own Times*

One day in 1987 Godfrey Bradman phoned and asked whether I had read newspaper stories about the Opren case. Opren was an anti-arthritic drug manufactured by Eli Lilly, an American pharmaceutical giant with a UK subsidiary; unfortunately, it emerged that it had a number of harmful side effects, and many sufferers, most of them elderly, had been seeking compensation. The company did not want to know. The newspapers Godfrey was referring to reported that the victims had tried to come together to pursue their cause in the courts with what was known as a Class Action, but the case was about to collapse due to their lack of money. Most could not get legal aid and, of course, they could not afford to employ lawyers, whereas Eli Lilly's resources were limitless.

As I mentioned earlier, Godfrey was so outraged that this colossal international company was refusing to help a relatively small number of mainly poor and vulnerable pensioners that he was offering to set aside £2 million of his own money to under-write the case. While I was, of course, immensely impressed by his compassion and generosity, I felt that it was wrong that he should have to do this, and proposed that before he did we should launch a campaign to force the company to settle.

For weeks we lambasted them in the media. We even took a full page advert in the *Wall Street Journal* naming and shaming the company's directors. They were extraordinarily stubborn, presumably not because of the money but because they did not want to set a precedent (they claimed they had warned of possible side effects). But in the end we drove them to the negotiating table, and eventually we got a £2.2 million out-of-court settlement paid to 1,200 people. The Judge admitted this was a small sum, but blamed it on the law:

'There is nothing wrong with critics questioning or condemning these levels, so long as they recognise that only Parliament can change them . . . so long as the present levels remain in force, the courts have no alternative but to apply them . . . '

We felt that the Judge was sending us a message, virtually provoking us into a campaign to change the level of compensation in such cases.

In fact, he paid tribute to those who had supported the victims and went on to say:

'When the Opren litigation is finally disposed of, those who have worked so hard on behalf of the claimants will have, I feel sure, a great contribution to make in finding answers to the problems which have come to light in the handling and financing litigation of this kind.'

It was clear that there were a number of serious flaws in the compensation system and we decided to set up, within Citizen Action, a small campaign called the Citizen Action Compensation Campaign – Citcom. We were given instant respectability by the decision of the distinguished former law lord, Lord Scarman, to be its President, by the sympathetic backing of key members of the Law Society, and by the involvement of a number of well known critics of the system, including the journalist Marcel Berlins, the National Consumer Council legal advisor Guy Dehn, and two others who had already been campaigning in the field, Marlene Winfield and Julia Cahill. But the star of the show was Henry Whitcomb.

Henry was to prove a campaigner in the Maurice Frankel mould . . . clever, dedicated, patient, superb at handling people, a highly competent writer and speaker – and, above all, he knew his law. And he was only 23. He qualified out to Bar School in 1988 and began looking for a way to use his skills promoting citizen rights. He wrote to me and, according to my then secretary Ann Paintin, his letter was in the process of being filed when I wandered in to the office saying that I needed a lawyer to run Citcom. From the moment he walked through the door, both earnest and enthusiastic, I knew we had found our man. What he achieved over a couple of years, with me banging the drum while he played every other instrument, was little short of miraculous.

Basically, the problem was that, when it came to seeking compensation for injuries, the dice were hopelessly loaded against the citizen. First, there were the difficulties of actually accessing the legal system. For instance, many of the claimants in the Opren litigation were not entitled to legal aid because they had pensions, often quite small ones, which were of course the result of a lifetime's work and all that they had to survive on in their old age. They simply could not afford a lawyer. Second, as even the Judge in the Opren case acknowledged, the levels of compensation available were far too low: the sums for the pain and suffering of injured victims were derisory; an award for bereavement of only £3,500 was an insult. And the approach adopted to calculate a claimant's financial losses and expenses which were often critical to their survival, for instance involving the funding of their nursing care needs for life, was rough and ready in the extreme.

So, with Henry as frontline campaigner, with Lord Scarman lending authority to our name, and with me, as chairman, orchestrating a series of newspaper articles, many in *The Times*, and speaking opportunities (I even addressed the Law Society's annual conference), we began to campaign to make the law work more effectively for victims instead of favouring those responsible for needless injury and death. Within a year we had parliamentary successes.

First we engineered an amendment to the Companies Act 1989. This gave thousands of victims of work-related diseases such as asbestosis, whose former employers had gone into liquidation, the right to continue to claim compensation from the insurers. This was a particularly hard fought campaign which succeeded only after a bitter fight with the backers of insurance companies, both in the committee rooms and on the floor of the House of Commons.

The Government at first defeated the proposed amendment amid acrimonious scenes with Francis Maude, then the Minister for Corporate Affairs, arguing that the amendment would place a huge burden on insurers. But it was re-introduced and passed at the third reading. Clare Dyer, of the *Guardian* reported:

'Thousands of victims of work-related diseases whose former employers have gone into liquidation are to be given the right to claim compensation . . . claims will be covered by insurers who covered the company at the time . . . the amendment, accepted by the Government after a six month campaign by Citcom, sets no time limit for firms which collapse . . . among the beneficiaries will be Mrs Doris Bradley, a retired cotton mill worker suffering from a lung cancer caused by inhaling cotton dust. . . after the company owning the mill was dissolved, she tried to sue Eagle Star, who insured the mill (but) the Law lords said she had no right to sue the insurers . . . now her solicitor said that (thanks to the change in the law) he would be able to issue a writ.'

Then, with the help of Lawrence Cunliffe MP, we introduced yet another Citizen Action private members' bill into the House of Commons, called the Citizen's Compensation Bill. While it eventually ran out of time, because some Conservative MPs talked it out, it was the basis for a significant achievement, the government being embarrassed into conceding that the level of bereavement damages should be reviewed. It published a consultation paper and this eventually led to an increase in the level from £3,000 to £7,500. (It has since been increased twice and is now £12,000, no doubt still too little, but an advance.)

Outside Parliament, Citcom campaigned for increases in the levels of compensation generally, for enhanced access to legal aid, for the funding of group actions, and to reduce the delays which plagued the system, chivvying the government through private members' bills, parliamentary questions and amendments, and by publicising cases of injustice. After sustained pressure by Citcom, the Law Society and the Legal Action Group, the rule which made many of the Opren claimants dependent on Godfrey Bradman for financial help was changed. In future, discretion would be used to allow pensioners with low incomes supplemented by a little capital, to receive legal aid.

During the course of the second reading of the Cunliffe Bill, the Attorney general, Sir Nicolas Lyell, was asked whether he was aware that children who had been catastrophically injured at birth and whose parents might have modest incomes were forced to wait until their sixteenth birthday before they could become eligible for legal aid in their own right and bring a claim. He was simply unaware of this and reeled when it was put to him. Following this, Citcom vigorously pursued with others, including the Law Society and the Legal Action Group, a revision of the legal aid rules so as to allow children to bring cases so that they could be given the compensation which they so urgently required. This campaign was also a success and transformed the access to justice for those children.

Over the years, one by one, the problems we had identified at the time of the Opren case were addressed. By Godfrey Bradman's action in taking up the Opren case, and thanks to the work of Henry, and the others we recruited to help Citcom, the issues were put on the agenda, some immediate improvements made, and a whole movement for reform set in motion. It would be wrong to claim that all the subsequent advances were initiated or caused by Citcom, and I make no such claim, but Citcom's activities over three years created the climate for change . . . and change there was. In particular the House of Lords eventually transformed the way whereby damages were calculated, thus increasing substantially the sums received by the injured, and then the Court of Appeal increased the level of damages that could be awarded for their pain and suffering.

Citcom was one of our least-publicised campaigns. It involved relentless research, close cooperation with many other concerned people, and much behind-the-scenes negotiation. But it did just what such a small campaign should do – it acted as a catalyst and inspired others, including those much better placed, to carry the baton on much further than we could hope to do, and achieve a series of victories that have made the citizen much more powerful when taking their cause to law.

Henry is now achieving what anyone who worked with him would have predicted, namely success at the bar, specialising in the kind of cases identified by our campaign. Chambers UK 2009 said of him: 'A very gifted practitioner known for his top-notch client skills, fantastic preparation and hard-working, intelligent approach. Whitcomb is sensitive, thorough and charming – he always comes up trumps.' In other words, the perfect campaigner.

15

The Tobacco Blockade – Story
of the PAT Campaign

'The attack upon the scientific and medical evidence about
smoking is little more than an attack upon science itself . . .
like every attack upon science from vested interests, from
Aristotle's day to Galileo's to our own, these attacks collapse
under their own weight.'
The Royal College of Physicians Report Smoking and Health 1979

In mid-1989 I was approached by David Simpson of the anti-smoking
campaign ASH. Despite overwhelming evidence of the damage to health
caused by smoking, he felt the anti-smoking movement had stalled. He
asked whether there was any way that my team at Citizen Action could
help. I was in two minds. On one hand, the importance of the issue was
beyond doubt. A recent opinion poll had shown that nine out of ten people
in Britain recognised that smoking could kill, a view clearly held by the
authorities who insisted that a warning appeared on every packet of
cigarettes. The World Health Organisation had said 'Some 50,000 studies of
all kinds . . . have irrefutably established the link between tobacco and
disease.' The Royal College of Physicians in the UK had described it as 'a
hidden holocaust'.

Despite this, tobacco men still talked about the 'alleged health risk of
smoking'. That word – 'alleged' – more eloquently reflected their cynicism
and explained their lack of credibility than any words we could deploy
ourselves.

So, I detested the tobacco industry, not only because of the nature of its
product but because of its cynicism in denying its deadly consequences, its
efforts to prevent restrictions on advertising and promotion, and, as health

warnings began to bite in the UK, its ruthless exploitation of Third World markets, knowing it had a better chance of selling cigarettes to the uneducated and a also better chance of corrupting those who governed the world's poorest countries so that their access was not impaired. My main reservation was a reluctance to tell others what to do with their own lives.

This may sound inconsistent coming from someone who was now seen, albeit not by myself, as an inveterate campaigner, but my and Citizen Action's campaigns had never been about telling individuals how to behave. It seemed to me that tobacco was an addiction; smokers would have needed to be blind and deaf not to hear and see the warnings; why else would someone continue to take cigarettes out of a packet containing the grim warning 'Smoking can kill' and then put them in their mouths, unless they were addicted beyond the point where logic or education could help?

So I told David that I was reluctant to launch a campaign hectoring smokers, no matter how foolish their smoking was. Anyway, there was little we could do to add to what the authorities were already doing; the message on cigarette packets could not be clearer. Later I was glancing at the materials David had given me, and I was struck by two things. The first was the problem of over 300,000 children known to be smoking regularly and nearly one fifth of fifteen-year-olds smoking at least occasionally. The effect was that their life expectancy was reduced, they suffered physical effects (coughing, lower resistance to infections, bronchitis) and they were in danger of an addiction that would stay with them all their lives. I found particularly alarming some American evidence that children between twelve and seventeen who smoked cigarettes daily were over one hundred times more likely to use marijuana and more than thirty times more likely to use cocaine than children who didn't smoke. The thought that cigarettes would not only damage children's health but make them more likely to become drug users was a sobering one.

The second thing that struck me was that the industry needed to expand, not only by trying to do so in the Third World but also by encouraging a new generation of smokers. As the WHO said 'the failure of a generation of young people to start smoking would devastate the industry within 10 years.'

There was striking evidence that the tobacco industry was indirectly but never-the-less deliberately promoting smoking to children and young people with its advertising and sponsorship. A voluntary agreement between the authorities and the industry had stated 'characters and situations depicted should not be such as to inspire the emulation of the young,' yet the European president of Philip Morris was quoted as saying about its sponsorship of motor racing ' what we wanted was to promote a particular image of adventure, courage and vitality.' Another Marlboro executive was quoted in a magazine as saying 'I think all who work on tobacco promotion realise deep down that the whole point is to create new smokers . . . '

Reading this and other material, I began to see that there was a way to attack the tobacco industry without getting into the business of telling adults what to do: that was to focus on children. I wrote down, literally on the back of an envelope, three thoughts:

First, a campaign aimed at protecting adults can add little to what is already happening . . . but a campaign aimed at children can help block the industry's ability to reach the next generation.

Second, the group most likely to throw themselves behind a campaign to protect children are their parents . . . and they will bring a fresh legitimacy to the anti-tobacco movement because of their indisputable right to do all in their power to defend the health and well-being of our children.

Third, the way to balance the tobacco industry's use of glamour and sport to reach the younger generation is to use glamour and sport against it.

From this came the idea of Parents against Tobacco (PAT), spearheaded by 100 leading show business and sports personalities. Parents, acting to protect their own children, had a special legitimacy. By inviting well-known personalities to support the campaign as parents concerned about their own children, we were able to break down the inevitable resistance from busy and over-stressed people to get involved in 'yet another cause'. Our approach to them was even more persuasive because we stressed it was to be just a one-year campaign, aimed at a particular result (a private members' bill), and intended to refresh the existing anti-smoking movement rather than replace it.

There was another special feature of PAT compared with my and Citizen Action's other activities – it was designed to be more aggressive, and even brutal in its assault on the industry.

We picked up a comment by a health researcher that 'It should go without saying that the tobacco industry is the largest, most determined and most devastatingly effective source of opposition to worldwide efforts at reducing smoking. But the irony is that this fact *has* gone mostly without saying . . . the tobacco industry is seldom the direct target of health workers' efforts.' We intended to change that.

To further contrast PAT with the existing anti-smoking activities we would draw on parental anger to make it really hard-hitting: we simply would not allow the manufacturers to position themselves as a respectable part of British business. We would campaign with the same anger as others did about the pushing of drugs to children. The industry would be described as 'pushers and traffickers'.

We would describe our aim as to 'build a blockade' between these ruthless and irresponsible industries and our children. And we would do so from a position of independence. Some anti-smoking organisations were limited by the controlling effect of DHSS funding. We would take no government money. Others were inhibited by charity status. We would not be a charity. We were going to make ourselves uncontrollable.

But this was not just to be about re-firing the anti-smoking movement; we wanted a practical result, one that would hit the industry where it hurt, at the point of sale. So, the objective in that year was to change the law to toughen up controls on sales to children. We had to make it more difficult for children to buy cigarettes. If they couldn't get them, they couldn't smoke them. This was not *the* answer to the problem, but it was a pre-requisite to solving it. Apart from making sense in itself, it would add credibility to laws restricting the sale of cigarettes to children and it would add credibility to parental warnings about the dangers of smoking. Why should children believe smoking was really damaging if they could easily purchase cigarettes from the nearest shop?

In late 1989 a survey of 418 shops that we commissioned showed that, despite laws – going back to 1904 – forbidding the sale of cigarettes to children below age sixteen, 224 shops – more than half – sold cigarettes to children as young as twelve. Retailers were ignoring the law. This contempt for the law was made more serious by confusion among the local authorities and the police over who was responsible for enforcement. So our key objectives would be

1 to make it mandatory for local authorities to maintain surveillance over the problem and to prosecute offenders;
2 to increase the fines to make them a genuine deterrent;

This would be the first time I had run a campaign with just one simple objective, achievable within a year: a private members' bill. Now we put all of our past experience and mobilised all of our potential resources behind what was to be my last 'public citizen campaign'. By now I and my team had developed a proven pattern of campaigning:

First, thorough research, not just to prove that we were right but to also test for ourselves that we were not wrong. This objectivity not only justified the demands we were making, but also strengthened our defences when we were counter-attacked. As I had believed with Clear and the other causes, a campaign should never be caught exaggerating or misrepresenting the facts; when a public debate took place it should be impregnable in this respect. The only way this could be done was to approach the research from a position of scepticism on every detail.

Second, fixing on a realistic objective . . . not an easy one – but one that could be achieved. There was no point in throwing away resources, using up energy and mobilising public opinion behind an objective that was unrealistic. (I was once accused on a radio programme of seeking 'soft targets'. My reply was that, if they were that soft, why had no one achieved them before? The targets were not soft; they were realistic, and I believed that if they were realistic we would achieve them.)

Third, the extensive planning of a programme of activities that would take place over a realistic time period. This was based on surges of activity followed by respite periods, both to enable the campaign to re-charge its batteries and to avoid public boredom. Thus, if we had six really great campaigning ideas, they would be spread over a year or 18 months or whatever was the logical period. This also had the effect that every time our opponents relaxed, thinking we had shot our bolt, we came pounding back from another direction.

Fourth, to devise a clear strategy and then a set of tactics to implement it. In the case of PAT, the *strategy* was to mobilise the right of parents to protect their children; the *tactic* was to hammer home the cynicism of the tobacco industry and prove with unanswerable research that current so-called safeguards were not working; to 'build a blockade'.

Fifth, to put together a coalition of support. My aim was always to have our troops assembled to their maximum possible strength before we launched, rather than use up energy after the launch by setting out to recruit them. Launching a campaign in the name of a coalition also provided it with additional credibility.

Then, and only then, would we think about the launch. The principle was to have the campaign won before that launch ever took place by having in place an unanswerable argument and supporting facts, resources, support, and a plan of campaign that was almost impossible for the 'enemy' to oppose.

Raising the money proved an easy proposition. Godfrey Bradman, as always, stepped up to the plate. But so did Richard Branson and Anita Roddick, who contributed £100,000 from their Healthcare Foundation. We went to Brussels and persuaded the EU health authorities to put some money into it. By the time we were ready to launch we had over £300,000. While we would not seek direct governmental money, we were happy to accept an offer from the the Health Education Authority to sponsor print materials and some other activities.

I then put together the best and most experienced campaigning team I had fielded since Shelter. Eileen Ware, Youth Director at Shelter, came back to run our schools campaign. My wife Jane drew her work with Clear to a close to become National Campaigner. One of the Liberal Party's best by-election campaigners Peter Chegwyn came on board to campaign with local authorities. A young London doctor, active on public health issues, called Sam Everington would lead our health team. To help recruit famous names we put together a team of convenors: Jane Asher would be convenor for show business and the arts, Anita Roddick would cover business, Claire Rayner would be health convenor, boxer Barry McGuigan would be sports convenor, and television campaigner Lynn Faulds Wood would represent the media.

We assembled a list of 100 founder members, all of whom were photo-graphed in our Pat sweater featuring a bright logo designed in a

Above: The Wilson family *c.*1950

Below: Oamaru with my first school in foreground

Above: the North Otago countryside

Right: Young reporter

Below left: My parents' 50th wedding anniversary

Below right: First day in London 1960, nineteen years old

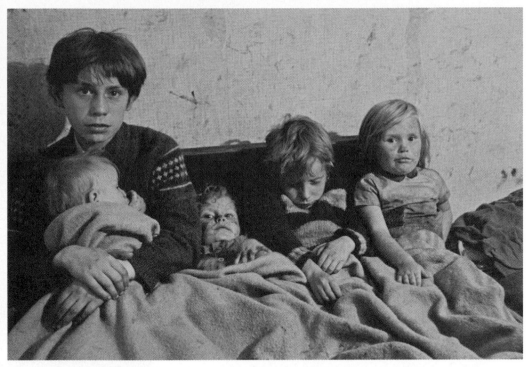

The homeless 1960s-style . . . 'three million families lived in slums, near slums, or grossly overcrowded conditions'.

Above: The inner team at Shelter: (left to right) Liz Wills (Groups Director), Eileen Ware (Youth Director) and Cindy Barlow (Chief Administrator)

Below: Speaking to the Shelter Rally at Church House. Lord Harlech in the chair, Lewis Waddilove beside him

Above: At a Shelter-supporting school

Right: Eamonn Casey, Shelter's dynamic
  and popular chairman

Below: With Prime Minister Harold
  Wilson

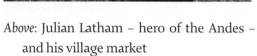

Above: Julian Latham – hero of the Andes – and his village market

Right: Padre Lira

Below: Managua after the earthquake

Above: with Godfrey
　　Bradman on the Clear
　　campaign
Centre: This van attracted a
　　lot of local publicity
　　when it called at schools
　　to collect lead samples
　　from playground dust
Below: Campaign won April
　　1983

EVENING STANDARD　　18 APR 1983

Government acts on petrol report
LEAD FREE GO-AHEAD

by Robert Carvel and Alan Massam

THE Government was this afternoon announcing that all new cars must eventually be designed to run on lead - free petrol.

Common Market country to commit itself to a reduction from 0·4 to 0·15 grams per litre.

With the car industry heavily dependent on export sales further progress towards

be required to run on unleaded petrol."

The report adds that improvements in engine efficiency make it unlikely that the removal of lead from petrol will produce "an overall

He believed this was due to the growing level of lead contamination from motor exhausts.

"Children and young people appear specially liable to suffer more or less permanent brain damage leading to mental retardation, irritability and bizarre behaviour patterns," he said.

Above: Cleared – Clive Ponting and wife leave the Old Bailey

Below: David Owen at the Ponting Rally, Ponting on my right, Chris Price on Owen's left

Above: some of the 100 famous founder members of Parents against Tobacco (*left to right*) Rula Lenska, Richard Branson, Hayley Mills and the Duke of Gloucester

Below: Kids joined their parents to see the PAT campaign bus

Maurice Frankel (*top left*)
Ralph Nader (*top right*)
Henry Whitcomb (*left*)
Archy Kirkwood (*bottom left*)
Jonathan Porritt (*bottom right*)

Above: with Michael Foot
and Ralph Nader

Centre: with Harold Evans

Below: Addressing the
'Secret Rally' in Friends
Meeting Hall

Campaigning in the 1973 Hove by-election when we had a 37 per cent swing from the Conservatives but still fell short in the eighth safest Tory seat in the country

EVENING ARGUS, Friday, November 9, 1973—1

CHEERS AND JEERS AS SAINSBURY SAYS 'I TOLD YOU SO'

DES IS BLOODIED BUT UNBOWED...

GLARING television floodlights turned 3 a.m. into mid-day outside Hove's Town Hall as the nation waited for the result of the by-election.

A crowd of 200, mostly Young Liberals, chanted slogans and sang folk songs as they waited in the cold. There was heated crossfire between Tim Sainsbury supporters and a large banner-waving mob of Young Liberals from Eastbourne and Oxford University. A lone National Front voice was drowned as officials unlocked the town hall doors at 2.55 a.m.

Police, who had been operating a strict security barrier from 10 o'clock last night, cleared a path to the specially-built platform in the forecourt.

Only the candidates and their officials had been allowed into the count. Press photographers and television crews, scrambling over the maze of cables, waited expectantly. A middle-aged house-wife, wrapped in a dressing gown, pressed against a pillar to keep warm.

After the results were announced Mr Sainsbury's victory speech, but he refused to be silenced. Des Wilson was acclaimed. Labour's Ron Wallis got a stormy reception and Mrs Carole Reakes (Communist Party of England, Marxist-Leninist) was shouted down.

INTERESTED

After the declaration, Mr Sainsbury said: "I said all along I thought the electorate were most interested in national policies, like prices, pensions and world peace."

by our political staff

Our supporters have been over-come by a mass of trendy propaganda from the Liberals—and if you tell people something often enough they begin to believe it.

"I don't believe this Liberal revival is going to carry over to a General Election.

"All it means is that a lot of our traditional supporters have had a temporary flirtation with the Liberals to get the Tories out. But I am sure they will come back to us next time."

The regional organiser for the Labour Party, Geoff Foster, who spearheaded Cr Wallis's campaign, said: "The Liberals have concentrated on the Labour vote and applied a lot of pressure. We always knew this was on the cards but we hoped we would keep our vote."

TOP RIGHT: Still smiling Des Wil-

The 1992 General Election

Above: at a morning press conference with Ashdown and Alan Beith MP

Centre: Speaking at the party conference

Below: A morning campaign meeting: Tim Clement Jones (*left*), Chris Rennard (*behind me*), and Graham Elson (*far right*)

Above: with Tessa Sanderson, who led the PAT United team and later became my joint vice-chairman of Sport England

Centre: The West End at last . . . with Ken Livingstone performing a sketch in a charity concert at the Piccadilly Theatre

Below: End of the ECB-Zimbabwe crisis

Wilson quits ECB because of Zimbabwe tour qualms

THE ENGLAND and Wales Cricket Board's ongoing dispute over England's scheduled tour to Zimbabwe in October claimed its first casualty yesterday when Des Wilson resigned from the Board. And the former chairman of the Liberal Party used the occasion as a platform for a scathing attack on cricket's governing body, the International Cricket Council, for the way in which it

ANGUS FRASER

Wilson leaves the shelter of ECB hierarchy after rejection

By Christopher Martin-Jenkins
Chief Cricket Correspondent

DES WILSON has resigned from the the management board of the England and Wales Cricket Board (ECB) after failing to persuade his colleagues to take a firmer line against the attitude of the International Cricket Council (ICC) to the sport in Zimbabwe.

"I am unable to share collec-

Left: Jane

Below left: Jacqui and Tim, 1990

Below right: with Sam Smith

Bottom: with Jane in South Africa, 2010

The end of a journey: After travelling to over sixty countries I finally achieve the ambition of a lifetime – to climb the Great Wall of China

competition by students of St Martins School of Arts in London. They included Brian Clough, Bobby Robson, Graham Gooch, Jonathan Davies, Bobby Charlton, Gary Linekar, David Moorcroft, Brendan Foster, Geoff Capes and Tessa Sanderson from sport, actors Tim Pigott Smith, Edward Fox, George Baker, Bill Oddie and Hayley Mills, yachtswoman Clare Francis, mountaineer Chris Bonington, film producer David Puttnam, broadcasters Esther Rantzen and Jonathan Dimbleby . . . and others. Finally, I decided to break my rule about involving Royalty and recruited the Duke of Gloucester to be our President; this was to prove fully justified because he did not pull his punches and even threw Royal conservatism out the window by coming to our press conference in a Pat sweater.

Despite this impressive list, we knew that if this was going to work we had to make an impact at local level; we set out to inspire the creation of PAT groups, or, at the very least, effective local PAT coordinators, to reflect in their own communities what we were doing and saying nationally. By the launch we already had 50 of them. We circulated all members of the House of Commons and got together a list of more than 200 political supporters of all political parties.

In January 1990 we launched the campaign at a major event in London. It was packed, not only with newspaper journalists, radio and TV, but with representatives of the supporting organisations and the hundred parents. The combination of the idea, the personalities, and the kind of subject the media love – bad retailers selling killer products to innocent children – had captured the imagination and virtually guaranteed huge coverage.

Before the press conference I appeared on the *Today* programme with the industry's paid apologist, a man called Clive Turner, who I had already met when he represented the petroleum companies defending lead in petrol. The confrontation was explosive – indeed so much so that it was repeated on radio more than once during the week and was much talked about. One newspaper described:

> . . . the story of a verbal clash between a Mr Clive Turner, spokesman for the Tobacco Advisory Council and a tough talking, combative New Zealander one morning in January . . . After a preliminary but indecisive exchange of statistics, the gloves came off. The no nonsense Kiwi went for the jugular. 'The last time I encountered you,' he told Mr Turner, 'you

were defending lead in petrol; now you are defending the sale of cigarettes to children; what comes next? Speaking for the Columbian drug barons?'

What Mr Turner muttered in reply was irrelevant as the encounter was lost. Des Wilson, Britain's foremost campaigner for good causes, was back in action.'

At the press conference we used our celebrity parents to make our case. Claire Rayner spelled out the special vulnerability of children. Lynn Faulds Wood reported on our surveys showing the extent of sales to children, stressing that more than 50 per cent of shops sold cigarettes to children under sixteen in defiance of the law. Hayley Mills talked about the lack of enforcement of existing laws. Anita Roddick reported on our specially commissioned opinion poll: it showed 95 per cent support for our demand that the law be strictly enforced.

I reported on our initial actions:

We have sent a letter to every Local Authority in Britain, to the majority and minority Leaders, to the Chief Executives, to the Chief Environmental Health Officers and Trading Standards Authorities, asking for the Council to pass a resolution undertaking voluntarily responsibility for the enforcement of the Act, and asking the Senior Trading Standards officer or Chief Environmental Health Officer to be responsible for conducting periodical surveys to establish the extent of illegal sales of cigarettes to children under sixteen, and to approve a Council policy of prosecuting offenders under the Act.

We are approaching all major supermarket chains and asking them to agree a policy for their chain. We are going to meet with all the major retailer organisations to persuade them that it's in their interest to educate their members. And, our local Parents against Tobacco groups will be encouraged to carry out surveys of all shops selling cigarettes in their area.

Richard Branson addressed the issue of tobacco advertising and the boxer Barry McGuigan said: 'the fact is that most sportsmen and women don't smoke, and it could make a real difference if we let our younger fans know that.'

The launch had been a success, but not everyone welcomed the new campaign. In his *Observer* column Richard Ingrams complained of the 'increasingly dictatorial and hysterical methods of the anti-smoking brigade.' Peter Mackay, in an *Evening Standard* column headed 'Deliver us from these busybodies' supported Ingrams: 'I do not need Media Moonies to lecture me about the upbringing of children and neither does anyone else. What we need far more than a crackdown on tobacconists is a purge on busybody campaigns launched by self-publicists which are accorded charitable status.'

But there was plenty of support: the *Guardian* also published a leader:

Yes, every person has a right to kill themselves by smoking cigarettes if they do so wish. But (surely no one) even can extend this right to children. The group has been intelligently designed to kick start the anti-smoking campaign back into life. It is not hard to see how the new pressure group has already recruited the support of 100 MPs, more than 100 leading names from the sporting world, the arts and business as well as 50 organisations. PAT deserves a pat on the back.'

And then we got support from a most unlikely quarter. My old foe, Mrs Thatcher, was questioned about the launch of PAT at PM's Question-time. She replied:

'We give our full support to the "Parents Against Tobacco" campaign. It will keep careful note of where cigarettes are sold to young children and give the information to the police. Knowledge of the campaign should already serve as an effective deterrent to those shopkeepers who perhaps do not take sufficient care to ensure that they do not infringe the law.'

It was enough to make a veteran campaigner blush.

I was told by a reliable source within the tobacco industry that there was widespread panic: they were accustomed to being on the defensive but never before to the hostility of our attack. Needless to say, they mounted their own campaign in retaliation.

First, they pretended to sympathise with our objectives. They had little choice as they could not admit to be deliberately seeking child customers. Second, while pretending to share our concern, they never-the-less suggested we were over-stating our case. We were 'emotive'. We 'exaggerated'. They, on the other hand, were moderate and reasonable. Third, they tried to switch the discussion to the right of adults to smoke and thus move onto their favourite territory, the rights of the individual – the very territory PAT was designed to avoid. Fourth, they stuck to the patently absurd argument that advertising did not increase consumption, but only promoted specific brands. This was, of course, contrary to the whole proposition of the advertising industry, namely that it increased sales. Finally, when all that failed, they turned to questioning our motives. Thus we were all described as publicity-seekers.

Of course, none of this washed with the public, the media, or the political world. We were winning the propaganda battle hands-down. What we now had to do was turn this support into effective, sustained pressure for legislative action.

The Private Members' Bill

As we had demonstrated with the Campaign for Freedom of Information, Private Members' Bills are not only the best chance a backbench MP has of changing the law, but the best chance a single issue pressure group has as well. With experience at Citizen Action of putting more PM Bills through the House of Commons than anyone in British political history, we were fairly confident we would succeed, especially as there was no effective opposition to it; even Mrs Thatcher was on side. There remained, however, one challenge: only the top six who emerged from the ballot for these Bills would have the parliamentary time to steer the legislation into law, so we had to get one of them – preferably – the number one.

We drafted a Bill and began to lean on our 200 backbench MP supporters to commit themselves to introduce it if they came in the top six in the ballot. But apart from lobbying at Westminster, we decided to apply pressure at grassroots constituency level with our Back the Bill campaign, our first of its kind. This became a big exercise. We did this mainly with our PAT Roadshow . . . our own Back the Bill double-decker bus: painted white with the PAT logo and campaign message all over it. This toured 137 towns. At each stop people had the chance to fill in a postcard to their MP and post it in our own post box. More than 5000 cards were sent.

Everywhere the bus went it was noticed. It was covered by 150 local newspapers, 38 radio stations and nine local television stations. Local mayors and other celebrities came to meet it. DJs from radio stations and actors appearing in local theatres were invited to have their pictures taken, surrounded by local children, with the bus. We also took the bus to Westminster and MPs flocked to have their picture taken at the wheel; we then sent the picture to their local newspapers: good PR for the MP and for PAT. This bus proved a huge success – as a collector of postcards, as a publicity-getter, but also as a focal point for activity by local PAT groups and other campaigning on health issues.

We also worked to get local authorities to apply pressure on national authorities and got more than 320 of Britain's local district, city and county councils to pass resolutions supporting PAT. We did this by circulating model resolutions to all councils. This resolution not only gave support to PAT but called on the council to take immediate action, such as banning tobacco advertising on council-owned land: which many councils did. And it raised a surprising amount of money.

Many local authorities really got the bit between their teeth and began to monitor illegal cigarette sales without waiting to see if we could change the law. The number of local council surveys soared. The number of prosecutions increased. From local authorities, the pressure on MPs grew. Early day motions were moved. MPs were falling over each other to publicise their support for PAT in their constituencies, helped by draft press releases and other easy-to-use materials we provided.

We now turned our attention to schools. We wanted to involve them because we wanted children to play a part in the campaign too, because we knew school activity would impact on local media and on parents. So we launched our schools competition. Apple Computers, who were anxious to raise their profile in the education world, were persuaded to donate $15,000-worth of computer equipment to the main prize-winning school. And we gave cash prizes for winners in other categories. The aim was to find Britain's top smoke-free school . . . the one with the most imaginative, wide-ranging and effective anti-smoking programme involving students, teachers and parents. The competition did much to mobilise schools behind the anti-smoking message while getting the additional momentum for our campaign we wanted.

We created our own team of sports stars, 'PAT United' and it was launched at a media photo opportunity at a London school. Led by Tessa

Sanderson, members included a number of Olympic champions, the captains of England's cricket and soccer teams, rugby stars, a former world boxing champion, and the champion steeplechase jockey. Indeed, of all the ideas that I and my fellow campaigners had from the Shelter days until I retired from campaigning, this was my favourite. To see the whole team in PAT sweatshirts doing a master class in a school was heart-warming.

So we had mobilised parents, organisations, stars, politicians, local councils and schools. One group remained: the retailers themselves. We decided to encourage the responsible retailers and further highlight the problem by publicising and rewarding shopkeepers who refused to sell cigarettes to children. We called it our 'PAT on the Back' scheme. Local groups gave PAT on the Back certificates to tried and tested local shops and arranged press publicity for the awards.

By the autumn of 1990, Jane – who from start to finish ran the political side of the campaign brilliantly – had secured firm promises from MPs of all parties that if they came high in the ballot they would introduce the Bill. We were also hopeful that many more would respond favourably. We had the industry on the run, and enormous goodwill behind our drive for legislative change.

On the MPs' Ballot day in November, we recruited the help of three MPs, one from each of the main parties, took over a room in the Palace of Westminster with our full team equipped with mobile phones and information kits and waited for the ballot. As each name was called we set off to find them . . . knowing we were 'competing' with about fifty other lobbyists with other cherished issues to pursue. I doubt whether in the history of private members ballots there has ever been such a determined and professional operation set up in the Commons; every single one of the top ten in the ballot were approached by a PAT representative before any other organisation could reach them. In fact we got the Number One.

Every campaign needs a bit of luck, and we got it. The number one in the ballot was a Labour MP, a genial, bearded former actor called Andrew Faulds, who was on our list of supporters. Helped by Archy Kirkwood, who knew his way around the place, I raced through the Palace to his office and found him dictating letters to his secretary. At that point he did not even know he had won top place and at first he was reluctant to commit himself. But I knew we had to get him committed to the Bill before others could get to him and applied every bit of pressure I could – including the fact that a TV crew was waiting outside to give immediate publicity to whoever took on the Bill. Faulds folded. We went straight out and announced he would introduce the Bill. He made the one o'clock news and we had got our MP – we were on our way.

We had a head start over other pressure groups competing for parliamentary time because we had built up public enthusiasm for the measure we proposed, we had a fully drafted Bill, and an experienced team to give the MP all the professional back up required. But that was still only the start. We had to build up a Parliamentary coalition behind the Bill, steer it through various readings and especially the detailed Committee stage discussions. We had to stop the Government from weakening it drastically as they were clearly inclined to do under pressure from the tobacco lobbyists, get it past the House of Lords, and finally see it working as the law of the land.

It was a long and tough process, involving many hours of negotiations with at least four different government departments, but Jane, who now took centre stage, was more than up to the challenge. She had already discussed the Bill with ministers at the Home Office, Health and Environment Departments and Trade and Industry, over a period of months, but she still had many late-night drafting sessions, going through clauses line by line with officials before each parliamentary sitting on the Bill. She wrote Andrew Faulds' speeches, drafted clauses and amendments, negotiated deals with those who had concerns. And eventually we won the battle – the Children and Young Persons (Protection from Tobacco) Act became law in June 1991.

It increased the maximum fine for the illegal sale of cigarettes six-fold. It extended controls to vending machines. It put the responsibility for monitoring and enforcing the law clearly on the shoulders of local authorities. It prohibited the sale of single cigarettes. It required a warning about the illegality of sales to children to be published on cigarette packets and in stores. In addition, although the UK Government was still standing out against a regulatory ban on print and poster tobacco advertising, we were influential in securing changes to the voluntary tobacco advertising agreement. Shop-front advertising, while not banned altogether, would be cut by 50% with shops near schools targeted first.

Was the problem of children smoking solved? Of course not! But when the legislation we introduced was fully effective, the law became much better known, it became much more dangerous for retailers to sell tobacco illegally, and it became clearer to children that parents really believe the message that cigarettes are bad news.

I accept that this was in some ways the less difficult of our campaigns. It was relatively easy to raise the money, recruit the support, and win. But it's surely fair to say that it was made easy by the impregnability of the campaign we designed; we chose our ground and our objectives well and we achieved in a year what we set out to do: we mobilised a considerable force behind our promise to get a private members' bill – and we did it. When we look at the controls over smoking today, and the reduction in the numbers who smoke, then the whole anti-smoking movement can take considerable credit for slowly and surely taking on and breaking down the power of this hugely powerful and wealthy industry. PAT gave it a much-needed stimulus and encouragement at a crucial time.

It demonstrated the power that parents have when acting to protect their children. And it was also an object lesson in teamwork. The generosity of the funders, the good-humoured support of the celebrity parents, the hard work of all the local coordinators, the cooperation of everyone in the anti-smoking world . . . it was superb. The team, some, such as Eileen Ware, with whom I had first campaigned over thirty years earlier, were fantastic. Jane's handling of the political side of it was awe-inspiring. It was she who took the baton on the final lap and, with Andrew Faulds, saw our parliamentary objective achieved. She emerged from PAT as a formidable campaigner in her own right. This teamwork, unity of purpose, trust in each other's reliability and skills, this fusion of energy and enthusiasm, friendship and self-sacrifice, it is this that made (and presumably still makes) campaigning in the voluntary sector so rewarding. But now I had to say goodbye to it.

I was headed for a more hostile terrain, a bloodier battlefield, where friends would be fewer, opponents more numerous, the stakes much larger . . . I was headed for party politics.

PART THREE
Politician

16

The Liberal Party, the Liberal-Democrats and a Lot of Hassle along the Way

'But I don't want to be an MP!'
'That's OK. You won't be.'

In 1970, in my last full year as director of Shelter and shortly after Harold Wilson was, after six years in power, removed from No 10 Downing Street by the surprise General Election victory of Edward Heath's Conservatives, I had lunch with Ron Hayward, then the Labour Party's Chief Agent, and later to be General Secretary of the Labour Party, who said that, from time to time, someone could be 'helped' to secure a safe Labour parliamentary seat, and he would like me to be that someone. I said that surely there were others who had done much more for the party, but he replied: 'You've earned the chance in your own way.' Looking back on it some four decades later, I realise this was one of the defining moments of my life. I was faced with what, I suppose, should have been for me a momentous decision. There was no doubt that he could deliver on the promise and if I seized the opportunity, who knew where it would lead? Yet, while I was flattered, I was not excited.

For nearly 25 years both the old parties had governed from the centre, yet they were still class-driven parties, many of their policies still derived from decades-old doctrine. I had at Shelter seen the results of 13 years of Tory rule. The poverty, the brutal absentee landlords of slum housing, the punitive hostels for the homeless – these were all a Tory legacy. To me at that time the Tories appeared illiberal. Their policies fostered social and economic injustice. And they were largely financed by and committed to the priorities of big business. Opposing the Tories would not be a problem. For me, the Labour Party was clearly the better prospect. In my time at Shelter I had made many friends in the Labour Party, I already knew most of its leaders on first name terms, and had spoken at Labour events, including twice to the Tribune rally at the party conference. And, to be fair, Labour had responded reasonably well to our campaign. There had been achievements in housing. If it was a matter of choosing between the two, Labour was the way to go. Labour's heart was in the right place.

But was this the real choice? In those days, my generation used to complain about what we called 'the system'. This had multiple meanings; I suppose if you were to try and crudely sum it up, it would be to say that the 'system' was the way things were done; it was what we also called 'the establishment'; it was the influence of vested interest, but to me it meant, at least in part, the divisive and often spirit-sapping effect of two-party adversarial politics. As an active political outsider, I had witnessed, via the housing problem, the undermining of sensible debate as the issue became a political football; in a later book, *Balance of Power*, I was to write of this 'two-party confrontation, with its polarising effect, its dependency on conflicting vested interests, its need to glean votes by dividing people, fostering envy and even hate.'

Yet in one respect these two parties were not adversaries; they were united in strengthening the state in relation to the individual. It was clear to everyone that the electoral system did not produce a result reflecting the way people voted, yet this worked for both parties so they kept it as it was; it was clear to everyone that the State was obsessively secretive, but both parties refused freedom of information and wielded the Official Secrets Act with equal force; it was clear to everyone that power was excessively centralised, but much of what both parties did was to concentrate it, not disperse or share it. It was clear to everyone that civil liberties were constantly under threat, yet individual rights had to be hard fought for in the face of political indifference. On behalf of Shelter, I went every year to the party conferences: you only had to see trade union leaders at Labour Party conferences waving cards representing the ' block votes' of millions of members (not, of course, in support of policies decided upon by those members, but by their leaders in smoke-filled rooms) to see how little democratic principles meant within the Labour

Party; you only had to see dinner-jacketed Tories at their conference, flitting from reception to reception while being content not to have a vote on issues at all, to realise democracy meant even less to them.

To me, and many of my generation, these parties, were separately and together, both part of the problem, not the solution. Was it any wonder that so many politically-committed but disenchanted younger people were rejecting either party and turning to CND or student protest, or Shelter, the NCCL and CPAG (or in my case, all three) to express their idealism? The Sixties had been a positive time for me because I had discovered fresh territory and flourished beyond the traditional party political boundaries – in the voluntary sector, where I had found one could make a real impact and achieve real results.

Thus, I let the weeks drift by, and then, while I was still mulling it over, there occurred an incident at the Shelter fringe meeting at the 1970 Labour Party conference that had a profound influence on me. With me on the platform were Dick Crossman, the Salford MP Frank Allaun who was chairing the meeting, and my PA at Shelter, Helene Middleweek, who had been the first woman President of the Cambridge Union and had parliamentary ambitions (she went on to become an MP and then Baroness Hayman, now Speaker in the Lords). I had become accustomed to a warm welcome at these fringe meetings, but Labour had just been voted out of office and from the start of the meeting I sensed a cooler atmosphere. Sitting glowering in the front row was Reg Freeson, the same Brent MP who had tried to undermine me when, as a junior Minister, he had attended the meeting with Anthony Greenwood a couple of years earlier. Full of bile, he rose and attacked me, the gist of his complaint being that we had never given Labour credit for all that it had done and we had lost them the General Election. Others joined him. The mood became extremely bitter, even ugly. It was clear to me that at this meeting at least, the homeless were irrelevant; I was not being judged on my arguments about housing, rather I was being found guilty and condemned as not having helped save the Labour Party.

This was absurd: it was not my function as a campaigner for the homeless to help Labour win elections, even if Shelter could be any influence on them, one way or the other, and this I doubted. When the meeting ended and I was leaving, a small, bald, round-headed man, his face full of hate, stood in front of me in the doorway. 'Bastard,' he hissed. Shaken, I pushed past him and walked down the stairs. I remember Nigel Spearing, the MP for Ealing, following me down the street and begging me to take no notice. 'They don't represent the best of the Party,' he said. And, of course, he was right, but at that moment he was not easy to believe. It may not have been the best of the Party, but it was the Party at its worst. Not surprisingly I had my enemies – you could not operate as I had and not make them – but this was my first experience of being trapped in a roomful of them and the hateful atmosphere stayed with me and still sends a shiver down my spine today. I know I could be accused of over-reacting, but that night I lost any appetite I may have had for a career in the Labour Party.

In the days and weeks that followed I compared that experience with the friendships and support I had always enjoyed from the Liberals. The party had always packed our fringe meetings at their annual conferences. David Steel had become chairman of Shelter's advisory council in Scotland. The Shelter full-time team contained a number of Young Liberals including a recent chairman of the Young Liberals, Louis Eakes. By attending their conferences I had become familiar with their philosophy and policies and felt comfortable with them. Like all political parties, they had their internal differences and disputes, but for a Liberal fringe meeting to behave as the Labour one had behaved seemed to me unimaginable. (I had not at that time met some of the Liberal parliamentary party!)

Up to this point I had quietly renewed my Labour Party membership every year; now I let it lapse. I did not actually join the Liberals but increasingly it was with them that my political sympathies lay. Some leading Liberals noted that. One slipped me a copy of a document called *The Creed of the Liberal*. I was struck by the overwhelming emphasis on the importance of the individual in relation to society or the State:

> We believe in people, and their slow, ascendant progress, and the autonomy of their spirit and in the primacy of their claims over the claims of all forms of human organisation . . . we believe in authority only when sanctioned by reason and consent . . . we believe that to be well-governed is not as important as to be self-governed . . . we believe that all truth is made manifest through the contact and clash of diverse opinions and that the very motive power of progress is the free exchange

of ideas and the exercised privilege of non-conformity.

A bit wordy it may have been, but I knew that of the three political parties of any consequence in the UK, only one could lay claim to represent these ideals, and that was the Liberal party.

Then in the Autumn of 1973, nearly three years after I had decided not to respond to the Hayward approach, and after my departure from Shelter to become an *Observer* columnist, I took a phone call from David Steel, now the Liberal Chief Whip in the Commons. The Conservative MP for the true-blue seat of Hove had died; what did I think about fighting the by-election for The Liberals? What did I think? I *thought* that I was not even a member of the Liberal Party. And I thought that Hove was probably the most unlikely seat in the country for someone of my controversial reputation. The Tories would have no difficulty in portraying me as a leftist, radical, semi-terrorist and the preponderance of old folk in that true blue constituency would be tripping over each other's walking sticks to get to the polling booths to keep me away.

But Steel had been talking to the party's by-election supremo, Trevor Jones, from Liverpool. Jones, a likeable political salesman, had achieved miracles with the Liberals up there and also been the architect of some impressive Liberal by-election performances. Rather than being the wrong man for the seat, he and Steel believed I was exactly the right one. Jones picked me up that Sunday and drove me down there. It was an eye-opener. At one point we saw an elderly woman stumble and fall on a pedestrian crossing. Jones put his foot on the brake and leapt out of the car. I was impressed by his concern until he produced a camera from his pocket and took a photograph. Only then did he help her to her feet. (The picture duly appeared on a by-election leaflet under the heading: 'Crossings that can kill!')

As we went up and down its wide avenues and past its tall, terraced mansions, he kept saying 'Look at the doorbells, Des, look at the doorbells. There are scores of lonely, neglected old people behind those doors. They may think they're Tories but what have the Tories ever done for them? You can reach them.' 'But I'm not a member of the Party.' He produced a membership form. 'Sign this and you are now.' 'But I don't want to be an MP.' 'That's OK. You won't be.'

He then explained that even he believed the seat could not be won. 'It's one of their safest seats, Des. They can't lose it.' But we could give the Tories 'a hell of a fight' and in the process galvanise the party and strengthen its credibility across the south of England. I said to him: 'Do you promise me I cannot win?' He said he couldn't promise that, but it was extremely unlikely. I was given the weekend to think about it. For the second time I was pondering a party political opportunity, this time with the Liberals.

For a start, I had meant it when I said I did not want to be an MP. If I pulled off a political miracle and won Hove, I would be stuck in the House of Commons, one of a tiny minority with hardly any influence, whereas as a campaigner, and then a campaigning columnist, I had become accustomed to being a political party of one. Nearly a million people read my views every week; millions more heard them from time to time on radio or television. This profile and platform were the envy of almost every backbencher I knew. And, unlike them, I could often have real influence.

But, then, becoming the MP for Hove was not going to happen. The Tories had a majority of 18,648. It was their eighth safest seat in the country. It was such a lost cause that the Liberals had not even bothered to fight the seat at the last General Election. As Trevor had promised, the most we could achieve would be a respectable result. But would it be fair on either the party or the constituency to fight a seat when I did not want to win?

The answer to that lay in the hopes of both Steel and Jones that, while we would lose – we would lose well. Fighting the kind of campaign which would unite and strengthen the party all across the South coast. The party did not need a candidate, it needed a martyr, but preferably one who had shown he could inspire enthusiasm, excite support – someone who would carry the Liberal banner to its inevitable defeat with honour.

It had been three years since I had been on the campaigning front-line; the *Observer* column was satisfying, but like a soldier who has been moved from the battlefield to a desk in Whitehall, I missed the drama of the battle, the sound of gunfire. This, I told myself, would be a mini-campaign: a few weeks to put my beliefs on the line, and then back to the *Observer*. So I decided to go for it. Trevor explained there was a small hitch. I had to be selected by the local Party and would I attend a selection meeting the following Sunday?

The local party consisted of three young people: one was about to leave Hove to return to university; one, a young woman, was about to leave the country to live abroad; the third, an unemployed young man, was lined up to be my driver for the campaign. After we met, I went out onto the balcony of the woman's flat while they pretended to consider the matter. I recall looking down upon the Sussex County Cricket ground and seeing John Snow bowling. Then I was called in and offered the candidacy. The student and the woman said goodbye. I never saw them again. The other one looked at me sheepishly. 'Well, it's just you and me,' he said. That was when I knew I had nothing to fear. With just him and me, we were not going to win this seat. Except that, one week out from polling day we *were* winning the seat!

Hove had never seen anything like it. It was the safest of safe seats. For years it had been taken for granted. The MP had hardly ever been seen. Elections were just a formality. And now, suddenly, the whole place was politicised. All the campaigning skills that I had developed at a national level were now concentrated on just one locality. Liberals poured in to help from all over the south of England. We pounded them with newsletters. We covered the constituency with posters so that parts of Hove were a sea of orange. We had meetings in every hall in town, culminating in packing Hove Town Hall with 1,500 for the biggest political meeting the constituency had ever seen. We took over the pages of the local newspapers with story after story of Tory indifference and neglect.

The Brighton and Hove Argus had the time of its life, thriving on the campaign, its editor, accustomed to obscurity, suddenly being wooed over lunch by national party leaders. (After I was accused of being pro-Arab in a constituency with an abnormally high number of Jewish voters, I admitted that my ship had called at Suez when I came to Britain in 1960, and that I had purchased a fez: the *Argus* headlined the story: 'Yez, I had a fez, says Dez.')

We set up an advisory centre so that I could help people, saying that as the Tories didn't care about their problems, I would – even in the middle of a by-election.

And, slowly and steadily, the old people began to come out from behind the doorbells and in all sorts of little ways indicate their support. The polls showed we were getting closer and closer. The people of Hove were loving the attention they were getting, and they were responding to the promise I was making that for the first time they would have a locally active MP instead of an absentee one. A week before polling day our canvassing returns and the public opinion polls were both telling the same story – it was either neck and neck or we were ahead.

Only too quickly I began to learn a few lessons about politics. One is that you became vulnerable to attack in a way that does not happen in the voluntary sector. While at Shelter, and even as a campaigner on the *Observer*, I had become accustomed to friendly coverage. After all, I was presumed to be on the side of the angels. But the day I crossed the line and became a party politician, I became a target – for the other parties, and for the more politically-aligned of the media. Up to now I had never needed to be thick-skinned; now I was having to learn to be. Another lesson was that in politics the more difficult problems and personality clashes nearly always came from your own side. The internal battle in Hove was whether I should cease to be the man who had made his name fighting for minorities, and instead pitch my message at the affluent majority in the constituency.

At a tense meeting, I was told I had to change my ways. John Holmes, the wily chief agent who had been sent down from London to over-see the campaign, led the attack, saying that I was there to achieve the best-possible result for the Liberals, not frighten the voters. I should stop talking about the poor and homeless and social injustice and civil liberties and 'concentrate on middle class issues'. To me, this was madness. They had chosen me for my reputation, but these party managers were now asking me to become a phoney character to win votes; I told them the Liberal Party was not worth my time if I was not able to stand on what I believed were both mine and the party's principles. And I reminded them I was the candidate and it would be my name on the ballot paper; if there was any danger of being elected, I wanted a mandate to be myself. In any case, they were being politically illogical; there was no way the most affluent in Hove would ever vote for me; my best chance lay in winning the latent Liberal vote, most of the Labour vote, and the group Trevor Jones had identified: those living in genteel poverty behind 'those doors'.

I decided to take the matter directly to the now growing number of local members and the other workers in the campaign, so I deliberately avoided further discussion with John Holmes until the adoption meeting when I could publicly hammer my stake into the ground. Usually there would be a motion to adopt the candidate and then the candidate would speak; I told the chairman I wanted to reverse the order and speak first. I wanted my mandate. I then told the meeting:

'I have been told that it is foolish to spend too much time talking about housing in this by-election because people here have a home. This assumes that those who have a home don't care about those who don't. I will not accept that. My experience at Shelter tells me it is not so.

'This is the problem with politics. Political leaders have not confronted people with the reality of our social problems; they have found it easier, indeed, to stir up prejudice, to foster ignorance . . .

'I will not be that kind of politician, nor I believe would the Liberal Party want me to be.

'We will tell the people of Hove the truth – the truth about the young families being exploited by outside developers and speculators; the truth about old folk being frightened by absentee landlords; the truth about disabled people living up flights of stairs because of poor provision for them; the truth about the need for better schooling and hospital facilities for the town.'

I was adopted unanimously. John Holmes came up to me afterwards and smiled. 'You win,' he said, 'but remember what I told you. It's your campaign now. Don't blame me if it does not work.' To be fair, John from then on proved a loyal and supportive partner and I liked him a lot.

Typical of him was the story of the bottle of whisky. To help raise money we had a raffle with a bottle of whisky as the first prize. About a week before the by-election I asked John where the raffle prize was. 'Oh,' he said, with a twinkle in his eye, 'I drank it last night with the Tory Agent!' Now the point of the story is not to say that John is a whisky thief. He replaced the bottle. It is to draw attention to John's particular style. The by-election had started to turn nasty, as the Tories panicked, and a lot of mud was being thrown at me on the doorstep by Tory canvassers. Rather than allow a particularly vicious public confrontation to develop, John sorted it out in his own quiet way by taking our objections and our evidence into the enemy camp and over a late-night bottle of Scotch, reaching an understanding with a fellow professional, the Opposition Agent. A lot of the mud-throwing stopped thereafter.

Unlike a General Election, when the candidate is lucky to be covered by one local reporter, by-elections attract the cream of the nation's political journalists, and they soon picked up on the contrast between my record and the nature of the constituency.

The *Observer* reported:

When he was selected as candidate two months ago, many Liberals believed he was the wrong choice for this graceful and almost change-less resort, and that his preoccupations would have been better suited to the glaring social problems of some neglected industrial con-stituency.

But Shelter, which he directed for five years before returning to journalism, is essentially a phenomenon of middle-class politics. Des Wilson is a more celebrated figure in Hove than he would be in, say, Manchester Exchange. As he points out, his success here has been the same as his success at Shelter: to have recognised that 'people who have homes care about people who don't.'

The *Financial Times* also understood what was happening:

It is astonishing . . . the deep fear close to panic that the high pressure campaign of the Liberal Des Wilson has inspired in the Tories in a constituency they have always regarded as theirs by right . . . Many thought that Mr Wilson . . . was an over-gimmicky choice for Hove, with its elderly conformist electorate . . . his technique is simple – it is to make voters feel that at last someone cares about them.

And the famous Walter Terry on the *Daily Express*, wrote: 'He is running one of the toughest by-election campaigns ever seen in recent years. He has demonstrated the incredible. That Hove, the last refuge of every true Blue, could actually be in danger of falling to the enemy.'

I was torn between elation at our success and apprehension at the prospect of getting elected.

And then, in the last week, the Tories now in a panic threw everything at it. It had for Heath and his administration been a hard year, fraught with difficulties with the trade unions. To lose this safest of safe seats was unthinkable. Helpers were bussed in from all over the country. Ministers abandoned Cabinet meetings and came down in twos and threes to dominate the local airwaves and newspaper columns. The message to the old folk was clear: 'You may like this Liberal, but defeat for the Tories could bring down Mr Heath and let the Socialists back in. This cannot be what you want.'

On the last Saturday of the campaign my team were convinced we had won, but I knew differently. The candidate can see and sense what no one else can: he sees it in the eyes of the people he meets on the doorstep and the street. If they are on side, they look the candidate in the eyes; if they're not, they look away. Now I could not help but notice people who had come towards me the previous Saturday with goodwill in their eyes were now looking embarrassed. They had changed their minds. The Tories were frightening them into the polling booths and there was nothing I could do about it.

Come the day the Liberals went from a nil vote at the General Election to 17,224 votes, a whopping 37 per cent swing from the Tories. The Tories majority had fallen by over 12,000 votes but they still won by 5,000. The result was announced in the early hours of the morning. Afterwards we had a party and for some unaccountable reason I drank rum and coke. The next morning I was violently ill and I arrived at our campaign headquarters feeling close to death. As I stood amid abandoned leaflets, empty coffee cups and discarded fish and chip wrappings, I heard a sound outside. I went to the door just in time to see the Conservative winner going past, standing on the back of an open van with a loud-speaker, thanking us for our support. As I looked at the smug face of the multi-millionaire winner I was, for the second time that morning, physically sick. Whatever I had felt about becoming an MP, at that moment I knew what defeat meant. And I did not like it.

The 1974 General Election

Three months later I kept a promise I had made to Hove and went back for the General Election in February 1974. Prime Minister Edward Heath had now picked a fight with the miners and reduced the country to a three-day week. He was calling an election so the country could decide 'Who Rules Britain?' The country decided it should not be Health, albeit not giving Harold Wilson a clear majority. My only bad moment did not happen in Hove, but in London. The Liberal leader Jeremy Thorpe was fighting most of the campaign from his constituency and being 'beamed' into the morning press conferences from there. To back him in case the communications fell apart, someone else was always there 'live'. It was just my luck that the day I was there, communications did break down. What was worse, the break-down was only one way; we could hear Thorpe but he could not hear us.

When it became clear we had a problem, I was asked to talk about housing. But every few words were interrupted by Thorpe's voice coming over the Tannoy: 'Tell Des Wilson to talk about housing . . . ' which, of course, I was trying to do. The journalists were virtually rolling on the floor laughing. I became more and more red-faced but stumbled on. At one point someone asked me if we could increase output when there were not enough bricks. Before I could answer this somewhat surreal question, Thorpe's voice came loud and clear: ' . . . for God's sake, tell Des to get on with it and talk about housing.' The press conference was now in hysterics. At that point we all gave up, and I fled back to the relative calm of Hove.

I will always be pleased that I fought those two elections. Being a candidate is a remarkable experience. You see for yourself how many caring, decent people give up days of their lives, sometimes whole annual holidays, to lick stamps and deliver leaflets and knock on doors . . . fantastic, committed, self-sacrificing, generous people. And you learn a lot about yourself. Because, particularly in a high profile by-election the candidate's character, ability and views are put on trial in a national courtroom. And you learn directly from the voters in a way that focus groups and polls can never convey, actually what people do think and feel.

And I learned for the first time what it was like to lose. To get up every day and fight until you drop, then to lose. To know you're winning the argument, to *know* you can do more for the constituency than your opponent, and then to lose. To go from light heartedly contesting the seat to the point where you want to win it, and then to the point where you desperately want to win it, because you have come to like these constituents and want to be their MP – and then to lose.

Well, for years I had been campaigning for minorities who were destined to lose, no matter how hard they had tried; now I had experienced it for myself. And it probably did me no harm.

But there were also light-hearted moments. We knocked on one door and my canvasser began rather pompously: 'Madam, you are on the electoral register.' 'Oh no,' she replied, 'we're on gas here.' I knocked on another door and suddenly windows, upstairs and downstairs, began to open and the house appeared to be packed with smiling Pakistanis. None of them could speak English, except for a 15-year-old who came to the door. I showed her my picture on the leaflet and explained that I wanted her family to vote for me. She spoke to everyone inside and they began to pour out, putting on their coats and scarves. 'No, no,' I said – 'not now. On polling day.' They all smiled and nodded. I began to walk down the road and they all followed. I turned back: 'No, you don't understand – not now. In a week's time.' They all smiled and nodded and I walked on. They still followed. I began to walk faster, then to run, and behind me I could hear them running too. It was like a Keystone Cops film. Finally one of our cars arrived and I leapt in and we fled, leaving our enthusiastic, if mystified Pakistani voters behind. I'm afraid after that episode they probably voted Conservative on the big day.

On another doorstep I was confronted by a man who saw my Liberal rosette and said, 'No need to talk to me, mate, I'll be voting Liberal. Always have.' I thanked him and was almost at the gate when I heard him calling after me: 'Mark you, don't send that Des Wilson round; I can't stand him'. I promised him I wouldn't. 'Never mind,' I said, 'just remember it's the cause that counts.'

My most memorable experience was to knock on a door and have it opened by a beautiful, dark-haired woman completely naked except for the most revealing of transparent short night gowns through which every detail of her spectacular body was displayed. As I stood there, frozen to the spot, she slowly looked me up and down and then smiled seductively and said in a husky voice 'Hullo there, do come in.' I thrust a leaflet into her hand and fled. I was, after all, a parliamentary candidate. But I could see why milkmen became milkmen.

With or without her support, I actually increased my vote to nearly 19,000, but the Tories recovered some ground from those who had stayed away in November. The Liberals nationally had a tremendous election, but, as always under our unfair electoral system, 19 per cent of the vote was not reflected in parliamentary seats. We only won 14. But we were now to share an experience not unlike that which was later to face Nick Clegg in 2010 – a hung parliament.

Heath, with more votes than Labour but less seats, over the weekend called the then Liberal leader Jeremy Thorpe to talks at Downing Street. Heath was to write afterwards that Thorpe was 'very keen to enter a coalition'. This Thorpe vehemently denied. According to Heath's biographer, Philip Ziegler: 'Thorpe was definitely attracted by the idea of a post in Cabinet and told Nigel Fisher that, though he was not very close to Heath, he "considered him by far the most able man we had" and one under whom he would be happy to serve.' It is probable that Thorpe would never have been allowed to take it further without a promise of reform of the voting system, but it was a measure of the distrust of him and some of his parliamentary team that Liberals in the country were deeply concerned. None more than I, because I had in the course of ten weeks fought two uncompromising battles with the Tories and had no wish to see my party now preserve them in power. While I was a new member of the party, I knew that the by-election had given me some influence so on the Saturday night in a speech to thank constituency workers I called on everyone to send telegrams to Thorpe urging restraint.

The following week, after Heath's overtures had been rejected, Thorpe called a meeting of candidates at the House of Commons. While speaking, he specifically attacked me for asking party members to contact him. Steel was in the chair and I indicated I wanted the right of reply. Steel looked away.

The Hove Liberals had by now gone from one member to hundreds, and now the issue that John Holmes had raised at the by-election was even more hotly debated, this time within the party membership when I was not there. If, it was said, a radical like Des Wilson could get this close, surely a more politically 'respectable' candidate, someone a bit more conservative, someone more comfortable in a suit, someone less frightening to the old ladies, could win it. So, while I was too popular with the locals to be forcibly dropped (I repeat, I had actually *increased* my vote from the by election), hints were dropped that they would like a chance to 'push for the top' with a more conservative candidate.

This did not worry me; I believed they were making a mistake, not about losing me as candidate but in seeking a more conservative candidate, but I understood their frustration at not winning, and, given that I did not really want to be an MP anyway, it would have been perverse to force myself upon them. I was more than happy to return to the columns of the *Observer* from whence I had come. So I announced that I was moving on, and the local party put its views to the test by selecting a decent, respectable, middle class, well-dressed doctor who was dedicated to fighting a decent, respectable, middle class campaign.

At the following General Election – just eight months later – the Liberal vote in Hove fell by over a third, from over 18,000 to just over 12,000.

Party President

I was acutely aware that I had been slipped into the Hove by-election by the back door and that, while I did the party proud, there were those who had for years dreamed of fighting a high profile by-election and understandably felt they should have been given the chance.

So it made sense all round for me to keep a low profile for a while, and for a number of years I did, 'earning my spurs' as a fee-paying party member. Then in 1981, after speaking at the annual Party Assembly in a debate about strategy and being touched by the warmth of the reception I received. I decided it was time to become more fully engaged and stood for the Party Council, nearly topping the poll. Subsequently the Young Liberals elected me their President (a symbolic post as I was far too old to be a Young Lib.)

A couple of years later, my friend Leighton Andrews (who is now a Labour member of the Welsh Assembly) suggested to me over dinner one night at a Harrogate Party Assembly that I should consider running for the Presidency (of the party, not the United States). Leighton reminded me of a famous conference resolution calling for 'a dual approach to politics, acting both inside and outside established political institutions' and for 'a primary strategic emphasis on community politics.'

Leighton pointed out that while the parliamentary party usually acted as if this twin track policy did not exist, the rest of the party had adopted it wholeheartedly with impressive results and was now winning council elections all over the country. A new generation of local Liberal leaders were becoming accustomed to managing huge budgets and governing big cities and counties. Now, with an Alliance with the newly-formed Social Democrats on the cards, the left-of-centre, or so-called radical wing of the party, wanted someone to stand for party President who could speak for them. Someone who would be a campaigning President for a campaigning party, someone with the credentials to promote the twin-track approach.

I was amazed. Since 1974 I had been low key to the point of non-existent in the party. How on earth did he think I could be elected its President? He was amazed that I was amazed: 'They know what you stand for from Shelter, from those years writing for the *Observer*, and for your other campaigns . . . You could be the first Liberal President for years that anyone has heard of.'

The President of the Liberal Party at that time was the most senior member of the party outside the House of Commons. As President-elect he made the opening speech at the Assembly, he chaired the Leader's Speech, and he chaired the Party Council and attended all meetings of the parliamentary party on behalf of the wider party. He had automatic access to the Leader at any time.

But it was a position that you made of whatever you were capable of doing and Leighton pointed out that with the party moving towards an electoral alliance with the newly-formed Social Democrats, the presidency could become very powerful. Indeed, if the parties formed an effective Alliance at the forthcoming General Election, a merger of the parties was on the cards; we could be talking about the last Liberal President, charged with the historic responsibility of helping to end the party and create a new one.

I had been present as a journalist at the historic press conference when the so-called gang of four – Roy Jenkins, Shirley Williams, Bill Rodgers, and David Owen – had, with a number of lesser known Labour MPs, announced they were leaving the party and forming the Social Democratic Party. Jenkins had, in fact, been initially planning to join the Liberals but it was Steel, of all people, who persuaded him to form a new party. Steel's rationale was that a new party would attract a lot of fresh people to politics in a way that the Liberals plus Jenkins would not do. A merger could follow later. I believed then, and still do, that Steel was right, and that his strategy would have been proved so, were it not for the leadership failures that I will describe shortly.

I waited for the results of the 1984 Party Council elections, and they confirmed my following in the party; I topped the poll with a decisive margin over all the other candidates. So I confirmed I would run for

President-elect in 1985–86 with the aim of being President in 1986-87 (1987 being the likely General Election year).

At that time, nearly half the small Liberal parliamentary party had been chosen by the Grim Reaper – they had won by-elections caused by the death of the sitting MP. Usually, they had been elected as a mid-term protest at the failings of the other parties. They were a mixed bag, most fully deserving of their place, but a handful only too obviously the Political Gods' idea of a joke. Their views and priorities differed wildly because they came from every corner of the British Isles, from Orkney and Shetlands in the north to the Isle of Wight in the south; they were united by one common purpose: to hold their seats at the next General Election.

But, no matter how they got there or how long they were likely to stay, in a party starved of MPs, they were 'the stars'. Whenever there was any sort of event in the party, the call went out: *Get an MP*. You could not have a by-election without *getting an MP* to come down and canvass, or speak at a meeting. You could not have a fringe meeting at the annual Assembly without *getting an MP* to address it. You could not have a constituency dinner without *getting an MP* as guest of honour. They were not so much revered for who or what they were, but because of what they represented. And what was that? It was hope. Everyone in the party wanted to be an MP, and these few showed it could be done.

Unfortunately, the effect of this is that some of the MPs (not all) actually believed they *were* stars. The MPs were later to be described by Paddy Ashdown as 'self-centred individualists: outstanding personalities in their own constituencies but unable or unwilling to play as a team'. He has also described numerous tantrums and vicious exchanges at parliamentary meetings. He was, too, to become the subject of a vitriolic attack from so-called 'colleagues' during the first Liberal Democrat leadership campaign. Steel, too, suffered from their self-centred, irascible behaviour from time to time; he once resigned after a particularly bad meeting and had to be persuaded back on board. My first difference with some of the MPs was over the role of the parliamentary party.

As President I was later to attend parliamentary party meetings. As I expected, most were a farce, devoted to deciding who would attend a debate or question-time on any given day. They were determined to play the traditional game of Government and Opposition, even though there were only 20 Liberal MPs out of 650. To me it was ludicrous that a small handful of MPs should share out 'shadow' positions and call themselves 'shadow Home Secretary' or whatever, and waste their time playing at big-time politics when, if they linked up properly with the whole party on the twin-track approach, they could become so much more effective. Why could they not sit down together and say: 'OK, we're here as members of a small group; we won't try and ape the main Opposition; let's see what we can do that actually makes a difference.'

And they *could* have made a difference. The House of Commons offered plenty of opportunities for a determined and well organised smaller party to make an impact. By prioritising their activities and becoming a dynamic parliamentary spearhead for national party campaigns, they could have raised the profile of the party, better defined what we stood for, and made the best use of all our resources, both local and national.

Some commentators said that my kind of Liberal wanted to turn the parliamentary party into some kind of single issue pressure group in the House; that is not what I was saying. I was saying they could and should have set specific, achievable and worthwhile goals and, in doing so, become an effective parliamentary expression of all that the Liberal Party stood for. One or two did seize their opportunities: Stephen Ross introduced legislation to help the homeless; Archy Kirkwood achieved two FoI Bills. But to the bulk of the parliamentary party, this was eccentric behaviour, to be patronisingly applauded but not what they were really there for.

For this unimaginative and sometimes absurd approach, successive leaders have to take much of the blame. Westminster knew how to seduce Liberal leaders: it allowed them to carry a wreath to the Cenotaph, meet new Ambassadors to the Court of St James, attend events at Buckingham Palace, travel to the funerals of foreign leaders; in short, it made them feel they were important. All the perks and privileges were enthusiastically accepted and jealously protected by all the leaders of my day. There were, too, a few crumbs for the MPs, just enough to keep them from becoming too hungry.

Anyway, most of the MPs intensely disliked my view of what they should be doing. Fair enough; I was not discouraged. Big challenges lay ahead, not least the 1987 General Election, the first to be fought by the

Alliance, and the possible merger being another. So, with the enthusiastic support of Leighton Andrews and all his many friends within the party, I announced my candidature, and was elected Party President unopposed.

I was then approached by the party's General Secretary Andy Ellis and asked whether I would be chairman of the party's General Election Committee as well. So it was that I found myself in Eastbourne in September 1986 about to become both President of the Party and its General Election boss. I could not believe that I had so effortlessly reached the top of this famous, albeit now minority British political party. It had all seemed so easy. But within days I was realising how difficult this was going to be.

The Eastbourne Debacle

By then I was married to Jane and living in Brighton where she worked, so we had a short drive in the sunshine to Eastbourne where the Party Assembly was being held in 1986. What I could not know was that a cloud was moving in over Eastbourne in the form of a controversial resolution that would the test the party's position on nuclear weapons. On the first day my own keynote speech was generously received and it was followed the next day by a stunningly supportive, but also prescient column by the distinguished *Guardian* commentator Hugo Young:

'Wilson is an unusual figure, a man who has arrived in front line party politics with a major reputation already made in another field. (He) made his name, of course, in para-political activity. He was the first and arguably the most effective of the Sixties single-issue activists. So he is well versed in the political skills. All this makes him an alien intruder into the orthodox political scene: unschooled by Parliament, unobliged to a party hierarchy, and yet a figure they cannot dismiss. Wilson's essential thrust is, if not anti-parliamentary, certainly anti-system and anti-Establishment. Now elected to high party office, he looms as a menacing invigilator of the stratagems of the party emollient wing: the managers and fixers who, operating with the SDP, now give more time to manoeuvre than substance, everything to the medium and almost nothing to the message.'

I was still basking in the warm glow from this when I found myself sitting beside Steel on the platform as the defence debate began. Within minutes I wished the ground would open up and swallow me.

The Liberal Party had never adopted a fully 'unilateralist' position, but Assemblies over many years had passed resolutions pressing for steps to reduce the dependence of the super powers on nuclear weapons, and for a policy (negotiated within NATO) that did not involve Britain having its own nuclear deterrent. In 1984 there was a famous Liberal Assembly debate on a resolution entitled 'Uniting for Peace'. This affirmed 'the party's opposition to the maintenance of an independent British nuclear deterrent' and committed the Party to a step by step process of disarmament which included cancelling Trident forthwith, including Polaris in arms control negotiations, and the removal of Cruise missiles from British soil. It was in this debate that David Steel took on the radical left of the Party and lost. During the debate, in which I spoke in support of the resolution, Paddy Ashdown made a brilliant and probably decisive speech opposing the retention of Cruise missiles.

The SDP leader, David Owen, on the other hand, was aggressively multilateral. A former Foreign Secretary, he had departed the Labour Party partly because of its inclinations to unilateralism. He believed that if Britain lost its nuclear status it would lose its status in the world generally. And he took that status seriously – his critics would say he took it too seriously. Owen had never been in any doubt that unless circumstances changed radically, we would need eventually to modernise and then replace Polaris. Not only did he hold these firm beliefs, but he actually took pleasure in discussing the various nuclear alternatives, often insensitive to the fact that when you talk with evident interest about weapons you can easily sound to others as if you would actually like to use them. In a speech, he said: 'I must tell you bluntly that I believe we should remain a nuclear weapons state.' All hell then broke loose.

Bill Rodgers, one of the SDP's founding Gang of Four, wrote an article for *The Times* flatly contradicting Owen's speech. Shirley Williams, another of the four SDP founders, also voiced her fury at Owen's initiative, 'It does not follow that what the Leader said is the same and identical with the policy of the party,' she said in a radio interview. 'The present policy of the SDP is that the party is willing to replace Polaris under certain circumstances but not irrevocably committed to doing so.'

Now in Eastbourne in 1986, Steel, sympathetic to Owen's position and anxious to maintain Alliance unity, wanted the Liberal Assembly to pass what was effectively an Alliance defence resolution. But many Liberals saw Eastbourne as a last chance to reinforce the Liberal position for final negotiations with the SDP on a joint policy programme. Three Liberal MPs, Simon Hughes, Archy Kirkwood and Michael Meadowcroft signed a report, *Across the Divide*, published on the eve of the Assembly that began from the position that 'the Liberal Party must make a strong Liberal contribution to the debate within the Alliance.' This contribution would build on the 1984 resolution.

This should have been a warning to Steel, but he and the majority of the parliamentary party still believed they would carry the day, and made no attempt to manage the debate. There was no consideration of persuading the movers to withdraw the amendment, or of tactics to rally support for the platform the following day. This was a bad mistake. The party, in a pre-election atmosphere, would in my view have been more than willing to settle for a compromise at this time – maybe a shuffling of the issue off for 'further consideration' – but the case was never made. So it went to the conference floor.

Early in the debate Ashdown retreated from his 1984 position, earning himself forever after the name 'Paddy Backdown'. Simon Hughes made the most telling speech against the platform, arguing that the party had to enter the negotiating process asserting a Liberal view. The Assembly was about reaffirming traditional Liberal policies. 'We have never voted for an independent deterrent. Not only must we not do so now, but our policy must be to do so never.' It was becoming clear the debate was not going the leadership's way and on this issue I was on the rebels' side instead of Steel's. I had, however, decided that I could respectably abstain on the grounds that the President would have to help pick up the pieces if it all went badly wrong.

But when every hand on the platform rose in support of Steel except mine, and I was sitting next to Steel, it was clear to me immediately that it would be seen very differently. And it was; it was interpreted in the media the following day as the President declining to support the Leader at a crucial moment. Never in my life had I so wished that I was some-where else – *anywhere* rather than sitting beside the defeated leader. The leadership was beaten by 652 votes to 625.

Afterwards Steel tried to shrug it off to the media but other Liberal MPs were in less generous mood. That night at a parliamentary meeting, chief whip David Alton led a brutal attack on the dissenters. He was supported by others, including Alex Carlisle, Cyril Smith and Russell Johnston. This was typical; they had not prepared for the debate, they had not sought to manage it by avoiding the confrontation, they had not bothered to even read the three MPs' pamphlet, and now, faced with the result of their own negligence and poor party management, they went ballistic.

Up to this point it may still have been contained, but David Alton now appeared to lose his head completely. Perhaps it was what he read in the morning papers. The headlines must have confirmed the worst fears: 'Alliance pact is shattered', said *Today*. 'Ban the Bomb vote shatters the Alliance' said the *Express*. 'Liberals rebuff Steel over nuclear policy,' said *The Times*. Alton compounded the problem. He missed no radio or television opportunity to attack the dissidents, and those who had voted with the majority. At a press conference he actually waved the tabloids in front of the television cameras. I happened to arrive in the press room while Alton was having his conference, and could hardly believe my eyes or ears. Surely the way to play it this morning was to cool it, to stress that the Leader was not overly perturbed, to emphasise the positive, that the party had actually approved 90% of the defence policy, to stress what steps could now be taken via the Policy Committees to establish final Alliance defence policy and so on. Alton was doing the opposite – throwing oil onto the flames.

That night, the eve of the leader's speech, I went to Steel's room to find him with his aides preparing an attack on the party. I advised them to cool it, pointing out that if Steel made an issue of it, the effect would be to confirm division, whereas if he acted in a statesmanlike way it would soon be forgotten by the public to whom internal debates within the Liberal party were not yet a matter of much concern. They were in no mood to listen. One said to me; 'we intend to crucify them.' I went away very alarmed. And with reason.

Steel was hardly on his feet the following day when he moved onto the attack:

'It is one thing to declare our goal of ridding our country, our continent, our world of nuclear weapons. That we must assert with all the passionate intensity of our command. But if we are ever to be in a position to influence our destiny in that direction, we must also convince the electorate that we have carefully thought through the painful steps we must take to reach that non-nuclear goal . . . The Chernobyl cloud drifting over Europe and over parts of Britain carrying its dreaded fallout in the wind should have taught us, if we didn't know it before, that you cannot create nuclear free zones by putting up signs on the lampposts of Lambeth. Our Assembly resolution as amended is the equivalent of one of these signs.'

There were shouts of dissent from the hall but Steel was determined to get what he called 'intellectual consistency and integrity' in our policy. He condemned the:

'no doubt well-intentioned but completely misguided belief that in some way it was this Assembly's task to accentuate the few remaining points of difference with the SDP in order to strengthen my hand in manifesto discussions with David Owen. That is a breathtaking mis-judgement.'

Once more there were cries of dissent – for this was the crux. Speaker after speaker opposing the platform on Tuesday had stressed that the debate was establishing a Liberal policy, and had talked about the need to strengthen our negotiators with the SDP and constitutionally they were right. A Liberal Assembly made Liberal policy. But Steel was concerned with the political realities, not the constitutional niceties. He forged on:

'We are either in alliance or we are not. We must live and breathe the Alliance. It is unthinkable that we enter the election with two defence and disarmament policies. But neither David Owen nor I are prepared to arrive at any election policy as a result of some botched up bargaining process. We wouldn't convince the country. We wouldn't convince you. We wouldn't convince ourselves.'

In that hall, and defiantly delivered, the impact of his speech was devastating. The assembled were told by the headmaster that the exam results were not good enough, and the majority didn't like it and didn't think it fair. I drove home in disconsolate mood. The week had begun on a high with my well-received presidential speech and ended on a low. Instead of a pre-General Election conference to unite and motivate the party, its members left Eastbourne divided and in low spirits. And the General Election was just over six months away.

Tragedy in Cornwall

The party suffered another trauma within a few weeks – virtually on Christmas Eve 1986, when my predecessor as party President, David Penhaligon, the popular MP from Truro, was killed in a car accident. It was a devastating blow to the party because he had the sense of humour, common sense, and ability to introduce a note of perspective when one problem or another was drifting out of proportion. An increasingly popular MP, he had built up his Truro majority from 464 to more than 10,000.

I will always remember a speech he made at a joint candidates conference of the Alliance when he waved a draft of the latest policy document and said . . . 'they say we have no policies . . . we have hundreds of policies and what's good about this document is that most of them aren't in it.' His memorial service in a packed Truro Cathedral was a memorable affair; as party President, I was one of the official party, with my SDP counterpart Shirley Williams. On the five-hour train journey back to London, Owen and Steel were sitting together at one table, putting together their 'shadow cabinet'. Every now and then an MP would be called over to be told his fate. There was plotting and whinging going on all over the train. If David Penhaligon could see it from above, he would have laughed his head off.

The 1987 General Election

The 1987 General Election campaign took place in May. It had been decided that a small Alliance team would plan and run the campaign. Owen included an old Labour Party warhorse and bore called Tom McNally, together with Lord Harris, the *Guardian* journalist Polly Toynbee, and the party president Shirley Williams. Steel included John Pardoe, Paul Tyler and myself. We were to meet regularly over the following few months and twice daily during the campaign. Harris and Pardoe were to be joint chairmen of the campaign. My task was to lick the Liberal Party into campaigning shape as chairman of its own General Election committee and then run the 'night team', a creature of my own creation intended to create briefing documents and draft press releases and newspaper summaries overnight ready for the daily meeting.

To keep the party in the news, Shirley Williams and I had toured the country promoting political reform. Based on a document *People in Power*, it made the case for electoral reform, a bill of rights, freedom of information, and decentralisation of power. It attracted a lot of positive publicity and we spoke to crowded halls wherever we went. Shirley and I were at this time working well together, even if there were a few hair-raising moments caused by her tendency to be disorganised.

Steel and Owen joined Shirley and I at a big press conference to drive home the constitutional reform. This, they said, was to be at the heart of the Alliance campaign. Except that it was not.

Once the campaign was under way, this, and almost every other policy, was filed away and forgotten as they for most of the time indulged in speculation about a possible balance of power, a topic they claimed to wish to avoid.

Inevitably, given the nature of the Alliance, it was a difficult campaign, and accident prone. The first setback came with our opening party political broadcast. As the main campaign manager, John Pardoe had turned out to be a tower of strength. For all his larger-than-life personality, he had no sense of self-importance and combined being suitably decisive with a capacity to encourage other opinions. He was amusing, realistic and apparently indestructible, and he performed brilliantly on radio and television. But he felt unable to impose himself on the advertising agency that was producing the broadcasts and came into our daily meeting looking distinctly nervous. 'What I've just approved,' he said, 'will either be a triumph or an unmitigated disaster.' It proved to be the latter. It consisted entirely of an appearance by an SDP by-election winner called Rosie Barnes. The opening shot was of her playing with her daughter and the family rabbit, and the rest of the broadcast consisted of a close-up on Rosie's face, and a series of what were obviously answers to questions, with the interviewer edited out, and brief fade-outs to the rabbit between each point. All everyone remembered at the end was the rabbit.

I was largely responsible for one success, albeit one that left me a bit shame-faced. The *Daily Telegraph* and the *Daily Express* led one day with reports of some extraordinary remarks by the Labour leader Neil Kinnock in an interview with David Frost who had suggested that if we didn't have nuclear weapons our forces would be subject to an unfair battle. Kinnock replied: 'Yes, what you're then suggesting is that the alternatives are between the gesture, threat, or the use of nuclear weapons – and surrender. In these circumstances the choices posed, and this is a classical choice, are between exterminating everything you stand for and the flower of your youth, or using all the resources you have to make any occupation totally untenable.'

Whatever he meant, these remarks were open, at best, to speculation, and, at worst, to misinterpretation or misrepresentation, and in an election it is wise to expect the worst. Commented the *Express* in a leading article: 'There has never been talk (in Britain) of surrender, even as a philosophical option'!

David Owen came to the following morning's meeting raring to go. He'd been wanting to take on Kinnock on defence at some point and surely 'this is it'. There was little enthusiasm because we had all hoped to move on from defence to domestic issues, but we had no choice but to accept the Kinnock gift. I suggested in a note to Owen that he should say that Labour was planning the recall of *Dad's Army* . . . Russian SS 20s *v.* Captain Mainwaring and the Home Guard!

With this we scored a hit. The *Dad's Army* line was the quote of the day. The Tory papers were particularly merciless. Building on an Owen speech, they ridiculed the Labour leader. The *Daily Mail* comment was typical: 'The idea of a latter day Dad's Army defying the mightiest military empire our continent has ever seen, beggars belief.' I should have been pleased, but actually I felt guilty; I liked Neil Kinnock and he deserved better than this.

One of our press conferences was a particular disaster. Simon Hughes was there to present our health policies. Beside the table was a mountain of computer print-outs, eight feet tall, intended to show what the waiting list for hospital beds would look like. Simon was carefully briefed to stress that these were not the real names, as these would be confidential; this was a simulation of the waiting list. Unfortunately, he did the opposite: 'These are real people,' he said, waving the top sheets of the print out at the journalists. I groaned inwardly, and Polly Toynbee who had set up the press conference and briefed Simon, went pale with horror. We both knew there was no way the reporters would let this pass. Sure enough, hardly had Simon finished than the *Evening Standard*'s then political editor Robert Carvel asked 'Where did you get the names and what do you intend to do with them?' Simon then replied that of course they were not real names. The press conference was in uproar. Paul Johnson, scenting blood, started calling out, 'So, it's phoney, it's phoney.' Others called out, 'So you're saying it's bogus?' Too late, Simon tried to explain that the print-out was there to represent the size of the list. 'Whose names are they?' cried the reporters. 'The names are irrelevant,' said Simon, digging himself ever more deeply into trouble. The press conference ended in disarray.

But our worst day occurred when the leaders contradicted themselves on the tricky question of what we would do if we held the balance of power. David Steel was not at all enthusiastic about holding the balance of power; he believed we would be the long term loser from a power-sharing arrangement and was ready to settle for a narrow Tory majority with the Alliance making an advance and positioning itself to replace Labour as the main opposition party. Owen, on the other hand, couldn't hide his impatience for power, and genuinely believed that we could negotiate a satisfactory deal if no party won a majority. Even if I misread Steel's ambitions, there's no question that he believed that tactically we could only lose from talking of a coalition, because he could see the damage caused by the widespread belief that Owen would be happy to work with Thatcher. And even if I misread David Owen's personal ambitions, it is beyond question that he believed that our main demand – proportional representation – inevitably led to coalition, and that we could only make sense if we campaigned positively for the result that was the logical conclusion of our argument. No matter who was right, what mattered was the timing. It was too soon in the campaign to be moving onto this ground.

Now, David Steel, asked whether he would back Mrs Thatcher in a hung parliament, replied, 'I find it unimaginable that there would be any circumstance in which a minority government led by Mrs Thatcher could be sustained in office by us. Her whole style and the nature of her policies is one which would not lead to the kind of compromise, the kind of search for consensus, the wider agreements, the healing of wounds that is required in this country. She would be disqualified for a whole range of reasons from leading such a government.'

This appeared to go beyond the declared position that, while we found it unimaginable that Mrs Thatcher would want to stay on, we would negotiate with the leader of whichever party had the most seats in the House of Commons. It implied that we would disqualify her, instead of she disqualifying herself.

David Owen, who had always argued that it was not for one party to choose the leader of another, initially responded to questions by saying he refused to discuss personalities or choose other party leaders, insisting that the real issue was forming a government on agreed policies. He acknow-ledged that David Steel had more determined views on Mrs Thatcher than he, but stuck to the party line that it was very hard to conceive, it was unimaginable, that Mrs Thatcher would want to serve in a coalition having lost a majority of 144 seats and having had her own way for eight years.

This was beginning to look like a split and the political media love splits. The two talked on their mobile telephones and issued a rather vague holding statement. It did little to avoid negative coverage. The following morning John Pardoe saw the leaders' security men checking their guns. 'Don't worry about assassins,' he told them, 'if you hear the leaders contradicting each other, just shoot the leaders.'

I have two memories of the end of the campaign. The first concerned Mrs Thatcher. Pressed on her view that 'there is no such thing as society', Mrs Thatcher told David Dimbleby: 'If people just drool and drivel that they care, I turn round and say "Right, I'd also like to see what you'd do?".' Dimbleby said: 'Why do you use the words "drool and drivel that they care"? Is that what you think saying you care about people's plight amounts to?' Thatcher looked stunned. 'No, I don't. I'm sorry I used those words. But I think some people talk a good deal about caring, about the policies which they pursue, and I am sorry I used those words.'

It was a striking moment, all the more so because having briefly let her guard slip once more, and suggested impatience with calls for compassion, she was at last looking vulnerable, saying she was sorry, admitting error. Asked if she had learnt any lessons from the last three weeks, she replied: 'Perhaps you have taught me one – that it is not enough to do things which result in caring. You also have to talk about it.'

My other memory is of the last night of the campaign. I sat in front of the television and saw pictures of David Steel looking tired and unenthusiastic, speaking in a shabby hall in Scotland. By contrast, at a school in his constituency in Plymouth, a defiant David Owen appeared on television still talking of his hopes of a coalition. 'On the anvil of the Cabinet table a new political metal will be forged. The Alliance will weld together the best government this country has seen for many a decade.' One had given up; one was fighting to the last breath. I thought, if ever I am sent to war, I know who I want on my side.

Battle for Power

The campaign ended with a difficult episode for me, one that was to poison my relationships with some of the Liberal and later Liberal Democratic MPs for another fifteen years. In a way it was a storm in a tea cup, but I need to tell the story because of its relevance to later events. I have already referred to my differences with the parliamentary party about their role. There had been other grumblings. Some had not liked me abstaining in the Eastbourne debate. I was seen by them as having stood with the dreaded activists, instead of the serious politicians. Some, frustrated by their obscurity in the House, resented the publicity I appeared to effortlessly attract. But none of this would have mattered if I had put myself out to butter them up, but, rightly or wrongly, I saw no reason to.

Before the General Election campaign began, I met with Owen and Steel and said that I would like to publish a diary of the campaign; would they have any objection? They did not. So within a matter of days after the polls closed it was published under the title *Battle for Power*. It is a book I remain proud of. But on the Saturday night before it came out, I was at home in Brighton and received a call from Chris Moncrieff, the veteran PA political editor. He wanted to know whether I had anything to add to the *Observer* article? 'What *Observer* article?' I asked. 'About your book,' he said, 'it's all over the front page.' I began to get an uncomfortable feeling in the pit of my stomach.

This became even more uncomfortable when I turned on the television set for the ITN News and the first item began with a picture of my book on the screen. The *Observer* headline then followed. It said: 'Liberal Chief blasts "arrogant" Owen. I had suddenly become the centre of a monumental row within and between the two Alliance parties. Robert Harris, then on the paper, had carefully selected a number of quotes which, out of context, appeared as unqualified criticisms of David Owen and had pieced them together so that the book could be represented as an attack on the SDP leader.

In fact the book was in no way an attack on Owen, as the following extract shows:

> I believe that David Owen made some misjudgements during the General Election, but we all made some, and they were borne of conviction, not of ill-intent. I believe many Liberals are unfair to David Owen; they underestimate his radicalism, they over-simplify his motives, they under-appreciate his value to the Alliance cause. As I have said earlier, he doesn't wear his heart on his sleeve, he doesn't try to be loved, and yet anyone of perception can see that the passion is there – it's there in the determination, it's there in the courage, and it's there in the sacrifices he had made. It must also be said that no one was more frustrated during the campaign than David Owen himself; he, as much as David Steel, was operating on half-power because he could not carry all of his colleagues with him on strategy. I have no doubt that he must feel now that if he is to be condemned for his strategy, he would at least have liked to put it to the full test. Abrasive and impatient, and, yes, sometimes difficult, as he is, David Owen is also a man of formidable talent and power and we should do all we can to encourage him to play a major part in a merged party.

But there was no way I was about to have a fair hearing from the parliamentary party at what was to be the nastiest meeting I have ever attended. Led by the chief whip David Alton and the former chief whip Cyril Smith, they attacked me on two grounds: first, in writing and publishing the diary 'behind their backs' I had betrayed trust; second, my alleged attack on Owen would further destabilise the Alliance. I stuck to the two points that I knew that in any rational court would be unanswerable.

The first was that, rather than betraying trust, I had been given the go-ahead to publish a diary by the two party leaders. My second point was that they were seeking to censure a book they *had not even read*. They assumed it would destabilise the Alliance, but if they had read the book they would know that was not so. I quoted three leading SDP members who only that morning had published reviews of the book, all praising my generosity towards the SDP. One of them, Ann Sofear, had even predicted that the book would be misrepresented. Saying that the *Observer* story was based on 'highly selective' quotes, she maintained 'read as a whole, as I have now had the opportunity of doing, this account is far from being a attack: it conveys a very good sense of David Owen's towering personality.'

What would the party think, I asked, if they knew that at their first meeting after the General Election they had wasted an hour attacking a book they had not even read? They all looked a bit sheepish and gradually mumbled their way towards a decision not to proceed with the vote of censure and to leave the matter there. To that extent it had been a success for me, but I had no illusions. I had not given them what they wanted, namely the satisfaction of putting me in my place. My refusal to be humbled by their attack – because that is all they really wanted, to reduce me to rubble – left them frustrated and, as we shall see, the episode was to poison relationships with the worst of them for years to come. (No less than fourteen years later, Ashdown was recording in his diaries that some of the old Guard of MPs were still referring to it.)

At that time, however, it was left there, and, while I was appalled by their illiberal and petty behaviour, I was determined not to allow it to affect what I now wanted to help make happen – because there was a much more important issue on the agenda – a possible merger between the two parties of the Alliance, the Liberals and the Social Democrats.

The Merger

Within a few days of the 1987 General Election, and while I was still President of the party, I made my position on merger clear in a final chapter of *Battle for Power* and, in doing so, was one of the first leading Liberals to make the case in full. I ended it with a call to action:

'We in the Alliance know that we could have done better in the 1987 Election – if we had devised a strategy we could sustain with passion and urgency until the end of the campaign,.. but we have all come out of the campaign in remarkable shape. We have won seven million votes.

We have a force in the House of Commons that can command attention. We have the opinion poll evidence that there are millions in Britain who wish the Alliance well, who want to believe that it is credible, and who are there to be won.

'. . . to everyone in the Alliance I say: let's put aside any minor differences: let's hammer out a merger that will work.'

Unfortunately, the person who really upset David Owen after the General Election was not me (Owen was good humoured about the book) but David Steel who, the weekend after Polling Day – and before my book was published – pre-empted any discussion between the party leaders by summonsing the television cameras to his home in Scotland and telling the world that he believed merger was now essential. What should have been obvious to Steel was that if he was going to get merger discussions off on the right foot, he had to quickly get together with Owen, if possible reach an agreement, and *then* arrange a joint call for negotiations to begin. Owen *had* to be seen to be as much a part of this historic initiative as Steel.

Steel's justification for promoting merger over David Owen's head that weekend was that Owen had implied in interviews that he would block it, and he believed a lead had to be given, echoing Macbeth's 'If it were done when 'tis done, then 'twere well it were done quickly'. Slightly in contra-diction, he also said that he did not talk to Owen because of a cock-up caused by the failure of a message to reach the SDP leader. This was hardly credible. If Steel had wanted to advise and consult properly with Owen before announcing his initiative, he could have. The cock-up was avoidable because there was no deadline to meet other than the one in Steel's head. So, given the non-applicability of the Macbeth quotation, what was the real explanation for the haste? One is that Steel had, rightly or wrongly, became so exasperated by Owen during the campaign, and so annoyed by the *Spitting Image* picture of him as Owen's puppet that he couldn't care less about antagonising Owen, in fact saw a need to lead the way to merger in order to establish himself as the genuinely bold and natural leader of the two.

Anyway, merger was the only story in town and over the summer dominated discussion in both parties. As President of the Liberal Party, and a leading advocate of merger, I devoted nearly all my time to it, consulting and working with Liberals, but also keeping in close touch with my SDP counterpart Shirley Williams and other Social Democrats.

It was over the summer that I believe David Owen made a huge personal mistake, one that not only would ultimately end his political career but have a profound effect on the merger and its aftermath. Owen made the miscalculation that he could not be elected leader of a merged party. You could understand his reasoning: There were more Liberals than Social Democrats and most Liberals did not like Owen. He thought he would lose to Steel. I have always believed he was wrong. He may not have been wildly popular within the Liberal Party, but his experience and public appeal were respected. The Liberals would by no means have unanimously opposed him.

Second, he over-estimated the popularity of David Steel, whose attitude to his own party over the years had created an element of alienation (as was proved when he discovered, after the merger, that he could not count on a majority, and had to stand down). Third, he also under-estimated the pragmatism of all involved; a merged party led by the heavyweight David Owen was likely to appear a much more formidable force than one led by Steel who was popular with the public but still perceived as a lightweight.

Some time later I met Owen at a *Spectator* party and said to him that I believed he would have been easily elected leader of the merged party; he laughed and said he did not think so. It was a big, big mistake.

In *Battle for Power* I discussed the personalities of Owen and Steel and why it was that Owen despised many Liberals as much as they disliked or feared him. As I wrote then many of Owen's problems with the Liberal Party were self-made. He had at times barely concealed his view of many Liberals as naïve, woolly, lacking in appetite for power and responsibility:

'I doubt if even Owen would pretend that in any circumstances he was an easy man to work with. He was abrasive and impatient. He could be devastatingly dismissive of others' opinions, arrogant, and moody. These characteristics did not endear him to many in his own party, let alone Liberals. Of course this was only one part of the Owen personality, but few got close enough to see the more attractive qualities. For instance, he would listen: even if he did initially attempt to brush it aside, if the advocate of a particular case had the strength to pursue it and it made sense. Owen was never too proud to be seen to change his mind. He also knew that the higher the stakes, the more you had to gamble, and he was always ready to take a risk or try a new approach. At first acquaintance, and even at the beginning of meetings with people he knew well, he could sometimes be abrupt and cold: when he relaxed, he demonstrated a surprising warmth. The point about Owen was that he was uncompromising. There was little light and shade. This was reflected in his speeches. He made little attempt to ingratiate himself with audiences, or end with a flourish to spark off a standing ovation.'

The Labour Party, aware of Liberal sensitivities, continually accused Owen of being right-wing. But it was a shallow analysis of Owen's politics. He was, in fact, a genuine radical, contemptuous of the establishment, and committed to wholesale constitutional reform.

But the main problem was his obsession with defence. It was arguable that if David Owen had never been Foreign Secretary he would have been a much more effective and popular leader of his own party and of the Alliance. But he had been Foreign Secretary and a member of the Cabinet. These were his credentials, and it is human to make your personal power base the area where you have unchallengeable authority and experience. The more Owen was asked to do radio and television interviews as a former Foreign Secretary, and write articles on major world issues, the more that base was strengthened. It is equally human to be most affronted when challenged by others in that area of authority and experience, and Owen barely disguised his view that he knew what he was talking about and that ninety per cent of Liberals (and probably ninety per cent of the rest of the population) did not. Furthermore, his pleasure in talking about the subject with which he felt most secure could at times make him sound far more hawkish than he intended. The problem was that it distorted his presentation of himself and the Alliance, so that the genuine radical and the man with an instinctive feel for the deprived was obscured from view. It was a shame because Owen's anger and impatience harnessed to the many social justice causes he genuinely shared, could have transformed his image.

Ironically, for all the Liberals' dislike of what they saw as Owen's arrogance, he was in many ways a more friendly leader than Steel, as the experienced political commentator Peter Riddell describes:

David Steel's behaviour during the conference contrasts with that of Dr David Owens, the SDP leader and reverses the common image of the two men.

Dr Owen is widely thought of as arrogant and aloof, on his own admission, not suffering fools gladly. Yet in practice he is approachable and open. He wandered around his conference in Torquay last week generally on his own, talking to any delegates and journalists he met.

For all his dominant style as leader, he is possibly the most democratic party head in his personal approach.

By contrast, Mr Steel has the more likeable image, relaxed and amusing, rather like Mr Neil Kinnock, whom he resembles in background and approach. Mr Steel is indeed agreeable and interesting company. Yet he is rather distant at a conference.

Unlike Dr Owen, he does not attend the preliminary meetings, leaving that to his entourage of staff and advisers. When he arrives, Mr Steel is seldom seen casually walking around the conference hall.

Instead, he spends much time in his hotel with advisers.

Ever since he was Liberal whip in the early 1970s Mr Steel has not disguised his impatience with some of the antics and ill-discipline of the activists.

Unfortunately Owen, unforgiving of what he believed was Steel's attempt to bounce him, hardened his heart towards merger over the summer and finally caused an uproar by writing to SDP supporters to say that 'I have no intention of being persuaded to become a member of the merged party.' As the *Sunday Telegraph* said at the time: 'He leaves them with a stark choice in which a merger with the Liberals would leave them without the man many regard as its greatest electoral and parliamentary asset.'

But, for all his power within it, Owen could not rally the SDP behind him; local parties were already merging; the SDP staff were strongly in favour; and informal polling of members showed that they were ready to vote for it. Accepting the way things were moving, having decided he could not become leader, and not wishing to find himself just another MP in a party led by a Liberal and dominated by Liberals, Owen then withdrew from the leadership of the SDP. It was the beginning of the end of a career that had initially been so dazzling – an unnecessary end in my view – based on a catastrophic misjudgement about how things would probably have turned out.

The SDP then elected Robert Maclennan as their leader, a bizarre choice. Maclennan, an uptight, tortured-looking character, had no leadership qualities whatsoever. As time would tell, he would prove a disaster. Things came to a head at the two party conferences in the Autumn of 1987.

The SDP conference came first. I had to go to Portsmouth to address it in my capacity as President of the Liberal party. In my speech I was anxious to reassure the Social Democrats that a merger would not be a takeover:

'Since the General Election I have received hundreds of telephone calls, and hundreds of letters, and have taken part in scores of conversations, and in scores of meetings, to discuss merger with the SDP. Not once . . . not once . . . has the word "takeover" ever been said. The overwhelming majority of Liberals already feel themselves to be colleagues and friends with you in the SDP . . . the drive towards merger in the Liberal Party is motivated by the practical realities, by a belief in what we have in common, by faith in our potential as one.

'We do understand what it feels like to discuss the end of a party. I, for one, love the Liberal Party . . . I am comfortable with its politics, and its members have honoured me in a way I will remember all my life. To contemplate its end, perhaps even the disappearance of the word 'Liberal' from the party title is heart-rending. So we are called upon to make a sacrifice too. And yet, I have to tell you, when it comes to the crunch, I don't find it all that difficult . . . for we all, in both parties, need to remember at this critical hour what we came into politics for . . . for political parties are vehicles for greater causes than their own survival . . .'

At this point I had to stop because this was greeted with thunderous applause. I knew then that the majority of Social Democrats there were going to support merger. Now it was the turn of the Liberals annual conference and I found myself in the extraordinary position of being the President of this famous old party and making the case that it should cease to exist:

'Never, never again must we approach an election in a state of endless debate and negotiation with ourselves, instead of dialogue with the country.

'Never, never again must we fight an election with two leaders with fundamentally different views on the objectives and strategy at the head of an uneasy coalition of two headquarters and two lots of members, with all the duplication and waste involved.

'Never, never again must we confront the country at an election divided and indecisive about our message, and afraid or unable to commit ourselves wholeheartedly to staking out our political ground and fighting on it.

'Fellow Liberals, provided there are philosophical and other reasons that justify a merger with the Social Democratic Party, the practical and organisational case is undeniable. That is why the issue of merger arose immediately after the General Election . . . that is what lies behind all that has happened this summer . . . organisationally, at least, there is no answer to the old saying "united we stand, divided we fall".

'But, of course, there are even greater issues. Not least, and we should not be apologetic about it, the difficulty we all have in contemplating the closure of our party . . . it is a huge responsibility for any generation to take upon itself . . . to end a tradition begun by illustrious predecessors in a previous century. But, no matter how much we love our party, our greater loyalty is to the wider community, to the country. It was that sense of responsibility that led to our involvement in the party in the first place.

'Also, there is a world of difference between closure of the Liberal Party and the end of liberalism . . . I don't believe anyone advocating merger would be doing so if they did not believe that the new party would draw strength from and would continue to represent the proven value of liberalism.'

Even so, I was aware that if there was to be an obstacle to merger it would be over perceived differences of philosophy and policy. So, I addressed this issue, making the point that we had just fought a General Election on a joint manifesto and surely this was a starting point for policy evolution. This point was largely passed over in the debate, and yet it was to prove crucial as the days went by.

At that conference, the Liberal party voted to initiate merger discussions and, while my Presidential year had come to an end, I was elected to be one of the negotiators. So started weeks of meetings, both of the Liberal team, and of the joint negotiating teams, as we agonised over every detail, from the name, to the role of committees etc, but all seemed to becoming to a head nicely, with all the organisation issues settled, until there occurred a monumental cock-up caused by one of two catastrophic mistakes by Maclennan.

Ignoring my initial proposal that we should adopt our General Election manifesto as the basis for policy evolution, he somehow persuaded Steel to appoint a couple of right-wing Social Democrats to produce a policy document. When they had done so he presented Steel with a copy and Steel now made his own catastrophic mistake. Never one to be concerned about policy, he didn't read it – or, at least, not properly. It contained some politically insane recommendations such as putting VAT on children's clothes. And he let it fall into the hands of the media. There was uproar. Four of the Liberal negotiators led by Michael Meadowcroft and Tony Greaves resigned. The parliamentary party went ballistic. The whole party was up in arms, and the media were having a field day. It was a fiasco. Even then Steel did not seem to think that the document was a disaster, so I dropped him a note, saying that 'the policy declaration is in my view barely literate, politically inept in electoral terms and represents a political approach that no liberal-minded or radical thinking individual could be attracted to.'

Later, after another fraught meeting in Cowley Street, I walked back to the House with Steel. 'Is it really that bad, Des?' he asked. 'Its worse, David,' I said. I went with him late that night to persuade Maclennan to withdraw it. He was looking even more tortured than usual and completely out of his depth. He initially refused. He said he would not change a word of it. He was so uptight that I said to Steel afterwards that we had better call for the men in white coats.

The following morning I was to appear on BBC *Breakfast Time* and found Maclennan there too, in the makeup room. He looked white-faced and shaky but appeared in more reasonable mood and indicated to me that he was, after all, open to some kind of compromise that would put the merger back on track. I suggested to him that a special small negotiating committee of three members from each party be asked to go away and come up with a document based on the General Election manifesto that would be a beginning point for democratic decision-making by the new party. He said that he could support that.

It was so frustrating because using the election manifesto as the basis for policy-making had been the approach I had proposed from the beginning. However, I knew that this was a significant breakthrough and immediately rang Steel and told him of the conversation and before the day was out, this plan was agreed. I was appointed to lead the Liberal team with chief whip Jim Wallace and Alan Leaman, a member of the radical Liberator group and a choice we knew would be popular with the activists in the party. McLennan appointed a former Labour minister Edmund Dell to lead his team which included McNally and the much-respected David Marquand.

While our task was to find an acceptable solution to the policy crisis, the real challenge was much greater: it was to save the merger. And we did. We met that weekend in my Citizen Action offices in Endsleigh Street under the glare of television lights and by the Sunday night had easily coalesced around a document. This we announced on the steps of the building and it led every television news bulletin and the following day's front pages.

We stated is aims as follows:

'Our 1987 Election Manifesto was designed to meet the challenges of the decade to come, and remains relevant and valuable. Our intention now is to bridge the gap between the past work and the policy-making to come and so create a starting point for the uniquely democratic yet careful deliberative policy-making process we have established for our members in our constitution. In this document we seek to do that by highlighting the shared beliefs and policies that have drawn us together while at the same time identifying those areas where early up-dating is most urgently required.'

We stuck closely to the manifesto but obviously all eyes would be on the defence section. Here we played a 'straight bat':

'We said in our 1987 manifesto that we would "maintain, with whatever necessary modernisation, our minimum nuclear deterrent until it can be negotiated away as part of a global arms negotiation process, in return for worthwhile concessions by the USSR which would enhance British and European security". We also said we would cancel Trident because it was ill-conceived as a minimum deterrent as well as being massively expensive. Unfortunately we did not win that election and by the time of the next, Trident will have been substantially paid for and will probably be ready to be deployed. The new party will, therefore, need to decide how to reconcile these changing realities with the manifesto commitment to "maintain our capability in the sense of freezing our capacity at a level no greater than that of the Polaris system".'

After a couple of irritating days while the committees of both parties met to approve it, we were back on track. Both negotiating teams gathered at a last meeting. Maclennan described it as 'a magnificent negotiation'. I could not help but smile. On the contrary, most of it had been depressingly petty and in the end he had nearly derailed it. Now he made his second catastrophic mistake, snatching defeat out of the jaws of victory. He announced he was leaving immediately by taxi to go and see David Owen and ask him to join the new party.

What on earth made him think he would succeed? Did he ever consider the disastrous rejection he was setting himself up for? No one said to this tortured man 'don't do it'. I desperately wanted to but it was clear everyone else in the room had reached the same conclusion that I was reaching, namely that he was beyond reason. He would not have listened. He took a taxi to Owen's house in the Docklands and knocked on his door. He was inside about two minutes before Owen turned him out in full view of the television cameras. He was publicly humiliated.

In a leader entitled 'A sucker for the punch', the *Guardian* said:

Recklessness is not the first quality that anybody would normally associate with Mr Robert Maclennan. But the SDP leader's capacity for pushing his political luck too far is getting to be a real liability. It was crass enough last week when he thought he could get the putative merged party to adopt a platform of policies which few Liberals could have been expected to tolerate. Now, just when Des Wilson, Edmund Dell and their colleagues seemed to have dug him and David Steel out of that hole, Mr Maclennan has been seized with another spasm of impetuosity. Anyone who knows anything about Dr David Owen knows that he is beyond reason or persuasion in his wish to separate himself from the majority of Social Democrats. For Mr Maclennan to beard him in his Limehouse lair on Monday night in the hope of signing him up in support of the Wilson-Dell package was therefore naïve. That it put Dr Owen on the defensive, showing Mr Maclennan as the man of reconciliation, was an advantage far outweighed by the humiliation which the Doctor predictably delivered to the new deal at the moment of its birth and by the free publicity which the visit handed him. Given the certainty of Dr Owen's rejection, there was something very childish about Mr Maclennan's instinctive wish to run home to show what he had done at school . . . not to mention the blustering twitterings at his press conference (afterwards).

However the *Guardian* did give credit for what our work had achieved over the weekend. Stating that the 'Wilson-Dell agreement' had given the merger renewed impetus,' it said, 'the single-minded desperation with which the Liberals and Social Democrats rewrote their policy declaration over the weekend was undeniably impressive.'

Now both parties had to meet once more to take the final decision, namely to accept the outcome of the negotiations and close the parties down in order to establish a new one. The Liberal conference took place in Blackpool the weekend after our Endsleigh Street negotiations and was a dramatic one, the final act in the long history of the Liberal party being played out before a huge, packed hall and live on television. I had to move the amendment to the original merger resolution, calling on the conference to accept the document I had helped negotiate. By now the opponents led by former MP, Michael Meadowcroft and Tony Greaves (ironically, later made a Liberal Democrat peer) had done their best to cite the discarded policy document as an indication of where we would be heading if we merged with the SDP. I set out to discredit the document: 'It's been described as being as "dead as John Cleese's parrot". Well, what did John Cleese say? "This parrot is definitely deceased. It has passed away. It has ceased to be. It is no more. It's . . . bereft of life, indubitably extinct, this is an ex-parrot!" Fellow Liberals, that document is an ex-document.'

I then made a passionate appeal to the party to rise to the challenge. The loudest applause came when I referred to the twenty or thirty years or more some of us had worked for the party to little electoral effect, and said that we had to do more than just pass that fate onto the next generation. Many others spoke, including Steel who admitted to a mistake over the policy document. And as the day went on it became clear there was overwhelming support. The resolution was carried, and subsequently the merger was endorsed by the SDP.

The Liberal Party was over. The SDP was over.

David Owen's career was over. Robert Maclennan's short-lived career as a party leader was over. David Steel's career as party leader was also about to be over. It was to be a new beginning.

The New Party

The first challenge was to elect a leader. Not surprisingly, David Steel had initially hoped that it would be him. But the handling of the issue immediately after the General Election, and the policy fiasco, had been seriously damaging, all the more so because they reflected a style of leadership, described by one Liberator critic as 'bunker leadership', whereby major decisions were taken within the leader's kitchen cabinet and office and bounced on the party.

I have already referred to Steel's preference for the media over his own party: the fact is he did not love the party he led. He undoubtedly subscribed to the Chesterton view of Liberals – 'they can't lead, they won't follow and they refuse to cooperate'. This was not my experience of the party; given the right kind of leadership they could and did achieve miracles by sheer self-sacrifice. In fact, considering his often distant, media-orientated and ungrateful style of leadership (you won't find many Liberals who remember being thanked by Steel for valiant service voluntarily rendered), the party remained remarkably loyal. To be fair, Steel himself enters a half-hearted plea of guilty to my main charges. 'I do not think I will ever be awarded full marks for either party management or pioneering policies,' he said later. 'Where I believe I made a contribution was in articulating our values and attitudes in a way which brought a huge public response. '

This was true. He was a superb television performer.

I think Steel became a classic case of power corrupting, not in a financial sense, but in the sense that his radical instincts and his willingness to act with courage to further unpopular causes were replaced by someone totally absorbed with the machinations of politics rather than its purpose. In his younger days as an MP I was a great admirer of his activities, whether it be opposing South African rugby tourists even in a rugby-mad marginal constituency, or his choice of abortion, a highly controversial issue, for his private members bill. He was an outstanding chairman of Shelter's Scottish Advisory Board.

He was not the first or the last talented and caring young Liberal MP to be made chief whip and, through that function, to move from being an issues man to a process man, and by the time he became leader in the aftermath of the Thorpe affair he had already lost much of his radical campaigning spirit. The Eastbourne defence debate underlined his isolation from his own party; he could easily have avoided it if he had been closer to the party – and he would have kept his party in better heart if he had not attacked it publicly to protect his own political face.

Yet there is much he can take credit for. He may have made mistakes, some spelled out above, but from the start, his main concern was the realignment of those on the centre left of British politics into a larger and more effective third force that would break the mould of the two-party system, and in the end it happened. In many ways he is the Liberal Democrats' lost leader. He was, at his best, the most likeable of them all, and he was immensely impressive on television and on the conference platform. If he had kept at least some of his earlier radical zeal and if he had been able to maintain a relationship with party members, he could easily have become leader of the new Liberal Democrats. Instead he ended up on the sidelines, and ultimately withdrew to Scottish politics.

I believe that Steel was persuaded by some of the MPs that I had not been a particularly helpful President; in fact, I had to frequently pick up the pieces, notably rebuilding party morale after the Eastbourne defence debate and in helping get the merger back on the road. Actually, I spent most of my Presidential year, from the first hour of my Presidency, when he attacked the party at Eastbourne, to supporting him and ensuring that the party rallied round when the votes were needed. Alas, my review in the *Spectator* of his book, containing many of the points I have made here, angered him and he now joined the other handful of MPs who were for me to become a constant irritant.

With Owen gone and Maclennan virtually a joke, the Social Democrat wing of the party had no one, apart from a too youthful Charles Kennedy, to field as a candidate for leader, so it would definitely be a former Liberal. It came down to a two-horse race, Ashdown or Alan Beith.

My first instinct was to support Beith. The MP from Berwick upon Tweed was a genuine liberal (small and large L), a decent man, approachable, a listener, more likely to be a consensus-builder within the party. His problem was that while being articulate and sound on television, he had no charisma. To put it bluntly, he came across as dull. What the new party needed was someone who would excite the public, especially those disenchanted by politics, someone with sparkle. Beith was the safe candidate; Ashdown high risk. I had dinner with Beith and found myself sympathetic to him and gave him reason to think he would have my support. But eventually I wrote to him to say that I was sorry but I felt that Ashdown had the better chance of capturing the public imagination.

So I supported the Ashdown campaign, albeit it in a preoccupied way because I had decided to run as party President. I did this partly from sheer obstinancy. The party establishment were all saying that if the leader was to be a former Liberal, then the president should be a former Social Democrat. My view was that we were now one party, and that the moment we started to take decisions on the basis of balancing people and policies between the two former parties, we were doomed; where would it stop? Should each former party have a fixed number of seats on the national executive? And so on.

Once more Leighton Andrews ran my campaign but this time the establishment opposed me to the man and woman, united behind the *Liberal leader, Social Democrat president* argument. It was that argument that prevailed. I took 38 per cent of the vote but would have done better but for a third candidate, most of whose votes would otherwise have come to me. So former SDP MP Ian Wrigglesworth became President (and to be fair, did it well).

Afterwards, one of the Liberator Group who produced the party conference revue, satirised my response: 'I can accept my defeat as President . . .

with an ex-Liberal leader and an ex-SDP president, we can now proudly say that, after merger, we are two parties.'

But, back to the Ashdown campaign. The older MPs could not see why this relative newcomer should emerge as the boss; the younger ones could not see why it should not be them. This turned nasty when they leaked a vicious anonymous letter they had circulated attacking the Yeovil MP. It provided 10 reasons why people should oppose him.

In a front page lead story, the *Independent* reported:

> Some points in the document are virulent in their contempt for Mr Ashdown's record and reputation. The paper says: 'Charisma can soon become boring if the shadow is not backed by substance: Beith has real political weight and substance.'
>
> Mr Ashdown is accused of a 'shocking record' on defence policy, having 'held three different views in 1986, in an attempt to be all things to all men'.
>
> The paper also reiterates the long-standing complaint that the former commando and diplomat is a loner. Mr Ashdown is further accused of a 'lack of general political experience as compared with Beith'; of 'poor understanding of economic policy and alternatives'; and of having a 'reputation as a poor debater in the House' because he 'concentrates on confrontation rather than argument'. Point nine states: 'Ashdown has a poor sense of humour, if any.' In contrast, Mr Beith's supporters are urged to make the most of their candidate being a Methodist, because 'abstemious godliness is a quality, not a disqualification'.

It was incredible that members of the parliamentary party could not be satisfied with circulating such a vicious attack among themselves, but had to make it public and so reveal the extent they would go to undermine one of their own. I was quoted in the newspaper as saying that 'this dishonest and vicious attack reflects badly only on its perpetrators'. In fact, to me none of it was surprising. It merely reflected my own experience of the viciousness of some of them, and the envy and jealousy of anyone who was achieving more notice than them. Welcome to the club, Paddy.

I realised that it was almost impossible for Ashdown to answer this attack directly and, feeling I had little to lose, decided to answer for him. That night Alex Carlisle (a Welsh MP who reminded me of Cassius – 'he of the lean and hungry look') appeared on *Newsnight* but only after insisting on a promise from the programme that he would not be asked about the authorship of the note. I was asked to appear with him and had every intention of confronting him head on with a demand to know whether he was one of those responsible, but Ashdown, who was maintaining a mature and statesmanlike silence, asked me not to and I reluctantly acceded to his request. It's a shame as Alex never got the chance to deny his involvement, as surely he would have wanted to do . . .

Come the day, the party ignored the parliamentary party completely and Ashdown won the leadership easily and became the first leader of the new party. With a few months he must have wished he had not bothered. He inherited a party that was on the brink of bankruptcy. To save it financially, he had to make brutal cuts, involving the redundancies of twelve of the thirteen campaign team, only Chris Rennard being kept.

Politically, it had been damaged in the public mind by the messy merger negotiations. Ashdown had to be constantly watching his back with the parliamentary party, who both opposed many of his ideas and treated him with disrespect at meetings. And he was finding it difficult to be taken seriously in the House of Commons. The whole enterprise just simply could not get off the ground. The party sank to only four points in the opinion polls . . . taking into account the three point margin of error, that could have been only one per cent. It all came to a head at the first electoral hurdle, the European elections: the new party polled only six per cent, and was humiliated by the Greens who took sixteen. There was a real danger that the party was over – before it had even begun.

17

Twenty MPs – Twenty per cent of the Popular Vote

> What we need is a rescue operation – a campaign to
> save the party.   ARCHY KIRKWOOD MP

I had come second only to Charles Kennedy in the election of the new party's executive, but from the first meeting found myself in difficulty. Ashdown had made an attempt to win back Owen and end the nuisance of the SDP by proposing that the new party (now called the Social and Liberal Democrats) and the Owenites engage in joint open selection for parliamentary candidates. This silly proposal was made without reference to the party executive or the parliamentary party, both of whom were deeply unhappy, not only by its nature but also by the way it was done. This bouncing of the party was just the leadership-from-the-bunker style that David Steel had been accused of, and I shared the view that it was an approach to the leadership of the new party that had to be stifled at birth.

I made my views clear at that first executive meeting, but Ashdown had some support, led by Tom McNally, who appeared to have only one approach to any debate, and that was to put the boot in. At a further meeting he and I clashed strongly and the meeting almost came to a halt. What was making my position impossible was that McNally kept implying that I was being 'difficult' because I lost the Presidential election. This was complete nonsense but it was damaging, and the effect of it was, as intended, to weaken my case.

It should be stressed that all my contributions to the party – the Presidential year, involvement in the General Election, promotion of the merger – had been as a volunteer. I was not paid. Yet my contribution was virtually full-time. In fact, I was performing two full-time tasks simultaneously, because this was also a particularly busy time at Citizen Action. Given that you're a volunteer, it is, I suppose, human nature to spend your time where you're welcome, so inevitably I now spent more and more time at Endsleigh Street, becoming increasingly preoccupied with our campaigns there, especially the Campaign for Freedom of Information. I did not stand for the Liberal Democrat executive after the first year and for some time watched what was happening to the party from afar. It was not encouraging.

The public image of the new party was still affected by the spectacle of the disarray during the merger process. Owen was still chipping away from the sidelines. Ashdown was being laughed at in the House, and ignored outside it. The parliamentary party, riven with the petty jealousies I knew only too well, were giving him a hard time (as I've said, the Ashdown diaries contain many references to dreadful parliamentary party meetings.) The party still had little money. And all of this was reflected in the catastrophic 1990 European elections when the party was overtaken by the Greens.

Most people in British politics assumed the General Election would take place in the Spring of 1991. In the Autumn of 1989, with probably just one year left, Ashdown was becoming desperate. The party had picked up a couple of opinion poll points, but, with few resources to fight with, his understandable fear was that after thirteen years of Tory rule, the country would so badly want a change that it would sweep the newly-professional Labour Party to power in a landslide, wiping out the Liberal Democrats in the process.

The 1989 Liberal Assembly was held in Brighton where Jane and I were living and on the Friday night, when it was all over, Archy Kirkwood came for dinner. Archy was one of the few Liberal MPs I really liked, a man incapable of the malice and malevolence of some of his colleagues. We had always worked well together within the party and he had been co-chairman of my Presidential bid. He had also helped in my other campaigns and steered two of the Campaign for Freedom of Information's private members' bills into law. It was good to see him.

After dinner he revealed his mission. It was to sound me out about running the party's first General Election campaign. I responded cautiously. My first thought was that I was being offered a poisoned chalice. Ashdown would not have asked Archy to put out feelers to me unless he had no alternative. He was having enough difficulty controlling his unruly parliamentary party without this. (In fact this was later confirmed when he wrote in his diaries that there would be an 'explosion' from most of the Parliamentary Party and the Party establishment if he appointed me.)

I did not spare poor Archy the bad news: The party was in terrible trouble. It was still in single figures in the polls. There was no voter base to build upon. There was no money. There was no national organisation of note: the party did not even exist in some constituencies. And there was no chance of wholehearted support for me from the parliamentary party, where some remained who, I contended, were unworthy of re-election anyway. To put it bluntly this was a loser. As I had my own campaigns and was enjoying them and achieving real results, why on earth should I do it?

Archy listened to what must have been a depressing review of the party's position with impressive patience and said simply: 'Des, no one is saying that we can win. That's not what this is about. What we need is a rescue operation. A campaign to save the party. This is about survival.' He now moved his ground, and gently, but rightly, pointed out that I had some obligation. I was the President of the Liberal party that helped to sell the merger. When the negotiations ran into trouble, I helped save the merger. And I was one of the movers of the merger resolution at the decisive party conference. To turn my back on it now would be the equivalent of helping to launch a ship and then watching it sink while making no attempt to save it or the passengers.

I did not send Archy away without hope. Apart from the fact that I liked him too much to send him miserable into the night, he had touched me with references to my relationship with the party as a whole. I recalled the pride I had felt when they elected me their President. Now they were coming to me and asking me to give them the one thing I had to offer – my experience as a campaigner.

There was another related factor, one that was personal to me: when all was said and done, I *was* a campaigner and this *was* a General Election campaign, a fantastic opportunity to put into practice for one last time all that I knew and all that I could do on the biggest stage of all. I felt like an athlete who had been on the point of retiring and suddenly found himself with the chance to compete in the Olympics. If I turned down the challenge, no matter how tough, would I ever forgive myself? So I said to Archy that I would not rule it out but there would have to be some tough conditions. The main one would have to be that I was genuinely in control of the campaign.

This was not about power, position, or prestige. If I was likely to be held responsible if we failed, I at least, wanted all the conditions in place to give me a chance of success, and genuine control over the campaign – the freedom to run it in my way – would be a prerequisite of success. This was not an outrageous condition; on the contrary, I was reflecting a decision already taken by the party itself – that the campaign would have 'a single controlling head with ultimate responsibility.' So all I now was asking for was an assurance that this decision would be adhered to.

A number of weeks slipped by and then Archy phoned and asked me if I would have dinner with him and Ashdown and we duly met for dinner at a corner table at Joe Allens in Covent Garden. I could tell Ashdown was on edge, even defensive, and after a few pleasantries he abruptly said, 'Well, what about the General Election?' Then he added: 'There's no money. We can't pay you.'

I told him that was no problem: my acceptance was conditional on being unpaid. He looked surprised. I explained I had believed from the start that my main problem would be his unruly parliamentary party. I had to make them powerless to undermine me or the campaign. I had to be unpaid so that they would not be able to treat me as an employee, and I had to have the authority that came from complete independence from them.

We talked about personnel. How did I feel about Alec McGivan an experienced ex-SDP man, as my deputy? I said he would be more than acceptable. He asked me how I felt about Richard Holme, his most trusted advisor and friend. It was assumed within the party that Holme and I did not get on. I reassured him; I respected Holme's political instincts and skills. He could be on the team. He then raised the name of McNally. I told him no way. I didn't respect him and did not want to waste my time in debates with him. 'Tell him to go away and put the boot into someone else.' He made a lot of notes and went away to think about it.

A little time passed and then he and Archy and I met once more at Joe Allens. It was now clear to me that he wanted me to do it, but he now admitted there would be hell to pay from some of the parliamentary party.

I said I could not care less. That was his problem. Once the deal was made, I would be beyond their control; they would either play a constructive part or I would ignore them. He looked a little taken aback at this but eventually we shook hands on the deal. Then came his final question: what did I think we could achieve? 'Well, you won't be in Number 10, if that's what you mean,' I said. 'But I see no reason why we can't at least hold the status quo – 20 seats and close to 20 per cent of the popular vote.' From that moment, 20/20 became my objective.

The *Guardian* later summed up the deal:

Ashdown wanted Wilson to have the job. Wilson accepted on the under-standing that there would be a formal written contract, that he could pick his own team and that he would receive no pay. Wilson is, above all, a man who likes to do things his own way and the value of these conditions is that they divest him of unwelcome obligations: they enshrine his authority, ensure his independence and, crucially, insulate his relationship with the leader.

Needless to say, the expected complaints came out of the parliamentary woodwork. Steel wrote a letter to Ashdown saying that he was strongly opposed and would spend most of his time in Scotland. He made himself look petty by attaching to his letter the rather critical review of his book that I had written for the *Spectator*, an admission that his views were based on personal pique rather than any issue of substance. Cyril Smith wrote a typically violent letter to the leader: 'Dear Paddy, I wish to register my STRONGEST POSSIBLE OBJECTIONS to Des Wilson heading the general Election team and I will NOT be prepared to assist nationally if he does so, yours sincerely, Sir Cyril Smith MBE, MP. He then added in his own handwriting: 'Count me out ! . . . I'm disgusted and will say so publicly.'

Unfortunately for these two and the other malcontents, the balance of power had changed. I was now in control with all the levers in my hands. Their views were irrelevant. I did think it extraordinary though that with the party on the rocks, these two prima donnas were prepared to put the whole enterprise at risk by refusing cooperation with the leader's choice of campaign director out of personal pique. As for the party in the country, it made clear in many ways that it was pleased and relieved. It was announced at the party's 1990 Spring Conference in Cardiff and when I walked onto the platform for the opening night rally I was rapturously received.

It was an emotional moment: I was deeply flattered by their confidence, by what could only be described as a sense of relief welling up in the room – relief that I was there. But, perhaps for the first time in my career, I also felt real apprehension. There was too much need. There was too much expectation. Did they know how hard this was going to be? Not only for me, but them? Of course, Ashdown, as leader, had the most at stake. But it was I who now had to deliver for him – and for the party. And if we failed, there was no question who the malcontent MPs would ensure got the blame. What had I done?

The Rescue Operation: preparing the plan

I did what I always did before a campaign. I went away alone to plan. This could not be a conventional General Election campaign. This was not about winning. So what was it about?

If it was a rescue operation, if it was about survival, as both Paddy Ashdown and Archy Kirkwood had said it was, then what did rescue and survival mean?

I decided it had to be about two things – a decent result and hope for the future: First, there had to be a respectable result at the General Election. The party had to emerge with political credibility. It had to be seen to exist; to me that meant no less than achieving the result I had promised to Ashdown at Joe Allens: 20 per cent of the popular vote and 20 seats. But even that would not be enough. For the party to survive and flourish it had to do better: it had to emerge with real hope for the longer term. To achieve this I had to create what I called a 'developmental election', one that was as much about re-laying the foundations and building the structure of the party as about achieving the immediate electoral result.

I now set about writing a 90-page campaign plan that was to form the basis of an hour and a half presentation I was to make, first to my chosen election team, then to the parliamentary party. I wanted it to be comprehensive and innovative. At least I knew there were some talented and hard-working people around to help me make it happen. To carry out the huge task of achieving the organisation on the ground I turned to an experienced former Liberal, Tim Clement-Jones (now Lord Clement-Jones).

Liberal Democrat News

o. 99   9th March 1990   *The paper of the Social and Liberal Democrats*   60p

Paper makes news!

HE four-page FOCUS supplement carried in this ek's *Liberal Democrat ws* will have a readership xcess of a quarter of a lion.

t the close of sales on esday afternoon, more n 110,000 copies of the CUS had been ordered by al parties for door-to-door tribution, taking news of campaign against Poll k to homes as far apart as ro and Aberdeen.

iberal Democrat News tor Mike Harskin says: e have been rwhelmed with the ponse. It is important that Party newspaper has a npaigning role in a npaigning Party. It is good t we can contribute to al election campaigns oss England, Scotland I Wales in this way."

reliminary figures from *eral Democrat News* for last financial year show paper making a profit for Party of several thousand nds. The accounts are yet e audited, along with the in Party accounts, for sentation to the ptember Conference in ckpool.

Des will lead election team

DES WILSON is to direct the Liberal Democrats' General Election campaign.

His appointment was revealed yesterday, Thursday, by Paddy Ashdown MP and takes effect immediately.

The post will carry sole authority for planning and directing the campaign, including the deployment of staff and financial resources.

In an exclusive interview with *Liberal Democrat News* this week, Des Wilson explains that he agreed to take on the job only after receiving an assurance that he would have "the authority and freedom to succeed."

Distinctive

He promises a "confident, distinctive and surprising" campaign.

Des Wilson will chair two new groups set up to co-ordinate the General Election efforts of the Party. The 'Planning Group' will consist of a team of professionals selected by Des, alongside Paddy Ashdown as Leader, Jim Wallace MP, Archy Kirkwood MP and Graham Elson (as Chief Whip, Chair of the Campaigns Committee and General Secretary respectively).

A smaller Finance Group will deal with financing campaign.

Des Wilson's first action as Campaign Director was to announce the

appointment of former SDP National Organiser Alec McGivan as his deputy.

Paddy Ashdown, Leader of the Liberal Democrats, said on Thursday: "I know the whole Party will be delighted that our campaign will be in the hands of such an able and experienced team of Des Wilson and Alec McGivan."

The first director of Shelter, the campaign for the homeless, and Chair of Friends of the Earth from 1983-86, Des Wilson was named 'Environmentalist of the Decade' by ITN's awards programme on New Year's Eve.

He is also a former President of the Liberal Party and fought Hove in the famous by-election of 1973, shredding a Conservative majority of almost 19,000 to one of just more than 4,000.

In 1987 he was a member of the Alliance's General Election committee, and responsible for the innovative all-night planning and strategy teams throughout that campaign.

Des Wilson's details:

1941 Born, New Zealand	1978 Author of 'So You Want to be Prime Minister'	1987 Member of Liberal-SDP merger team
1967 Director of *Shelter*		● In addition, Des is Chair of Citizens Action, Co-Chair of the Campaign for Freedom of Information, Chair of the Citizen Action Compensation Campaign and Chair of Parents Against Tobacco, his latest campaign.
1968 Regular *Guardian* columnist	1981 Established CLEAR, Campaign for Lead Free Air	
1971 Editor of *Social Work Today*	1983 Chair of Friends of the Earth	
1973 Fought Hove by-election for the Liberals	1986 President of the Liberal Party	

Ashdown reshuffles Parliamentary pack

SIMON Hughes is to become the Party's new spokesperson on the Environment following a mini-reshuffle announced by Paddy Ashdown on Monday evening.

He moves from Educatio to a role he has often been identified with as one of Parliament's 'greenest' MPs with a long track record of environmental campaigning.

Matthew Taylor moves to Education, and his place at Trade and Industry will be taken by Lord Ezra, former Chairman of the National Coal Board.

And Malcolm Bruce moves from Environment to team up with Ray Michie to speak on Scottish affairs.

Alan Beith and Menzies Campbell will add Trade and Industry matters to their present portfolios in the Commons. Menzies Campbell has also recently joined the Trade and Industry Select Committee.

Speaking at a public meeting in Edinburgh, Paddy Ashdown stressed the importance he gave to ensuring a strong voice for Scotland from the Liberal Democrat benches in Westminster.

He said: "I believe that these changes will considerably enhance our effectiveness, both in Scotland and at Westminster and I look forward to increased success for the

Liberal Democrats in Scotland."

Malcolm Bruce combines his new role as spokesperson on Scottish Affairs with leading the Scottish Liberal Democrats. And Ashdown added: "With Malcolm and Ray Michie both speaking for Scotland, we have a powerful team."

The announcement is timed to coincide with the decision of the Scottish Labour Party on adopting a system of proportional representation for a future Scottish Parliament.

The reshuffle takes effect from the start of Parliament's Easter recess on Thursday, April 5.

Tim was company lawyer for Kingfisher, a man of unlimited enthusiasm and energy, and he was to perform magnificently. (At one point Kingfisher took exception to some remark I made and asked its company lawyer, Tim Clement-Jones, to write to me complaining; I then asked a party lawyer, namely, Tim Clement-Jones, to reply. He loyally wrote both letters!)

Tim and his team were asked to set a specific objective for every constituency. The aim was to field a candidate everywhere and to use the local campaigns to recruit members and accumulate resources for the longer-term. This he did brilliantly and thus laid the foundations for greater success at General Elections to follow. In this he was ably supported by Chris Rennard, who had an astonishing record of by-election success, and had become an authority on assessing the potential of seats; he took charge of our target seats campaign and went on to be a key player as the party in later elections concentrated more and more of its efforts on these seats and as a result began to win a substantial number of them. Not well-known outside of Westminster, Chris is respected by his own party, other parties, and the political media alike as one of the most astute of the country's political operators.

As communications director I appointed a bright former Young Liberal called Olly Grender. She, too, did brilliantly. Alec McGivan would be my deputy, Richard Holme would produce the manifesto, and some of our best party 'gunslingers', Gavin Grant, Simon Titley, John Read, would organise the leader's tour and the rallies.

In the preamble to the plan I spelt out the size of the task:

1 We may well begin the campaign in single figures in the polls, and these polls could
   (a) adversely affect our media coverage as the election is perceived and promoted as a 2-horse race.
   (b) increase our traditional "wasted vote" problem.
   (c) adversely affect our ability to raise money and motivate support generally.
1:2 Our resources will be a fraction of those available to the two main parties. This will:
   (a) make it comparatively difficult for us to make an impact.
   (b) create the danger that we look comparatively down at heel.

(c) Rule out activities/initiatives our workers hope for or expect, possibly causing a corresponding fall in morale.

1:3 We will be considerably hampered by our own weaknesses – notably:

- few 'saleable' national figures (i.e. could we really run the country?)
- uneven strength on the ground
- the legacy of merger difficulties
- no established constituency of support
- the popular perception that we're a wasted vote

We would fight every seat. In particular, we would resist the temptation to hope for some kind of deal with Labour. 'Pursuing deals isn't necessary, won't work, and is essentially negative and is contrary to the whole approach of our campaign.'

A controversial element was the timing of the morning press conference in London. I was determined that ours would be the first one and thus have the best share of the morning radio and television coverage but Labour and the Conservatives countered this by fixing times for theirs that were very early. To beat them we would have to have ours at 7.15 a.m. and I was told, not least by the journalists themselves, they would simply not turn up at that hour. I ignored them, taking the view that when push came to shove, they would have no choice. Were they really going to tell their editors that they were missing our press conference because they would not get out of bed early enough? How would they defend themselves if they missed a big story? In fact, they did turn up and the objective, to take the initiative from the other parties every morning, was achieved.

Ashdown called his parliamentary party to a meeting at the National Liberal Club to hear the plan. Their behaviour was typical. Steel did not even attend, but other of the malcontents, like Alex Carlisle and Russell Johnston, deliberately turned up late, talking loudly as they came into the room while I was in mid-presentation. I completely ignored them and as the 90 minutes ticked by they were cowed into sullen silence by the sheer extent of detail and by an inability to find fault.

In so much as they had the chance to demolish the plan and couldn't, they, by virtue of not opposing it, endorsed it.

The *Guardian* picked up on the mood in a profile of me:

Part of the problem for Wilson's critics is that they see him as an autocrat and inveterate self-publicist, a non-politician who gets on television more often than they do. Another is that he is not, and never has been, the sort to flinch from getting up the establishment's – any establishment's – nose. Wilson offers stout defence to such charges: 'Yes, I court publicity. It is the lifeblood of the business I am in. But it's purely business. It's not personal.' Further, he insists, his incursions are guided only by the imperatives of broader strategy – 'this party is not used to strong direction' – and he has no doubt they are inevitable if the greater good is to triumph.

So we were all set to go. Soon we had candidates in every seat, a record number of them women. We were hitting out fundraising targets. The team was in place and working well. A coherent message was beginning to get through. We were beginning to rise in the polls. The 1990 party conference was a resounding success. Thanks to the efforts of its new chief executive Graham Elson and his team and the conference committee, the party looked professional and credible. My own first conference speech as campaign director for the General Election was well-received.

The months passed, then a year, and there was still no General Election. In one way I was pleased; with every month we were building up our resources and perfecting our plan – and rising in the polls. In another way I was discomforted; my determination to be unpaid meant that I was running down my resources. I had to ask Jane to do more than her share (politicians' wives make huge sacrifices and never get any credit). Six or seven years earlier I had found the money to buy a small flat in Spain and I loved going there; now it had to be sold. My refusal to be paid had cemented my control, but at an increasingly heavy personal price.

The 1991 conference was critical and it went fairly well. For the second consecutive year my speech won a standing ovation. The *Guardian*'s Hugo Young, who had been so kind about my Presidential speech back in 1986, gave me another boost:

'There was something almost anarchic about Mr Wilson's manifesto yesterday. The demagogic gleam in his eye might have been calculated to infuriate the primmer members of the parliamentary party, and their response was noticeably more restrained than the roars from the floor. Besides, there are a few contradictions to be worked out if this thing gets serious. Stable government, for example, is touted as the prime good that will come of it: not a commodity obviously consistent with such root-and-branch terrorising of the status quo.

All the same, the message is a sound one. What Mr Wilson had to say about the condition of politics was largely true, and is likely to become still truer if we wake up and find ourselves in the middle of two decades of one-party government. More relevantly, the message connects. It is not hurled into the void of good intentions. It supplies a hard reason for voting Liberal Democrat.'

Could the parliamentary malcontents contain their envy and bile? No way. The next day the *Guardian* reported:

There was a feeling among MPs that the speech overstepped the demarcation line between organisation and politics by an un-reconstructed Liberal of the 1960s school. 'Only flower power was missing,' a senior MP sniffed.

What some of Paddy Ashdown's colleagues fear is that Mr Wilson's populist instincts and strong political views may encroach on the leader's role in the coming election campaign to create the sort of confusions that dogged the two Davids – Steel and Owen – in 1987.

However, the *Guardian* added:

On the face of it the risk is remote since Mr Wilson, former director of Shelter and many other pressure-group campaigns, is not even an MP, and his critics admit he is a brilliant organiser who has put the party machine streets ahead of where it was before Mr Ashdown appointed him . . .

The so-called fears of the MPs concerned were, of course, a nonsense. Whatever reservations I was to develop about Ashdown never got in the way of the deal we had made, that he would run the party and speak for it, and that I would run the campaign and speak for it. To his credit, he kept his promises about our relationship, as did I, and he took no nonsense from the MPs. In nearly two years of partnership at the head of the party, he as leader and me in charge of mobilising its resources for its first great electoral test, we never once had an argument about who did what or about the strategy of either the party or the campaign.

What was it about these people who, when the party was being so united and full of optimism, and when so much was at stake, simply could not control their need to cause harm? As a student of British politics from the Sixties, I have never ceased to be amazed at how politicians have allowed petty jealousies and bitter rivalries to take precedence over what was right for the party and country. Harold Wilson, whilst trying to run the country, had to deal with a lot of back-biting, not least the extraordinarily disloyal, intemperate, and often drunken behaviour of his deputy George Brown. John Major was undermined by the Euro-sceptics and other critics in his party to the point where he was forced to call an election to re-establish his authority; they finally destroyed his party's chance of re-election. Tony Blair lived for years with a brutal campaign to force him out by Gordon Brown. Brown himself lived with almost weekly stories about one attempted coup or initiative to force him out of office.

I have often reflected on the good-humoured comradeship and unity that existed in all of my non-party-political pressure group campaigns; in these, everyone understood my role. I never had one row with anyone in all the years I was involved in them, and I have often speculated on what this says about the difference between politics and the voluntary sector. I have come to the conclusion that, in politics, so much of the destructive inter-action between those supposedly on the same side surely derives from ambition, jealousy and the needs of self; in the voluntary sector, so much of the harmony and good nature surely derives from a focus on higher goals – the needs of others.

When later I was to work in business I was once more struck by the generally constructive and cooperative approach of those I worked with. Indeed, I was once asked about the fundamental difference between working in business and working in politics and replied: 'If you are walking down the road and you see a man lying on the pavement full of bullet holes, how do you know whether he is business or politics? The answer is if the bullet holes are in his front, he's in business; if they're in his back, he's in politics.'

It is notable that this debilitating and petty behaviour is nearly always at the top. I never had a problem with the Liberal Party as a whole; on the contrary, the evidence of my popularity is overwhelming. I always either topped or nearly topped the poll in party elections, was elected Party President unanimously, and was given 100 per cent support throughout the country for the General Election. As President and then General Election campaign director I went and spoke to hundreds of constituency dinners and was always given a wonderfully warm welcome.

It is an honour to be elected by your fellow citizens to anything; it was a particular honour to be repeatedly entrusted with influence by people who had worked so hard and sacrificed so much over so many years for the political cause they believed in. I may not have fond memories of all the parliamentary party, but I felt only liking for, and loyalty to the party as a whole.

Paddy Pantsdown

As someone wrote: 'fiction has to avoid bizarre coincidence; real life doesn't.' I'm no stranger to coincidence, but have never experienced a greater one than occurred on the evening of January 28, 1992. Ashdown and I were having a planning meeting over a Chinese takeaway in his flat in south London (he also had a home in Yeovil and another in France). After we finished both our discussion and the takeaway, we talked about the trials and tribulations caused to Bill Clinton by his involvement with women and in particular the Jennifer Flowers affair. Ashdown said to me: 'It's time someone stood up to the media's intrusion into the private lives of public figures. If ever it happened to me, I would defend my right to a private life. I would take them on. I would face them down.'

Now to the coincidence: *at that precise moment* the phone on the wall beside me rang, causing me to jump. Ashdown answered and expressed some surprise at the caller's identity and then went very quiet and, after a few moments, said 'Let me think about this. I'll call you back.' I could tell he didn't want to share the details with me, and, anyway, it was late, so I left.

At the time I was sometimes staying at the Royal Horseguards Hotel. This was beside the National Liberal Club in Whitehall Place, with a side entrance directly into it, and was to be our base for the General Election.

Having left Ashdown, I went back there, only to be woken by him early the following morning. Could he call in on his way to the House of Commons and have a word? I knew immediately this must be to do with the phone call the previous evening, and when he turned up, it all came out: four years earlier, he had had a brief affair with his former secretary Tricia Howard. It was she who had been on the phone. Even as Ashdown had been spelling out to me how he would approach a Clinton-type crisis, the *News of the World* had been at her door. They appeared to have the whole story. Ashdown says in his diary that I acted 'typically well'. In fact I was shocked – not by his behaviour – that was his business – but by the fact that we were now weeks away from the General Election and I could not at that moment begin to imagine how it would play out.

At this point only Ashdown and I knew about this, and he asked me to keep it that way (he has subsequently published his account of the whole affair, so I feel free to do the same. I will identify where our accounts differ.) He also asked me to accompany him to a meeting at the office of Andrew Phillips, a veteran Liberal (now Lord Phillips), who often advised the party on legal matters and was Ashdown's personal solicitor. While I waited for the meeting I went for a stroll on the banks of the Thames and tried to put it into perspective.

According to him, it had been a brief affair five years earlier, before he was elected party leader. This could not be too bad. It definitely did not represent a reason for resignation. Also, having observed political life on both sides of the Atlantic for over thirty years, I knew that it was nearly always not the sin that caused a crisis but the mishandling of its revelation. A candid, contrite admission was manageable; a cover-up rarely was. So if Ashdown was still of the same mind that he had been when we discussed the Clinton affair, it was possible he could deal with the potential media coverage quickly and effectively by, to use his words, 'facing them down'.

My guess was that if it was handled well it would be more personally than politically embarrassing. Above all I was convinced that it was only a scoop for a newspaper if it broke the story first for such a story could run for several days. But a frank admission of all the details, an apology to those affected, and then a show of determination to 'move on', gave the media little to play with. So Ashdown had to take the initiative.

Clear in my mind what we had to do, I joined Ashdown at the meeting with Andrew Phillips. There came a surprise, for, if anyone was contrite, it was Phillips. It turned out that there had been a threat of publicity of this affair a couple of years earlier and that Ashdown had called on Phillips for advice. The solicitor had placed a note of the meeting in his safe. Now he told us that only recently his offices and safe had been broken into and the contents, both money and documents, stolen. The irony was that he had put the Ashdown note in there for 'safekeeping'; had he just filed it in the ordinary way under 'A for ASHDOWN' in a filing cabinet, it would not have been found because the thieves had, of course, only been after what was in the safe.

In any case, the thieves, reviewing their haul, had stumbled across the Ashdown note and realised they were sitting on a potential goldmine. And so it was that the *News of the World* was now its proud owner. However, said Phillips, there was a positive aspect of this; because the document had been stolen, it was probable that we could obtain an injunction preventing its publication. This would probably only be a holding operation but it would create time for us to develop a strategy and brief everyone who needed to know. At this point the Ashdown 'I would face them down' policy went out the window. He did not appear to see that this was, as Phillips had said, just a holding tactic; instead, he clearly believed there was a chance it could all be contained. In fact in his diary he admits this, saying it was a 'triumph of hope over expectation'.

Over the following 24 hours two things happened: first, the *News of the World* offered Tricia a substantial sum of money (I think £50,000) for her story and to her great credit she turned them away; second, the paper contacted Phillips to confirm his signature on the note, thus itself confirming how it had obtained the document and making the injunction more likely to be granted. By now the matter was the only one on Ashdown and my agendas. I have to admit I was myself of two minds. On the one hand, I still believed we should break the story ourselves. There was no question that this was politically the right thing to do. On the other, I could not but feel for Ashdown who was going through hell and clearly desperately hoping the injunction would save him.

In his diary Ashdown claims that I was 'overjoyed' at the probability of an injunction; I fear what he was actually hearing was what I knew he wanted to hear, because I had come to the conclusion that for his sake, as a human being, husband and father, rather than our leader, we had to give the outcome he desired a chance to work. By now Ashdown was facing up to the fact that he would have to tell his wife Jane, his family, and probably his closest constituency officers, many of them friends. Indeed, it appeared to me that he was far more concerned about having to share the story with Jane and the others than he was concerned about the media or the public. To me this was understandable; given my view of the whole matter, I felt that if there was any lasting damage, it would be to his personal relationships, not his political standing.

On the Thursday afternoon we met with Tricia in Phillips' office. It was the first time I had met her and my first thought was how unlike the tabloids' idea of a 'mistress' she looked. This was no Jennifer Flowers, attractive and assured; this was a nice-looking but hardly glamorous woman who looked hopelessly out of her depth and desperate for support and reassurance. (Jane Ashdown was later, in an unguarded moment, to describe her as 'looking like an old trout'; this was unfair, an understandable but rather catastrophic contribution to the handling of the matter.) I had the task of telling her that from now on she could not be in direct touch with Ashdown. There were too many dangers. She would have Phillips's full support and she could contact me whenever she liked. (She did, indeed, phone me once or twice and I developed considerable respect for the courage she was showing.)

Later that day a judge granted an injunction. It included forcing the newspaper to name its source and the police were preparing to move in on the thieves (not that this was much help to us).

By Friday it was clear that the whole of Fleet Street was aware of the story. Everywhere I went I could sense the close looks. We were being tipped off of all sorts of possible stories. Sure enough, on the Sunday the *News of the World* ran a clever story about the theft of sensitive documents involving a senior politician from the office of a solicitor. Others picked up on the story. Newspapers have their own way of hinting at the truth: they print a story without a name, and then, 'by sheer coincidence', a picture of the relevant personality appears with another story close by. The ordinary reader may not pick up on the link between the story and the picture, but the rest of the media and the country's political life undoubtedly can. Now the *Independent* did just that.

We now made what I believe was our only major mistake in handling the whole affair. We took Phillips' advice to widen the injunction to all of the media. What I did not realise, and I don't know whether Ashdown did, was that the terms of the injunction would include all the details. So we were doing two things: first, we were confirming the whole story to all of the media in maximum detail; second, we were now being clearly seen to be engaged in a cover-up, the very thing Ashdown had said to me he would not do just seconds before Tricia's call the previous Tuesday and the one thing that I had calculated would make the position worse.

By the end of that day I knew this had been a mistake. I recall being at a party in Whitehall, trying to keep up appearances, when the late Peter Jenkins of the *Guardian* took me aside. 'Des, you are going to have to come clean,' he said. 'Your position is unsustainable and with every day its getting worse.' I knew he was right. Now the media were crowding Ashdown wherever he went. An innocuous speech to the coal industry, usually unlikely to be attended by even one journalist, other, perhaps, than the editor of *Coal News*, was packed with reporters and photographers. It was time to use the space the injunction had bought to get ourselves in shape. Ashdown began to widen the number who were in the loop. I began to prepare a statement that he could make if he decided to disclose the affair himself and another should it break before he could act. Ashdown went down to Yeovil and had a sad meeting with his constituency officers.

On the Sunday the *News of the World* ran a careful story under the heading 'Votergate' predicting a scandal brewing in Westminster. On Tuesday February 4 Ashdown was in the Commons and overheard some remarks from Dennis Skinner, the Labour parliamentary party's vicious attack dog. Ashdown heard the words 'bloody injunctions' and 'marital infidelity'. (Ironically, Skinner was to have an affair of his own revealed in due course.) Then, that evening, it all came to a head at a surreal dinner at the BBC which had been in the diary for some time, and involved their full political team and, from our side, Ashdown, myself, Alan Leaman (Ashdown's main aide) and our communications director, Olly Grender. As I say, it was surreal.

They all knew the whole story. They knew that we knew they knew. But, of course, no one said a word. Ashdown had said to me in the taxi on the way to the dinner that I would have to do all the talking because he could not concentrate. But as he sat there, miserable and largely silent, he realised this could not go on. He passed me a note asking that Alan and I go back to his flat with him afterwards. There he said he had decided to break the story himself. In his diary he says I was 'rather nervous'. Once more he had misread my reaction; I may have been nervous about how it would go, but otherwise I was hugely relieved. I believed that despite the injunctions and the delay we still had a chance, maybe not with the media who knew there had been an attempt to cover it up, but with the public who would still hear it first from Ashdown.

Just how right we were to act was revealed the following morning when the *Scotsman*, not covered by the injunction, broke the story that the media were being suppressed by an injunction and named Ashdown. By then though, we were on our way. We had called a press conference for eleven o'clock and decided on the few words he would say. We decided on the Jubilee Room. We knew there was a side door to it that the media would not necessarily know about, so that while the photographers and others were all over the main entrance, Ashdown could slip in, say what he had to say, and leave before any questions could be asked and any pictures taken. (It worked like a charm and I was rather proud of that.)

While we waited for the press conference, I witnessed two impressive exchanges. The first was a call Ashdown made to Roy Jenkins. He began to give him the details when Jenkins interrupted him. 'No need to explain to me, Paddy,' he said, 'you have my sympathy and full support.' I could see how much that unequivocal support meant. Even more impressive was a call from the Prime Minister, John Major, wishing him luck and assuring him that no political advantage would be taken of it. There are times when politicians rise to the occasion.

And the strategy worked. Whitehall and Westminster is a world of its own; everyone there knew all about it, but to the public, not educated in the 'nods and winks' approach of the media, it came as a surprise and in the form of what appeared as an honest, contrite confession rather than a 'shock . . . horror . . . disclosure'. How could they become all hot and bothered when Ashdown had seemingly himself decided to break the story and was obviously apologetic and regretful and fully supported by his wife and family and party ? Of course, there was a bad day in the media, with the *Sun* devastatingly providing the affair with its lasting title, 'Paddy

Pantsdown', but after the Sundays had reviewed the whole story one more time, it died.

Ashdown's ratings went up and the Liberal Democrats rose four per cent in the opinion polls. It had been a personal nightmare for Ashdown but it actually became a positive for the party. The lesson was clear: don't let the media break the story. Do it yourself on your terms.

That may have been the end of the public end of the story, but privately it was only a beginning and, for me, what followed caused my enthusiasm for the leader to wane. The first incident occurred immediately and it concerned Tricia Howard. She had been superb; she had followed advice, taken the controversy on the chin, turned down the money, and in every way proved a real 'trooper'. I was, therefore, angered by a reference to her in a leader in *The Times*. For two or three weeks she had been ducking photographers (once her car was nearly pushed off the road by one) and, on our advice, she had appeared on the steps of Andrew Phillips's offices for a photo call. We told her that if she fed the frenzy, it would stop.

The Times, in its leader about the affair, commented harshly that she had not appeared averse to publicity. Given that she had turned down a small fortune to tell her story, this was outrageous. I spoke to Ashdown about it. 'Someone should write to *The Times* and defend her,' I said. 'At the least they should be told she acted on our advice and that she rejected £50,000,' He stood looking at me for a moment, then said: 'Well, I'm not going to do it.' I could not but feel that Tricia Howard had been thrown to the dogs. I walked out and wrote a brief letter to *The Times* which to its credit, it printed at the top of the letters page the following day:

> I believe that you were inadvertently harsh when you stated of Ms Tricia Howard . . . that 'the right to privacy of the lady in the case, which at first was surely close to total, was also surrendered by her when she summoned reporters and photographers' for a photo call.
>
> The fact is that Ms Howard has been hounded for days. Her family and friends were being harassed. And it was even more likely to be the case that her life would be made a greater misery from now on until the tabloids had drained every bit of blood from the story.
>
> She reluctantly took the view, having taken her lawyer's advice, and

also our advice, that it would be best – to put it bluntly – to let the dogs have their day. 'Surrendering' her privacy was done with the utmost reluctance, but I believe was as sensible a course as it was courageous.

Incidentally, Ms Howard has turned down considerable sums of money and acted with remarkable integrity and that, too, should be a matter of record.

Then, hardly had the public focus on the Howard affair ended, than the media began chasing another story, namely that there were more women involved. Fleet Street was on fire with rumours. If all the women suggested had been involved with Ashdown, he would have had no energy left for the General Election, and as the election approached an army of reporters spent days sniffing around his private life. By the time the election was called, the story doing the rounds was that there were at least five women, but the stories differed wildly as to who the alleged five were. Reporters and photographers were despatched round the country to doorstep any woman whose name emerged from the rumour-mongering. At least one victim of the feeding frenzy telephoned me for help: she had found a national newspaper reporter and photographer encamped outside her door. Eventually the *Sun* ran a story that Westminster was alive with rumours about a senior politician and five women.

With the General Election under way I took the view that my role was to keep the leader away from this as much as possible, not tell him all the horror stories we were hearing, and thus allow him to concentrate on the campaign. I instructed Olly Grender that any calls to the Press Office on the issue should be diverted to me.

There then began a vicious campaign of psychological warfare. It had clearly been decided within the offices of more than one of the Tory tabloids that if they could not prove a story, they were going to make us sweat, and hopefully as a result they would destabilise our campaign. So day after day we were 'warned' that a story was about to break. On every Friday of the campaign we received warnings that one of the Sundays had a big Ashdown story. Papers even called press conferences, then cancelled them. It appeared to me that they were trying to force us to panic. Jane and I were living in Lincolnshire by now and on Saturdays I would go home for 24 hours with her. We would have dinner at the local pub, but I could never relax until one of the Press Office team had seen the first editions and telephoned me to say there was no story.

The scare stories came to dominate my role in the campaign. It was a nightmare. And it was ruining the experience. Instead of enjoying running what would be my only General Election campaign, I was reduced to skulking in my Cowley Street bunker awaiting the next bit of dirt. I have never discussed it with him, but I have no doubt it ruined Ashdown's campaign too. Instead of flourishing in the limelight, he must have been weighed down by pressures only he could know.

It did all end with a laugh, however. On the last Sunday I received a call from Jonathan Dimbleby, who I had known since Shelter days when he was a junior reporter on *The World at One*. Jonathan told me he had become appalled by the rumour mill and wanted to warn me that there was a story doing the rounds that the *Sun* was going to turn up at our press conference on the Monday morning and name a woman and challenge Ashdown to deny it.

I took immediate steps. I decided to keep the press conference short and take questions only from bona fide political reporters who I personally knew. We would also talk longer than usual to reduce the opportunity for questions. And I told Simon Bryceson, our communications number two, to keep an eye out for the *Sun* reporter and to tell me where he was sitting. Finally, just a minute before the press conference, I told Ashdown of the warning and said that he must not answer. I would deal with it. I had prepared my response: 'You are in the wrong place, sir. The gutter is outside in the street. Next question.'

Seconds before we went in, Bryceson came up to me and said 'I think he's here. I've not seen him before. Untidy, dishevelled looking, if ever I saw a *Sun* reporter this is it.' I asked where he was. Bryceson replied: 'Four rows back, four seats in from the left.' We walked in and before I opened proceedings I glanced to my left. Four rows back. Four seats in. I recognised him immediate. It was Pierre Salinger, former Press Secretary to President Kennedy.

The Campaign

On the whole it was an uneventful campaign, for me dominated by the rumour mill over Ashdown. One parliamentarian who was a tower of strength was Alan Beith. As shadow Chancellor of the Exchequer, he had to carry the burden of appearing with the Tories' Ken Clarke and Labour's John Smith and he did so with distinction. He was always available when I needed him.

Because he was in London, Simon Hughes was also useful. This was another MP I liked; a bit of a maverick, a bit unreliable when it came to dates and times, he was invariably helpful and good-humoured. His main failing was that when he was on his feet making a speech, you could not stop him. During the campaign I went to Southwark to speak at his adoption meeting. As his speech went on and on, members of the audience began to disappear. At one point four Muslim members of the audience, in the front row, rose and said: 'Sorry, Mr Hughes, we have to go and pray.' His own mother, who was on the platform, interrupted and said, 'Sorry, Simon, I have a train to catch.' Still he went on, until he and I were just about the only one's left.

Now you would think that, given the radio and television opportunities, the MPs would be rushing to London to take their share of them, and to stop me doing them. No way. Once in their own constituencies, where they had each built up their own following and developed their own way of winning, they had no desire to leave. This meant I had to do a lot more than I wanted to. I had never bothered to swot up on every detail of party policy because I assumed the MPs would handle those programmes. More than once I had to bluff my way through programmes I would have given my life to have avoided. On one radio phone-in programme, I had someone next to me whose task it was to open the relevant page of the manifesto so that I could read answers to the callers' questions. The trick was not to sound as if you were reading. The most dodgy appearance was when I had to step in late to do Adam Boulton's morning phone-in on Sky television. I could not have any help because viewers would have seen it, so I pleaded with Adam to give me some protection. When one question came in and Adam saw the panic in my eyes, he began feeding me the answer: 'I believe your policy is such and such . . . '

I nodded eagerly: 'Absolutely.' 'And I think your party also thinks such and such . . . ' 'Quite so.' 'And you take the view that such and such . . . ' 'Indeed.' How we got away with it I'll never know.

My main critic from within the hierarchy of the party was Shirley

Williams who felt she was an asset that was not being used. From the start I had taken a decision to sideline some of the famous but the older party names, Williams, Roy Jenkins, Bill Rodgers, and even the immediate past leader David Steel. My reasoning was that if we were to present the party as an alternative to politics as the public had known it, as a fresh, vibrant political force, we could hardly do so with names that had been around for decades. Jenkins accepted this philosophically, telling *The Times* 'the younger generation will be coming to the fore . . . I have had a good run.' Bill Rodgers could not care less. But Shirley was offended and sent me letters pointing out that she had been an election winner in the past. I didn't like to point out that she had also subsequently lost every seat she had won.

One of the more controversial moments of the campaign was the affair of Jennifer's Ear. In his book *Packaging Politics*, Bob Franklin describes it:

The most significant PEB of the 1992 campaign was undoubtedly the Labour Party broadcast on 23 March about the National Health Service, which featured the case of a young child's wait for minor surgery to her ear, to illustrate the wider argument about hospital waiting lists; the PEB became known as 'Jennifer's Ear'. The broadcast prompted an outcry but, many reporters suggested, brought the election to life. The tabloid press alleged that the Labour Party, but Neil Kinnock in particular, had been unprincipled in exploiting a child's personal suffering for political gain. The Conservative Party made similar claims with Chris Pattern suggesting that the affair exposed Kinnock as an unsuitable person to be Prime Minister. The debate quickly moved on from health issues to a row about who had leaked the identity of the child to the newspapers. Both of the major parties pronounced the other guilty; the Liberal Democrats, on the advice of Des Wilson, decided not to enter the debate.

The issue dominated press, radio and television election coverage for days, with one analysis of the television election agenda suggesting that 'the war of Jennifer's ear came in fifth' If the function of PEBs is to place issues which favour the sponsoring party on the election agenda, then the broadcast must be judged a success. But, given the unsavoury allegations and acrimony which followed the broadcast and the public distaste they engendered, it is uncertain whether or not Labour benefited electorally from the broadcast. By the end of the week, however, polls were showing a considerable increase in support for the Liberal Democrats.

From the start I decided to make our television coverage a public issue. We were entitled to fair coverage and in my view we were not receiving it. There was a row with Channel 4 when they decided on the day we published our manifesto that they would lead on Labour's shadow budget rather than our policies. There had always been an unspoken understanding that on a party's manifesto day it would be given a bigger than usual share of the day's coverage. I took the view that reducing Ashdown to the number two story was unacceptable and decided to make a stand by withdrawing him from the programme. Channel 4 News complained forever afterwards, but I remained unapologetic. I felt I had to make a stand and I believe that subsequent coverage reflected some success. ITN's editor Stewart Purvis wrote to the newspapers refusing to accept that the broadcasters were responsible for properly 'balanced' coverage of the parties. My case is best summed up by my reply, published the following day:

> The Liberal Democrats are fighting every seat in England, Scotland and Wales, and mounting a major campaign on a distinctive manifesto. This has been acknowledged by the provision of four party election broadcasts (compared with five each for Labour and the Conservatives).
>
> However, it is not acknowledged in coverage by either the BBC or ITV news programmes.
>
> While we accept that the stopwatch should not be the only criterion, and news values should apply, the quantity of coverage remains the only precise way of monitoring how the broadcasters are treating us. In the first week the Liberal Democrats received only 23 per cent of time on main BBC television news programmes, and in the three days of this week 18.5 per cent. The respective figures for ITV news coverage are 21.5 per cent and 23 per cent.
>
> If the 5:5:4 criterion was being applied, we would be receiving 28.5 per cent. Given that we have no tabloid newspapers with mass circulations supporting our party, this represents a seriously damaging media squeeze.
>
> All complaints are dealt with by a bureaucratic brush-off from the

BBC and indifference from ITV. Why should they care? At the end of the day the election is just a story.

The public should know that just because we have decided to fight a positive campaign and not throw dirt about, just because we have decided to concentrate on real policies instead of emotive case histories, just because we refuse to lower the tone to raise the 'news value' decibels, they, the public, are being denied adequate coverage of what we have to say.

Another controversial decision that I believed worked out well was to take head-on the issue of the wasted vote. Polling showed that 40 per cent or more of voters would support the Liberal Democrats 'if they thought they would win.' We decided to use a party political broadcast to take the issue head-on and across the bottom of the screen we displayed the names of every constituency where we were lying second. Charles Kennedy fronted it to make the case that, if people really wanted a Liberal Democrat, and if they voted Liberal Democrat, in many more seats they could have one.

The *Guardian*'s Ian Aitken gave his verdict on the campaign I was running:

The 'wasted vote' gamble is only the latest in what is regarded in Cowley Street as a series of accumulator bets which have – so far – come up trumps. Behind most of these wagers is Des Wilson . . .

The first of his long-shot bets was the decision to upstage the other two parties and go for the first of the three daily press conferences. This entailed starting at 7.15am, which clearly risked the possibility that nobody would come.

In the event, the hacks have indeed turned up, albeit rather sleepily. But the advantage has been that issues set by the Lib Dems have helped to fill time on breakfast TV, not to mention the car commuters' friend, BBC Radio 4's *Today* programme.

The second gamble was to encourage the idea of putting the extra penny on income tax right up at the sharp end of the Lib Dem campaign. There were those who regarded this as madness, bordering on the suicidal. In the event, recent polls suggest that it has given the Ashdown campaign a special moral cachet during the squabbles over taxation between the two main parties.

The third gamble was the decision to stay out of the big row between

Labour and the Tories over the health service and the notorious Jennifer Bennett broadcast. This entailed sacrificing actual air time under the rules of "balance".

But the move seems to have paid off. Opinion polls conducted immediately after the so-called "War of Jennifer's Ear" suggested that both main parties had lost ground while the silent Lib Dems had gained a couple of points.

Then there was Sunday's day trip to France, when Paddy Ashdown and his team took a ferry to Boulogne. The Cap'n (he who speaks Mandarin Chinese as well as fluent Malay) stumbled through a school-boy text about our 'avenir en Europe'. It was an occasion pregnant with opportunities for comic disaster.

In the event, the preposterous example of the modern philosophy of the sound bite scored several notches on the PR Richter scale. It got Paddy on pretty well every Sunday night television news bulletin, without a trace of a smile from anyone.

This isn't a bad record by anyone's standards. By the standards of the ultimate amateur's party it is remarkable.

We had been slowly climbing back from the six percent before the General Election was actually called and by the last week were near my target of 20 per cent. By then the Tories and their tabloid supporters were mounting a brutal attack on Neil Kinnock who made things worse for himself by an over-the-top performance at a triumphalist Labour rally in Sheffield. Over the last weekend I began to receive messages from the constituencies that the Tory message that 'a vote for the Lib Dems will help put Kinnock in' was having some resonance. We were slipping.

On the day we got nearly 18 per cent per cent of the vote and 20 MPs. It was, I suppose, about as close to my target as the fates made possible.

As always, the party suffered from a corrupt electoral system. With nearly one vote in five we should have had over 100 seats; instead we more-or-less returned the existing parliamentary party. I could not help but consider the irony that my achievement had been to ensure the return to the House of Commons of all the MPs who had done so much to try and undermine me.

But I believed we had achieved what Paddy Ashdown and Archy

Kirwood had been looking for nearly two years earlier: we had rescued the party. It had survived. It now had four or five years to move on and show it was a serious player in British politics. When the campaign was over, I spoke to a conference of political aficionados that takes place after every General Election at Essex University.

'Our aim was a party hammered into shape and fit to make a stronger challenge later in the decade. That's why Ashdown began talking publicly about a staging-post election . . . he was seeking to condition the party, the press and the public to that kind of result.

We knew we would have a fraction of the resources of the other parties. We did. Our expenditure was in the region of one pound for very thirty pounds of the combined Conservative-Labour budget.

We knew we would get a raw deal from the media. We did. The broadcasters allocated us only 80 per cent of the other parties peb's and, by implication, 80 per cent of coverage generally. This has to be compared with parity in 1987. As for the mass circulation newspapers, they more-or-less ignored our existence, our manifesto getting two paragraphs in one tabloid with a huge readership. To a whole section of Britain's newspaper readership our involvement in the election was all but kept a secret!

And we knew Labour would enter the election with more credibility than in 1987 and fight their most professional campaign ever. On the whole they did

Those were the "circumstances" we faced.

That's why my outside hope – my ambitious objective – throughout the last 18 months to polling day was 20 per cent of the popular vote – one in five votes – and 20 seats. We got the 20 seats. We got one in five voters – to be precise 18 per cent of the popular vote – but I believe we lost between 3 and 5 per cent over the last few days as many soft Tories returned to the fold, fearing that a vote for the Liberal Democrats would put Labour in.

I don't present that as a triumph; I do think it was a considerable achievement given the daunting and difficult context I have described.'

Inevitably, given the vibrancy of the campaign, the party was disappointed not to have done better, but this was unrealistic. Jim Wallace wrote to me to say: 'I know that given our rising expectations during the campaign, the immediate reaction to the result was one of disappointment. Nevertheless when I think back to the first meeting which we had in June 1990, there can be little doubt but that the main campaign objectives were fulfilled and that, in no small way, was due to your own constructive approach and the drive to see it through. Certainly, comments which I have had from people in constituencies which were never among our targets, have been to the effect that, for once, they were proud to own up to the National campaign.' Jim was one of the parliamentary party's good guys. I was happy to rest on his verdict.

The Aftermath

Shortly after the General Election, Ashdown made a speech at Chard in which he sought to ditch the party's position of equidistance between the two main parties. It was not well received by either the parliamentary party or the party in the country. It was in my view a mistake, short term and long term. This radical change in approach would inevitably come to dominate the politics of the party, and prevent it from focusing on building further from our 'developmental' General Election and striking out on its own with its own alternative case. And it was an admission of weakness at just the point when we should have been showing strength.

Labour had just failed to win when all the circumstances – the shaky economy, the desire for change etc. – were in its favour. The Tories were surely in their last term. This was the moment to build from the base we had established at the General Election and try to overtake Labour as a genuine alternative. And even if we failed, and even if it did come to pass that only a Labour-Liberal alliance of some sort would replace the Tories, at least we would have strengthened our position for the negotiations to create it.

In the longer term, Ashdown's dream was to combine Labour and the Liberals into a party that he believed could hold power for many years, with the Tories as the only opponent. In other words, back to the old two-party adversarial system I had joined the Liberals to help challenge. I had already said publicly before the General Election that I would probably retire from public affairs after it was over. I had been campaigning, with the occasional break, for over 25 years. I felt, too, that with the General Election campaign I had passed a kind of break-off point with the British public;

another campaign would be one too many. I did not want to move from someone who had achieved some respect as a campaigner on national issues to becoming a national bore. But Ashdown's strategy added another factor. If I stayed active in the party, I would be at odds with the leader over his fundamental aim. There was no way that the leader and the recent General Election campaign director could take opposite sides in this debate without it becoming a personalised issue.

Ashdown and I had dinner at Joe Allens, and I raised questions about his Chard speech. In his (from my experience) somewhat unreliable diary, he recorded that I appeared convinced by his arguments. My memory is that I expressed my view so strongly that he ended the discussion by pleading 'please don't say anything publicly, Des, that will make it impossible for me to work with you again.'

I had been asked to be the final speaker at a rally on the eve of the party's Harrogate conference that year. No one knew that it was likely to be my last-ever speech on a political platform for eighteen years. Without mentioning Ashdown, his Chard speech, or his ambitions, I decided to make one last plea for the party to pursue its destiny as a genuine alternative to the other two, at least for the time being.

Over the summer I had been to Atlanta, Georgia, to the place where Martin Luther King is buried. I found inscribed – on a wall there – these words of his: 'We must make a choice. Will we continue to march to the drumbeat of conformity or respectability, or will we listen to the beat of a more distant drum . . . and march to its echoing sound? Will we march only to the music of time? Or, will we, at the risk of criticism and abuse, march to the soul saving music of eternity?'

I now quoted this to the party (for the majority of those at the conference were also in the hall for this rally, including Ashdown himself):

'It appears that we, too, are debating a choice: whether we march to the drumbeat of conventional political ambition and practice – maybe even to another party's beat – or whether we forge ahead to our own distinctive sound. If we do face that choice, I'm for marching to our own beat.'

'Some co-operation between political parties on specific issues should always be possible and may even be desirable,' but in my view

the party should resist the calls for so-called political realignment: . . .
it's in present circumstances politically unrealistic – it just won't
happen . . . and it denies our distinctive and historic role as the
upholder of principle in politics and the only credible advocate of
radical change.'

It had just been a few weeks since one in five voters had the courage and
the independence to reject the huge propaganda campaigns of the other
parties and their newspapers and to invest it in our long-term promise.
Was it really possible that some Liberals had less faith in what we could
achieve than those voters? I talked of the way the old parties were wedded
to a corrupt political system. This is why I had chosen the Liberals. This is
why we needed an alternative:

> 'Does that mean we forsake power in order to stay pure? No it does not.
> It means that we create a system that restricts power, that reduces the
> probability of corruption – and that means a more open system, a more
> democratic system, a more decentralised system, a system that
> reduces patronage and limits rewards for what is supposed, after all, to
> be public service. These are the things the other parties do not rate as
> of importance; we alone – ALONE – understand it is that its no good
> changing the people or the party running the country if you don't
> change the system too.'

I concluded:

> 'We came to this party . . . we came to this conference . . . driven by a faith,
> by values that are our own . . . our party is distinctive and valuable . . . So
> let's march – as King said – not to "the drumbeat of conformity and
> respectability" . . . instead let's say that if respectability is to conform to
> the standards of the others then it just won't do . . . '

Of course, read today, some eighteen years later, with a Conservative-
Liberal coalition now in place, this all sounds anachronistic. But now is now,
and then was then. And, at that time, I believe I did speak for many, many
members of the party, especially former Liberals. And so it seemed from the
response; when I had finished the whole hall rose in a standing ovation. I
should have been exhilarated. But, even as I listened to the applause, I knew

that this was the end. "Don't make it impossible for me to work with you," Ashdown had said. That is what I had now done. The *Guardian* reported the following day: 'Des Wilson . . . last night threw a hefty spanner into Paddy Ashdown's strategic works . . . ' I could not help Ashdown on the course he was now set, but nor did I want to lead a campaign that split the party. I had been one of those who had created a united Liberal-Democrat party; I did not now want to be one of those who divided it.

I stayed behind for a few minutes to talk to one or two of the other speakers. I eventually said goodbye to them, only to find the hall was now empty. I suddenly found myself completely alone. I could hear the chatter and laughter from the bars nearby but I no longer had the heart to go there. I walked back to my car and set out on the six hours drive back to London.

While I drove I recalled so many amazing experiences over thirty years: the Hove by-election that fired the energy and enthusiasm of the party in the South; the presidency of the party that helped it survive the Eastbourne defence debacle and participate constructively in the Alliance campaign; the merger with the SDP and the last minute policy negotiations that saved it and finally, the recent General Election campaign that had left the party with an electoral and organisational base it could build on.

No fair-minded Liberal could deny that I had done my bit – responded to the call. Put myself on the line when it was needed. And, I believe, always been constructive. But, once more in my life, it was time to move on. For me, this particular party was over.

18

Is the Party Really Over?

> Power tends to corrupt and absolute power corrupts
> absolutely.   LORD ACTON

Of course, the party wasn't over: far from it. But if, as Harold Wilson said,
'A week is a long time in politics' – a couple of decades are an eternity. As
I write this, nearly nineteen years on from that last speech, the Liberal
Democrats are in power, in coalition with the Conservatives; the political
landscape has been transformed and party loyalties are being tested on a
daily basis.

For some, their party's survival matters above all else; for them, it is a
tribe; once a member, always a member. My party – right or wrong! I understand how and why that happens and I don't mock it. There's a lot to be said
for loyalty and persistence. And I know, as a former Liberal President, I
would probably be expected to fit that mould. But I never have been a blind
follower of the party line. If I had, I could not have been one of those who
presided over the end of the Liberal party in 1988. It is a daunting experience
to look at the list of former Liberal Presidents and realise you are drawing a
line under that list – forever. Yet, for me it was liberalism that mattered; that
is what I meant when I went to the famous 1988 Social Democrat conference
and told them that 'political parties are vehicles for greater causes than their
own survival'. And, to their credit, both Liberals and Social Democrats understood that: they killed their parties in the greater cause; that cause was to
create a new party with a new constitution and new policies, one offering a
credible alternative to the old, unchanging parties of the past.

Yet having said all that, in my career as a minor public figure, being
elected President of the Liberal Party had been *the* moment; you would be a
hard man not to be moved by being given the confidence of the membership of a historic political party, especially this one. So, even at moments of
despair or disillusion over the past nineteen years, I have kept the faith. I

believed – and believe – that we need a liberal Liberal Party, and that we need a minimum of three parties to make our democracy work.

I want to say four things though about the Liberals (and later, the Liberal Democrats).

The first is that they are good people. They are remarkably resilient. I still see veterans at the annual conference who were there in the Seventies; together they've suffered defeat after defeat, even disasters; been battered by an unjust electoral system and belittled by media indifference; been the victims of countless leadership let downs (one leader, ending in the Old Bailey accused of attempted murder, another forcibly retired because of drink, others – as we shall see – just straight-forward failures). They've had their quarrels, because they're involved and opinionated people, and some have moved to other places, and then come back. But even the hard bitten hacks from the political press admit that you have to like them: they're hard-working, good-humoured, idealistic, loyal, patient, self-sacrificing, tolerant, and, above all, liberal.

Secondly, I want to nail the lie that Liberals never really wanted power . . . that they preferred the safety of the sidelines to engagement on the pitch. Liberals have not consciously avoided power – they have been denied it by a corrupt, deeply unfair and undemocratic electoral system, cynically propped up and preserved by the other two parties for their own purposes: A system that, election after election, cheated the Liberals of a fair return on their votes.

I can still remember the anger I felt after the first General Election campaign in which I was centrally involved, the Alliance one in 1987; the Tories had won only 43.3 per cent of the popular vote, two people in five, but obtained 57.6 per cent of the parliamentary seats, nearly three seats in five – a minority of votes, but a majority of nearly 100 seats. While the Tories with 43.3 of the popular vote had 375 seats, the Alliance with 22.5 per cent of the vote had 22. Who but a political charlatan can defend that?

Unfortunately, this libel – that the Liberals don't want power – has become part of the mythology of contemporary politics. It is a constant refrain of the other parties and the media. As recently as its 2010 conference, a *Guardian* columnist described the Lib Dems as 'reared on the purity of powerlessness and the warm glow of self-righteousness that comes with it.' Tony Blair in his memoirs refers to the Liberals' lack of the necessary fibre to govern – 'unwilling to take on the mantle of responsibility for the hard choices and endure the rough passages.'

The party has nearly always been most savagely attacked and accused of 'enjoying the self-indulgence of protest' when it is, in fact, most courageously making a stand on principle. I have already described the 1986 Eastbourne debate: this was a classic case of the party, determined to defend its distinctive position on defence, yet being asked to sacrifice its beliefs in order to make life politically more comfortable for its leader and to make the party more acceptable to a sceptical and largely right-wing media; that debate was for years cited as evidence of the party's lack of realism about power and how it could be achieved; in fact, it was evidence of the media's lack of understanding about principle and how it is defended.

If Liberals had wanted to do and say what the other parties were doing and saying, they could have joined those parties; but they had joined an alternative party because they had an alternative view. When they held to that view, they were accused of avoiding responsibility. In fact, this slander on the Lib Dems is disproved by what the party has actually been doing . . . because, given the obstacles to a national breakthrough, Lib Dems have taken every opportunity to seek and exercise power wherever they could get it.

They have for thirty years been advancing in local government, taking no prisoners, seizing power, handling huge budgets, and taking tough decisions. At the time of writing the Lib Dems are more powerful in local government than the Labour Party. They have nearly 4,000 local councillors and control the cities of Sheffield, Newcastle, Bristol, Hull and Portsmouth, and two London boroughs, and are in coalitions running four more councils. As partners in coalitions, they have shared in the governing of the countries of Wales and Scotland.

Denied political power, many party members have also worked hard in the voluntary sector. Many senior people in charities and other voluntary organisations have been leading Liberals too. And, finally, but surely conclusively, they have taken the first opportunity to share national power by entering into a Coalition at an exceptionally difficult time. The charge that Liberal Democrats are afraid of power just does not stand up.

My third point is that the party has suffered from another lie: that 'the party does not stand for anything'; 'All things to all people'; 'No policies'. Perhaps it is easier to define a party as red or blue, working class or ruling class, public sector or private sector, capitalist or socialist, collectivist or conservative, left-wing or right-wing, tweedledee or tweedledum – than it is to define a party that does not think in this simplistic way, that does not seek to divide, but rather to unite, that puts doing the right thing before the doctrinaire thing. But, in fact, the party has always had a clear philosophy, principles, and a coherent platform.

I always knew why I was a Liberal in the last three decades of the 20th century: Because I disliked the two-party adversarial system and the crude, over-simplistic choices it offered, I wanted to join a party that fostered partnership, not division. Because I believed in Britain being a constructive contributor in Europe, whereas both the other parties whinged and whined on the sidelines so that for thirty years we were positioned as outsiders there. Because I believed in a freer and more open and liberal country, while the other parties refused fair votes, laughed off a Bill of Rights, increasingly centralised power, and institutionalised secrecy. Because I opposed the mindless adherence to the idea that to be respected in the world we had to be a nuclear state; we were wasting billions on a macho defence policy that was not about defence, but about the political status of our leaders in the world. Because I believed that there was no contradiction between a free enterprise system and a strong public sector and because I believed in the importance of creating a ecologically sustainable economy and society at a time when the other parties treated conservationists and environmentalists as weirdos.

By the time of the 2010 General Election many of those causes had been achieved, or were now shared by one or other of the other parties, but Liberal Democrats continued to be lone voices for electoral reform and for really radical political change, for the non-replacement of Trident, and on a variety of other issues. Which brings me to my fourth point: in the nearly forty years since I first became involved, the party has always been better than its leaders.

As a campaigner on the national scene I know how vital it is to have a clear, comprehensible and convincing message. A political party should be able to project what it's about, and the Lib Dems, and in particular, Lib Dem leaders, have not always made clear: *This is what we stand for. This is who we are. This is what we will do.* Voters have to know these things. If they do not, they will go elsewhere.

The failure to clearly and passionately convey a big message has, in my view, been the fault of successive Lib Dem leaders, too absorbed with the politics of politics and not sufficiently communicative about why they wanted power and what they would do with it. They never seemed to be able to capture public imagination with a Big Idea – probably because they did not have one. In particular, I believe there were at least three occasions the party was poised to make a huge advance on the national scene, and on each occasion it was let down by its leaders.

Owen and Steel

Steel handled the emergence of the SDP brilliantly – in fact, by persuading Roy Jenkins not to join the Liberals but to create a new vehicle for dis-illusioned centre and centre-left politicians, he could claim to be an unofficial founder of the SDP. He always envisaged the SDP and Liberals becoming an Alliance, and ultimately part of a united party that could credibly challenge the two-party monopoly. This vision, and its achieve-ment are enormously to Steel's credit. Owen, too, by deciding to leave the Labour Party when, having been Foreign Secretary at 38, he appeared to be set on a glittering career within it, showed immense courage and integrity.

So they had courage and they had vision. But, when the moment arrived when they could make it all happen – bring the parties together into a convincing alternative to the old parties – they lacked the generosity of spirit that was called for. They were not big enough men. Their personalities and rival ambitions got in the way. Under the political microscope of the times, their fallibility was exposed to devastating effect.

The opportunity after the 1987 General Election was enormous. Thatcher had been re-elected for a third term, but with diminishing support. The country, as it always does in a third term, was beginning to yearn for change, almost for its own sake. Labour, having lost under its new leader Kinnock, was not convincing. Voters consistently told opinion pollsters that they were fed up with politics and both the old parties. But, most significantly, over 40 per cent also told the pollsters that if a third party could prove it could be elected, they would support it. (A bit unfair, this, because if they just went out and voted Liberal Democrat, the party would be elected – but that's the way it was.)

A combined Liberal and Social Democrat party stood a real chance. It would be a more substantial party with impressive resources of money and membership. It would have personalities like Owen who had held national office. It would, by combining, have shown that its members would sacrifice their tribes in the national interest, that it was a grown-up party genuinely seeking power. There was no reason to believe it could not quickly become a major political force. Faced with the exciting prospect of a merger with the support of an overwhelming majority in both parties, it was the duty of Owen and Steel to make it to happen, and in a way that would both unite the memberships and excite the public.

They needed to step forward together and speak with conviction and enthusiasm about the potential of a merged party. They needed to tell the country: 'Here is what you have wanted: A new party, big enough to win, with enough experienced heavyweights and bright young talent to offer you real change. This is not just our moment – this is *your* moment.' Instead, they failed to rise to the occasion. Instead of coming forward together with a message of hope, they headed in opposite directions, dividing the parties and the members within the parties and trampling all over the hopes and dreams of those who had worked to create a united Alliance campaign and who were ready to move forward to merger.

Steel's only too-typical decision to summons the media to Scotland after the 1987 General Election, and to try and 'make it happen by media', could not have been more ill-judged. Owen's petulance in response could not have been more inappropriate. They turned what was about to be a major piece of political theatre, the creation of a genuine third political force, into a soap opera. Maclennan made matters worse with his Dead Parrott document, an error compounded by Steel's once more too-typical failure to pay attention to the detail and, thus, to let it happen. What should have been a major political moment, the emergence of a credible alternative to the two old parties, became a humiliating shambles.

And as for Owen's suicidal splitting of the Social Democrats, this culminated in his polling only about a third of the votes of the Monster Raving Loony Party in a by election, surely the most humiliating rejection in the history of British politics.

Ashdown

Fortunately, the Liberal and SDP memberships behaved in a much more mature way than their leaders; their common sense and resolve saved the day and led to the formation of the Liberal Democrats, but it was a party already damaged by the nature of its birth. Ashdown did inherit real problems when he became the first leader. Inevitably, members of the two old parties were having inevitable difficulties bedding down. The parliamentary party was divisive and often disloyal. There were difficulties over the name. There was no money. There was little public support; thanks to the Owen-Steel debacle, the public remained unconvinced that these were serious people. And, as we've seen, its initial electoral results were catastrophic.

Never the less, the General Election offered him a chance. He was guaranteed attention, coverage, notice. One night in Joe Allens (my main London watering hole, as might be clear by now) he asked me what was the one piece of advice I would offer him with respect to the General Election. I replied: 'Paddy, you will have the attention of the country focused on you in a way you have never had before or can even imagine. You don't know whether this will be the only time or not, but you cannot waste it. Whatever it is you stand for, whatever it is you want to say to the country, do not hold back. Say it. There would be no greater tragedy than for you to spend the rest of your life saying "I had a moment, a moment when everyone was listening, and I did not say what I really felt and thought." ' His tragedy was that, when the time came, he had nothing to say.

If there was a failing in our campaign it was that the leader did not convey to the public a clear and compelling reason why they should vote for him and his party. That was because he did not have one. When I had run my campaigns I had always taken responsibility for defining and communicating the fundamental message; that to me was an essential role of the leader – to explain why he is there, what he believes, and why he should have the public's support. But I was not the leader of the Liberal Democrats. Ashdown was. This was his role. He was the one who dreamed of being Prime Minister; he had to tell the country why he should be.

I must, of course, take some of the responsibility. I should have insisted it happen. I just assumed – wrongly – that he and his team of policy advisors and speech-writers would do it. Unfortunately, this was not what they were practised at doing. Westminster activity is driven by events. The leader has little time for thought and depends enormously on his team to produce sound bites. For the Liberal Democrats, hardly taken seriously by the media, this was an opportunistic business. The team spent all their time acting on the spur of the moment desperately trying to get Ashdown and the Lib Dems a mention here, a paragraph there; they had not been responsible for producing a set of clear messages and major speeches to a clear and compelling theme to underpin a General Election campaign. So it just didn't happen.

It was only a week before polling day when I realised that, while he was drawing big crowds to his rallies, no clear message was emerging from them. And while he was dutifully speaking to the briefs we had written for the daily press conferences, each related to a policy position, and especially to our five E's – education, economy, environmental protection, Europe, and electoral reform – there was no sense of a man with mission, campaigning with barely suppressed excitement because of what he wanted to do for the country.

And, to emphasise an earlier point, if you want to persuade the public to support you, they have to know what they are supporting – what you will do. During the General Election campaign we established that Ashdown was there. But we never did communicate what he was there for. The country wanted a man with a plan; Ashdown was giving them sound bites and pictures. I had hundreds of conversations with Ashdown over the two years of the campaign, many of them lengthy; we talked endlessly about politics, about political personalities, and about the campaign; I do not recall him once talking with any passion about any issue.

Only much later would my fears that Ashdown stood for little other than the pursuit of power become obvious to everyone else. It emerged with the publication of his diaries and the revelation that he spent almost every waking moment between that 1992 General Election and the 1997 one pursuing his dream of a realignment on the left of British politics, an ambition that involved the permanent sharing of power with Labour and, incidentally, a return to the two-party adversarial system.

He pursued this proposition despite the opposition of both his parlia-

mentary team and the party in the country, meeting privately with Tony
Blair, and sharing what was happening with only a handful of advisors.
The more he failed to win support, the more he operated in secret, sometimes deliberately misleading his highly sceptical colleagues. In this he
was showing serious lack of judgement. First, it was all based on the
belief that Labour could never win again on their own. Yet, from about a
year after John Major's 1992 victory, it became clear that the Tories were
beginning to self-destruct and it became even more clear that Labour,
especially after Tony Blair became leader, was going to win convincingly.

Of course this all suited Blair who to some extent shared the Ashdown
dream (why wouldn't he? Labour had little to lose), but was also happy to
have the option to call on the Liberal Democrats should Labour not win
a majority. However, once Blair was sent to No 10 Downing Street in a
landslide, a desperate Ashdown became half-joke and half-liability. In an
effort to appease him, Blair set up a series of meetings between Labour
Ministers and a small group of Liberal Democrat MPs, and this led to a
Commission headed by Roy Jenkins to look at electoral reform but, of
course, there was no way Labour either needed or wanted this to actually
happen. With the exception of Robin Cook and one or two others, what
Labour Ministers were saying about all this behind the scenes was un-
printable, and the best that Peter Mandelson could say in his memoirs was
that he saw the possible broadening of the base as 'a useful insurance
policy if we needed to ward off a Tory revival'. What a reflection on Ashdown's sense of reality that his great dream was seen by one of Blair's
most influential advisors as an 'insurance policy'!

It was not only a fantasy because Labour did not need that 'insurance',
but because the Liberal Democrats had a much braver vision for itself. One
Liberal MP describes a parliamentary away-day when Charles Kennedy was
cheered by the others in the room when he told Ashdown that they should
seek to try and replace the Tories as the main Opposition party, thus going
head-to-head with Labour. In the end, the party, becoming more suspicious,
passed an Assembly resolution that, in effect, put handcuffs – actually, a
'triple lock' – on the leader. The game was up.

Sky Television's political editor Adam Boulton was to sum it up in an
article in *Sunday Business*:

The staggering achievement of (the Ashdown) diaries is to confirm a cynic's worst fears. However well he served his constituents, or turned his speeches, (Ashdown) became obsessed by the pursuit of political power pure and simple, for himself and his party . . .

In pursuit of that power, Ashdown lied repeatedly to most of his party, to the press, to Labour politicians and to the public about the secret negotiations with Blair.

Boulton concluded: ' . . . After Ashdown, the bigger challenge for his successor Kennedy (who emerges from the diaries unsullied by back-room dealing) is to prove that his party stands for something more than the craven pursuit of position.'

The Liberal Democrats did win more seats at the following General Election, largely thanks to Chris Rennard's brilliant target seats strategy and the anti-Tory swing, but there was still the same problem: the public liked what they saw of the Liberals, but could not say what they stood for. That's because Ashdown, busy producing memos and lists of possible Cabinet posts, having cozy chats with Blair, and negotiating in his own vacuum, did not have the time to do what the leader should have been doing, namely taking the marvellous opportunity between 1992 and 1997, with the Tories divided and in disarray, to come up with a coherent and convincing case for their replacement by the Liberal Democrats. Having, to his credit, held the party together and steered it past the worst, he diverted his energies to a foolish and ultimately doomed mission. In doing so, without any mandate from the party, he betrayed it, making a mockery of its members' hard work and sacrifice.

Kennedy

Opportunities to win the respect of a majority in the country at a historic moment don't come often, but one came with the Iraq war and I believe Charles Kennedy missed the moment.

Greatly to their credit, and unlike the Tories, Kennedy and the parliamentary party refused to buy the Blair case for war, and in the House of Commons voted consistently against it. But unlike Labour under Hugh Gaitskell, at the time of Suez, who established himself as a national leader by the way he opposed that equally flawed military action, Kennedy, in my view, went about it too carefully, too cautiously, restricting his concerns mainly to a Westminster audience, instead of giving them real resonance in the country. One problem seemed to be that he wanted to keep his more conservative foreign affairs spokesman Menzies Campbell on side and Campbell was a constraining influence. Another was that there were a number of members of the parliamentary party who had military bases in their constituencies and were understandably sensitive about being seen as too anti-war when the husbands or sons of constituents were in Iraq putting their lives on the line.

But it would have been no reflection on the troops, nor ungrateful for their valour, for responsible opposition politicians back at home to have made the case as forcibly as possible that they should not be there. This war was costing lives and it was costing a fortune in resources and it was costing our relationships with many other countries; it was, and has increasingly been seen to be so, an illegal and unnecessary and amoral war, and vast numbers in the country were opposed to it; over a million marched in protest and millions more supported them – and the Liberal Democrats had not only a unique opportunity, but every right to give it voice.

In my view, the Liberal Democrats should have not just have posed awkward questions and voted against it in the Commons (sadly, unnoticed by many outside), but should have led the opposition in the country, made a huge issue of it, nailed its colours to the anti-war mast, and, in doing, so changed their image from the 'nice but ineffectual other party' to the 'tough and challenging voice of the people'.

In September 2002 Kennedy performed well as the only questioning voice in the big parliamentary debate on the war; when met with jeers from the Tories, he turned to them and said 'I am only asking questions unasked by the leader of the Conservative party.' It was one of his best moments. At that time he and his colleagues were the parliamentary 'Opposition' to two parties voting for war; Kennedy was the one major figure in the House of Commons who could be said to represent the concerns of the British people. He then went on to effectively use PM Questions week after week to press Blair on the details.

Then in February 2003 there arose a big opportunity to reinforce his national leadership on the issue. There was to be a huge demonstration in London and Kennedy was asked to speak. On this he dithered for some time. The *Guardian*, in a leader, spoke for me and no doubt many other Liberal Democrat supporters, when it said: 'Remarkably, no senior or significant figure has managed to place themselves anywhere near the head of this oppositional movement . . . this ought to be Charles Kennedy's moment . . . but he is not going to be there and he does not appear to want to be there. This is an extraordinary mistake on Mr Kennedy's part.'

Eventually, under pressure, he decided to attend, but not to oppose the war as such. He would attend as pro-UN, not anti-war. His main pitch to the crowd was that there should be no war without another UN resolution. It helped that he was there, but it left many frustrated. In what was the last really crucial debate in the House of Commons, Kennedy and his war cabinet rightly decided to vote against the war but, if the Commons were to vote for it, as it would undoubtedly do, then it would accept that decision and 'support British troops in the field'. It was a measured position, an understandable position, but, alas in terms of the party's opportunity, a weak one, in effect: 'We don't think you should be doing this, but, if you do, we're with you.'

By then the rationale for war was becoming less and less credible, the need for a powerful voice for national concern was urgent, and Kennedy, well liked, articulate, should have become it. In doing so he would have answered the question: what are the Liberal Democrats for? Why do we need a third party? The answer could have been that when the two major parties became, in effect, one, driven by the same vain-glorious views of international statesmanship and the same vanities, there could be an alternative voice to put forward an alternative view.

Despite his drink problem and one or two sleazy friends, Kennedy was not a dishonorable man. He had better judgment than Ashdown (who, incredibly, supported the Iraq war, and did not help his successor by writing to Blair to say so). There will be many who will think my criticism is too severe, but this was *the* test . . . this was a special moment here, and Kennedy was too careful and cautious to fully grasp it.

Nick Clegg

If you add Jeremy Thorpe and Menzies Campbell to the above, then Nick Clegg is the sixth Liberal (or Liberal Democrat) leader since I joined the party. If the bar is set high, it is not because of his predecessors, but because of the circumstances he and the party find themselves in.

I accept without reservation that partnership government was the inevitable and logical outcome of what the party had been about for years. Liberals (me included) had complained about the two-party adversarial system and had called for more cooperation and more sane and sensible debate in politics. They had advocated a voting system that would be more likely to lead to shared power than control by one party. And, in any case, there was never going to be a moment when the party would receive such a colossal vote that, despite the electoral system, it was going to be swept to power over both other parties; there was always going to be at least a period of partnership politics of some sort, and the party had shown it could make it work in both Scotland and Wales and on many local authorities. To refuse in 2010 to assist one of the other parties to establish a stable government would have made no sense; indeed, it would have confirmed to the sceptics that the Liberal Democrats 'are not serious'. The Lib Dems had to step up to the plate.

Sadly – because it would not have been my preference – I also believe that when the moment came, the partnership had to be with the Conservatives. When the Lib Dem parliamentary party first met after the General Election, a majority of its members wanted to explore a coalition with Labour, both because they felt more comfortable with Labour, and because many of them had been elected by persuading former Labour voters that a vote for the Lib Dems would 'keep the Tories out'. But, apart from the fact that some of its key personalities did not want a deal, the reality was that Labour did not deserve another chance; it was shockingly divided at the top, looked tired, and it had lost the election. In fact it had lost 97 seats and won only 29 per cent of the vote. It had lost over 5 million votes since 1997. The country may not have given the Conservatives a majority either, but, the momentum was all in their direction. They won more votes and parliamentary seats than Labour; they were the winners.

So Nick Clegg's first two big decisions – to help establish a Government, and to do it with the Conservatives – were surely the right ones. But, a third question – how should it be done? – was one that had to be addressed in both the national *and* the party's interests.

One option was to enter a Coalition. On this, he could, of course, draw on the lessons of history. Four times between 1794 and 1933 the old Liberal party (earlier, the Whigs) entered into coalitions and each time the party became divided and virtually destroyed. Even when the Liberals declined coalition but agreed on a deal to keep Jim Callaghan in power in 1978-79, the party paid a heavy price, its vote falling by a fifth at the 1979 General Election. The evidence, both in the UK and elsewhere, is that when a coalition ends, as it always will one day, the junior or smaller party emerges as the loser.

But no one ever appears to want to learn from history, so let's stick to the present-day:

There was more than one workable option; coalition was not the only game in town.

It would have been possible to serve the national interest and protect the Liberal Democrats' independence by signing up to exactly the same policy agreement as that reached by the Coalition, but on what is called a 'supply and confidence' arrangement. Additionally the party could have made exactly the same deal on a referendum on electoral reform.

The second would have been my preference, *but* I fully accept that a powerful case could have been made for either option. Anyone who is adamant in saying that, in choosing to enter a formal Coalition with the Conservatives, Clegg made a mistake, stands to be proved wrong by events. We are, as they say, in uncharted waters. So, I, for one, am not adamant. On the contrary, I accept that this is what has happened, and I hope for the country's sake and the party's sake that it succeeds. But, for it to succeed for the Liberal Democrats, it must enable the party to emerge from the Coalition to fight the General Election with its credibility intact, its independence clear, and its integrity beyond doubt. David Cameron has said the Tories will seek a clear majority and sole power at the next General Election. And he has expressed a preference for 'the first past the post' system. This is not promising.

As I write, at least one question has been answered. When asked at the 2010 party conference, 'Will you field candidates in every constituency at the next general Election?' Clegg replied 'Yes.'

In that one-word answer he committed himself to the independence and integrity of the party. In that answer he gave every party member a reason to continue the fight, to contest seats at local level, to continue to develop its own policies and positions. It was an answer without ambiguity, from which there is no escape route – an answer which is surely beyond betrayal. Now the party is asked to believe that a credible escape route will emerge. They are asked to be loyal. They are asked to trust. And they will, because they are constructive and loyal and trusting people.

But it is worth remembering that Nick Clegg only won the Lib Dem leadership by a small margin. Those who knew him best, his own party members, had their reservations. And, despite winning the first leaders' debate and having a generally impressive General Election in 2010, he actually led his party backwards; it lost six seats. The public, having had a much closer look at him than ever before, also had their reservations. Now – by no means all – many already feel their trust betrayed; they had believed the Lib Dems who told them 'vote for us to keep the Tories out'.

During the 2010 General Election I spoke for our local Lib Dem MP, Andrew George (we met on the beach and he threatened to turn his dog on me if I didn't help; as it was a big dog, it was not a difficult decision). Andrew had lost six thousand Lib Dem voters in boundary changes; he was fighting for his political life. Indeed, come the General Election, both his neighbouring Lib Dem MPs were defeated, one in a seat the Lib Dems had held for thirty years. Andrew hung on, not thanks to my minimal help, though it was good that the old campaigner was still on the winning side, but because he persuaded local Labour voters that if they voted for him, he would keep the Tory out.

That was the winning strategy. Next time it will be a non-strategy.

It will take unprecedented political brilliance for Clegg and his colleagues to bring the Lib Dems out of the Coalition at the next general Election in a way that saves Andrew George and many others like him. Until then, all the party can do is try to maintain its independence . . . and hope. It's now all about trust. Trust cannot be demanded. It has to be earned. Will Nick Clegg earn it? What a fascinating few years these will be.

And my own view? It is that Lord Acton was right. Generally speaking, all power corrupts. It's not only me but every other Liberal Democrat who is hoping Nick Clegg proves there can be exceptions to the great historian's rule.

PART FOUR
Corporate Citizen

19

Time to Do the Business

'When I hear businessmen speak about the social responsibility of business (I say) they are unwitting puppets of the intellectual forces that have been undermining the basis of a free society.'

MILTON FRIEDMAN

On March 5, 1991, I woke up to find I was 50 years old. This came as a shock. I felt as it if were only yesterday that I had been nineteen and on a boat from 'down under'. How had this happened? And what was I to do? I was, in effect, unemployed. I was working, but unpaid, on a General Election campaign that appeared to have no end. I had no savings and had sold my only asset, a flat in Spain, to help pay our way. Jane had heroically offered to be our main earner while I helped rescue the Lib Dems, but soon it would be my turn and I hoped to repay my debt by helping her become a full-time artist. To make this happen, to eventually have some kind of pension and ultimately fulfil my childhood dream to travel and see the world – to achieve these three objectives, there was no option: I had to make some money.

But there was another factor: I felt that I had to cease to be an issue-by-issue campaigner. It was already 25 years since the launch of Shelter; I could only promote another cause so many times before people crossed the road when they saw me coming. I had watched Ralph Nader lose some of his impact as the years passed; I too was bound to become less effective with each campaign.

There was, of course, journalism; that would probably keep the wolves from the door, but, as another price paid for all the campaigning, I had not pursued it as a career, and even in journalism there was a ladder you had to climb, and there were a lot of younger men and women than me already competing with each other on the top-most rungs. There was no option: I had to go into business.

I knew, of course, that I was setting myself up: I could almost hear the cries of 'sell out' and 'poacher turned gamekeeper' from media and political cynics. I had no qualms myself. I was not, and never had been, anti-business. I may have battled with some companies and even some whole industries, but that did not make me anti-business as such; that would have been plain silly. Over 20 million people were employed in the private sector and just over five million in the public sector. To put it another way: the four-fifths of the workforce who worked in business and industry were funding the fifth who worked in the public and voluntary sectors, of whom, for a lot of my career, I was one. But I had to be realistic: whether it be fair or not, there was a credibility test I would have to pass. At the very least, I had to avoid inconsistencies with what I had campaigned for in the past.

I was mulling all this over when, a few weeks after the 1992 General Election, I was chosen by the communications industry as 'outstanding individual of the year' in their annual awards and found myself at the Grosvenor House being presented with it by Andrew Neil in front of over 1000 people. Everyone who was anyone in the communications and public relations industry was there. I realised that if I was going to make a break into business, this was the moment, so the following day I let my availability be known. This led to an offer from the London office of Burson Marsteller (BM), at the time the world's number one PR agency.

I made it clear to them that they would have to accept a condition, namely that I could decline to work with any client or industry with whom I had previously been at war, or of whose activities or product I disapproved. This condition may sound sensible enough, in fact – for me – essential, but news of it caused considerable debate and disquiet within a public relations industry that did not want to set a precedent. Generally speaking, PR practitioners worked on the same principle as lawyers, namely that everyone was entitled to their day in court and to be properly and professionally represented; that's how they saw themselves, as advocates for their clients. As the head of the London office of BM said to me: 'If everyone was like you and decided only to work for clients he personally approved of, the whole business would collapse.'

Fortunately, they saw the sense of it in my case and made the deal, and it all worked out even better than I hoped, because I was given my own unit with the freedom to build a business in the sectors where I would be comfortable, and soon was winning clients with whom I was fully in sympathy, beginning in the area of employment. First we won the Training and Enterprise Councils, and then Investors in People, and finally, the TUC, where I worked with and became friends with Brendan Barber, now its General Secretary. We were then hired to run a campaign for a University of Lincolnshire.

Jane and I were now living in a Lincolnshire village and it made sense for BM to recruit Jane to help me with this local client. We ran a high profile campaign culminating in a spectacular event at the local show grounds attended by a thousand influential people from the county, covered live by Radio Lincolnshire, backed up for a major supplement in the *Lincolnshire Echo*, and involving the local youth orchestra and choirs from a number of local schools,. The climax to our presentation was a surprise appearance by Richard Branson, who arrived by helicopter. The local newspaper described it as 'a triumph of showmanship and sound business sense'.

The university project succeeded and the area is now served by the University of Lincolnshire and Humberside. By now I had achieved the ideal, earning a decent living in business, but still devoting nearly all of my time to campaigning for causes I believed in. We now became involved in two particularly high profile campaigns, one for Sunday shopping and one in support of Richard Branson's lottery bid.

Sunday Shopping

I had initially been recruited to this cause back in 1990, pre-General Election and pre-Burson Marsteller days, by Sir Basil Feldman, a friend of Godfrey Bradman and a senior figure in the Conservative Party. A Royal Commission had recommended de-regulation of shopping hours but even my old adversary Margaret Thatcher, armed with a majority of 140, had failed to achieve it, beaten by her own backbenchers in the House of Commons. But Basil was an optimist: he had now persuaded a number of major High Street retailers to join in a fresh campaign for reform and they had poured considerable sums of money into what they called the Shopping Hours Reform Council (SHRC).

He asked me one day where I stood on the issue. I replied that I didn't stand anywhere, in the sense that it was a hardly a cause I would lay down my life for. But I was reasonably sympathetic; apart from being riddled with absurdities and inconsistencies (on Sundays, you could sell the *News of the World*, but you could not sell the Bible. You could make money from stories about naughty vicars and choir boys, but not sell the *Book of Common Prayer*). But the real point was that the ban on Sunday shopping simply no longer reflected our lifestyles.

The old days of Morning Service, followed by the Sunday roast, and then a doze in the deck chair, a tea of scones with strawberry jam, and off to Evensong, were past, if, for most, they ever really existed. In particular, the lives of women had radically changed; the majority no longer stayed at home and did the shopping while their husbands worked to pay for it; now women were going out to work too. Polls showed an overwhelming majority of women wanted the convenience of being able to shop on Sundays. In fact, no less than 30 national opinion polls over an 18 month period averaged 65 per cent support for reform. Incontrovertibly – and this was the clincher for me – this was what the public wanted. So, I allowed myself to be hired by the SHRC as a fairly low-key advisor, earning a fee that just about covered my rail fare from Lincolnshire to London (thus, Basil, former chairman of the Conservative Party, was unwittingly contributing to the costs of the Liberal Democrat General Election campaign!)

I just had time to discover that a fervent minority in favour of the status quo, championed by an organisation called Keep Sunday Special, was winning every skirmish, when we were all swept up in the 1992 General Election campaign and SHRC was put on hold; when the election was over, and I was at Burson Marsteller, I found that one of the SHRC's main funders, David Sainsbury, then head of the famous family business, had reached the pessimistic conclusion that the cause could never be won. Sainsbury's main point was that, if a powerful Prime Minister like Margaret Thatcher, with a majority of 140, could be defeated on the issue, then a weaker John Major, now Prime Minister with a majority just over 20, stood no chance.

So he called what became, for me – but also for the issue – a momentous meeting. I knew it was out of the ordinary when I arrived by taxi to find a whole line of big, expensive cars with chauffeurs lined up outside the Sainsbury head office. I was even more impressed when I entered the board room to find about a dozen chairmen of the main High Street retailers; I think nine of them were Knights of the Realm . . . Sir Asda, Sir

Kingfisher, Sir Safeway, and so on. They included the major supermarket chains, but also High Street familiars such as Boots and WH Smith. These men were Britain's retail giants; they employed vast numbers of people; everyone in the country spent money in their stores; their purchasing policies could make or break other major companies. Every one of their companies was a household name; most of them in the FTSE 100. This really was Big Business.

As I looked round, I realised that no one from the SHRC had been invited, not even Basil Feldman or its impressive chairwoman Margaret (later Baroness) Jay. Clearly David Sainsbury wanted the kind of frank exchange with his peers that could more easily take place if the SHRC leadership was not there. But, why was I there? I felt a bit like Norman Wisdom as the office boy in *Trouble in Store* in the presence of these immaculately dressed men, comfortable in their certainties. No one knew why I was there, including me, but no one was so indelicate as to ask, especially me. After only a few minutes, another thing became apparent: they did not have a clue what they were talking about.

I was to discover this many times as my career continued in business: men and women can be exceptional in their chosen field; they can be highly intelligent; they can be outstanding leaders of others – and yet, take them out of their particular sphere, and especially into the world of public affairs, and many of them would be left standing in a contest with a first year student in politics at a second-level university. So it was at this meeting. These men, knighted for their services to industry, were brilliant retailers, brilliant at positioning their companies and their stores, but when it came to positioning their company in the community and to understanding politics or how the world beyond their business actually worked, it was they, not I, who were the innocents abroad.

There is no question what so ever that, had I not been there, these men would have closed the SHRC. Had they done so, no one else would have had the temerity to have another try for years, possibly decades. Shops would still be closed on Sundays. After what seemed only a few minutes, David Sainsbury summed up their views: This could not be won. It was time to call it a day and save their money. SHRC should be closed down, wound up, its cause abandoned, defeat accepted, and the field left to the victors, Keep Sunday Special.

'Sir Asda', 'Sir Kingfisher' and 'Sir Safeway' and so on – all nodded. Their role at the meeting appeared purely ceremonial, to jointly wear the black cap, pass down the sentence, formally observe the execution. Sainsbury then turned to me and said 'That's right, Des, is it not? This cannot be won.' I was thinking: this was crazy. They could win. 'No, David,' I said, 'I don't believe it's lost. I believe this can be won. But the problem is not the House of Commons, and its definitely not Keep Sunday Special. The problem is you – and it is the companies represented in this room. You lost when Thatcher was in power because you took success for granted, and you made no concessions to the genuine concerns being expressed; you were so busy thinking and talking about what you wanted, that you did not listen or hear what others were actually saying.'

I asked them to look carefully at each of their three main opponents: First, there were the trade unions. They had to be won over because, on what was a non-doctrinaire issue, the Labour Party would vote prag-matically, whichever way the trade unions wanted. The trade unions were not totally opposed to reform, nor were the workers themselves; they just didn't want to be *made* to work on Sundays. All they wanted was for Sunday working to be optional . . . voluntary . . . and they wanted protections guaranteed. Second, there were the small shop-keepers, especially in rural areas, who needed those three hours from seven till 10 o'clock on Sunday mornings, when – as in my own village in Lincolnshire – people came to buy the Sunday papers, but also pick up a few other essentials, bread, milk and the like. This was a big time of the week for these village or corner shops. Protect them for those three hours and they would have less reason to oppose reform, and their main parliamentary supporters, Tory MPs in rural constituencies, would have more reason to support it. Third, there was the Church. Hardly anyone was going to its early morning and early evening services now; the last thing the Church wanted was another reason for them to stay away. Its influence may be disproportionate, but if the SHRC was to win, then it had to protect its main 'business hours' too.

'So what precisely are you saying we should do,' Sainsbury asked. 'Restrict the hours you open,' I said. 'The SHRC has already been moving towards this position; you now need to firm up on it: aim for partial de-regulation. Open from 10.00 a.m. to 4.00 p.m. to protect the church and the

small shops. And then make Sunday work voluntary. If people don't want
to work on Sunday, they won't have to – guaranteed.'

And there was one other thing. 'You are throwing away your number
one asset – the public. They want this. Instead of talking about what *you*
want, you have to mobilise them to call for what *they* want. You are coming
across as big business wanting to change the law to make more money,
but this has to be about your customers, their convenience, their needs. Be
conciliatory. Help your customers speak. This way they, and not you, will
give their MPs permission to support you.'

So, instead of closing the campaign down, 'the meeting of the Knights'
decided to consider a plan for its revival on those principles, and I was
asked to put together a plan and present it to all the companies involved in
the SHRC. This I did, and I think it fair to say this meeting of about fifty
retailers became genuinely excited; for the first time, they saw a real chance
of winning. So the SHRC appointed me and BM to handle the campaign.
The objective was partial de-regulation: opening on Sundays from 10.00
a.m. to 4.00 p.m.

The Home Office decided to allow the House of Commons to choose
from four options; our task was to win a parliamentary majority for the
SHRC option – and to ensure it subsequently became law. From the start,
we set out to undermine the belief that this was the Big Business option.
We had to get ordinary people, the 'consumers', to campaign for it, with
our coordination and support and, if necessary, resources.

We set about mobilising existing consumer and women's organisations,
but also set up two of our own, Working Women for Sunday Shopping and
Consumers for Sunday Shopping. People became members of the latter by
signing a form at supermarkets; before we knew what was happening we
had three million 'members'; we appointed one woman in Wimbledon as
secretary and she ended up with hundreds of sack-loads of signed forms in
her garden shed! Never the less, it was impressive when she wrote to *The
Times* and began 'I write on behalf of my three million members . . .' which
she could legitimately do; these people *had* queued up at supermarkets to
sign the forms. They wanted this. Sympathetic workers were recruited to
another organisation we established, the National Association of Sunday
Shop-workers. Local authorities joined CLIFSS (Council Leaders in Favour
of Sunday Shopping). The SHRC was given the jazzier name of Sunday

Shopping Campaign and became the coordinating campaign for all these already-established and newly-created groups.

We now had to convince MPs that they were 'safe' to support it; that it really did have the public behind it. We commissioned a whole series of polls, and even asked every major polling organisation to conduct a poll on the same day to create a super-poll, a 'poll of polls'. These polls never varied; every one showed overwhelming support for the cause. Ironically, considering that it was the one that least had me tossing and turning in bed at night, this was rapidly becoming my most popular cause ever.

It was also crucial that we reached MPs in their constituencies, where they would be hoping to get a sense of what their own local voters really wanted. Some of the supermarkets had decided to test the law and prove the demand by opening on Sundays anyway, and paying the fines if they were prosecuted. While I was not entirely comfortable with this, as I had always made it a principle to try and win campaigns with activities within the law, it proved a success. The public were voting with their feet. MPs were persuaded to go to the opening shops and see the popularity of Sunday shopping for themselves. We set up a nationwide grassroots campaign to get constituents to write to MPs and go to surgeries. We hired a former *Mirror* journalist to produce a tabloid newspaper for hand-outs at supermarkets and in the High Street; for a time it was the highest-circulation newspaper in the country. We assembled the top employers to publicly sign a charter of employees' rights. The main shop workers' union then withdrew its opposition. Once it had done that, the shadow Home Secretary, one Tony Blair, felt able to commit the Labour Party to back reform.

As the parliamentary debate got nearer, Andrew Currie, the bright, young lobbying head of the campaign (who later went with me to BAA) had the names of every one of the 650 MPs on his wall and a prediction as to how they would vote (on the night he was right about 648 of them). When the whole issue eventually came to the House of Commons in the form of the four options, one of which was full de-regulation and one of which was as near as possible to the status quo, there was an enthralling debate and at the end of it our option won easily,

Today Sunday shopping is part of the British way of life, another freedom, another right, that we all take for granted. There will be those who say that it was the retailers' money that did the trick. But it wasn't. On the contrary, after investing a lot of their cash, the retailers, whose resources were virtually unlimited, had been on the point of giving up. It was won by a campaign based on two essential ingredients: we listened to the voice of the people, and especially those directly affected, and met their concerns. And instead of speaking for the public, we helped the public to speak for themselves. (Incidentally, money is never the number one factor in campaigning. Many citizen campaigns have defeated opponents who have been much better-resourced. Just from my own experience, if money was the key factor, the lead industry and the oil companies would have wiped the floor with Clear and the tobacco companies would have done the same to PAT. The Lib Dem 1992 campaign was widely judged to have been the best, but we had a fraction of the resources of the larger parties. Campaigns are won because of the energy and ideas behind them, and usually because they are right, not because they are the best-funded.)

These were lessons for business, but also for me. I was beginning to envisage a new kind of relationship between business and those it affected (I had not yet learned to call them 'stakeholders'). It was a relationship based on finding common ground and working together to create change.

Richard Branson and the Lottery Bid

Richard Branson asked me whether I and my team at BM would take on the communications and campaigning for his bid to run Britain's first lottery. For whoever was permitted to run it, the lottery appeared to be 'a licence to print money'. That was because, unlike almost every other major lottery in the world, the operator would only have to hand over some of the profits to the state and to good causes; they would be allowed to keep for themselves hundreds of millions of pounds over the first seven years of the licence. Richard Branson argued that this was never the intention of those who campaigned over the years for a National Lottery. And it hardly reflected the title of the White Paper called *A Lottery for Good Causes*.

Richard wanted all the profits from the lottery to serve the public, and announced a bid for the licence by a company that would be non profit-making; instead, all the 'profits' would go into a Foundation he would set up to help good causes. He believed that the public-spirited nature of his bid would make him an inevitable winner. He would create a People's Lottery.

From the start, I had my doubts about Richard's chances. While we had a good team, I could tell by the 'body language' of the all-important OFLOT regulator and his staff that they were less than enthusiastic about Richard running the lottery; my guess was that they were nervous about the lottery getting off the ground without mistakes, and were inclined to play safe by awarding it to our main rivals, Camelot, who had recruited a company with vast experience of running big lotteries in America. I also sensed that OFLOT feared it would become too much Richard's lottery, rather than the National Lottery. But Richard's bid was a good one and I was determined to do all I could to help.

Richard had been involved in Parents against Tobacco which was the first time I had worked closely with him. I quickly saw why he got the best out of people; he was careful to show he trusted them. He would phone me on a Sunday morning to discuss the campaign, and sometimes he had suggestions, but he always went out of his way to stress they were only suggestions; in my area, I was in charge. He gave you the confidence to act and this, in turn, inspired loyalty.

He was a remarkable mixture of efficiency and informality. When you went for a chat at his house in Holland Park he would be sitting on a sofa in bare feet, often with his son playing on the floor in the same room. He was always accompanied by a big notebook and he wrote down everything you said that he believed to be of consequence. The system obviously worked because everything you agreed on then happened. Richard was tough – he had to be tough to build the empire he did – but he was also a team player, open to any idea, and always ready to listen. For all the flamboyance of his publicity activities, he often gave the impression of hesitancy; He was a surprisingly nervous public speaker.

Richard was totally committed to the public service nature of this bid. He saw it as the biggest thing he could ever do for his fellow citizens, his legacy. He stood to gain not a penny; the nation, and its neediest, stood to gain a fortune. He became emotionally involved with it. For a time it was virtually all that mattered to him. You could not help but want him to succeed. 'I was standing beside him the day he received the fax from OFLOT. It was brutally brief. Thanks, but no thanks. While I had feared this result, Richard was genuinely shocked, virtually in tears; he had to slip away from the media assembled outside of his house and walk round the block to calm down.

Even so, in his interviews he came across as a bad loser, which was true, but not entirely fair, because it was not he who had lost, but thousands of charities and sports clubs and art facilities and other good causes that would have received the huge sums of money that have subsequently gone to Camelot's shareholders. Richard is both a popular and controversial figure. You can, however, only judge someone on your own experience of them. I liked Richard.

PR Week said in an editorial that Branson lost the bid, but had won the public relations war. I think that is fair. I cannot think of what else we could have done. So despite the result, my first 18 months at BM had been for me a success, and the company now asked me to become their world wide vice chairman for public affairs. But, while I had only been there 18 months, I was impatient to move on to a wider playing field. Partly as a result of the Sunday shopping experience, and partly from reading, I had become aware of a new way of doing business, and I could not wait to become involved.

I had discovered a new cause. It was corporate social responsibility (CSR), and the concept of stakeholder companies.

Corporate Citizen

In 1993, the Royal Society of Arts launched an inquiry into the qualities that would help a company succeed in the 21st century. After consulting with more than 8,000 business leaders and opinion formers, it concluded that while profit and long-term value for investors remained crucial, understanding stakeholder needs and including them in business strategies was central to achieving those objectives. Even more controversially, it stated:

> Business has the potential to act as an engine of social change, using its creative thinking, economic resources and cultural power to improve lives . . . Conservatives dismiss this as 'adding to the burdens of business' . . . They're completely out of step with social trends: a new generation of managers is rising to the top of many leading companies – individuals who are socially concerned and have progressive ideas about what their companies could do to make the world a better place. Not

because they're altruists but because they recognise the tremendous economic and cultural power they wield, and want to find creative ways of using that power for good while delivering financial returns.

The debate that now took place was far from one-sided. Thus Nobel Prize winning economist Milton Friedman:

> When I hear businessmen speak eloquently about the social responsibility of business in a free enterprise system ... that business is not concerned merely with profit ... that business has a social conscience, and takes seriously its responsibilities for providing employment, eliminating discrimination, avoiding pollution and whatever else may be the catch word of the contemporary crop of reformers. [I say] they are unwitting puppets of the intellectual forces that have been undermining the basis of free society.

A later column in the *Financial Times* by the influential Martin Wolf acknowledged the popularity of corporate social responsibility ('To attack it is like assailing motherhood'), but continued:

> The idea is not merely undesirable but potentially dangerous . . . it accepts a false critique of the market economy, it endorses an equally mistaken view of the powers of multinational businesses; it risks spreading costly regulations world-wide, it is more likely to slow the reduction of world poverty than accelerate it; it requires companies to make highly debatable political judgments ...

But they were speaking for the past; they simply did not appear to understand that a younger, better-educated, more articulate, more self-confidant generation was becoming more sensitive to environmental threats, to risks to health and safety, to abuse of financial power, and to the power of companies to affect their lives without proper accountability to, or involvement by the public or consumers.

Companies that did not act responsibly were beginning to face devastation to their reputations – some already faced consumer boycotts, and others were finding it harder to recruit talent, losing the trust of customers or business partners, facing hostile neighbours, and having their plans blocked by hostile regulators and public authorities or opposed by campaigners and the media. All this was distracting managers, limiting the company's freedom of manoeuvre, handicapping its ability to grow its business, and threatening its long-term profitability.

In a nutshell, companies could no longer act as if they were isolated from the world around them: they were becoming increasingly accountable to higher social expectations.

Not only did CSR make sense of my involvement in business, but it was highly motivating. I was really excited about it. And I was positioned to make a real contribution, because my reputation meant it was easy for me to get to speak on public platforms and at business conferences; I could place articles in newspapers and magazines, and I could be a credible advocate because I had worked on both sides of what some called 'the divide'.

Enthusiastically, I wrote that this was a historic change to match the revolutions of the past. In the nineteenth century, we had the industrial revolution. In the twentieth century, we had at least two huge human resources changes: first greater industrial equality driven by the rise of the trade unions and the Labour movement, then in turn, greater employee involvement as management came to understand that it needed to harness the employees' brains as well as their brawn in order to remain successful. Towards the end of the twentieth century we had also experienced the information and technological revolution, whose full outcome was probably still beyond our imagination to appreciate. Now, approaching the twenty-first century, we had a potential revolution in the way business perceived itself: no longer a law unto itself, but instead, accountable to the community and its highest values By keeping industry free to create wealth, but also involving it in the wider social cause of improving the quality of life for people everywhere, this revolution was as crucial as the earlier ones.

I was particularly attracted to the concept of stakeholder companies, and set my heart on finding a company where I could develop it from scratch and show what could be done. But, where was I to find the company? This is where the Wilson luck kicked in once more. I found myself in the right place at the right time. And I met John Egan.

John Egan

I owe it all to Jonathan Porritt. In 1993 he had been unable to travel to Budapest to speak to a conference of chief executives of international companies in travel and tourism, and he recommended me. The top men from hotel chains and airlines were to be there, and others from companies like American Express. We're talking about chairmen and chief executives; some of the world's leading business figures, men with the clout to have Henry Kissinger as one of the other speakers. As I arrived in Budapest and looked out the window of the economy section of the aircraft, I could see expensive private jets landing all around me. This reminded me of the Sunday shopping meeting at Sainsbury's, except this was bigger – this was on a global scale.

My mission was to persuade them they had to go Green and commit themselves to sustainability. I won't say they rose to their feet, cheering and waving their order papers, but the speech was at least politely received. But what made the event a memorable one for me was that, while I was there, I met the boss of BAA, Sir John Egan.

John and I had actually lived in Earls Court at the same time, way back in 1960, but while we must have passed each on the streets, we never met – probably because I was from the old Commonwealth and he was English, and in Earls Court in those days that made him a foreigner. John subsequently became internationally known when he saved Jaguar and subsequently led a management buy-out of the company. He became chief executive of the recently privatised UK airport company BAA in 1991.

John built his companies around three main beliefs. First, to him 'mission statements' were not a trendy idea; the company's mission statement had to mean what it said. To him, it was the route map that enabled everyone in the company to travel together to the same destination. It was widely debated at every level of the company; to change so much as one word called for intensive discussion. There had to be total sign up. If you had a new idea, his first question was 'where does this fit with the mission statement?' The effect was to create a company that really did pull together. Second, there had to be a process of 'continuous improvement'; today's achievement was never good enough – the whole point of today was to improve on yesterday, and the point of tomorrow was to improve on today. Third, the company had to be dedicated to customer service: 'If you don't know what else to do, start satisfying your customers'.

He revolutionised the way BAA worked. Continual surveys showed both airlines and passengers becoming increasingly satisfied. Employee relations were good; in its first 20 years after privatisation there was never a strike in any part of the business. It was consistently profitable; it had to be, because over a number of years it was consistently investing £1 million every day in national infrastructure. In John's day, it was a good company. And it had values. (There was a meeting when a middle manager, spelling out the details of an overseas deal, mentioned a 'payment' to someone. 'I hope you don't mean a bribe?' John asked. 'Well, I would not use that word, but . . . ' the middle manager began. John interrupted. 'If that's what it takes, the deal's off.' Meeting over.)

John was immensely popular with the staff at the airports, but his relationships with his senior managers were more complex. He could come on heavy to get his way, but like all such men, he respected anyone who withstood the heat of the argument and held their ground. For someone with the reputation of being a business buccaneer, he was actually quite cautious. He was not afraid of change, but he needed to be persuaded. His best quality was that he delegated. He expected his managers to take responsibility, and he did support them. And he was not a blame merchant; if you made a mistake, he did not waste energy and time explaining why you were at fault. He assumed you knew that. He was more likely to sympathise, especially if you were clearly determined to repair any damage yourself.

Given that, apart from him, I was the spokesman for the company, I needed to be able to act with confidence; he gave me that confidence. Finally, he understood that while BAA was a private company, it was still perceived by the public as belonging to them. This is because it was delicately positioned at the interface between the public and private sector, responsible to its shareholders, but also to the nation, as the company entrusted with an essential part of the national infrastructure, the airports, gateways to the country. To put it bluntly, it would be allowed to do what it wanted as a private company as long as it behaved in a way that was consistent with the public interest . . . John was walking a tightrope.

This was the man I met in Budapest.

The BAA Challenge

Shortly after Budapest, John had a bad evening in Richmond, Surrey. At that time (the early 1990s), there was plenty of runway capacity at Heathrow, but nowhere to park extra planes and for people to embark and disembark. It needed a fifth terminal. Whereas these days the main objection to additional aviation activity is its input to global warming, in the early Nineties the issue was more likely to be aircraft noise and traffic. Some of the more vocal opponents were centred in Richmond and Twickenham, articulate, affluent areas on the flight path. John was asked to attend a public meeting in Richmond Theatre and went out there on a Sunday night expecting 40 or 50 people. Instead, it was packed to the rafters with hundreds, and they gave him hell. He was shaken, and the next day told colleagues: 'I've always been told our opponents were environmentalists or citizen activists. But these are ordinary people, our neighbours. 'They're not promoting an environmental or political cause; they're just upset by the noise and the traffic. We can't ignore this: these people have a right to be heard.'

That night John also realised that the rules had changed; in the past BAA had been able to count on getting planning permission with the help of lawyers, technical arguments and sympathetic Whitehall civil servants. Now he was faced with a vocal local community, and unlike many leaders of other industries, he actually understood that he could not ride roughshod over them; he had to listen to them and try and find an answer to their concerns. By coincidence, I was scheduled to speak at a London First meeting, and John was also speaking. We afterwards reminisced about the Budapest conference, and some days later we had lunch, when he shared with me his Richmond experience and what he saw as 'the T5 challenge'.

He also told me that BAA needed a new Director of Corporate and Public Affairs and he was beginning to believe that what he needed was not a traditional corporate man but, as he put it, 'a street fighter.' I then talked about corporate social responsibility and my ambitions to see how far the stakeholder concept could be taken in a big company. Why not BAA?

So, later that week, after I had met some of his fellow directors, a deal was struck. I would leave BM and become a member of the executive committee of this FTSE 100 company, my mission to develop a stakeholder approach with investors, employees, business partners, neighbours, national and local authorities, and anyone else who was directly affected by the activities of the company, and to help promote at every level of the company the concept of corporate social responsibility.

John was taking an even bigger risk than he realised; because our direct contact had removed head-hunters and the usual human resources machinery from the hiring process, the relevance of my experience to the totality of the role was never properly questioned. In fact no one asked me for a CV. (I recall having a chat with John one day a year or so later, and he casually remarked, 'I would never hire anybody without a university degree'. I said, 'Well, John, you have – I left school at 15.' He went white).

John assumed that if I had a world-wide post with BM, I must know what I was doing. John's colleagues assumed that if John wanted me, he knew what he was doing. I never really thought about it . . . until I arrived, and found everyone expected me to know things that I had never come across before.

It was, for a while, hair-raising. I had to learn the aviation business. And for the first time I had to deal with numbers as well as words; I even had to hire a tutor to show me how to read a balance sheet, and lean on others to teach me how the City worked. If my executive committee colleagues had known the extent that I was playing it by ear, they would have had a communal heart attack. How did I get by? The answer is by working extremely hard. As we were still living in Lincolnshire, I stayed on weekdays in a hotel 100 yards away from the office and was at my desk by 6.00 a.m. I had three or four hours to carefully study and understand the papers for every meeting. If I did not always have answers, I at least knew the questions.

Once when I couldn't sleep, I actually came in at four in the morning. The security man was so impressed that he told everyone in the company when they arrived at nine. This did my reputation no harm at all. In fact, it became the stuff of legend . . . years after, when new corporate office staff asked about me, they were told 'He comes in at four in the morning, you know.' Such are reputations made.

By dint of putting in the hours and getting round the company and asking the right questions, I soon learned the bread and butter part of my role, but this was only the starting point: if I was to justify working for BAA, it was not me who had to change; the whole company had to change, and even the whole industry. And a lot of people were watching, some of them not uncritically.

This was reflected in the widespread newspaper comment when I joined, with the *Guardian* in a front-page headline describing me as a 'former environmentalist' and its story was headed 'Poacher turned Gamekeeper?' The *Economist* wrote about both my move and a similar one by the environmentalist and television celebrity Dr David Bellamy:

> '... Both men are gambling their reputations on being able to influence companies from inside, rather than outside. It is Mr Wilson whom environmentalists will watch most closely. Companies increasingly want to work with environmentalists; if he succeeds, with his reputation intact, others will find such co-operation easier. But he could hardly have picked a more delicate issue. There must be easier ways to earn a pension.'

Were all this happening now, fifteen or more years later, I could probably not have joined BAA, because the aviation industry's contribution to global warming has become such a major issue. But, it was hardly on the horizon in the Eighties and Nineties. In the whole time I was chairman of Friends of the Earth, the aviation industry was never mentioned to me – not once. Even in 1994, when I joined BAA, no one who had worked with me in the environmental movement at national level, questioned my action: in fact Jonathan Porritt, Charles Secrett and others all came to lunch at BAA at various times to discuss the issues. Friendships were maintained. They understood my hopes for what I could achieve; they may have been sceptical about my chances of pulling it off, but they were more than ready to give me space. I was grateful for that.

So it was all high risk, but at the same time there was no industry I would have been happier to be part of. I loved travelling, and rejoiced in the fact that I now lived at a time when it was possible for people to fly – to holiday overseas, to explore the world, to visit family and friends who live abroad, to participate in international cultural sport and political events, to do business, and to generally broaden our life experiences. I was not a hypocrite: I was not going to deny to others what I enjoyed and wanted for myself. I also believed that the only way you could curtail air travel was by making it more expensive; that meant restricting it to the well off. I did not want the first generation of low income people who could afford to fly to also become the last.

To me this was a big test of the sustainability concept: if an industry that was basically a popular and necessary one, was to be allowed to grow to meet demand, it had to be made sustainable. In the case of the aviation industry, that meant quieter planes. It meant lowering of emissions. It meant reducing road traffic around airports. And all of this, BAA believed, was possible. But my first challenge was T5, and on this I made my most critical impact before I even joined the company, at a memorable dinner at the Goring Hotel near BAA's Victoria offices in the summer of 1994, when for the first time I met the BAA team handling the inquiry.

Up to this point the inquiry team was acting on the principle that it should make no concessions at all, but instead allow itself to be grudgingly forced to make them, one by one, as the inquiry proceeded. This meant it would concede the minimum but at the same time allow its opponents a few small wins. This was the traditional way whereby industry faced public inquiries. But I came in with the view I had expounded to the High Street retailers on Sunday trading, namely that it was better to identify the real issues up-front and deal with them. While there would always be some objectors left, they would be minimised.

My argument was that BAA should not see problems such as noise and traffic as inquiry obstacles to overcome with minimal concessions, but as real community problems to be dealt with by real solutions. In so much as the airports directly affected the quality of their lives, our neighbours were stakeholders, entitled to the same consideration as the other share-holders . . . employees, business partners, passengers, and so on. All this was put to the test at this first meeting. The team explained that the T5 Inquiry was, in effect, more than one inquiry. It would also deal with per-missions for a number of road works and other operations associated with the project, including how a terminal access road would connect to the M25, and all would coincide with the highly contentious governmental proposals for a widening of the M25 to 14 lanes, a step that BAA was saying was not needed for T5.

I asked why, if the 14 lanes were not needed for T5, the company was supporting the plan. 'Because the Government asked us to,' was the reply. I then argued that, with the widening of the M25 being one of the main complaints of T5's opponents, it made no sense for BAA to support it. 'It's hugely controversial, we don't need it and we're being blamed for it. Why don't we support our neighbours instead?'

So it was decided at that meeting that the company would withdraw its support for the 14-lane M25. Its new position proved a key factor in the 14-lane scheme eventually being ruled out and more restricted widening being concentrated on a few key congestion points. And it eliminated one of the main objections to T5, for instead of testifying as opponents to the local community, BAA had become a key agent on their behalf: their solution instead of part of their problem.

I now proposed we should examine the whole T5 proposal to properly appreciate opposition concerns and see how we could address them. We began by polling local people to establish exactly what they were concerned about. The polls were conducted by Gallup within the noise footprint and a five-mile radius of the airport, and were slightly weighed towards the most affected areas. At the same time the company representatives attended scores of local meetings to discuss the proposal and its implications and to listen to local concerns.

There were a number of surprises. To begin with, despite the fact that opponents had to this point virtually had the battlefield to themselves because of BAA's concentration on its technical case, more people in the area supported T5 than opposed it, not least because many of them worked in the aviation industry and the whole local economy was based on it.

This surprised the company, so much so that we decided to repeat the poll a few weeks later; the second one replicated the findings of the first almost exactly.

There were other interesting findings. People's concerns differed according to where they lived but, on the whole, aircraft noise was not as important an issue as the company had expected. The major local concerns were:

- the fear that T5 was 'just another step' that would lead to a third runway and an ever-enlarging airport with ever-increasing impacts on local communities
- the fear of increasing traffic on the roads
- the fear of more night flights.

So, just as the retailers had done with the Sunday shopping issue, we now set out to address those concerns. The company began to look for answers – real answers – and then . . . to communicate that it had been listening and was responding.

The first sign of our change of approach was a letter from John delivered to 500,000 homes in the Heathrow area on the first morning of the inquiry. In it he wrote:

> I want to make a firm promise to you, on behalf of the Board of Directors of BAA plc and on behalf of the management of Heathrow Airport that we will:
> Address the concerns raised by you, our neighbours.
> Take practical steps to minimise our impact on the community.
> Report to you annually on our progress.

The letter reassured members of the local community that:

- T5 does not call for another runway
- T5 will not lead to a fourteen lane M25
- T5 will not cause more noise than today
- T5 will not increase the quota of night flights.

The company began an internal debate into how it should set about keeping its promises to listen and to respond.

From the start, we were determined: the answer could not be a cosmetic one. The company had to make real concessions to local concerns: it had to come up with practical solutions to real problems. As one senior colleague Michael Maine said at the time, 'You can't tell people they can't hear noise when they can, that they can't see cars when they can . . . If they're to believe you're acting on these issues you have to achieve a real result.'

For two or three years we worked at establishing better relations with the community, making concessions within the inquiry, and working with them on all sorts of local issues, and on the last day of the inquiry John Egan was able to write back to the 500,000 households:

> I'm pleased to confirm that we have kept our word. Every specific pledge we made in that letter has been repeated formally to the inquiry: every practical step has been taken. T5:

- Won't lead to more overall noise – We are prepared to be legally bound to ensure that the area affected by aircraft noise will be kept below what it was in 1994. This is possible because aircraft are getting quieter.
- Won't lead to a huge increase in the number of planes – While the terminal will handle around 60 per cent more passengers, the increase in flights will be around 8 per cent. This is because as well as getting quieter, the average aircraft at Heathrow is carrying more passengers.
- Won't lead to an increase in the night flight quota – We have invited the inquiry inspector to recommend this to the government.
- Won't lead to huge increase in road traffic – Just as there will be more planes, there will be more cars, but only 3 per cent more at peak times throughout the area. In addition, we have offered a cap on car park spaces under our control, so that the number will never exceed what is predicted with Terminal Five.
- Will lead to an increase in rail capacity – Terminal Five creates an opportunity to increase Heathrow's rail capacity from 10 to 16 trains an hour each way.

By then a graph of our opinion polls showed the extent that we had won back many in the community.

Eventually, the Secretary of State for Transport, Stephen Byers, announced that T5 was approved. Byers told the House of Commons it was in the national interest. It is significant that the result led to little protest locally, and construction of Terminal Five proceeded with none of the disruption caused at, say, Manchester Airport, where there was all sorts of protest activity when it extended its runway. We had helped the majority of local people to become comfortable with the result.

Contact with the Community

The T5 campaign had only been part of what I had been doing, in fact, a small part. My main contribution was a new CSR programme called 'Contract with the Community'. We launched the proposal at the annual meeting of the company's top 150 managers in late 1995, advocating a progressive approach to corporate citizenship, the adoption of an open, expansion-by-negotiation approach to planning, and a commitment to sustainable growth.

In a nutshell, building on the T5 experience, the company would ask for permission from its neighbours to develop its airports, in return for sharing their concerns about the negative effects and coming up with practical solutions. Where the negative could not be entirely balanced, the company would compensate its neighbours for the downside by a positive contribution to community life.

In recognition that attitudes can take years to change, Contract with the Community was launched internally as a pragmatic programme geared to the areas where the company's growth aspirations were, and to what it could deliver at any particular time. There was good reason for this. We were concerned to carry the whole of BAA with us. I well remembered a few years earlier attending a management conference of Monsanto and hearing a top international board director extolling a corporate-citizen approach, only to be openly attacked by his middle managers who argued that they had enough problems meeting the board's bottom-line objectives without being stuck with this 'do-gooder stuff'. This was not surprising. They had for years been educated to believe that those who obstructed the growth of their industries were unrealistic eccentrics, extremists, trouble-makers, and 'nutters'. There were many in the middle rank of BAA who had always felt I was an environmentalist who had slipped past the security guards to distract them from their real work; it was critical therefore to build up a team of traditional BAA people who believed in CSR and would 'front' the cause within the company. And it was equally crucial, at the beginning, to stress the business benefits. The social benefits could be stressed later.

I was very proud of our contract (*see over*). Few companies could match it. To me it was vindication of my belief that I could create real change within business, just as David Bellamy, FoE UK founder Graham Searle, former Greenpeace director Peter Melchett, and Jonathan Porritt, with Forum for the Future, were all trying to do. When John and I launched it at a major management meeting, I proudly told my colleagues: 'This is not about PR. It is about the values of the company, the kind of people in it, the kind of ethical and other beliefs at its core.'

A simple first step was to increase the company's charitable giving by 50 per cent and create and register our own charity, the Twenty-First Century

**The ten key principles underlying
Contract with the Community were:**

1 Promote a vision for cleaner, smarter growth in aviation which maximises the positive benefits for society – facilitating prosperity, regeneration, regional and UK competitiveness, cultural exchange and social inclusion – while minimising negative social and environmental impacts.

2 Pursue a stakeholder partnership approach to the decision-making process on new developments and other issues affecting the wider community, listening to and understanding the concerns of stakeholders, and developing practical programmes of action to address them.

3 Integrate strategies, incentives and reward systems to ensure that sustainable development priorities are reflected in day-to-day decisions and operations at each of our airports.

4 Improve performance through objectives, externally audited targets, key performance indicators and by reflecting these priorities in relationships with business partners and suppliers.

5 Influence solutions for wider environmental improvements and aviation's contribution to climate change directly through the industry as well as government and bodies such as Airports Council International and the UN International Civil Aviation Organisation.

6 Proactively engaged in global, EU and national government consultations on the sustainable development of the aviation industry.

7 Act responsibly as a corporate citizen and employer.

8 Think long-term and seek to be challenged by leading experts.

9 Communicate our performance within the company and externally via a process of integrated annual sustainable development reporting supported by annual external audit and verification.

10 Explore the environmental and financial gains to be secured through innovation and technology.

Communities Trust, to channel donations to specific causes in the airport communities. This was the company saying: 'We belong here, many of our employees live here, your problems are our problems.' It was also a way of saying: 'OK, we're not the easiest of neighbours, but we want to be good neighbours and this is a positive thing we can do.' More importantly, a group led by Richard Everitt explored what we should be doing to make the industry more sustainable. In 1998, BAA reported its environmental, social and economic performance in its first sustainability report. This addressed the company's neighbours and other stakeholders in the same way as its annual report and accounts addressed its shareholders. BAA became the first to publish its sustainability and annual financial reports side-by-side on the day of its financial results, and to have the sustainability claims independently audited.

The approach won BAA in 1998 the award for Best Site Reporter in the prestigious Association of Chartered and Certified Accountants (ACCA) Environmental Reporting Awards. The award recognised BAA's 'fully-developed site reporting package' of individual airport reports charting progress against specific environmental targets and objectives. It won another ACCA award the following year, and then in 2000 received an exceptional accolade when it achieved the highest score of 50 leading international companies surveyed on their sustainability reporting record. The Global Reporters survey was undertaken by the UN Environment Programme and SustainAbility, the world-renowned think-tank committed to encouraging sustainable principles in business and the highest standards of accountability.

After John Egan retired as chief executive in October 1999, John's successor, Mike Hodgkinson and I decided to go a stage further and promote the sustainability agenda to the whole industry. In a ground-breaking speech to the Aviation Club, Mike said:

'The question that we have been debating, 'Should the UK have a vibrant and growing aviation industry or protect its environment?' is the wrong question: What we should have been asking is how the aviation industry can be encouraged to develop sustainability, so that the benefits can be reaped for the environment, for society and for the economy. There are real challenges to face up to, but I believe that sustainable growth can be achieved if we address the issues openly and constructively, and if the right incentives, structures and resources are put into meeting the challenge. The environmental challenge is to address the contribution of aviation to climate change bringing it within the international framework of the Kyoto agreement to reduce greenhouse gas emissions . . . '

By the time I was due to retire from BAA, it was becoming a leader in the whole aviation industry. We had not only established Contract with the Community and the sustainability approach, but there had been a huge change in the company's culture, mission statement, and way of doing business.* Both retired, John and I carried on our campaign beyond BAA: we jointly wrote a book on CSR called *Private Business, Public Battleground – the case for 21st century stakeholder companies*; John became President of the CBI and we worked together to make CSR the theme of his Presidency. I wrote articles for the *Financial Times*, *Sunday Business*, and other publications promoting it.

Our efforts at BAA were summed up in an article for the *Observer* by Steve Hilton, who now works alongside David Cameron in No 10 Downing Street as his chief advisor on strategy. In an article beginning 'I'd like to tell you about one of the "good guys",' he wrote:

> BAA has been at the forefront of the corporate social responsibility movement: not as a substitute for running the business properly, nor as a fluffy feel-good add-on, but as just another component of giving good service. If you look at BAA's social report, it is a model of its kind, detailing a sophisticated range of initiatives that help fulfill BAA's stated mission to grow the business with the trust of local communities.

The 'Doom'

Before I move on, I must refer to the Millennium Dome (or Doom, as I like to call it). While I was at BAA, John Egan attended a meeting called by Michael Heseltine to persuade companies to sponsor the Dome. One of those present was Bob Ayling, the abrasive and unpopular chief executive of British

---

*   My references to BAA, customer service, etc, may not square with my readers' more recent experiences. I return to this subject in my final chapter.

Airways, who had accepted the chairmanship of the Dome Company. Given that BA was our biggest customer, John felt bound to offer help and came back to the office to rather shame-facedly admit he had promised £6 million. I, in turn, persuaded John this was too much and we should cut the sum in half. He kindly offered me the task of telling Ayling this. The message was not well received, but reluctantly accepted. From then on, we were stuck with the Dome whether we liked it or not, and we did not.

It should never have happened. Labour inherited it from Michael Heseltine and, when it first came to Cabinet, they still had time to pull out. A majority of the Cabinet wanted to, but as history shows, over Iraq and other issues, this was a Cabinet not noteworthy for the strength of its spine. What happened at that meeting has been well recorded in diaries and elsewhere: Tony Blair, who had typically hyped up the idea and has to take prime responsibility to history for it, had to leave early, and John Prescott was in the chair. Apart from Peter Mandelson, no one was enthusiastic, but nor was there anyone who was ready to rock the boat. Finally, it was Prescott, who liked to position himself as Labour's bluff, no-nonsense voice of common sense, the representative of the working man and the ordinary Labour constituency worker, but actually maintained his position by cheerleading for Blair, who helped Mandelson carry the day.

The Dome ultimately cost well over £750 million. Of this, £603 million came from the National Lottery. It was a colossal waste of money and was not even a creative success. They anticipated 12 million visitors in the year 2000 and they got just over 6 million. Above all, it was an abuse of power. Blair and Mandelson wanted it, so that was that: we all paid. Any business confronted with such a financial failure and such a mismanaged project would fire its chief executive and everyone else responsible. But there is no such thing as political accountability these days. (They did, of course, fire the Dome chief executive.)

From the start, I felt very uncomfortable; I thought the Dome was insanely expensive, a London-based project that was being paid for by the rest of the country. But BAA was committed as one of the sponsors. It was happening, no matter what I felt about it. So, as the company's spokesman, I had to hope and pray it would surprise me and that it would be a success, and I had to speak positively about it. I have never represented a case so unenthusiastically.

New Years' Eve, 1999, should have been for Jane and I a night of celebration. We had made it to the 21st century. Instead, it all became a nightmare. It should have been so easy. The impressive new Jubilee Line ran directly from the centre of London to the Dome itself. All that the many thousands attending the big night had to do was catch that train from Victoria or a nearby station and travel a few stops down the line to the Dome Station, climb on the escalator, and they would be inside the Dome within fifteen minutes. But that did not allow for the unbelievable arrogance of the Blair administration and the ruling elite and the even more incredible incompetence and cowardice of the Dome management.

What happened was that someone decided that it would not be safe (or seemly) for the Queen, Blair, Mandelson, and a handful of others to travel to the Dome on a train occupied by ordinary people (in fact, the 'ordinary' people were mostly extraordinary, mainly an elite themselves, specially asked for this celebrity opening). So, for so-called 'security reasons', they closed the whole London-Dome service down for the night, except for one train occupied by that tiny handful of our 'betters' (who apparently were judged to be immune to the effects of a bomb or whatever) and everyone else was told to find their way to Stratford Station, miles away, from where they would travel back on the train to the Dome.

That conceivably would have worked if anyone in the Dome management ever listened to anyone else. I had specifically offered the services of BAA to advise on, and, if necessary, oversee the security for the night; after all, BAA handled hundreds of millions at security machines every year and could easily have got everyone into the Dome on time. Instead the Dome managers took no notice, turned the offer down, and on the night, at Stratford Station, had just one machine. Everyone had to go through this and have their bags searched, one by one. The result was chaos. Huge queues. Many famous people, powerful people, newspaper editors, MPs, top business leaders, celebrities – were all trapped there in the rain, their husbands, wives, boyfriends and girlfriends furiously complaining about being there instead of being with their families or at some party somewhere. BAA's company secretary, representing a company that had put £3 million into the Dome, queued outside the station in the rain for four hours!

It is fascinating to read Blair's account of all this. Obviously no one dared tell him the truth that it was all due to their own incompetence, so they told him that the train from Stratford had broken down. What says it all about the elitism involved is Blair's fury when he found out that newspaper editors were trapped in the shambles: *'Please God, tell me you didn't have the media coming here by Tube from Stratford just like ordinary members of the public'* (my italics)

What an end to the century. What a beginning to the new one? I saw a lot of anger at that supposedly happy event . . . anger that carried over into the newspapers and led to a catastrophic start for the Dome. For instance, they had promised everyone a quarter bottle of champagne to toast in the New Year. Ours were stacked in a box at the top of my staircase and someone forgot to hand them out. I saw a corporate figure in dinner jacket begin to open the box. An attendant stepped forward. 'You can't do that.' The red-faced corporate figure grabbed him by the throat and lifted him into the air. 'Give me six bottles or I'll kill you,' he said. And he meant it.

Happy New Year! Happy 21st century!

On the Board

In the days when I spent many hours as a reporter in the courts, I could not help but notice that whenever a down-at-heel, seedy, furtive-looking man came into the dock to plead guilty to some petty fraud, or to exposing himself to women in the High Street, he was always described as 'a company director'. Little did I know that I would end up as one of these myself – no, not exposing myself to women in the High Street, but 'a company director' . . . or, at least, a non-executive director. The first evoked memories of where my career in London began, way back in 1960.

Earls Court and Olympia

When I came to London with only £5 in my pocket, one of my first jobs was to sell ice cream at Bertram Mills circus at Olympia. I felt I had come full circle when in 2001 I was contacted by Andrew Morris, whose family had taken over the Earls Court and Olympia complex. He was facing a serious challenge from the newly-built Excel centre in the Docklands and needed a plan to fight back. I had been recommended by a former BAA colleague as someone who could possibly help.

As always, I advised listening to his stakeholders, so we decided that I should tour his Customers – around twenty major conference and exhibition organisers – and independently seek to establish their views of his two venues. It was a fascinating project, and my report must have made sense, because shortly after Andrew asked me to become a non-executive director.

The aim was to build up the business and sell it and, sadly, this duly happened; I say 'sadly' only because I loved working with Andrew and his enthusiastic team and was sorry when control changed hands. Many in the public sector assume that all the idealism is to be found in their sector and that those who work in business have to settle for more material rewards. It is not true. I have already commented on the fact that I found people in business worked better together, with less back-stabbing and all the other shenanigans of political life. I also found many, especially younger people, to be tremendously idealistic about their work. I found that at BAA. I found it later at Carphone Warehouse. And I found it at Earls Court and Olympia, where the team was a joy to work with.

Andrew presented me with a superb gift: he had found in the basement – an old seating plan created for Bertram Mills Circus in 1960, the year I was there as an ice cream salesman. He had it framed. To this day I have it in my den and can see exactly the spot where I sold a chocolate ice cream to Prince Charles.

The Carphone Warehouse

Way back in 1992 when my first novel, *Costa del Sol*, was published, I became friends with a young man living near San Pedro, a few miles east of Marbella. His name was James Ross and he was starting an English book-selling business there. At that point he was running up and down the coast placing books in racks outside supermarkets. I wanted him to promote my book but he could not afford to buy it, so I made a deal with him: I would buy copies of the book from the publisher at a discount and James would pay me back over time. It worked out well; James sold a lot of copies. It actually topped the best-seller list for English language books in Spain.

In those days I had a small flat in a restaurant village called Benhavis, five miles from the coast, where James also moved, and I was spending a lot of time there writing. James and I would hit the local bars and restaurants in the evening. I eventually became best man at his wedding, an event that came close to being a disaster. For weeks before I had been phoning him from London to ask what I could do to help, and he kept assuring me that there was 'no problem' . . . all was under control. On the day of the wedding I was just walking out the door of my hotel room when the phone rang. It was James. 'Are you coming to pick me up?' I said, of course I would if he wanted me to. He said 'Well, you are the best man. It's one of your duties.' One of my duties! I began to have a sinking feeling, all the more so when I drove to his house and he handed me a leaflet: 'Duties of the Best Man'. I now discovered that I had failed to do a number of crucial things – like organising the cars, including that of the bride, who didn't turn up. She finally arrived an hour late, by which time the priest's car had been towed away, the guests had been become bored with waiting in the church and were wandering around Marbella, and James was in a terrible state. The priest looked at the chaos and said to me: 'This wedding should be in the book of Guinness'.

Anyway, finally everyone was corralled into the same place, they were duly married, and we went off to what turned out to be a terrific dinner over-looking the beach. Even then my failure to read the leaflet on the best man's duties cost me some popularity; it turned out that James' step-father had spent weeks writing and polishing his speech proposing the toast to the bride and groom, only to have to sit and hear me do it instead. To this day the debate rages about who should have done it.

Anyway all this is but a prelude to introducing James' brother David. James had often talked about his younger brother and mentioned that he was making a lot of money in the cell-phone business with a company called The Carphone Warehouse but I had taken little notice and, while, I was meeting David from time to time, usually on the golf course with James when he too was holidaying near Marbella, I had not taken on board just how brilliant and wealthy he was. Then James became involved in David's business and told me that David and his partner Charles Dunstone were planning to float it on the stock market. James thought my experience with BAA, especially in the areas of public affairs and corporate social responsibility would make me an ideal non-executive director of the new publicly-quoted company and suggested it to David, who in turn set up a breakfast meeting with Charles. Afterwards I was asked to join the Board.

The company floated in 2000 and Charles and David immediately became massively wealthy. (My friend James, who I had met selling cheap paperbacks in Spain, also made millions and bought a huge mansion on top of a hill near Marbella.)

Unfortunately, soon after the flotation, the cell-phone business, together with much of the rest of the economy, went into recession and the CPW shares collapsed. I was most impressed with how calmly Charles faced up to the setback. In fact, he saw it as an opportunity and bought up shops that were closing all over the country, thus positioning the company to do well when the recovery came.

Two things soon became clear to me. First, while the company was always linked to the names of both Dunstone and Ross, it was Charles who was the senior partner. I remain a huge admirer of Charles, who was brilliant, visionary, a superb leader and inspiration to his young staff, and generous, but he was not always as open to suggestions as I had hoped. Nevertheless, we eventually joined forces in the main contribution I made to CPW. Inevitably it was in the area of corporate social responsibility and it eventually won CPW an award.

At a Board meeting I recommended an almost unique partnership with a charity called Get Connected. Charles had already helped it in the past and I investigated further. I found that 100,000 under 16's were running away from home every year . . . 270 every day . . . 11 every hour.

One in seven would be hurt while away from home. Of those taken in by a stranger, half would be physically or sexually abused. Get Connected aimed to reduce the risk of physical and emotional damage to these kids by providing a free number – a help-line – that would be answered by trained volunteers who would, in a way the runaways could trust, connect them to the best service to advise, help and support in each individual case. It had handled 1000 calls in its first year, 6000 in its second, and expected it to increase to 30,000 within the next two years.

Now I proposed we become a full partner of Get Connected, building up its volunteer base and thus the quality of the service, and marketing it to the young. It would be housed in the spectacular CPW offices in North Acton. Every one of the hundreds of North Acton employees would be given the opportunity to train as volunteers (new employees as part of their induction) and asked to commit themselves to a few hours every quarter. The helpline would then be enabled for the first time to become 24 hours a day, 365 days a year.

The Board approved the idea and I joined the Board of Get Connected for the time I was a non-executive of CPW. We launched it with a big presentation at the CPW offices with Home Office minister Jeff Rooker and television's Esther Rantzen present to underline its importance. Today it is still there, in the CPW office, dealing with nearly 50,000 phone calls and 5000 e-mails a year.

The British Tourist Authority

When in 1995 John Egan ended a term on the Board of the British Tourist Authority, Chris Smith, the then Secretary of State for Culture, Media and Sport, who was also responsible for tourism, asked me to take his place. I was to spend six years on it and became briefly its longest-serving member.

The chairman for nearly all of my time there was David Quarmby, who as number two to David Sainsbury at the supermarket chain had been on the Shopping Hours Reform Council. David was an exceptionally enthusiastic and conscientious man and, unlike many appointed to chair quangos, he worked hard for his fee. Others on the Board included the former England cricket captain and television commentator Tony Lewis, and Patrick McKenna, who as former chairman of the Really Useful Group and now head of his own company Ingenious Media, made two fortunes before he was 50. (Patrick became a friend and took a liking to my wife Jane's paintings and furnished both his London office and his French home with them, a big boost for her.)

The Board usually met at the BTA office in Hammersmith, but once a year held a meeting in an overseas city to support the work of its team there. This took me to two places I had not seen, Dubai and Stockholm, as well as back to cities like Madrid and New York. I was also asked to undertake a speaking trip to Australia and New Zealand, an opportunity I jumped at. This did, however, cause me one exceptionally uncomfortable evening.

On my schedule was a speech in Sydney. I was told that this was to be a reception and that only three or four minutes of generalities were called for. I asked 'are you sure about this ?' and they replied yes, definitely, only two or three minutes. When I arrived I was disconcerted to see a poster advertising a lecture, one of the 'Wyatt Conservation Series.' This was to be delivered by one Des Wilson and the subject was 'Gardens and the English National Trust'. I was stunned; they had allowed 50 minutes for it. What I knew about gardens would take 50 seconds maximum; what I knew about the National Trust was even less.

I decided to make a run for it and phone from a call box and say I was ill. But, before I could, an embarrassed Sydney BTA staff member took me by the arm, and ushered me into the hall, where I had no choice but take the event's chairwoman into a corner and explain the dilemma. She kindly began the meeting by telling the audience that I had been asked to speak on the wider subject of 'the state of the UK' as tourists would find it that year.

I then lectured a bewildered audience for 50 minutes on current British politics, the state of the national psyche, and the latest tourist attractions. For this last part I read directly from a BTA leaflet. Somehow I got away with it but I still remember one man in the audience watching and listening to me with increasingly intense disbelief as I droned on; as I kept glancing at him nervously, it was only too obvious that he knew that I knew that he knew that it was all total bullshit. When it was over I could not face the reception and fled with the BTA staff member to a bar on the waterfront and sank two bottles of Shiraz while she assured me that in the circumstances my performance had been 'awesome', as, to be fair, it had – even if I say it myself.

(This was not the first time this had happened to me. Away back when I became a candidate in the Hove by-election I was asked to step in for the deceased MP and open a national conference of the catering industry that was being held in Brighton. I was told 'two or three minutes . . . welcome to Brighton, hope you enjoy your time in our hospitable town' . . . that kind of thing. As I listened to the chairman welcoming the packed hall, I glanced at the programme. It said: 'Prospects for the catering industry in Europe – keynote address by Des Wilson'. They, too, had allowed 50 minutes. To this day I cannot recall how I survived without being forcibly ejected by a jeering audience.)

I left BTA on a funny note. There was a big tourism fair in Birmingham and the Duke of York was to attend the buffet lunch. I arrived to find a crowd at the buffet, so to fill in the time until it dispersed I wandered over to a corner where there was a band playing. As I stood there, tapping my foot in time to the music, I noticed a plate of delicious looking goodies sitting on a window ledge. I looked around. Nobody appeared to own it. So I picked it up and began to enthusiastically devour it. Suddenly a man came rushing across the floor and snatched the remains from my hand. 'Oh my God,' he said, 'you've just eaten the Duke of York's lunch.'

The English Sports Council

We had a dinner party one Saturday night and Chris Smith was there. He told me he was having problems finding a chairman of the English Sports Council (the ESC) to replace Sir Rodney Walker who was moving to UK Sports. The obvious replacement was the former England and West Ham footballer Trevor Brooking who had done well as one of the two vice chairmen, but Chris was unconvinced. Emboldened by one glass too many of wine, and ever the volunteer, I jocularly told him that I was his man. I was astonished when the following Monday I was called and asked if I would submit my name.

What I did not know was that, in an attempt to keep all his options open, Chris had somehow convinced at least two other people they were to be chairman, one being Brooking and the other being the former Olympic javelin gold medalist, Tessa Sanderson. After dithering for days, he now found himself due at an ESC Board meeting with three people expecting to be named. In a series of panic phone calls he appointed Brooking as chairman and persuaded me to be senior vice chairman but also to be chairman of the ESC Lottery Panel, a powerful position because the panel distributed a small fortune to sport every year. (I was also later made a member of the Board of UK Sports.) Tessa was asked to be junior vice chairman. Given that she had expected more, she was very upset, but in the end we all settled on these posts and it became clear that Chris had made the right decision. Brooking was not only hugely popular but a genuinely committed and capable chairman. As for Tessa, she was even more popular than Trevor and was a terrific ambassador for the Council, She and I hit it of from the start and working with her was great fun.

There was so much sporting experience and talent on the panel, I was almost embarrassed to be chairing it. It included round-the-world sailor Sir Robin Knox Johnston, a lovely man, three times world record holder Steve

Cram, former Olympic swimming gold medalist Anita Lonsborough, the popular footballer Garth Crooks, and the prolific gold medal winner at the Paralympics, Tani Grey Thompson, as well as a number of sports administrators from around the country, and one or two local authority leaders, including a former mayor of Leeds, Bernard Atha. The panel was immensely conscientious and, well-served by the main administrator, David Carpenter, it had earned a survey rating of 89 per cent for the efficiency of the operation.

My first responsibility was to announce a new strategy for the distribution of lottery funds. This had been worked out before I came but I had no problem accepting it. The basis of it was that 75 per cent of the funds would be given to community sport and 25 per cent to a programme to help world class competitors.

While I was chairing the panel we gave away £750 million over three years to over 60 sports. While there were major projects for me the real satisfaction was in the small grants to hundreds and hundreds of sports clubs all over the country – for lighting so that athletes could train at night, for pavilions, for basketball and tennis courts, for sailing equipment . . . the list went on and on. Every grant meant a boost for those who were working all over the country to inspire kids to play sport rather than take to the street corners. I would often think of people receiving letters telling them they were receiving Lottery money and the boost they would get, and I was immensely proud of what we did.

I was also anxious to make the operation as accountable as possible. I set up an annual report-back meeting so that we had to meet sports leaders in one hall, tell them what we were doing and why, and deal with criticisms and questions. I tried to cut back on the bureaucracy and speed up the responses. I asked for plans to be made to decentralise decisions, using local panels. I invited the national administrators to come and do presentations on their sports so that the Panel could better understand their strategy and their problems.

From the start I could see that the operation was not helped by two things: first, constant political interference. It seemed to me that ministers and civil servants in this area did not have enough to do, so both in tourism and in sport they entertained themselves by being too hands-on. Also, it appeared to me they were always looking for some initiative to publicise for political reasons, and this could actually influence decision-making. (The worst case was that of Tessa Jowell, when she took over from Chris Smith. She was due to speak to a major athletics conference and wanted some good news to announce, so we were put under immense pressure by her then sports minister Richard Caborn to make a grant to UK Athletics that we were not at the time keen to make; it cost millions to get her a round of applause.)

Towards the end of my three year spell, I was one day at Lord's and Hugh Morris, who was at the time the man who ran cricket's developmental activities, asked me into his office and showed me some alarming correspondence between the ESC chief executive Derek Casey and the English Cricket Board. Casey was offering cricket the ESC facilities at Bisham Abbey as a base for its academy. What alarmed me was that I knew Casey had written a similar letter to the Lawn Tennis Association offering them the facilities for tennis. I had to step in to sort this out, first by calling a meeting of both sports to see if they could share the facilities, and then finally having to take the uncomfortable decision that, as tennis had been offered the facilities first, their needs must prevail. This, together with a clumsy attempt by Casey and Trevor Brooking to cover the whole business up, caused me considerable concern and I was gearing myself up for internal warfare when I was relieved of the need by the arrival of Richard Caborn as Minister of Sport.

I knew Dick Caborn well. We had played golf together, both in Cyprus, where we found ourselves on holiday at the same time, and annually when we both escaped for an afternoon from the Labour Party conference. (We were due to play one day at Bournemouth and, as we were driving to the golf course, we ran into thousands of marchers who were descending on the town to protest at Labour's policies on the countryside. Their chief steward waved at us, and Dick wound down the car window. The steward, unaware he was talking to one of the despised Labour ministers, wanted to check the way to the conference hall and Dick enthusiastically gave him directions. Happy that the marchers had Tony Blair in their sights, he drove on to the golf course.)

On the day he was appointed Sports Minister, I phoned Dick to say how pleased I was, and he proposed we have dinner that night. We were hardly in our seats before he made it clear there were to be changes.

It turned out that Caborn had long-standing concerns about the way Casey exercised his quite considerable power at the ESC and had persuaded his boss, Tessa Jowell, that it was time to move on.

Twenty-four hours later Trevor Brooking phoned me. 'Derek has decided that with a new Minister coming in, this is an opportune time to leave and make way for fresh energy and ideas,' he said. I said I was sure it was the right decision.

After my three year spell, I received a letter from Bernard Atha:

'I had become so dispirited by the bureaucratic way it was being operated and the way in which commonsense or sound judgement was being ignored that I had intended to withdraw from the panel. Your arrival changed that and though you may not think it so, the effect you had on the morale of the panel members was invigorating . . . I think you should feel satisfied that your time with the lottery was well spent and the effect will I believe be long lasting. Panel members are now exhibiting signs of independence and a determination not to be shrugged off. Vive la revolution!'

I would rather receive letters like that than be paid the millions that bankers are paid to screw up the world.

PART FIVE

Time to Declare

20

The last (and losing) Campaign . . . 'who knows cricket who only cricket knows'

'You would do well to love cricket. It is more free from
anything sordid, anything dishonourable, than any game in
the world. To play it keenly, honourably, generously, self-
sacrificing is a moral lesson in itself . . . protect it from
anything that would sully it, so that it may grow in favour of
all men.'

LORD HARRIS 1932

This chapter should come with a health warning. It ends badly. Blood will
be spilt over these pages – mainly mine – and to understand why this
became one of my darkest hours, you need to appreciate how much I loved
cricket when I was younger. There was a park near my home, bordered by a
small river known as the Oamaru Creek. From when I was about ten, I was
there in the summer, every Tuesday and Thursday evening, about forty
yards away from the men's cricket nets, ready to field and return the ball. If
it went into the creek, I was the one who paddled after it. If it went across
the road, I was the one who risked his life, weaving between the cars to get
it. Then one night, after I had been fielding for three hours, they let me
have a bat. The pads came up to my chin, so that I could hardly walk into
the net to take guard. But, who cares. I had become a cricketer.

Looking back at them now I can see that I became passionate about
cricket towards the end of a vintage twenty-year era that began just before
the Second World War and ended in the late-Fifties. There have been
generations of illustrious cricketers since then, but for me, the stars of the

1950s, including our own new Zealanders, Bert Sutcliffe and John Reid, will always top the list. There are no heroes like childhood heroes.

My abiding memory of cricket in those days was a 1955 Test in Dunedin. I was fourteen and had travelled the 72 miles to see Len Hutton. He was by then 37, and suffering from back troubles that caused him to retire a year or so later. Compared with his tall, straight-backed partner Tom Graveney, he looked small and bent – an old man. He only scored 11. But my journey to see this man, who in 1938 had set the world Test record of 364 when playing the old enemy the Australians, who scored 40,000 first-class runs, who made over a century of centuries, who was the first professional to captain England, was justified by just one stroke . . . a cover drive for four. Not so much a drive – that implies force – but a caress. He just leaned into the ball and it rolled at increasing speed across the grass to the boundary fence like a Rolls Royce accelerating on the open road. It was a classic shot, the effortless, flowing, majestic shot of a master. In his superb book on cricket *A Last English Summer*, Duncan Hamilton writes: 'Age wearies and the years condemn, but we still see old cricketers in our mind at the point at which a stroke was played, or a ball bowled, that made our senses come alive. We preserve them in the high summer of their life.' Well, Hutton was already in the autumn of his career, approaching winter, but, in addition to numerous pictures of him in my scrapbook, that cover drive preserves him for always a special place in my lexicon of heroes.

In later years I was to meet some of the big names of that time, all by now old men. More than once I found myself with the famous Alec Bedser, fabulous England bowler of the Forties and Fifties. He and his twin Eric, always dressed alike, were often in a box at Lord's and the Oval. For some reason they took to me, asking me to sit with them. This was a mixed blessing because they could see little to admire in contemporary cricket, or in the world generally ('no discipline') and could be depressing company. Back in 1953 the Essex amateur Trevor Bailey and the Yorkshire professional Willie Watson had saved England from defeat at Lord's with a partnership that lasted most of the day; I also found myself with them in a Lord's box one day. Willie was looking old and unwell (he died shortly afterwards) but Trevor Bailey was alert and spry and was a joy to talk to. I asked him about that day and he began 'Well, my wife and I left Southend in the train . . . ' I interrupted him: what was he doing in Southend when he was due that day to play for England at a packed Lord's and with the eyes of the nation on him? 'Oh in those days we went home every evening, and that's where I lived.' 'So, in order to come to London to play that famous Test innings, you sat on the train with many of the crowd who were coming to see the match?' 'No, we stood – the train was full.' I found myself comparing that with today's millionaire Test players who stay in a first class hotel near the ground and are driven there in a special coach every day.

But, back to the scrapbooks: between reports of county and test cricket, are pages solemnly devoted to my own early career. In 1953–54 I batted 25 times for 121 runs, averaging 7.3. In 1954–55 I took 22 wickets for 133. And in 1955–56 I took to recording commentaries on my performance. For instance, in one match I scored 4 and 3 not out. Commentary: 'Batting well.' The mind boggles at how poorly I played when I had 'a bad day'.

Even as a kid, I also frequently found myself at No. 11 for the Union club's first team, because there was always at least one man who didn't show. Of course, I was completely out of my class; the scrapbook reveals failure after failure. Wilson out – o. But one innings is described as 'a great knock' . . . and it was. I had fielded in the absence of one Union's star players; now, at the end of the afternoon, with nine wickets down, we needed 15 runs to win. My name was in the scorebook at No. 11. Then the missing player arrived. Technically he could have batted instead of me and, if he did, the team's chances would be vastly improved, but the captain must have seen my face fall and, to his eternal credit, when the ninth wicket fell, he sent me in as last man. Is this not what makes cricket an exceptional game . . . that a captain would rather lose the game than walk over a kid's dreams of glory? And did I reward him? You bet I did. With an experienced batsman at one end and me, a determined 12 year old at the other, we battled it out and won the match. The local paper reported it, 'No 11, D. Wilson, five not out.' Do not under-estimate the importance of that day in my life.

Compare my captain that day with Ian Chatto, a name to be recorded in the annals of cricket infamy. He was my captain when one day I was batting particularly well and had reached 79. He came out to the wicket and said, 'Maybe you would like to retire and let someone else have a bat, Des.' Now, I had never scored a coveted century . . . this was my chance, maybe my only chance. And I wanted that century desperately; it was as if every second of my life had been about this moment. But he did not think about that. And I was too young and inexperienced to challenge him. So, I walked slowly, feet dragging, back to the pavilion. I never did score a century. And I have never found it in myself to forgive him. Asked many years later to list the worst tyrants in world history I wrote down the names of Attilla the Hun, Adolph Hitler, Idi Amin . . . and Ian Chatto. No cricketer would blame me.

From boyhood, I began building a collection of cricket books, helped by the practice of the library to sell old books at a shilling a time. No game has inspired its own literature the way cricket has. It is the 10,000 and more cricket books that give the game its uniquely timeless quality, that guarantee that no match or series is a story in itself, but just another chapter in its history. In this respect it's like Shakespearean theatre. No one sees a *Hamlet* or a *Henry V* without comparing the latest actors in the roles with the Hamlet's and the Hal's of the past, and so it is with cricket – Boycott has to be compared with Hutton and Hutton with Hobbs, and so on. It is this placing of today's game in a historical context that makes discussion of both Shakespearean theatre and cricket so absorbing.

Much of the literature and poetry dwells on the beauty and calm of the game, the peaceful Sunday afternoons on the village green, white-clad local tradesman, the blacksmith and the butcher, revelling in their intensely played-out encounters with traditional rivals from the surrounding countryside, their families enjoying a picnic on the boundary. That is the cricket I played when a kid in New Zealand too, the only sport that can match poetry, or for that matter produce such poetry as Newbolt's famous 'There's a breathless hush in the close tonight . . . ten to make and the match to win' or Bullet's description of cricket as 'civilisation under the sun'.

But the encounters that have made cricket history were more brutal affairs: the Bodyline series; Hutton facing the Australian pacemen, Lindwall and Miller; Brian Close, his chest black and blue with bruises, after facing the West Indies attack, or a famous confrontation between England's Mike Atherton and the South African fast bowler Allan Donald, a duel that reminded me of the bull ring – the bowler (the bull) charging, full of destructive malevolence; the batsman (the matador) waiting . . . still, calm, defiant in defence.

This brings me to a particularly dramatic hour in the history of New Zealand cricket, one that still makes my heart pump faster. I was twelve and it was Boxing Day in 1953; New Zealand were in South Africa, and I was listening to the Test match on our wireless. The news was devastating. The South African fast bowler Neil Adcock, aided by a bumpy pitch, struck the New Zealand opener Miller who left the field coughing blood. We were told he could not return. New Zealand were down to 10 men.

Then New Zealand's best-ever batsman, Bert Sutcliffe, as gentle a sportsman as you will ever meet, an artist with the bat, was hit a crushing blow on the head and taken to hospital. We were told that he, too, could not return. New Zealand were down to nine men. Now the match was affected by some terrible news. Only two days earlier, on Christmas Eve, New Zealand had suffered our worst-ever train disaster. Over 140 were killed, many more were injured, and hardly a town or village was not affected. It now emerged that one of those who died was the fiancé of the New Zealand fast bowler Bob Blair who, distraught and inconsolable, was also now assumed to be out of the match. New Zealand were down to eight men.

Unable to concentrate, the team collapsed, and soon were nearly all out for 80-odd runs . . . still needing 40 to avoid the follow-on. As the fielding side turned to the pavilion, from its shadows came Sutcliffe, face white as parchment, head heavily bandaged and slowly turning red with blood from a split ear. Applauded all the way to the wicket, he now abandoned his customary elegance and proceeded to hit seven soaring sixes to score 80 not out. But even that would not have been possible if it were not for another act of heroism. When the last wicket fell, and the South Africans turned for the second time towards the pavilion, they were once more stopped in their tracks.

A New Zealand cricket writer who was there describes what happened next:

'The crowd were cheering the South African bowlers . . . and cheering Sutcliffe, but now the cheering faltered and died away. Bob Blair was walking out into the sunshine, hands trembling so much that he found it pathetically difficult to pull on his gloves. The huge crowd now rose slowly in silence. The New Zealanders, looking down on the scene, wept openly and without shame. Sutcliffe was obviously distressed as he greeted his partner. Blair struck out blindly at the first ball, hitting a mighty six. The two then added 33 in 11 minutes before disappearing, arms about each other, into the darkness of the tunnel, leaving behind an emotional cheering crowd, and a light and inspiration that would remain forever with those who were there.'

John Reid comes to town

John Reid was playing in that match. He became New Zealand's greatest cricket captain. I was thrilled to bits when he came to live in Oamaru to manage the local Shell depot. He was the town's first – and last – Test cricketer. Neville Cardus once described Reid as 'a club cricketer in excelsis' and that's what he was: a club cricketer who from time to time slipped away to do what club cricketers dream of. For years he stood alone between New Zealand cricket and humiliation. His greatness is not fully reflected by the statistics, impressive as they are: he averaged over 40 in 246 first class games and took 466 wickets, and played in 58 tests averaging 33 and taking 85 wickets. What those figures don't reveal is how many momentous performances were produced in desperate circumstances or when he was virtually without support (in 1951, for instance, he scored a century for Wellington while the remaining ten players contributed 39 between them).

Like Ian Botham or Freddie Flintoff (or Australia's Keith Miller), Reid habitually scored runs when they were most needed and took wickets or a blinding catch at just the right time. He was that kind of cricketer – an aggressive all-rounder who made things happen. Shortly after he came to Oamaru, I was one of a handful who gathered one Saturday morning to bowl at him so that he could prepare for the New Zealand tour of India and Pakistan. As he politely and sensitively patted back this 14-year-old's innocuous medium-pacers he must have wondered how on earth this could be described as 'preparing'. Yet in the first match of that tour, in Karachi, coming from the chill of a South island winter to steamy heat, he took for 7 for 28 and then scored 150 not out. It was a difficult tour, yet he hit 1024 runs, averaging more than 50, and took 39 wickets. He made 493 runs, averaging 70, in the tests.

The following year, while still in Oamaru, he led New Zealand to its first-ever test win – over the West Indies in Auckland in 1956. I can still recall the thrill of listening to it on the radio. For ten years he carried the burden of leading a sub standard Test team. When he eventually retired he had played in 58 of the 86 tests New Zealand had played in its entire history and led it in 36 of them. Sprinkled throughout that time there are some particularly memorable Plunkett Shield moments: in 1952 he hit 283 for Wellington including a century before lunch; in 1957–58 there was an innings of 201 with five sixes and 22 fours; in 1958–59, having taken 7 for 38, he hit 191 not out of the 330 required for Wellington to beat Canterbury; and in 1962–63 struck a stunning 296 with a world record 15 sixes against Northern Districts.

When I was last in touch with him, he was quietly running a bed and breakfast place in Lake Taupo on New Zealand's North island.

The MCC – then the ECB

Once I became involved in Shelter in 1966, I had little time to watch cricket. In the late Seventies, while I was living in Worcestershire, I did turn up at the county ground on Sundays to see Basil D'Oliviera play and I was at Lord's in 1976 when he made his test debut, batting with Tom Graveney who was making a comeback, and who I had first seen in Dunedin way back in 1955. Watching cricket at Worcester was a treat. You could sit in the ladies pavilion, from where you had an unrivalled view of the cathedral across the river, and where you were able to eat the best date loaf in all England. Often, while I sat there on a summer's day, I would think back to Don Bradman, the most prolific run-scorer of all time. In the old days Australia always began their tour of England with a match at Worcester, and in 1930, 1934 and 1938 Bradman began each tour with a double century. Of all the places where I have watched cricket, it was at Worcester where I felt closest to its history.

And then there was – and is – Lord's, the home of the game, the cathedral of the game, a magnificent cricket ground, with its beautiful old pavilion, its museum, and its library of thousands of cricket books. When I first went to Lord's, I tried to slip in to the pavilion wearing jeans and a jumper, just hoping to catch a glimpse of its famous long room, but I was hastily intercepted by an attendant. 'You're not a member?' he asked. 'No,'

I said. 'Then go,' he said. 'We don't let people like you in here.' He did not remember me when, many years later, I became a consultant to the MCC and was issued with a pass that allowed me to stroll past him and into the pavilion as if I owned the place.

The MCC used to be a dreadfully right-wing organisation, banning women from membership, insisting that amateurs and professionals change in different dressing rooms and take to the field from different gates, and causing any number of injustices within the game. But over the past twenty years or so it had changed dramatically and become the conscience of the English game. I became involved with Lord's before the ICC absconded for Dubai (what does it say about the administrator of world cricket that, to save a few quid in tax, it ends up in a Middle Eastern country where cricket is not played?) At one end you had the MCC, the gentlemen. At the other end you had the ECB, the tradesmen. And, to one side, suspiciously watching both, you had the ICC, the politicians. Often they were at war, especially the ECB and the MCC.

The divide derived from the increased commercialisation of cricket. The ECB became big business, all its decisions over-shadowed by the money it needed to raise, to satisfy increasingly poverty-stricken counties and pay increasingly wealthy test players. The MCC remained dedicated to the game itself, selflessly funding 'missionary' tours of other countries where test cricket has never been played.

A key man at the MCC was Roger Knight who, as chief executive, came with real cricketing credentials – 19,588 first-class runs, with 31 centuries, and 369 wickets. That, together with his values, won the members' trust. When I was proposed as a public relations advisor for the MCC, Roger and I hit it off immediately. Apart from advising Roger at times of crisis, my main contribution was to act as advisor and sometime ghost-writer for speakers at the annual Cowdrey lecture.

The first of these was the famous South African opener, Barry Richards. Barry knew what he had to say but had no experience of public speaking so I not only had to write his speech but teach him how to deliver it. The result was a triumph and he would always greet me enthusiastically whenever we subsequently met at Lords.

I also helped the former West Indies captain Clive Lloyd and we became good friends; for years afterwards he would phone when he had a tricky speech to write. I also helped, to a lesser extent, Martin Crowe and Geoff Boycott. The cricket world is sharply divided between Boycott fans and those who can't stand him. I was a fan. Once I went to Worcester just to see him bat. I waited outside the dressing room, camera and binoculars around my neck, and when he came out I was so excited I tried to take his picture with the binoculars. (It doesn't work.)

There were advantages of being an advisor, and also a friend of Roger; the main one was being invited into the box for a test match day. Another benefit was getting to know so many old English players, including the old England cricket captain Ted Dexter. We had a most enjoyable lunch one day in St Johns Wood. Ted told me a lovely story about the even older England batsman Bill Edrich. Ted found himself sitting beside him at a cricket dinner and said to him 'Mr Edrich, I know you were a great player of fast bowling. Can you give me any advice?' Edrich looked at him closely. 'Have you ever been hit on the head by a ball bowled at 90 miles an hour' he asked. Ted said, 'well, no.' Edrich said: 'Well, it doesn't hurt a bit.' Ted has never forgotten that advice. He never has worked out what it means, but he has never forgotten it.

One night I attended a dinner at Lord's. After the final course I found myself sitting out on the pavilion balcony with the former England opening batsman Dennis Amiss. The famous field was at our feet, dark and silent. We sat there for several minutes and said not a word to each other. No word needed saying. We both knew we were in a special place.

On the English Cricket Board

By 2003 I was fairly well connected in cricket circles, both because of the MCC and as a result of my dealings with the English Cricket Board on behalf of the Sport England lottery panel, so, when a vacancy arose on the ECB for someone who would combine board membership with chairman of their commercial and public affairs committee, it was not difficult to find a couple of counties to nominate me. There was no rival and so, a couple of years after my 60th birthday, I completed the 47 year journey from secretary of the Oamaru Cricket Club to sharing in the running of English cricket. My enjoyment of this was to be short-lived. I was about to become engulfed in a controversy that led to my most crushing defeat and an early end to my ECB innings.

Before I joined the Board of the ECB, there had been a political debacle at the 2002 World Cup in South Africa caused by the players' reluctance to play a match with Zimbabwe. The ECB handled it dreadfully so that the players, instead of practising in the nets with peace of mind, were drawn into endless meetings and forced to more or less take the decisions themselves. They eventually decided to forfeit a World Cup point and not play Zimbabwe. Now, in 2003, a full-scale tour of Zimbabwe was rapidly coming down the runway and, as chairman of the public affairs committee, I offered to maintain an overview of the matter.

At one of the first Board meetings I attended, I was surprised to hear a contribution from the affable, but none too bright deputy chairman, and chairman of Surrey CCC, Mike Soper, who in a remarkable outburst told us we should abandon the Zimbabwe tour 'and to hell with the consequences'. If only I had immediately supported him, and helped him force it to a vote, much that was to follow may have been avoided. But I felt at the time that it was more than possible to engineer an acceptable escape route that would meet the *force majeure* element of our contract to tour; for that reason I suggested we delay any discussion, and it was left there.

Zimbabwe

In view of what was to come, I should spell out what made Zimbabwe such an exceptional case. Mugabe was brutal even by the standards of despots. He was rigging elections, suppressing criticism, intimidating and even killing political and media opponents, politicising the judiciary, denying fundamental human rights, and carrying out political programmes that were devastating its economy causing widespread poverty, hunger and disease affecting nearly everyone who lived there.

There were those who said that critics of what was happening in Zimbabwe were racially motivated, angered by the fact that Mugabe had been seizing the properties of white farmers. As someone said to me at the time, if it were blacks being persecuted, no one would care. This was the opposite of the truth: as a British diplomat working in Zimbabwe, Philip Barclay, relates in a recent book:

The most horrifying consequence of Mugabe's onslaught against agriculture is not what it did to whites – who nearly all escaped with their lives and most of whom now live a life of tolerable comfort – but what it did to black farm workers and their families . . . Since 1998, over a million of these people have been made homeless and have lost their access to the needful things of life. An estimated 40 per cent have died – several hundreds of thousands of avoidable premature deaths. This toll of around 400,000 deaths caused by malicious policy-making is more than ten times greater than the number killed during the massacres in Matabeleland during the 1980s. But the deaths were silent and invisible – wheezing, malnourished, homeless individuals dying from treatable diseases.

The 2003 Commonwealth conference was portrayed by some as a black versus white confrontation; it was not. To quote the UK Prime Minister in the House of Commons on December 9, 2003: 'Every single Common-wealth country signed up to (the suspension of) Zimbabwe, including the other 19 African members of the Commonwealth . . . nor did any African member of the Commonwealth take up Mr Mugabe's invitation to avoid the summit meeting.'

In fact, so appalling was the Zimbabwe regime that the country became totally isolated. After its suspension from the Commonwealth, the European Union in February 2004 reconfirmed an arms embargo, a travel ban on many members of Mugabe's ruling party ZANU (PF) and an assets freeze on the same people. Every EU country signed up to these sanctions. The European Parliament passed a resolution urging tough international action including calling 'upon the sporting federations of EU Member States which are due to play matches in Zimbabwe this year to refuse to play sport in that country at this time.' In short – and to repeat – there was an exceptional problem in Zimbabwe. And the international response was to isolate it and thus apply maximum pressure for change. That was the background to the drama that was now to take place.

The main members of the cast in the drama that was to unfold were to prove a shabby bunch: Jack Straw, Foreign Secretary, and Blair's Foreign Secretary during the Iraq war, who had it within his power to prevent the Zimbabwe tour by the force of his advice to the ECB not to go; David

Morgan, a Welshman who, like so many British sports administrators, had 'risen without trace' in his chosen sport by just sticking around and worked his way up from the Cardiff County Cricket Board to the ECB and ultimately won its chairmanship by telling the counties who had the votes whatever they wanted to hear; the afore-mentioned Mike Soper; Tim Lamb, a former county cricketer and now ECB chief executive; Rod Bransgrove, a self-made millionaire who virtually 'owned' Hampshire country club and helped it build the Rose Bowl, a new contender as a venue for international cricket; Eshan Mani, who had somehow got himself elected as President of the International Cricket Council (ICC), a Board notable for having not one member with first-class cricketing qualifications but all of whom – and no one more than David Morgan – loved travelling the world at their Board's expense to entertain each other with canapés and cocktails in the ICC box.

I do not deny that from the start I could not see how a tour by England to Zimbabwe could be defended. It was not just because I was shocked by what was happening there; it was also because the Zimbabwe cricket authorities were themselves a dodgy bunch who were politically 'in bed' with the oppressive forces there. They had already forced out most of the team's best players for racial reasons.

Two of those players, one white and one black, had acted with tremendous courage at the World Cup by taking the field wearing black armbands to show their distress at what was being done to their fellow citizens back home. They did this, they said, because 'we cannot take to the field and ignore that millions of our compatriots are starving, unemployed and oppressed . . . we are aware that many people have been unjustly imprisoned and tortured simply for expressing their opinions . . . we are aware that people have been murdered, raped, beaten and had their homes destroyed because of their beliefs . . . '

Movingly they concluded, 'although we are just professional cricketers, we do have a conscience and feelings.' Both had to come to live in England because it was no longer safe for them in their home country. There was no question, therefore, that a full England tour would be interpreted and represented by Mugabe as, if not an endorsement, at least evidence that he and his regime were not as internationally despised as was being stated . . . and it would be welcomed by the Zimbabwe authorities as an international stamp of approval on their mal-administration of the game. I began my campaign full of hope because I believed there was a majority on the Board for cancelling the tour. I was told this by Morgan, who I assumed should know.

Of course, we both knew cancellation was never going to be easy. As a member of the ICC, the ECB was committed to a 10 year programme of international cricket. If countries cancelled tours other than in exceptional circumstances, the programme would lose credibility. There were also practical implications that were too easily discounted by those who don't care about the game. Cancelled tours cost money. This was particularly hard on the host country, but it also affected English cricket, which had become totally dependent upon its earnings from international cricket. Without that money most of the 18 counties would be bankrupt.

No, this would never be an easy thing to do. Just the same, most people in English cricket wanted a way out of the Zimbabwe tour; unfortunately, they wanted an easy way, and there was no easy way. Unless, that is, we could recruit the help of the Foreign Secretary, Jack Straw.

Force Majeure

While the ICC rules did not allow tours to be cancelled on 'political or moral considerations', it did allow force majeure – tours could be cancelled because of factors beyond anyone's control, such as earthquakes or hurricanes, but, in reality, it meant a tour could be cancelled if the touring country's government issued a clear instruction to that effect. This was the ideal solution.

There was, however, a problem: the ICC members, many of whom came from dictatorships or near-dictatorships, did not understand (or did not want to understand) that in a genuinely-democratic country governments could not easily ban sportsmen and women from travelling; the most we could hope for in our democracy was advice from the Foreign Secretary that was so firmly written that any reasonable person or country would accept it was the democratic equivalent of force majeure. While I knew Straw slightly, having appeared on occasional television programmes with him, I decided to begin my approach with a call to Peter Hain, the Secretary of State for Wales, an old friend who was now in the Cabinet. He phoned me back from his car as he was being driven across the Welsh hills and, after I explained the position, he offered to speak to Straw. This he did and the upshot was that I was called to the Foreign Office to confer with Straw's political advisor Ed Owen.

Owen confirmed that Straw would be reluctant to create a precedent by a straight-forward ban, but he hoped a strongly-worded letter would come close to it. I went away encouraged by this, He then sent me a draft approved by Straw. It said, in part:

> I draw your attention to the appalling human rights situation in Zimbabwe and the resulting isolation of that country's government by the international community.
>
> The situation in Zimbabwe is bleak, and is deteriorating. Political repression remains a daily reality for many Zimbabweans, particularly those who are active in civil society, the independent media or opposition politics. Hunger is widespread, largely as a result of the disastrous policies of the Zimbabwe regime . . .
>
> This would be the background to any sports tour taking place in Zimbabwe this year.
>
> . . . it is the Government's view that the overall situation in Zimbabwe is worse today than it was during the cricket world cup last year.
>
> Zimbabwe is increasingly isolated from the international community. In December, following the Commonwealth's decision to maintain Zimbabwe's suspension from its Councils, the Government of Zimbabwe withdrew from the Commonwealth. At around the same time, the IMF voted to begin the process of expelling Zimbabwe. The EU, the US and others maintain targeted restrictive measures against leading members of the Zimbabwean regime, and the UK has taken a leading role on this issue.

This was strong. The message was clear enough – to reasonable people. But we knew the ICC would not be reasonable people, and the Zimbabwe cricket authorities, even less so. I decided to draft a final sentence. It said: *'You may wish to consider whether a high profile England cricket tour at this time is consistent with that approach.'* I sent it to Ed Owen and after a day or so, Owen came back to say that this was acceptable to Straw. It was also agreed that the Straw letter would be held back until the most suitable time; this, I was clear, would be after the ECB had the chance to debate the wider issues in relation to tours and before a specific debate about Zimbabwe.

In the meantime, I also contacted the Lib Dem foreign affairs spokesman Menzies Campbell and the Conservative shadow foreign secretary Michael Ancram, both of whom I knew well. They both also sent letters, much stronger than Straw's, calling for the tour to be abandoned. I felt the three letters uniting all three British political parties represented an unanswerable case that the ECB would be defying all UK political advice if it proceeded with the tour. With these letters in hand, I then set out to write two papers.

Sport had never had a blueprint for how to take decisions on political issues of this sensitivity. Each sport had dealt with each problem as it arose, nearly always in crisis mode; hence the shambles when the ECB faced the issue at the previous year's World Cup. So I decided to draft for debate what I called 'a framework for decision-making' on the cancellation of tours; my hope was that, before a decision on Zimbabwe was necessary, we could thoughtfully discuss this framework and, if it proved acceptable, the actual Zimbabwe decision could be taken in that context, and would be a relatively straight-forward matter.

I spent weeks working on the paper. I can barely touch on its contents here, but in essence it took on the over-simplification that there was 'no place for politics in sport'. Ever since it kept trying to play South Africa in the apartheid era, English cricket had never moved from mindless adherence to this doctrine, yet, even within the game itself it was a nonsense. The ICC was riddled with politics, much of it motivated by dislike of England. For instance, English concerns about Zimbabwe were interpreted as reflecting old Colonial attitudes and superiorities. Rather than being sympathetic to England's difficulties over Zimbabwe, the Asian countries in particular could barely-disguise their glee.

But there was even more to the politics of the ICC than that; the organisation was desperate to expand, both for its own self-aggrandise-ment and because it hoped to become a global sport and possibly even get on the Olympic gravy-train; the last thing it wanted was for Zimbabwe to resign its membership in protest at the ICC's failure to protect the tour. Also, there was a racial divide within the ICC; India and Pakistan wanted to keep the two minor test countries Zimbabwe and Bangladesh on board to ensure a majority for the Afro-Asian bloc over the old white Common-wealth countries.

But, that apart, my main point was that, even if sport believed it could somehow be free of 'politics', politicians did not seek to be free of sport. Sport was too big a factor in peoples' lives for politicians not to want their bit of it. Sport in the UK, was political, with Sport Ministers and ministries dictating policies and priorities and taking political credit for sport's achievements. In the UK, politicians determined the overall policy for distribution of both Treasury and lottery funds to sport, and appointed and determined the priorities and policies of the various UK sports councils. Politicians did more than interfere with sport; they literally controlled it.

Some senior officers of ICC member countries were directly appointed by or had the closest links with the ruling politicians in those countries. This was undoubtedly the case in Zimbabwe. The Chairman of the Pakistan Cricket Board was – and still is – appointed by the Prime Minister of Pakistan and answerable only to him. From the days of Hitler and the 1936 Olympics on, dictators in particular had sought to demonstrate they had world approval by staging international sports events. Furthermore some tours have been abandoned not in protest at the behaviour of politicians, but on the orders of politicians. Whether India and Pakistan played each other at any given time was dictated by their Governments. Countries, had been withdrawn from Olympic Games on political grounds . . . as the USA team was at the time of the Moscow games. Thus, sport was never going to be allowed to be 'an activity apart' . . . it both affected and was affected by politics, and it was disingenuous to pretend otherwise.

But the key contention of my paper was that it *should not seek* to be an 'activity apart' . . . to try to 'isolate sport as an activity that "stands alone" in human affairs, untouched by "politics" or "moral considerations" and unconcerned for the fate of those deprived of human rights, is as unrealistic as it is self-serving, and is in the 21st century so divorced from society's expectations of it as to be untenable. I then identified the more obvious justifications for abandoning a tour on moral grounds: The first was racism: 'it is unimaginable that the ECB could contemplate a tour if players or spectators were excluded from participation by the host country solely because of their race.'

A second reason would be if the host country's political leadership intervened in the selection of its team. (This happened in the famous D'Oliviera affair, when South Africa in Apartheid days refused this coloured cricketer permission to tour with the England cricket team; the tour was abandoned.) The third reason would be if restrictions were placed on freedom of movement and expression by the players, but perhaps especially if it applied to the media's ability to report what it saw and heard.

But the key and more controversial issue was this: if a dictatorship was inflicting on its people death and disease, hunger and human misery, and a disregard for all civil liberties and human rights, so as to be totally unacceptable to any other civilised country, and so as to have it expelled or suspended from all major international institutions, and if a tour could be interpreted or represented by that dictatorship as suggesting the touring country was either indifferent to or, even worse, endorsed its behaviour, that tour could surely not be defensible.

The paper – and it was too lengthy to be more than briefly summarised here – never mentioned Zimbabwe. It asked the ECB to accept the above principles.

The big blunders

Perhaps it would never have been possible to discuss this paper separately from the Zimbabwe issue. Maybe I was naïve to think it could be. But if there was any chance of it, the behaviour of Straw, plus two blunders, one by Morgan and one by me, now made it impossible. I went to considerable lengths to properly involve Morgan and Lamb. I provided them both with drafts of the 'framework for decision-making' paper, and we met in a bar in London to discuss it. Morgan, in particular, was impressed; he had even ticked some paragraphs he specially approved of. I left them knowing that the paper, if not officially endorsed by the ECB chairman and chief executive, was approved by them to be circulated for debate. At that same meeting they approved its release to the press.

I asked them to do this because Straw was about to take a step that threatened to destabilise all that I was doing. Faced with questions in the House about the Zimbabwe tour, he had decided to cover his back by prematurely releasing his letter to the ECB. I pleaded with Straw's office to hold it back, reminding them that I had initiated the whole process and had even drafted the key last sentence, and therefore that I was entitled to some consideration, but once politicians decide they have their own political reasons to act, appeals are usually hopeless, and mine was in this case. This was difficult: of course we wanted Straw to be seen to be giving us a firm instruction, but, ideally, we wanted it at the right time.

My aim was for English cricket to be seen to be clearly in control of its own affairs, taking its own decisions, and reaching a principled position of its own, and then for the Straw letter to strengthen, or, if you like, complete its specific case on Zimbabwe with the ICC. If the Straw letter was released ahead of time, the story that would emerge would be that the ECB was being forced to do the right thing under pressure. So, for these reasons, but perhaps mistakenly, we decided that night – Morgan, Lamb and I – that we should be seen to be out in front on the issue, and the way to do that was to beat Straw to the press.

I therefore asked my friend John Read, the ECB public affairs director, to set up a dinner for the key cricket writers. The plan was that they would be given an embargoed copy of my paper but not allowed to publish it for two days, thus allowing plenty of time for it to be sent to the Board so that they were not taken by surprise and would have a chance to read it and feel fully informed and properly involved. In our dealings with the media we would stress it was a *discussion* paper, not an ECB policy, and that it would be widely circulated for others to add their views. At this point, we made our two self-destructive blunders. For one, Morgan was responsible. For the other, I have to take the blame.

Morgan decided it would be only courteous for him to walk across Lords to the ICC offices and present the paper to its chairman, Eshan Mani, and his thick-skinned Australian chief executive Malcolm Speed. I was appalled. As far as I was concerned I had produced a paper to help *English* cricket reach a position. It was, at this point, no one else's business, least of all the ICC. Only if and when adopted, would it create a platform from which English cricket would negotiate with the ICC.

True, the ICC would know about the framework document, because it would be publicised, but it would not be formally placed on their agenda; there would be no reason for them to address it unless it was. But the unctuous Morgan, who it quickly became clear was hopelessly out of his depth, was now making it the ICC's business too, for there was no way that Mani and Speed would not use the opportunity to make it an ICC issue and immediately begin their fight back. And, of course, they did. As far as they were concerned, the ECB chairman was presenting it to them; what were they supposed to do? Pretend they had not seen it?

From that moment it became impossible for English cricket to unite behind a thoughtful framework document and become the voice of conscience in world cricket. Morgan had mobilised the opposition, before his own forces were armed. There were cables and calls all around the cricket world. Pressure began to be applied on ECB Board members. Threats were made. The green playing fields of Lords were being covered in blood. And it was to be mainly mine.

And I'm sorry to say that my own mistake was even worse; I failed to organise the distribution of the document to make sure the Board received and read it before it made the newspapers. If there is something I had learned from politics, it is that, when it comes to controversy, *process* matters as much as the substance of the argument. People's sense of propriety has to be respected. Rights have to be protected. Egos have to be massaged. Get the process wrong and the argument gets lost. I got the process wrong.

The fiasco was partly caused by my distance from Lords. I had spent many weeks working on the document and believed that it was of such importance that I wanted everyone to read an impeccably-printed version, and not just receive it by e-mail. I was at the time in Cornwall and had the document printed there, but I did not allow for the problem of getting it to the ECB office and then for the vagaries of Post Office delivery. To cut a long story short, it arrived on the desks of Board members on the same day as, but after it had been all over the *Today* programme and they had read about it in the newspapers. The effect was inevitable: so furious were some at what they assumed to be a deliberate act to 'bounce' them, that the document never stood a chance. Some did not even read it.

As far as they were concerned, a rogue member of the Board, clearly with an agenda of his own, had wrong-footed them, pre-empted their debate, and made any decision to tour even more publicly unpalatable than it otherwise would have been. And, of course, the way they perceived themselves to be treated played into the hands of those who wanted the tour to proceed, above all Bransgrove. He was immediately working the phones to other Board members. Even Mike Soper, who had a few weeks before told the Board it should abandon the tour 'no matter what the consequences', went bananas over the publicity and joined the protests.

It was a cock-up that reduced the value of my work to zero. A blunder! A disaster! And it need not have happened. It was unintentional, but I did not take sufficient care to get the order of events right. There's no other way to look at it; I screwed up on a major scale. The publicity itself was overwhelmingly positive. The paper was widely-praised in the media and won the Board a lot of plaudits, but, alas, it had become irrelevant.

One supporter was Lord (Ian) McLaurin, former ECB chairman and chairman of Vodaphone, who wrote: 'As the main sponsor of the England side, Vodafone . . . would prefer them not to go to Zimbabwe both on moral grounds and because of the deteriorating situation in the country.

'I am delighted that Des Wilson of the ECB has drawn up his paper. He is a very capable and sensible man and I am sure that what he has written will enable the full ECB management board to have a good discussion . . . ' The *Mail on Sunday* described the paper as 'scrupulously argued and utterly persuasive' and added 'we should inform the world that a tour of Zimbabwe is unthinkable so long as the psychopathic patron of its Cricket Union holds sway . . . and that, instead of trying to enforce a fraudulent unity, the ICC should recognise practical and political reality. Zimbabwe is way beyond civilised bounds.'

But despite this and much more support, as the next Board meeting approached, I was seriously on the defensive. If I was saved, it was thanks to the extremism of the man now emerging as my main opponent. Bransgrove wrote a letter to the Board. In it, he accused me of stirring up the whole controversy for personal publicity. (Where had I heard that before?) Morgan tried to calm things down by having a private dinner on the eve of the meeting attended by about two thirds of the Board. At this, I made it clear that I was mortified by how they had, accidentally but carelessly, been treated. I explained what had happened and the intentions behind it, but took full responsibility for the cock-up. Morgan at least confirmed his involvement. But Bransgrove now repeated his attack, questioning my motives. He was now obsessed with the view that it was some kind of conspiracy between me and my 'journalist friends'. Fortunately for me, Bransgrove had a problem: while the Board may have been dismayed at my handling of the matter, they did not actually dislike me (they did not at this point know me well enough), but many of them were not too fond of Bransgrove. Now he was so crude in his attack that he lost the other Board members who, led by Roger Knight and the former test cricketer Dennis Amiss, told him that they felt he was wrong to question my motives.

Deciding that I had Bransgrove on the back foot, I told him that he either must move a vote of censure on me next day, or withdraw. I requested a meeting with him and with Morgan before the Board meeting the following morning. At this meeting I tabled a resolution that I insisted be considered by the Board; while it would express regret at the manner of the paper's publication, it would note that that I had acted in good faith. I said if it was not passed I would, of course, resign. I had called Bransgrove's bluff (and bluster). Aware that he had gone too far, he reluctantly accepted it, and sat silent and humiliated as it was duly tabled and unanimously accepted. For the time being I had seen Bransgrove off. Unfortunately, that had never been the aim of the exercise. This was about much bigger things than the defeat of Bransgrove, and in the wider arena, I was losing.

The Zimbabwe decision

Morgan, armed with the Straw letter, now went to a meeting of the ICC. I told him I did not mind if he allowed me to be used as a punch bag, if that helped. By all means, blame the way it had been handled on me, but never-the-less he must insist that the Straw letter was force majeure because it was all that Straw could do in a democracy. It was vital that he get across the irony that, because we were a democracy, the Foreign Secretary did not feel he could order us to abandon the tour; BUT, if the boot was on the other foot, and Mugabe wanted to ban us from touring, as a dictator he could do so. In other words, the ICC force majeure clause was loaded in favour of dictatorships.

But, Morgan stood no chance. Without him being given any warning, the other countries tabled a resolution giving the Board the right to suspend countries that did not adhere to the tour contract. They had ganged up on Morgan, who was completely wrong-footed. He was, in effect, being blackmailed: 'tour' or we suspend you'. The ICC now makes much of the fact that Morgan didn't argue the moral case at that meeting, but in this I defend him: even I accept that moral arguments would have been wasted on men without a moral bone in their bodies.

Morgan was aghast; suspension could cost England tens of millions if enforced for just one season. Also, he hated being the outcast. This was not the way Morgan worked; he was the ultimate insider, the committee man, the careful climber of stairways to power, a man who loved oiling his way from hospitality box to box, canapé to canapé, dinner to dinner. So he came back full of apprehension. We had to be careful. They meant business.

But did they? Could they really have got away with suspending England? Some argued the ICC would never do it. Others argued that it would never survive legal challenge. Were Morgan and the ECB Board being too weak in running scared? Probably, but once more I feel bound to enter a small defence for them: it was at least possible that English cricket would pay a price. A malign and morally-bankrupt ICC, an organisation that could insist on ruling out moral considerations from the game's deliberations and back that up with draconian measures, was capable of almost any injustice.

It has to be stressed that, even more than the ECB, the ICC's role in this affair was unforgivable. England's case should have been sympathetically listened to, its difficulties as the founder member of the cricketing family recognised, and some compromise – a postponement with financial compensation for Zimbabwe cricket – properly negotiated. Their refusal to even consider moral issues is beyond belief – a least until you met them.

I still shudder at the memory of being introduced to the head of West Indies cricket in Barbados – 'Ah,' he sneered, 'so this is Mr Morality!' I told him he should look the word up in a dictionary; it could widen his horizons. It soon became clear to me that Morgan and Lamb had jumped ship. They were not only unsympathetic, they were mobilising to defeat me. So, realising there was no chance of getting the tour abandoned. I decided to move my ground – I proposed a compromise approach – a 'work to rule' attitude to the tour which would at least leave English cricket with some dignity.

In a letter to the Board, I said if we were forced to go to Zimbabwe, we should at least find a principled route capable of winning public support and uniting the game:

In my view the three minimal criteria for an acceptable and sustainable ECB position are:

First, that we should be seen in the UK as having the courage to 'live in the real world' and being willing to struggle with tough choices. This means publicly expressing our repugnance at the circumstances in Zimbabwe . . . stating officially that it is our preference not to tour there at this time . . . but at the same time drawing a line at what we can and cannot ask the game to do in support of that view.

Second, should the tour have to go ahead, we should rightly direct the blame where it lies, communicating our anger at the moral inadequacies of the ICC position, and the injustice whereby the force majeure clause favours dictatorships over representative democracies.

Third, if we are forced to tour on legal/financial grounds, we should back up our concerns by doing so under protest in a way that captures the imagination and sympathy of the public.

I proposed a whole series of political moves to establish an ECB position and to embarrass the ICC, but without affecting our membership or giving them reason to suspend England from international cricket. I also proposed legal and other initiatives to reform the unfair force majeure clause. And I proposed that if we proceeded with the tour, players should not be required to tour and should not be financially disadvantaged, nor their careers affected, if they did not; the ECB management (chairman, chief executive etc) should not travel to Zimbabwe; the team should be advised it was not required to attend any official receptions or events other than the cricket fixtures, nor was it expected to meet or, if faced with him, to shake hands or converse with President Mugabe or other members of his 'governing' regime. I really believed there was still a chance this approach would win the day.

The issue was now a huge story, with the debate raging in the newspapers and behind the scenes. For my part, I felt that, as we approached the Board meeting and a decision about Zimbabwe, I had overwhelming support, including:

- All three political parties
- The media – every newspaper
- The public (on opinion poll evidence)
- The MCC
- The Professional Cricketers' Association
- The England cricket team sponsor, Vodaphone

On the Board itself, surely I would have the support of Mike 'to hell with the consequences' Soper. And then there was Phil Edmonds, former England spin bowler and now chairman of Middlesex.

Earlier the outspoken Edmonds, had attended his first meeting of the Board (the ECB) and been wonderfully uncompromising on the issue. The tour should be 'cancelled forthwith'. The Board was 'obsessed with money'; it was time to make a moral stand. One Board member, he said, 'sounded like a Nazi'. It was gloriously over the top, but welcome to me. I now looked forward to Phil's support when the debate was renewed. With Soper and Edmonds on board, I still had a chance.

But as I entered the gates of Lord's for the meeting, I saw Phil climbing into a car and disappearing at speed in the opposite direction. At the meeting all was explained: someone had pointed out to Phil that he had a business interest in Zimbabwe and he was, therefore, withdrawing from the Board until the Zimbabwe matter was resolved. He had been seen off. I haven't seen him since. The ease with which he was dispatched told me all I needed to know.

Bransgrove was not there – he was in the West Indies – but sent a letter. It was a typically coarse attack on me. I was using my political and campaigning experience to manipulate the debate. I was preoccupied with what the press had to say. He questioned my continued membership of the Board. Soper made a useless contribution, wringing his hands and saying it was the most difficult decision he had ever faced – so much for abandoning the tour 'no matter what the consequences'. And now even the MCC let me down: Morgan had been to see them, and now Roger Knight reported they had been frightened into believing the English game faced a huge financial threat and they reluctantly decided not to oppose the tour.

(This led to the furious resignation of one of its most popular and influential members, Robert Griffiths, QC, one of the most distinguished lawyers in the country, who launched a powerful attack on the ICC over its threatened sanctions, arguing that any financial penalties could be found illegal by a court of law. He told *The Times*: 'The ECB have got to tell ICC that they have grave reservations whether the ICC can legitimately impose these heavy financial sanctions and must dig their heels in. They must say,"if you damage English cricket, that's a matter for your conscience."')

I looked round the room and could see no hope. I could see sympathy – even guilt – on some faces. I knew I had some friends there and they were not enjoying it. But there were no votes. I was alone. I left the room after the debate and walked over to the Edrich Stand and climbed to the top to look across the empty ground. I thought of the great battles fought on this hallowed turf for over a century and more. Of all the great cricketers who had played there. Of how, as a small boy, I had hidden under the blankets at home, with my transistor radio, to listen to the test match commentaries far into the New Zealand night. Of how I had come to see Lord's on the first day I arrived in England, way back in 1960. And I knew for me this place would never be the same. I had achieved so much to come from secretary of the Oamaru Cricket Club to advisor to the MCC and member of the ECB Board; now I was bowled, stumped, run out.

I would always despise Mani and Morgan, and the cynical bunch of free-loaders on the ICC who were rejoicing they had seen off 'Mr Morality'. But I could not avoid one harsh and hurtful truth: It was partly my own fault. I had made too many mistakes. With all my experience, I had not handled it as well as I should have. I had lost my last campaign.

The final betrayal

In my resignation press release, I said:

> I welcome the freedom I now have to say what I think about the ICC. It is supposed to be the international family of cricket but has not acted like one. There has been no genuine sympathy or understanding for the position of the ECB, and no attempt to encourage Zimbabwe to com-promise, although postponement – not cancellation – with generous compensation was on offer. When the ECB responded positively to a request by the ICC President to delay its decision to allow the ICC to debate the matter, it did so, assuming good intentions; in fact, ICC

member countries merely employed the additional time to plot even more draconian retaliatory measures, including the ability to suspend countries from international cricket. And to enforce their will, they have cynically enforced an interpretation of force majeure that they know works for dictatorships, but not democracies such as our own.

In all my years in public life, in one capacity or another, I have never experienced such an avalanche of support. The newspapers were unanimous in their praise of my decision to resign. I had more letters, e-mails and phone calls than in all my other campaigning years put together. Old friends came out of the woodwork; new ones emerged. At least I had the consolation of knowing that I had spoken for the country. Or at least that was what I thought. But there were more betrayals to come. Jack Straw now jumped ship too.

He, and that other great survivor, the culture secretary, Tessa Jowell, hosted an appalling press conference, attended by Morgan and Lamb. At it Straw said he understood that the ECB was in a very difficult position, and he gave the tour his blessing. Then this man, Foreign Secretary when Zimbabwe were suspended from the Commonwealth, supposed guardian of a foreign policy based on real values, sat benignly by while Morgan said the ECB accepted it should not allow 'moral considerations' to influence its decisions. (The ECB had never discussed my framework document and had never decided that; Morgan was just interpreting the ECB's frame of mind as he believed it to be, and helped it to be.) Morgan strengthened his stand later, saying 'Our business, our trade is cricket. If we want to trade in international cricket, then we have to do so by the rules of the ICC. It's crystal clear that members of the ICC are not permitted to pull out of tours for political or moral reasons.'

Later Morgan had one last chance to put it all right. Mugabe's men banned some English journalists from entering the country to cover the tour. He had actually provided a legitimate reason to cancel the tour – a safe reason to walk away. For a few days the cricket world held its breath. And then Morgan acted – not to cancel the tour, but to go to Zimbabwe and persuade the Zimbabwean cricket authorities to lean on Mugabe to allow the journalists in. This he finally did. The tour went ahead. Morgan then forced out both the ECB chief executive Tim Lamb and the communications director John Read, leaving himself the only survivor of the whole affair. For his efforts he was rewarded with the presidency of the ICC.

At the end of the season I was given a unique opportunity to speak to everyone in the game at the well-attended Cricket Writers' Dinner. I knew it would be my last word, and that by the following summer I would be a forgotten man:

> 'Cricket is not played on a planet of its own, but on this place where human beings live, and from time to time put each other to the real test . . . in that test . . . conscience and principle come into play – and conscience and principle can have no boundaries. Our game is synonymous with doing what is right – that's why the whole world, pointing to wrong-doing, says "its not cricket."
>
> 'Even our great game must have a sense of perspective. Even it must know its boundaries. Even it must know that beyond all of its dreams there is a prior human dream – the right to food and shelter and basic human rights – that no one can set aside as irrelevant. I find in the MCC anthology of cricket verse a remarkable poem by Lewis Carroll – written some 130 years ago. It could have been written for this moment:

> > Amidst thy bowers the tyrant's hand is seen,
> > The rude pavilions sadden all thy green;
> > One selfish pastime grasps the whole domain,
> > And half a faction swallows up the plain;
> > Adown thy glades, all sacrificed to cricket,
> > The hollow-sounding bat now guards the wicket.
> > Sunk are thy mounds in shapeless level all,
> > Lest aught impede the swiftly rolling ball;
> > And trembling, shrinking from the fatal blow,
> > Far, far away thy hapless children go.

'We all love this game – we all want it to flourish, free of malign influence . . . but C. L. R. James really did say it all when he wrote: "What do they know of cricket who only cricket know." '

21

I did See the World – but did
I Make a Difference?

'Perhaps the whole root of our trouble, the human trouble, is
that we will sacrifice all the beauty of our lives, will imprison
ourselves in totems, taboos, crosses, blood sacrifices, steeples,
mosques, races, armies, flags, nations, in order to defy the fact
of death, which is the only fact we have. It seems to me that one
ought to rejoice in the fact of death – ought to side, indeed to
earn one's death by confronting with passion the conundrum
of life. One is responsible to life.'

JAMES BALDWIN

One warm Monday morning I found myself relaxing on the back steps of
our house in London, still in my dressing gown, coffee in hand. I had no
plans for that day, nor, come to think of it, did I have any for the whole
week. It was only then I fully realised I had retired. I had made it. And,
while I had never felt myself in any way to be a prisoner of anyone or
anything, I suddenly felt wonderfully free.

Jane soon found a home in the middle of a farm in the south-west of
Cornwall; there we have now been for nearly ten years, our lives overseen
by a herd of impassive-looking cows. A pheasant has taken possession of
our lawn. The postman calls most days. Otherwise we are left in peace. We
each have a studio in the garden: for me to write and for her to paint. She
has sold paintings for private homes and offices in the UK, Ireland, France,
and the United States. A small show in Cornwall in 2009 was a success. Tim
and Jacqui are both in their forties now, Tim running his own business
in London; Jacqui, a senior manager in the NHS on the south coast. My
mother reached 94 before she followed my father to a peaceful corner of

the Memorial Gardens in Oamaru; their six children all made it home for her ninetieth birthday, the last gathering of a family that is scattered across four countries, but that has held together well for three quarters of a century, earning its own living, and – apart from me – minding its own business.

The kid from New Zealand may now be a white-haired seventy-year-old old man who wanders the country lanes of Cornwall, waving a friendly walking stick at passing cyclists, but I have not lost my appetite for the adventures and opportunities life has to offer. A number of cherished ambitions have been fulfilled. I finally got to watch cricket in the West Indies, choosing by a miracle of timing a historic match when the home team scored a world record 418 in the fourth innings to beat Australia amid unbelievable scenes of joy and jubilation. I got to spend a whole week in the mad house that is a Democratic Party convention; believe me, after that experience, there's little about American politics that can surprise. And I got to play in the main event at the World Series of Poker, surviving a whole 16-hour session with the best players on the planet.

And thereby hangs a tale. I was watching television one night and stumbled across *Late Night Poker*. From the first minute I was hooked. Ever since I had played poker with the older newspaper reporters in New Zealand, I had loved this game of patience and nerve, psychology and skill, but *Late night Poker* revealed a world I didn't know existed, that of the poker professionals, characters out of Damon Runyan, who in the old days would have played for a few dollars in illicit back-alley clubs, on Mississippi river boats, or in Western saloons, but now were competing under the glare of television lights for millions of dollars. The veterans – the been-there, seen-it-all players – were now under attack from kids in baseball caps who had read scores of books about the game, played for thousands of hours on-line, and took the game to new levels of sophistication. Who *were* all these people? It awoke the reporter in me; I decided it would be fun to research and write about them. Within eighteen months this had become a book called *Swimming with the Devilfish*. It became a poker best-seller and led to me being commissioned to write over fifty magazine articles on poker, mainly player profiles, and then to write a second book, *Ghosts at the Table*, a history of the game. These books, also published in the United States, together with a 'celebrity' appearance playing in the *Poker Million* on television, and various other appearances on poker programmes, helped make me, for a few years, well-known and well-connected on the poker scene. As a result Ladbrokes signed me up to write for their on-line poker site and that's how I found myself playing in and writing about the World Series of Poker. Imagine my surprise, however, when someone showed me my entry on Wikipedia: after an all-too-brief summary of my career, it concluded: 'He is now a professional poker player'. I did not know whether to be flattered by the implication that I knew what I was doing on the green felt or embarrassed by the suggestion that my career as a minor public figure had ended so frivolously, but . . . well . . . what the hell? It *was* fun. I even found myself playing in a Deadwood saloon near to where Wild Bill Hickock was shot with a pair of Ace's in his hand, and in Tombstone, just round the corner from the OK Corral, and in a poker club called the Rainbow in California that was accused by a local newspaper of fostering cheating; the manager's defence was: 'These aren't Sunday schools, you know.'

Yes – I WILL see the world

But, as much as possible, I've been on the road – or on planes, boats, and trains, keeping the promise I made to myself back when I was nine years old: to see the world.

As a child I had a book full of pictures of man-made miracles, geographic spectacles, and colourful people who did not look like New Zealanders – Arabs bartering in bazaars, skinny African kids minding cattle in the desert, Chinese peasants in cone-shaped hats toiling in rice fields. The book cost twelve shillings and sixpence, but really it was priceless, because it unveiled to me the world and its wonders. I read and re-read it until the pages fell out. To see the world became for me an ambition that over-rode all others, but if it was to happen, I first had to believe it was *possible*, and that was the importance of that night in 1950 when our local builder shared the pictures of his trip to America: he showed *it could be done*.

I went on to become the first of my family to leave New Zealand, and I have now been to over 60 countries spanning every continent. I have had the luck to travel to nearly half of them for work: as a writer for the *Observer* or the old *The Illustrated London News*, and as a speaker for various causes, or on business. When I've done so, I've always added on time to experience the place I've been sent. But, once free of any day-to-day cares, I have travelled more, and to more out-of-the-way spots, accompanied by Jane when I could entice her away from her easel, but more often alone. (To pay for this, I was much-helped by three years of public affairs consultancy engineered by my New York friend Larry Smith – no relation, but also a friend of Sam's).

I love the whole adventure of travel – the challenge of landing in a strange country, spending its currency, coping with its language, taking risks with its food, adjusting to its climate, respecting its customs and cultures, and dealing with all the uncertainties and misunderstandings that inevitably arise. I even like planning the trip and making the reservations; my career has been a mistake – I should have been a travel agent.

And I make no apology for wanting to see mankind's big 'set pieces', the monumental achievements of design and construction that have survived centuries and make today's architects and engineers look pedestrian by comparison. For me, it is not just wanting to *see* the man-made wonders of the world, the Sphinx and the Pyramids, the Acropolis, the Angkor Wat, the Great Wall of China, the hidden city of Petra, the Taj Mahal, the great cathedrals and mosques; it is more like fulfilling a *duty*. They were not built only for their time or the piece of land they stand on; they were built for eternity, they were intended to speak to and inspire the whole world. I simply would not have felt I had lived if I had not actually been to share in my ownership of them.

And what I have discovered is that, if you want to, you can have these wonders to yourself. The answer is to be there first. The overwhelming majority of those who travel vast distances to see these places do so in groups, usually arriving by coach, and by the time they are assembled and travel to the site and have to stop at the entrance and listen to a lecture from their leader, you can, if you are first there, have some of the world's greatest treasures entirely to yourself for at least a precious half hour. I was first into the museum in Cairo and had the fabulous Tutankhaman exhibition to myself; in Xian in China, I stood alone in front of row and row of silent Terracotta warriors until I began to have the spine-tingling feeling that they were alive and awaiting my orders; a stunning experience. There is a cafe about fifty yards from the Sphinx where you can sit alone as the sun rises and have a coffee and a completely undisturbed view of the Pyramids as they must have looked for thousands of years. The Grand

Canyon is at its most awe-inspiring if you walk around the brink as dawn breaks and before the crowd comes to disturb its peace and diminish its grandeur. There is no better time to lean on the rails of boats and look at life on the banks of the Nile, the Yangste and the Volga than when the sun is coming up and communities are beginning to awake and come down to wash and gather water for their families and cattle. I have shared hundreds of miles of Jordanian desert with one distant Arab on a camel, meandered across Red Square, the Grand Place, and St Mark's Square with only the birds for company. I have clambered all over the Acropolis, the Angkor Wat and the Colosseum as if it were I who was discovering them for the first time. I have stood at the foot of Mount Cook and on the top of Table Mountain, walked in the meadows and woods of Yellowstone and Yosemite, marvelled at the rainbows and waterfalls of Iceland, meditated in the temples of Japan and Thailand, revelled in the spectacle of wildlife in the Masai Mara or polar bears in the Arctic . . . always either alone or with a few other world-wise adventurers. It's the way to do it – and it is still possible. What compensation for being, when travelling, both a loner and a non-sleeper.

And what is so rewarding is that by travelling at out-of-the-ordinary times and to off-the-beaten-track places, you do not just cross boundaries and countries and continents, you travel back in time. When not surrounded by twenty-first-century tourists, these places look much as they must always have looked. You don't have to imagine what life was like a thousand years back on the steppes of Mongolia, in the Bedouin settlements of Jordan, in the wooden huts and rice fields of China, in the mountain markets of Peru, and in the floating villages of the Mekong Delta; even today you can experience it just as it always was. Jane and I were once out on a South African game reserve just as dusk was descending and we found ourselves on the edge of an expanse of plain surrounded by trees. As we looked across it we saw an elephant emerge from the trees, then another and another, until there was a herd of at least thirty, male and female and babies, making their slow and dignified way in single file across the other side of the plain. In no way would this immensely moving and impressive scene have changed in centuries.

Of the many countries I have been to, I have over the years spent more time in Spain, in the United States, and in South Africa than anywhere else.

The travel writer Jan Morris described Andalucia as *sol y sombre* – 'sun on one side of the street, shadow on the other.' It is the most dramatic part of Spain, its colourful and violent history carved out of a rugged landscape. This is just the kind of place where you can shut your eyes, then open them, and believe you are in the sixteenth or seventeenth century. Widows, short, bent, broad-bummed, still wear only black. Donkeys still carry goods across the plains, following trails into ravines and valleys alive with sunflowers, wild herbs, and cork and cypress trees. Its white towns, many perilously built like forts on the top of hills and mountains, were key stop-over points on the old smuggling trails, and in the moonlight you can still imagine the shadowy figures of mule and man making their laborious way up during the night to disappear into the narrow streets to shelter behind these white walls.

It is not only a country of both sun and shade; it is also one that combines the solitude of lonely farm houses out in the sierra with arresting spectacle, especially the Semana Santa processions that make their way from every local church into the centre of Seville at Easter, a time when that city becomes at night a great, glittering open-air theatre . . . and this scene is re-enacted in every small village and city across the land.

Andalucia, with its dramatic music and dance, its secretive hill-top towns, its stunning Mosque of Cordoba, the Alhambra in Granada, the Cathedral in Seville, its joyous local fiestas, stubbornly refuses to allow time to steal its history or replace its culture and traditions. It is impossible for anyone with an appetite for life and with imagination not to love Andalucia.

In over seventy visits, I have travelled across nearly every American state, walking across cities like New York, Boston, Seattle, San Francisco, New Orleans, and Chicago, holidaying on the eastern seaboard, with its grey clapboard houses, its lighthouses, and summer season repertory theatres, not to mention its lobster rolls; driving the coastal road in northern California with the Pacific crashing onto its rocky shore, admiring its forests of giant redwoods and its spectacular mountain-parks, St Helen and Rainier; reviving memories of all those childhood cowboy films in journeys to Monument Valley, Death Valley, and the ghost towns of Arizona and Nevada. But I first went to the US in 1972; to travel there now, nearly forty years later, is a more sobering experience: because when I first went there I was attracted by the sense of power throbbing in the streets of the cities, and the beauty and calm of the country; now what strikes me forcibly is not its power and wealth but a sense of dereliction, with whole areas of cities now near-ruins and rural areas, especially as I have travelled west, that are rundown, farms with collapsing barns and rusty machinery, deserted roads dotted with abandoned gas stations and roadside cafes.

America has been diminishing and dividing itself by wasting its resources on its fears and fantasies abroad instead of doing what made it such a powerhouse in the first place, namely investing its energy and wealth on its economy at home, as the countries that are overtaking it, most notably China, have been doing. There is a tall skyscraper on the banks of the East River in New York. It is called the United Nations. If only America had poured all its good intentions and more of its political and financial capital into making that institution really effective, instead of casting itself as world super power and policeman and seeking to impose its ideology on other countries, how better off both America and the rest of the world would be. Yet, ironically, while we would benefit if America as a country stayed more at home, both we and Americans would be better off if more individual Americans travelled abroad. When you talk to many ordinary Americans you cannot but be dismayed at how little they know about the rest of the world, making them vulnerable to manipulation and misinformation. This is partly why they have allowed their leaders to send their sons to die in country after country they have never even heard of. If only more Americans spent a few hours on the Mekong delta and saw the Cambodians and Vietnamese at work and play on the water, living in houses on stilts, fishing for food in self-made canoes and selling their products in floating markets, their children paddling themselves and their friends to school, they would surely wonder: *what in God's name were we ever doing there?* Nor would they be so surprised that the most terrifyingly equipped war machine in the history of man could be beaten back by Asian peasants or Afghan Arabs who knew best how to control their own terrain. When you travel around America, and especially as you move from the relatively sophisticated east coast further west, you realise that there is no difference between the hopes and dreams of ordinary Americans and almost every other race in the world; most of them only want to work to pay for their families and raise their kids and keep a roof over their heads.

They just want America to be like it used to be: a place where there was work, and if you worked, you lived well. But they have been let down by the corruption of the political system, corporate power and the media, all of them inter-related, and all of them deeply manipulative of the innocence of a basically decent people. They are educated to a world of black and white, good and evil, and to people as stereotypes, instead of the wonderous place it actually is. America was the place I most wanted to live; now I feel sorry for it. It has lost its confidence and one of the things about it I liked the most: its sense of fun. And that can't be good.

In *Observer* days, I was asked by a New Zealand organisation to travel to New York and speak to a special meeting of the Anti-apartheid committee of the United Nations, an experience special to me both because I met Oliver Tambo there, and because I won a real battle to do what my sponsors asked of me, namely persuade the committee to complain to the New Zealand rugby authorities about a racist tour by South Africa. A few weeks later I received a letter from South Africa informing me that I was banned from entering the country, and I stayed banned for nearly twenty years until Nelson Mandela was released. I first went there as part of a BAA expedition to explore a possible purchase of the country's airports. It was to be the first of over fifteen journeys to a place that I have come to love, especially Cape Province.

The world rightly worships Mandela for the way he helped change to happen in South Africa without violence. Having been there, it does not surprise me at all: taken as a whole, the South African blacks are a warm and gentle people, this illustrated by one experience: I was driving alone down a dusty back road and had a puncture. This caused me to lose control of the car and it ended up in a ditch, with three of the tyres torn from their wheels. Somehow I manoeuvred it back onto the road and limped onwards until I came to a crossroads at the same time as a truck-load full of young black men. We sat looking at each for a few minutes, and then one pointed to the road immediately ahead and told me that I was three miles from a town where there was a 'tyre works'. I limped on and eventually found a hut, a pile of tyres, and six or seven kids chatting in the sun. Within minutes they cheerfully and efficiently repaired the tyres, and I was on my way. Now the point of this story is that, if some of the white South Africans who still lived in gated communities with security guards were to be believed, I should never have been there and I should have been beaten and robbed by the men on that truck. But it isn't true. I have been there enough times now to know that I was never in danger. How could I know this and the white South Africans not? It comes back to the old story: education and manipulation.

With every trip to South Africa I have become more aware what a tragedy its past has been; the two races didn't really know each other. I talked to a young white woman about apartheid and asked her how she felt about it, and she explained that from when she was a child she was educated by her parents, by her friends, by her school, by the media, by the police and by the authorities to despise and fear blacks; she now realised she had been cheated out of what would have been a better life. A leading business figure told me the same: 'I just feel a sense of loss,' he said, 'all those years we wasted.' Of course there are still serious problems caused by the legacy of poverty and injustice: there are still a dispiriting number of awful shanty towns, there is still too much unemployment fostering too much crime, and black people are much more likely to be waiters in restaurants than customers, but their willingness to forget and forgive, their cheerfulness and their friendliness, and their optimism in the face of every setback fills one with hope. The whites of South Africa wrecked decades of their own lives to keep at bay people they have now found to be as decent and hardworking as its embattled economy allows them to be. My feeling about South Africa is that the rest of the world hated apartheid and forced its end, but then assumed its work in South Africa was done; what it needed to do was invest and create work there and help build its economy. From a distance we told them how they should behave; when they listened and did what we wanted, we abandoned them to their fate. God knows, South Africa still has its problems, but this beautiful country is also a beacon of hope for all humanity. We should stay close, and help it shine.

Whether it be in the United States or in South Africa or many other places I have been to, what strikes me is that the problem is always power, and its corrupting influence on those who have it or seek it. Its worst manifestation is the way so-called leaders divide to rule, turning people on each other. They do it be spreading fear – fear that one group will be deprived or harmed by another. So the worst horrors are caused not in wars between countries but by division within them. If it was sobering to see Dachau in Germany, it was even more so to see reminders of the activities of the Kymer Rouge in Cambodia. In Phnom Phen I went to an old school in the back streets that had once been the infamous S-21, or Tuol Sleng. It is now a museum of horror: in room after room the walls are covered from floor to ceiling with rows of harrowing photographs of many of the thousands who were imprisoned, tortured and killed there – literally thousands of faces full of foreboding and terror. The Killing Fields were even worse, all the more so because my first impression was of a peaceful park with an impressive monument in the centre that appeared to be made of glass. It's only when I approached it that I realised that it was a tower made of skulls of some of the nearly 9,000 people whose remains were found there. And what remains inexplicable is that this is what the Cambodians did to each other.

There are reminders of external invaders as well. In Siam Reap I saw a small orchestra by the side of the road; about twelve people playing traditional Cambodian instruments. I was standing there, enjoying the music, until I realised with horror that not one of them had legs. They were just a dozen of thousands who have been victims of American landmines. In Saigon I went to the War Crimes Museum, full of more harrowing detail of what the Americans did there. A young American woman was taking photographs. Once more, I had to contain myself from grabbing her camera and shouting: 'What were you doing here? Why are you not asking yourself that question: what were you doing here?'

What you end up wondering is not only how and why humans can do terrible things to one another, but how they can be so resilient. As I travelled down the Mekong delta, I not only marvelled at life on the river, but how this physically small, deeply religious, poverty-stricken, hard-working people could have survived those assaults by the world's most sophisticated weapons of war and emerged stronger in spirit than the all-powerful invader. Vietnam was pounded with all that the American war machine had to offer, but you would never know it only a few years later. The Cambodians under the Kymer Rouge carried out acts of unspeakable savagery on one another and yet you would not know it now. Their towns and cities are bustling, cheerful places. Their countryside beautiful and peaceful. They are an amazing illustration of the ability of human beings to forget and forgive, and to move on from any catastrophe and resume their daily quest for a good life for them and their families.

I would like to say that travel allows me to explain why people do what they do to each other, but it hasn't really. I don't pretend to know what turns good people into monsters, except that local people and communities don't suddenly decide to turn on themselves with hate and violence, as the Russians did under Stalin, the Germans under Hitler, the Chinese under Mao, and the Cambodians under Pol Pot: instead the people are corralled into countries or races or religions and 'led' to do it. The People don't decide that some of their number are only fit for torture and death; so-called leaders order it, exploiting fear or desperate human need to motivate. The People don't declare war on other countries; their so-called leaders do it. The world is a complex place and any comment upon it can in my view appear naïve, but our leaders and institutions, countries and religions are far too often the problem, not the solution, and that is because we give too few people too much power and too much incentive to do whatever is necessary to maintain it.

As you travel widely you see that the overwhelming majority of the human race are born, live and die in the same small place – whether it be a small town in the back country of Texas or a collection of mud huts in the Kenyan bush or dwellings on stilts on a swamp near Saigon. They have never left their country, many have never left their district. And, when all is said and done, the overwhelming majority of human beings – 99.999 per cent – share the same objective: to survive . . . to eat, drink, keep warm and sheltered, and live free of disease and violence. They want to provide and care for their families. They want laughter and love. And for all the horrors, or memorials to horrors, that I have seen, my journeys leave me convinced that the overwhelming majority are also good people; in all those 60-odd countries, and often in places where few Westerners would dare go, I have never once felt afraid of ordinary people. If you come in peace, if you look cheerful and friendly, you will find the locals the same.

I do not live without some fear: I fear some countries. I fear some leaders. I fear their armies and their police forces and even sometimes their administrators. I fear some corporate power, and I fear centralised power. But as I have explored and experienced our world, I have never once seen reason to fear ordinary people in the places where they live, work, and play: reach out a hand for help; someone will usually take it.

And that leads me to my final story.

End of a Journey – The Great Wall of Journey

If my whole life has been a journey, from challenge to challenge, experience to experience, place to place, then one of the climatic hours of that journey came when the picture in my book of the Great Wall of China finally came alive. On a beautiful sunny winter's day, in a place out in the country where the tourists rarely travel, I had the Wall virtually to myself. Alone, I sat on a step 900 metres up a hill, and traced its course down from where I had come, across a valley, and then across hills and mountains as far as the eye could see.

The Wall took nearly two thousand years to build, beginning in the seventh century BC, and involved millions of workers, tens of thousands of whom lost their lives. It is 50,000 kilometres in length. These are the bare facts, but they don't even begin to convey the magnitude of the feat or the magnificence of the results. In some places it is now rubble, in others astonishingly well-preserved. And what is amazing about it is that the builders remained loyal to the contours of the land; it does not wind around hill and mountains, it goes straight over the top. Dotted with watchtowers and blockhouses, it varies from five metres to eight metres high. It is magical, monumental, and, to someone who has crossed the world and waited 60 years to see it, deeply moving.

The place where the vast majority of tourists see the Wall (and where world leaders are pictured when they visit China) is about 40 kilometres from Beijing. It is a well preserved and spectacular section of the Wall but is surrounded by what has the appearance of a whole town of souvenir stalls and these, together with the crowds, mean it has no atmosphere.

I found myself a driver and, abandoning the tourist track, we drove over 140 kilometres to Miyun County. Our destination was a place called Simatai. This section of Wall was built in the years 550 to 577 and re-built between 1368 and 1644. The Wall climbs the Yanshan mountains on either side. There was no one there: at least no one from overseas, but at the foot of the Wall stood a girl carrying a satchel full of guide books. Alas, I already had the one she was selling, so I smiled and shook my head and began to climb. It was steep and at each watchtower I had to pause for breath. Each time I did so I would hear a polite cough, and looking behind me, would find the girl with her satchel. I tried to indicate that she would be wiser to wait at the foot of the Wall for someone who did not already have her book, but to no avail. As I climbed, it began to narrow and become much rougher. I continued on more slowly, but eventually, after I had passed my tenth watchtower, I reached a sign that told me I could continue no further. I was as near the top of this section as I could hope to be. I sat on the top step and looked with wonder at all below me and then across the valley to the mountains on the other side. On it went, over peaks, down into valleys and then reappearing, until it was beyond my ability to see.

It was a great moment. The Great Wall of China! This was it. I WAS THERE. And it was all my picture book had promised, all I had ever dreamed of. I recalled a Chinese saying: 'One who fails to reach the Great Wall would not be regarded as a hero'. So maybe I was a hero after all, but my heroism did not last for long. As I finally got my breath back and, after one last look at the unforgettable scene, I rose to go down and only then realised how steep the climb had been. The way down looked terrifying. It was almost vertical, with steep drops on either side. I realised I had been so overpowered by the spectacle that I had not grasped that with every step upwards, I was creating a nightmare journey back down. I hastily sat back down and reviewed my options, though there was really only one; somehow I had to make my way back down the 900 metres, knowing one slip and I could tumble the rest of the way into the valley. I was particularly worried about the first 70 or 80 metres; the steps had virtually disappeared for that section and the rubble was loose; the chance of a slip was high. As I summoned up the courage, I heard a familiar little cough. The girl was still there. Only now she held out a hand and took mine, and slowly she guided me down, pointing out every danger, identifying every little and safer detour, until eventually she had returned me safely to the ground.

I thanked her. I bought a book. Then I bought all the books. Then I bought the satchel.

And on my way back I told myself that I had not only seen the Great Wall of China but also met my match. She was the ultimate campaigner.

But . . . did I make a difference?

And speaking of campaigners, occasionally, as I walk the lanes of Cornwall, I think back on the activities that consumed more than half of my life and the furies and passions that drove me in younger days, and I wonder whether, in the words of my Preface, I really did 'make a difference' . . . whether I will 'leave the world even fractionally a better place'.

Does it matter? Well, it does to me, if only because I believe that the Autumn and Winter of one's life are more likely to be mellow if the earlier seasons served a useful purpose. I love Dylan Thomas's insistence that we should 'rage against the dying of the light' . . . but, while I still tear my newspaper to shreds at least once a week in response to one folly or another, the truth is that I did my 'raging' when I had the energy – raging, like campaigning, is probably best left to the young: they inherit what we fail to do, or are too old to change.

Anyway, in order to answer my own question, while writing this memoir I returned to old battlegrounds, revived old friendships, and reviewed the current status of old campaigns and causes, beginning with Shelter. There is still a housing problem; I suppose there always will be, but it's not as it was in the Sixties; the worst of the Dickensian slums have been wiped out and the inhumane hostels for the homeless closed for-ever. But reduced house building in recent years meant that we are once more significantly short of decent homes for those on low incomes and that means there are still families living in overcrowded conditions, or even split up.

But at least we built Shelter well. It's still there, now its forty-fifth year. From time to time, on anniversaries, it takes me out and dusts me down and kindly reminds everyone that I was once there. I take those chances to reassure both my contemporaries and my successors that we may not have solved the *national* housing problem, but we have solved scores of thousands of *individual* ones . . . families rescued from squalor, families kept united, families given a better chance because we were there.

When I last looked into its busy office in Old Street, its income was over £40 million, half as a result of voluntary giving and it had a nationwide staff of over 800 – a far cry from the £1 million and staff of about 70 of my time. But its role had changed: with housing associations no longer so dependent on charitable funds, Shelter was now concentrating mainly on providing advice, information and advocacy to people in housing need, including legal aid from 50 local offices, and also on a variety of projects aimed at special housing needs or problems. Its free housing advice help-line was dealing with more than 50,000 calls a year and its advice online service with around six million page views. Perhaps cutbacks in what is now called 'social housing provision' could require it to revert back to the aggressive pressure group activities of the Sixties; if it is so, it can be counted on to have the desire and the flexibility to do it. I was pleased to see it to the fore in the recent protests over cuts in housing benefits.

The full-time team look much the same – young and committed. I walked past their desks unnoticed. Just some old guy . . . well, that's as it should be.

As for the Clear campaign, the guns have been stilled for many years; nearly everyone drives on lead-free petrol today. And just as well. Recently, the *Independent on Sunday* reported new studies from the United States that: 'add to a growing body of research which shows that lead . . . is having far wider, longer-lasting and more devastating effects than anyone suspected when it was originally removed . . . The danger to children's brains has become incontestable and new consequences of the pollution are emerging.'

There's also fresh evidence that we were right about Associated Octel: In 2010 the BBC's *File on Four* and the *Guardian* separately reported that the company, now the only one in the world still selling tetra-ethyl lead, the product used in petrol, had transferred its attention to the Third World. It had changed its name to Innospec and, in 2010, had to admit to bribing officials in Indonesia and Iraq, blocking health campaigns and even sabotaging field trials of an alternative to TEL. The British judge at its trial complained that the £40 million fine added up to leniency in the face of what he called 'massive criminality'.

Britain has now had a Freedom of Information Act for a number of years. One of its main impacts has been to expose the abuse of parliamentary expenses, a disclosure few MPs can have imagined when they voted for it. On the act's fifth anniversary, the *Guardian*, in a leader, said: 'It has enabled the public to get its hands on information which was always nominally held in its name. . . It is unimaginable for any serious politician to overtly propose a return to the dark days . . . but the battle for openness is one that will never be won. There are still too many exemptions, and new ones could be introduced. Five years of FoI has proved its worth. But without perpetual vigilance, the victory of light over the dark side can never be secure.'

Thanks to the continued work of the remarkable Maurice Frankel and the still lively campaign, that vigilance exists. Maurice can be found in an office near Holborn, surrounded by files and thousands and thousands of pieces of paper, still minding the shop twenty-seven years after we opened it, as dedicated as ever. In his memoirs, Tony Blair declared that introducing freedom of information was one of his mistakes. He says he must have been mad to do it. To Maurice and I, and many others who had worked to achieve it, this was a coveted endorsement. If FoI made it difficult for politicians like Blair to keep their secrets, and for so-called public servants to rob the public, it was valuable indeed.

As for smoking, the number who smoke in the UK, and the opportunities for them to smoke in public places, have been hugely reduced. Of course PAT, with its one year campaign and the legislation it inspired, cannot claim credit for that, but few in the public health lobby will deny that at the time it provided a useful boost to the anti-smoking cause. Even so, in 2010 the industry was still claiming that it was only promoting cigarettes to adults and still arguing that many of the measures being taken to reduce smoking were 'unreasonable and lack sufficient health evidence'. Incredibly, the chief executive of Imperial Tobacco was still able to publicly say with a straight face that 'there is no credible evidence to support the idea that children start smoking or that adult smokers continue to smoke as a result of the display of tobacco products.' These people will never change. Just the same, they *are* losing the debate.

Friends of the Earth UK thrives. So close to collapse in 1983 when Godfrey Bradman and I moved in, it had by 2011 over 200 local Groups and was the biggest environmental network in the UK, The international FoE movement encompassed 77 countries. By then its main cause was one that had hardly surfaced in 1983 – climate change – and FoE was credited with forcing Labour to include a climate change bill in its Queens Speech in 2006. The Bill became law in 2008.

No one is always right. Even when we were active at the Sizewell inquiry, I had my doubts whether environmentalists should be totally opposed to nuclear power. I still think that, provided we can satisfactorily deal with waste disposal, it should be an option. I also had my doubts about wholeheartedly opposing genetically modified food; even today nearly a third of the world is hungry; if real, safe answers can be found to reducing ending famine in the Third World, this has to be a positive. But, that said, the environmental movement has been right far more than it has been wrong; whatever else, someone has been needed to ask the questions. FoE remains a valid and valuable organisation.

By 2010 nearly every one of the aims of Citcom had been achieved; our campaign can only claim to have been a minor contributor, but still an essential one: you can trace the beginning of the unstoppable momentum towards reform to the words of the judge in the Opren case and the launch of Citcom. Claimants now have a much better chance of obtaining fair compensation more quickly, and Henry Whitcomb has become one of the country's most respected barristers in the field.

All that is the good news; the news from the business community is more mixed. The freedom to shop on Sundays is now a well-established feature of the British retail scene, and Heathrow's Terminal 5 is open and providing a superb gateway to the country. But, apart from T5, the BAA story has been all downhill. Alas, and unaccountably, a Spanish company was allowed to buy the company and thus become the owner of a vital part of our national infrastructure. The new owners undermined much that was special about the company, including the emphasis on customer service and the best of the corporate social responsibility programme. As a result, they lost public confidence, and paid a heavy price: the ownership of the country's airports was forcibly split up. For those of us who had taken pride in the company, it was awful to watch. For other companies, it was a lesson.

As for corporate social responsibility, that's a mixed story too. Business has notably improved in terms of health and safety. There have been some encouraging steps towards greater environmental sustainability, and there is much better information available on products and services. In many ways, the balance of power has moved to the consumer. And some major companies have become genuine corporate citizens. But there are still too many companies that refuse to accept accountability beyond the bottom line. In particular, there is still an unacceptable gulf between the way employers reward themselves and the way they treat their employees. As far back as 2003, I was writing in the *Financial Times* about the way, when management makes mistakes, it is usually the less powerful in the company who pay the price in redundancies or low pay settlements. I once observed a major company purchase another business, discover that it had paid too much for a 'lemon', and then compensate by a draconian series of cost-cutting measures including redundancies; needless to say, the executives who took the decision to buy the 'lemon' survived. As for the banks, well it's obvious that the corporate social responsibility message has never reached them. Apart from their determination to fill their own pockets even after they had to be bailed out by the taxpayer, two of them were in 2010 found to be undermining economic sanctions on Iran. The cynicism, the thick-skinned insensitivity and the greed of bankers is beyond belief. I would have hoped by now the cause of corporate social responsibility would have been won; probably the best that can be said is that all the movement is in the right direction.

That, then, is a brief update. And that is my story.

It is said that 'a man lives happily and in command of himself, who from day to day can say *I have lived.*' Well, I think any fair-minded reader will grant me that. I *have* lived.

And if my campaigning activities have made a difference and I have, therefore, served some wider purpose, I ask no more than a friendly nod in my direction, for let it be said, re-stated, and *underlined*: this achievement has not been mine alone; it is to the credit of all the other campaigners I have identified in this book . . . it is their dedication, idealism, loyalty, hard work, and, above all, generosity, that has allowed and enabled me to become all that I can ever claim to have been . . . a minor public figure.

Author's note

Sometimes you can't improve upon what you wrote in the heat of the moment. I have never kept a diary but I have over the years written two to three million words, and where what I experienced at the time could not be better described – at least not by me – I have drawn on and woven those words into this memoir; I thank all my editors and publishers over the years for making that possible.

It goes without saying that I am in debt to all who work for my publishers Quartet, but I especially thank Naim Attallah and David Elliott for their confidence and help.

My thanks to Harold Evans and Peter Hennessy for their Forewords; they honour me.

Thanks also to those who have helped by commenting on chapters, especially Tim Wilson, Maurice Frankel, Henry Whitcomb, Archie Kirkwood, Andrew George, Tony Holden, Andrew Currie, Matthew Engel and Sam Smith.

For help with photographs I would like to particularly thank Nick Hedges. (Gathering the pictures for this book was not easy, because many photographs in old campaign files are not stamped with the photographers' names; my apologies to any photographer who as a result is not properly credited for his/her work. We would be happy to do so in any later edition.)

My thanks are also due to Les Burrows, who created the Shelter archive, and to Shelter's current director Campbell Robb for his help and support.

Finally, thanks to Mary Vyvyan who has been an exceptionally fast and impeccable typist.

DES WILSON
March 2011

Chronology

1941   March 5 ... Born in Oamaru, New Zealand

1956   Left school (Waitaki Boys' High School) at fifteen with school certificate

1956–59   Reporter, *Otago Daily Times*, then *Evening Star*, both Dunedin newspapers

1959–60   Reporter and sub-editor, *Melbourne Sun*

1960   Arrived in London, June 10.

1960–63   Worked for AAP-Reuters and on local and trade newspapers, London

1964–66   Worked in public relations agencies, London
Joined Labour Party

1966   Helped plan and launch Shelter ... director 1967–71
(1968–71 – Columnist the *Guardian*)
(1970 published first book – on Shelter)

1971–74   Columnist, the *Observer*
(Joined Liberals ... 1973 Fought Hove by-election)
(National executive member, NCCL and CPAG)

1974–76   Head of Public Affairs, Royal Shakespeare Company

1976–79   Editor, *Social Work Today*

1979–81   Deputy Editor, *Illustrated London News*

1981–83   Chairman, Clear campaign for lead-free air

1983–90   Chairman of Friends of the Earth
Campaign director, FoE Internatiional
Chairman of Citizen Action
Chairman of Campaign for Freedom of Information
Chairman of Parents against Tobacco
Published a series of campaigning books

President of the Liberal Party 1986–87
Member Alliance General Election Committee, 1987
Published Battle for Power on the 1987 campaign
Member, Liberal merger negotiating team 1987–88

1990–92 Director of the Liberal Democrat General Election Campaign
wrote two novels, *Costa del Sol* and *Campaign*)

1993–94 Director of public affairs, Burson Marsteller

1994–2000 Director of corporate and public affairs, BAA plc
Six years on Board of the British Tourist Authority
Three years deputy chairman of Sport England, chairman of
the Sports Lottery Panel
Two years, columnist on *New Statesman*
Co-authored Private business – Public Battleground with Sir
John Egan

2000–2003 Board of The Carphone Warehouse
Board of Earls Court and Olympia

2003–6 Advisor to the MCC

2005–6 Member, English Cricket Board

2006–2010 Retired to Cornwall, wrote two books on poker, travelled
extensively.

Index